SOCIAL CHANGE AND SOCIAL CONTROL

Rajendra K. Sharma

ATLANTIC
PUBLISHERS & DISTRIBUTORS (P) LTD

Published by

ATLANTIC

PUBLISHERS & DISTRIBUTORS (P) LTD

7/22, Ansari Road, Darya Ganj, New Delhi-110002
Phones : +91-11-40775252, 40775214, 23273880, 23275880
Fax: +91-11-23285873
Web: www.atlanticbooks.com
E-mail: orders@atlanticbooks.com

Printed & bound in India by Atlantic Print Services

Preface

This book covers syllabi in the papers Social Dynamics; Social Change and Social Control, prescribed by Indian Universities. Part I on Social Change includes the discussion of Social Change, Social Selection, Theories of Social Change, Social Development, Social Evolution, Social Revolution and Factors and Sources of Social Change including Population; Fashion, Style, Fad and Craze; Education; Culture and Civilization; Social Progress, Social Interaction and Social Processes. Part II on Social Control includes discussion on Social Organization, Status and Role; Individual, Society and Socialization; Suggestion, Imitation and Sympathy, Meaning, Types and Agencies of Social Control and Factors and Sources of Social Control including Social Groups, Family Group, Political Institutions, Economic Institutions, Religious Institutions, Propaganda, Public Opinion and Social Codes.

Thus, the author has left no stones unturned to make this Volume an ideal textbook on the subject for students and a reference book for the teachers. Suggestions for improvement are, however, invited from the indulgent readers.

RAJENDRA K. SHARMA

Contents

PART I

SOCIAL CHANGE

CHAPTER 1

Social Change and Social Selection

Social change is the change in social structure. Social structure is a web of social relationships. Hence, social change as a change in social structure involves social relationships. It is the change in these which alone we shall regard as social change. What are social relationships? Social relationships include social processes, social patterns and social interactions. These include the mutual activities and relations of the various parts of society.

Definition of Social Change

1. *Jones.* "Social change is a term used to describe variations or modifications of any aspect of social processes, social pattern, social interactions, or social organisation."[1]
2. *K. Davis.* "By social change is meant only such alterations as secure in social organisation — that is, the structure and functions of society."[2]
3. *Merrill and Eldredge.* "Social change means that large numbers of persons are engaging in activities that differ from those which they or their immediate (forefathers) engaged in some time before. Society is composed of a vast and complex network of patterned human relationships in which all men participate. When human behaviour is in the process of modification, this is only another way of indicating that social change is occurring."[3]

Human society is constituted of human beings. Thus, whatever apparent alteration in the mutual behaviour between individuals takes place is a sign of social change. This fact of social change can be verified by glancing at the history of any society. Man is a dynamic being. Hence, society can never remain static. It undergoes constant variation.

FACTORS OF SOCIAL CHANGE

What are the factors due to which social relationships undergo constant alterations? Some writers regard diffusion to be the main factor of social change while some other writers consider invention in a similar capacity. Actually, both diffusion and invention

1. Jones, Basic Sociological *Principles*, p. 96.
2. Davis, K., in *Human Society*.
3. Merrill and Eldredge, *Culture and Society*, pp. 512-513.

have a hand in the change which besets social relationships. Roughly, the main causes of social change are the Cultural, Technological, Biological, Population, Environmental, Psychological and Other Factors,

1. Cultural Factors. The main cause of social change is the cultural factor. Changes in the culture are accompanied by social changes. Max Weber has proved this hypothesis by a comparative study of religious and economic institutions. Actually, no one can deny that changes and variations in culture inevitably influence social relationships. Culture gives speed and direction to social change and determines the limits beyond which social changes cannot occur. This, however, does not warrant the conclusion that there is no distinction between social and cultural change. Actually, the field of social change is limited in comparison to the field of cultural change.

2. Technological Factors. The technological factor has immense influence in social change. To quote Ogburn, "Technology changes society by changing our environments to which we in turn adapt. This change is usually in the material environment and the adjustment we make to the changes often modifies customs and social institutions."[4] In this way, the incessant increase in new machines and methods due to new discoveries has had a very great influence upon social relationships. The form of society is undergoing change as a result of the development and invention of electric, steam and petrol driven machines for production, the means of transport and communication and various mechanical appliances in everyday life. Even institutions like family and marriage have not remained immune to the effect of these developments. The explicit effects of technological advance are labour organisations, division of labour, specialization, high speed of life, increase in production, etc. In the modern age technological factors are among the predominant causes of social change.

3. Biological Factors. Biological factors too have some indirect influence upon social change. Among the biological, factors is the qualitative aspect of the population related to heredity. The qualitative aspect of population is based upon powerful and great men and their birth is dependent to a large extent upon heredity and mutation. Hence, biological factors play a part in social change to that extent. In addition to this, the biological principles of natural selection and struggle for survival are constantly producing alterations in society.

4. Population Factors. Even changes in the quality and size of the population have an effect upon the social organisation as well as customs and traditions, institutions, associations, etc. Increase and decrease of population, a change in the ratio of men and women, young and old, have an effect upon social relationships. Decrease or increase in the population has an immediate effect upon economic institutions and associations. The ratio of men to women in a society affects marriage, family and the condition of women in society. In the same way the birth and death rates, etc., also influence social change.

---

4. Ogburn, W. F., *How Technology Changes Society,* Annals of the American Academy of Political and Social Science (Jan., 1947), p. 81.

5. Environmental Factors. The geographists have emphasized the impact of geographical environment upon human society. Huntington has gone so far as to assert that an alteration in the climate is the sole cause of the evolution and devolution of civilizations and cultures. Even if these claims of the geographists are to be discarded, it cannot be denied that floods, earthquakes, excessive rain, drought, change of season, etc., have significant effect upon social relationships and these are modified by such natural occurrences.

6. Psychological Factors. Most sociologists regard psychological factors as important elements in social change. The cause of social changes is the psychology of man himself. Man is by nature a lover of change. He is always trying to discover new things in every sphere of his life and is always anxious for novel experiences. As a result of this tendency, the mores, traditions, customs, etc., of every human society are perpetually undergoing change. This does not mean that man always considers the new to be superior to the old. While he is always attending to what is new and unique he also wants to preserve what is old. The form of social relationships is constantly changing in the process of interaction between these two tendencies. New customs and methods which replace the old traditional customs are being formed. Old traditions are respected but time demands change and adaptation to changing conditions. Change is the law of life. When changes do not occur at the appropriate time revolutions take place, wars are fought, epidemics spread and changes are violently introduced.

7. Other Factors. In addition to the above-mentioned factors, another factor of social change is the appearance of new opinions and thoughts. For example, changes in the attitudes towards dowry, caste system, female education, etc., have resulted in widespread social variations and modifications. In fact a majority of the social revolutions take place as a result of the evolution of new ways of thinking. Similarly, war is also a cause of social change because it influences the population, the economic situation and ratio of males to females, etc. In the same way, social changes are introduced by the advent of great thinkers as Gandhi and Karl Marx, etc.

RESULT OF SOCIAL CHANGE

The form of each aspect of social life is being continually transformed due to the effect of the above-mentioned factors which cause social change. New institutions and associations are being formed and destroyed in the social, economic, political, cultural, and verily, in all spheres. The form of family, marriage, state, religion, culture, educational system, and economic and social structures is continually clanging and transforming, as a result of which, a change occurs in the life of the individual and subsequently in his relations with others. To take an example, the results of social change can be well understood and realised by studying the history of the objectives, structure, forms, importance and functions, etc., of the family from the early past to the present day. Similarly, all the changes and differences that can be seen between the tribal society and the present day society can be attributed to social change.

LEVELS OF ADAPTATION

Man has to adapt himself to society and nature. Environment, be it social or natural, has an important role in man's development. Life, vegetative, human and animal, all adapt to environment. There are many kinds of environment such as physical, biological, social, etc. Similarly, there are many levels of adaptation also. Mainly, there are three levels of adaptation to the environment in man:

1. Physical adaptation,
2. Social adaptation,
3. Biological adaptation.

Physical Adaptation

Physical adaptation is a term signifying man's adaptation to his physical environment which is natural. Man has neither to employ his will power nor to make any effort for this adaptation. It is based on human nature and the structure of the human anatomy. For example, air atop a high mountain is rarified and has a smaller oxygen content, as a result of which the man has to exert more in breathing. Consequently, in order to adapt to this environment, people going to high mountainous terrain carry oxygen cylinders with them. One adapts to the physical environment by wearing warm clothing in winter and cotton garments in summer. It is natural to do so. When a person feels cold, he wants somehow or the other to escape if. In this he has no alternative and hence, naturally, wants to adapt to the environment. Physical adaptation is governed by natural or physical laws. One finds it difficult to breathe in a stuffy atmosphere and makes an effort to get into clear air. Despite all his desires, one will become diseased if he lives in dirty lanes. Death too, is just another form of physical adaptation. Having become too feeble the body loses its ability to cope with heat and cold, and its temperature is reduced to the temperature of the natural environment, in others words, it becomes lifeless matter.

Social Adaptation

Man's adaptation to his social environment is called his social adaptation. There is a saying that when you go to Rome, do as the Romans do. The young men who go from India to England to continue their studies learn to eat meat and drink, besides acquiring new habits. In this way, a man on going to a new society adapts himself to it because man wants to concur with society and he has to suffer derision and sarcasm if he strikes a note of discord. It is doubtful if there are many men who do not desire to earn a name in society and avoid infamy. It is man's nature. On joining a new society, individuals not only acquire the various habits, peculiar to it, they also adopt new values. The environment in Hindu, Muslim and Christian societies is different and the people who live in them become adapted to it.

Some differences between physical and social adaptation must have transpired from the foregoing description. There are the following distinctions between the two:

1. Physical adaptation is a biological process while social adaptation is a social process. For example, the colour of the skin of British people undergoes some change through continued exposure to the sun in warm countries like India and Africa. This is their physical adaptation. Children acquire bad habits through playing in dirty lanes, an example of social adaptation.

2. The question of the individual's wish does not arise in connection with his physical adaptation. The natural laws are continuously influencing him. On the other hand, the individual's wish does have some influence on his social adaptation.

3. In physical adaptation man cannot introduce any modifications whereas in his social adaptation man is not only influenced by his environment but he, too, in his turn influences and affects it.

4. In addition to the above mentioned differences between physical and social adaptation, yet another difference exists in that the former is governed by natural laws while the latter takes place in accordance with the social values. For example, every man resorts to some cure or the other when he feels warm but when a foreigner visits various countries, it is uncertain whether he will adopt the culture of these countries, such a contingency depending on his own social values. All the Indians going to Rome do not behave like Romans. Some people will behave in their own way wherever they may go.

The following table is intended to clarify further the difference between physical and social adaptations:

Physical Adaptation	*Social Adaptation*
1. Biological Process. 2. Wishes of the individual ineffective. 3. The environment is not changed. 4. Based on natural laws.	1. Social Process. 2. Influence of the individual's wishes also. 3. The environment is modified. 4. Based on Social values.

Biological Adaptation

Biological adaptation is explained with reference to two principles — struggle for existence and survival of the fittest.

(i) Struggle for existence. In 1842, Charles Darwin stated his principle of struggle for existence in his famous treatise *Origin of Species.* According to this theory, the rule of the force reigns supreme in the biological world. Every living being struggles for its existence. In this struggle only those survive who are strong or those who can adapt themselves to their environment, while all others perish. In this way, this earth witnessed the gigantic dinosaurs and mammoths struggling for existence, but these species became extinct because of their inability to adapt to the environment. Thus numerous species of animals originated and decayed. They struggled for their existence but became defunct, having failed in their struggle. Only those remained alive whose struggle was crowned with victory.

(ii) Survival of the fittest. Thus living beings have to struggle to maintain their existence and this struggle is governed by the principle of the survival of the fittest whereby it is decreed that victory shall go only to those who can achieve the maximum adaptation. In the world of nature one living being feasts on another. The lion eats the goat, the cat does away with the rat, the snake eats the frog who in turn makes the insects his food. There are many aspects of this struggle for existence, there are many problems involved, such as adaptation to the quick variations in climate and season besides the supply of adequate food for the living beings, death caused by the effect of germs, power to resist them and increase in this power through injections, obtaining of victims by the hunting beings and efforts of the hunted to escape and struggle for a mate, etc. The struggle is universal. It functions continually among the atoms, molecules, individuals, living beings and societies. Among the animals this struggle is in two forms: (i) elimination in which the inefficient are excluded, and (ii) absorption whereby successful ones are included in the group of living beings. This is explained by the principle of natural selection.

NATURAL SELECTION

The principle of natural selection states that biological factors and environment are engaged in perpetual conflict. A struggle for existence is found even among the animals and plants. The elements of inheritance are also being changed and modified. The chromosomes are sometimes completely changed. This process of modification is called mutation. Those genes which can adapt themselves survive this process of mutation while the unsuccessful ones are eliminated.

Pearson has diagnosed four major premises for this natural selection, all of which are important for both man and animal alike:

1. Qualities are variable.
2. Qualities are inherited.
3. Death rate is selective meaning that those who do not possess the power of adaptation, die. In this Nature selects only those efficient beings to live who can successfully adapt themselves.
4. Those who die later procreate more while those who die earlier have comparatively fewer progeny.

Many mutations take the form of natural defects and are inefficacious for some particular species. Before the birth of the living beings, Nature, through death, performs the function of natural selection. Accordingly, a fly with a small wing mutation could not survive. Mutations are beneficial to the maintenance of the life of the living beings under certain conditions and for this reason receive encouragement in the process of natural selection. Possession of a long neck facilitates the giraffe in its quest for food. Consequently, in this condition, the mutation is not eliminated by natural selection. In this way Nature selects from among the mutations. The mutations which assist in adaptation are allowed to continue while those which hinder adaptation are eliminated.

Natural Selection is Influenced only by the Death Rate. Those individuals who appear inefficient are destroyed in natural selection. In tribal societies, children with defective eyes, teeth and ears were destroyed since that environment allowed only those to exist who had all these three organs in good condition. In natural catastrophes like rainstorm, typhoon, etc., Nature selects through death, since in this catastrophe the able survive while the disabled die. The ability to survive is the ability to adapt and does not depend on the gigantic or enormous size of the anatomy. In this connection an experiment conducted by Dr. Bumps of the American Museum of Natural History is very interesting. Following a very severe storm, he weighed and measured the wings of all sparrows who had been killed when they had fallen from their nests and found that most of the dead birds were either too big or too small. It is true that as a result of the progress of civilization and development in the science of medicine even the disabled beings live long in the modern world. In this connection it is difficult to understand how the feeble minded survived in the tribal hunting conditions, though modern culture looks after them and helps them to live. But the process of natural selection through death can be clearly seen, however much the science of curing may have progressed. The number of Americans, for example, who died because of influenza in the same years was 3,50,000 more than the number of Americans killed in World War I.

Criticism of the Principle of Struggle for Existence

There are many objections to the application of the principle of struggle for existence to human society. The major ones among them are as follows:

1. The principle of struggle for existence is one-sided because in human society co-operation exists along with conflict and is equally important. Human beings can neither be born without co-operation nor can live in the absence of co-operation. Some scholars have proved that mutual co-operation can be found even in birds and animals.
2. As a consequence of the importance accorded to the standard of living and other factors in modern society, the birth rate in the higher class is lower than in the lower class. In this way, the more useful individuals procreate less while the less useful procreate more. This fact contradicts the principle of struggle for existence.
3. According to this principle only the powerful survives but sometimes even among the animals there is evidence of the survival of species which are less strong.
4. The existence of the species is maintained not only by success in the conflict but also through a high birth rate and low death rate.

Criticism of the Principle of Natural Selection

The criticisms levelled at the principle of struggle for existence are applicable to the principle of natural selection also. Other objections against the latter are:

1. The principle of natural selection does not apply without qualification to even the animals world. It cannot be said that all plants and animals are engaged in an incessant struggle with other living beings.
2. According to this principle natural selection takes place through conflict but when human groups wage conflict with each other it is the efficient and able

individuals who are killed while the weak ones survive because only the able-bodied are selected for war.

3. According to this principle, Nature carries out its selection through the medium of the death rate but there can be many factors other than the natural which influence the death rate.

4. The principle of natural selection can apply only in a natural environment. Today the control of Nature over man is continually being decreased, due to developments in science. Thus, the principle of natural selection does not apply properly to human society.

5. In the book *History of Civilization* Prof. Toynbee has proved that social change is the result of many natural and social factors and causes. The application of the principle of natural selection is restricted by the social conditions which are equally important. Selection in human society is more social than natural and the cause of this is the predominantly social environment.

6. According to the principle of natural selection, the offspring of the weaker individuals should not get the opportunity to live or to develop. But in civilized human societies, all citizens have equal opportunity to live and to develop.

7. The great defect of the natural selection principle lies in its endeavour to explain human activities on a biological principle while completely disregarding the difference between the animal and the human societies. The principle of natural selection will lose its force as human culture and civilization progress. To quote Lloyd Morgan, "...Natural selection is a constantly diminishing factor in the evolution of civilized man."[5]

SOCIAL SELECTION

What is Social Selection?

Defining social selection, MacIver writes, "In so far as forces generated within human society and operating through social relationships create conditions which affect the reproduction and survival rates of the population as a whole and differentially with the various groups within it, we can term the process social selection."[6] In this way social selection is a process which generates circumstances which influence reproduction and survival. Various conditions carry out selection in various forms.

Modes of Social Selection

Social selection functions in a society in a number of ways. For example, the economic conditions influence the marriage rate. More marriages are contracted during inflationary periods than during depression. In the same way, the birth rate is influenced by the standard of living. As the standard of living improves, the birth rate decreases. Generally, two modes of social selection are recognised. The two are:

5. Loyd Morgan, *Habit and Instinct*, p. 324.

6. MacIver and Page, *Society: An Introductory Analysis*, p. 342.

1. Direct Social Selection. Under this mode, man himself creates those social conditions which affect the birth and death rates, exampled in family planning, contraceptives, suicides, abortions, etc.

2. Indirect Social Selection. Under this mode, no individual makes any conscious effort to increase or decrease the birth and death rates. It is the organisation of society which causes changes in the birth and death rates. Accordingly, this is indirect social selection since it is caused by those social activities of individuals which have been created by man for achieving other objectives. For example, the cause of excessive number of tuberculosis patients in Kanpur is industrialization and insanitation. Both these causes indirectly and unintentionally augment the death rate.

Forms of Social Selection

Social selection encourages social change in a variety of forms, the major ones being described below:

1. Military. It is the first fundamental form of social selection. In times of war, the strong-bodied are selected and sent to the war field and the number of superior persons in society is drastically reduced. In this way war selects the healthiest of the population. Lapouge has written that wars increase with the progress of civilization. But it is difficult to accept this opinion in the light of existing circumstances. The invention of atomic and nuclear weapons has created such a situation that war will have disastrous consequences not only for the entire world but even for the generations to come.

2. Political. Political conflict leads to the selection, on the one hand, of opportunities for wily people since often they succeed in becoming leaders and of the destruction of the intelligent and honest, on the other, since it is they who are killed in revolutions and domestic conflicts and wars.

3. Religious. The religious form of social selection originates in religious conditions. In most religions, the religious leaders or saints do not marry and ostensibly lead a life of celibacy. As a result, the society is deprived of the offspring of such intelligent, pure and capable individuals.

4. Moral. In addition to its religious form, social selection also takes a moral form. It is intimately related to the religious form. It is in its ethical or moral form that social selection appears to be a complete contradiction of natural selection. Due to moral dogmas, the imbeciles, injured and diseased persons are continually protected in society and no restrictions are placed upon their cohabiting or begetting offspring. In this way they increase the burden of weak people upon the society. Harmful traditions find value and existence in society only due to moral dogmas, even though they have a bad effect upon health.

5. Judicial. The judicial form of social selection is caused by the methods or activities of the government. As a result of government policy, prostitution is at one place allowed to flourish while at another it is prohibited and curbed. Criminals are punished by the state. In serious crimes, many people are prevented from begetting children by being sentenced to death or life imprisonment.

6. Economic. The economic form of social selection is the result of conditions of economic conflict. Often, in the economic sphere, advertisements, chicanery and deception hold greater sway than do intelligence and honesty. Consequently, the superior persons are not financially successful and they endeavour to restrict the number of their offspring.

7. Occupational. Different studies have revealed that the individuals engaged in superior and intellectual occupations beget lesser children than those whose occupation is common. As a result the number of lower class people in society constantly increases.

8. Urban and Rural. The urban and rural forms of social selection are caused by the different conditions of towns and villages. Due to these causes fewer children are born in cities than are born in the villages.

DISTINCTION BETWEEN NATURAL AND SOCIAL SELECTION

The distinction between social and natural selection would have become apparent from the foregoing description of the modes and forms of social selection. The distinctions between the two are the following:

1. Natural selection works only through the death rate. It eliminates the inefficient and useless individuals from among all those born. The more direct influence of social selection is upon the birth rate.

2. In natural selection there are only two ways — adaptation and death. Those who adapt, survive while those who do not, are destroyed. There are many alternatives in social selection. Along with preventing the birth rate from rising, it provides also for the existence of the maximum possible number of people. It is preventive as well as creative.

3. Natural selection demands that an individual should adapt to a particular environment. In social selection there are many environments. This social environment is constantly changing and can be changed.

4. In this way, in natural selection, the living being has to come to terms with Nature which he can alter to a very limited extent. On the other hand, the social selection is made by man's effort and industry. In this way the path of natural selection is unchangeable while the path of social selection is susceptible to variation.

5. The sphere of activity of natural selection is limited in comparison with that of social selection. In it the weaker can win on the strength of his intellectual capacity.

6. Natural selection is the way of competition and conflict while in social selection co-operation and benevolence too have importance.

7. Natural selection is based upon natural conditions and social selection upon social conditions.

The above described difference between social and natural selection is further clarified in the table given below:

Natural selection	*Social selection*
1. Based on natural conditions.	1. Based on social conditions.
2. Path of competition and conflict.	2. Importance of co–operation and benevolence.
3. Determination of the limits of development.	3. Indication of direction within these limits.
4. Unchangeable.	4. Can be changed.
5. A definite environment.	5. Many environments.
6. Adaptation or death.	6. Many alternatives.
7. Destructive.	7. Preventive as well as creative.
8. Influence only on death rate.	8. Influence also on birth rate.
9. Man generally suffers it.	9. Man can, by his enterprise, change it.

SOCIAL CHANCE AND TECHNOLOGY

In the words of Karl Marx, Technology discloses man's mode of dealing with Nature and the process of production by which he sustains his life and thereby lays bare the mode of formation of social relations and of mental conceptions that flow from them."[7] In this way technology is a systematic knowledge which facilitates the use of machines or tools. A locomotive, for example, is a machine and the process of its application is technology. In this way man, unlike an animal, does not behave towards Nature in an effortless, indolent and straightforward manner, but rather in a definite and methodical way making use of Nature's secret acquired by his knowledge and power of intellect. This constitutes technology. By means of it man produces food and other commodities of daily consumption from the earth. According to Karl Marx, even the formation of social relations and mental conceptions is dependent upon this. Technology differs from scientific processes. Scientific processes try to discover the truth, which is made use of in technology, so technology is practical. Keeping in view human ideals and needs means are developed in technology. In this way technology is a tool for man in his behaviour towards Nature. In capitalist countries this means is controlled by capitalists and by the State in communist countries. Economic interests can be insured only by retaining control or right over the means. In this way, technology is the means of economic production which is an end.

Technology is constantly developing and with its development the structure of society is also changing. Increased division of labour and a higher degree of specialisation are the results of a constant development in technology, so much so that one sees specialists in every conceivable subject in the society. The advance of technology has played a major role in the development and progress of human civilization. Today, the means of transport and communication such as post, telegraph, rail, aeroplane, ships, automobiles, motor cycles, the tools for agriculture

7. Marx, K., *Capital*, Vol. 2 (1954), p. 342

and the thousand and one machines producing other commodities useful to life, that one comes across, are all fruits of technological advance.

Technological Factors

The following are the main technological factors in social change:

(a) Introduction of machines in industries.

(b) Development of the means of communication.

(c) Development of the means of transport.

(d) Development of new agriculture techniques.

(a) Introduction of machines in industries. The introduction of machines in industry has resulted in some fundamental changes in the social structure. The major changes thus created are:

1. Birth of Factory System. The most apparent and dominant effect of the introduction of machines in industry is the replacement of the system of individual production by the factory system. The invention of machines has led to the creation of huge factories which employ thousands of people and where most of the work is performed automatically. In India till recently, the weavers used to make cloth on their looms at home, while sugarcane juice was turned into gur in the farmer's home. Today there are may sugar and cloth factories in which millions of labourers find employment.

2. Urbanization. Industrialisation and the birth of gigantic factories led to urbanization and big cities came into existence. With the advent of industrialisation many labourers migrated to the sites of work and settled around it. As the industry grew, so did this community of labourers and with it was felt the need for all the civic amenities which were essential for them. Their needs were fulfilled by establishing market centres, schools, colleges, hospitals, recreation clubs. The area further developed when a new business came to it with the formation of large business houses. In this way large cities grew up where there had been large factories. Towns like Kanpur, Modinagar, Ahmedabad, in India owe their birth to the factories established there.

3. Evolution of New Classes. Urbanization and Industrialisation transformed the structure of society. The social organisation divided itself into classes between which a fierce conflict raged. The capitalist and the labourer classes came to blows often and under numerous pretexts. A middle class of white collar aristocrats also evolved.

4. New Conceptions and Movements. All these factors culminated in the generation of new currents in the prevalent thinking. Trade Union movements came into favour as the socialistic and communistic thought gained in popularity. Lockouts, strikes, processions became the stocks in trade of those who wanted to promote class interests and are regular features of economic activity.

5. Improvement in the Condition of Women. The burden of work in the family which falls on the women has been decreased by the increasing use of mechanical appliances. With the domestic work being facilitated, they were left with adequate time for mental and occupational activities and they too competed with men in the economic field. In India, household mechanical appliances are not so popular. Hence, the Indian women have not reached the same status which the Western women have achieved.

(*b*) ***Development of the Means of Communication.*** The introduction of machinery into industry led to the development of large scale production which necessitated communication between traders situated far apart. In this connection much benefit was reaped through postal service, telegraph, telephone, etc. Newspapers, radio, television, etc., helped to bring news from every comer of the world right into the household. It became unnecessary to stir out of the house to learn the news. These means also led to mutual exchanges between the various cultures. They also facilitated the spread of new principles and became propaganda machines for political parties.

(*c*) ***Development of the Means of Transport.*** Along with development in the means of communication the means of transport also progressed at a surprising rate, and the advent of the jet aeroplanes made it possible for people to go from one country to another at the speed of more than 500 miles an hour. The development of the cycle, motor, rail, ship and aeroplane made transportation of commodities much easier. As a result, national and international trade made unprecedented progress. The intermixing of people belonging to various countries led to the removal of much misunderstanding, and feelings of hatred and jealousy were replaced by sympathy and co–operation. Feelings of benevolence prevailed between different races and nations. This assisted in the progress of the sense of universal brotherhood and world government.

(***d***) ***Development of*** *New Agricultural Techniques.* An important factor in technological advance is the development of new techniques in agriculture. New agricultural tools have been developed and designed. Agricultural production was increased due to the use of new chemical manures. The quality was also proved by the use of superior seeds. All these factors had resulted in the increase of production. Fewer people were needed for agriculture. Consequently many people shifted to factories and mills and many devoted themselves to trade. In India, the effect of technology is most apparent in this direction because India is pre-eminently an agricultural country and its future depends upon the progress of agriculture.

Social Effects of Technology

From the foregoing description of the effect of the main technological factors it would have become apparent that these factors have a very appreciable influence upon social change. The effects of technological factors are the following:

Changes in Values. The extension of economic limits and the areas of states, formation of new classes in society, development and progress of democracy, spread of fashion, urbanization, introduction of novel thoughts and the formation of new associations have had profound effect on the beliefs, tendencies and thoughts of human beings. This has led to a vast transformation in the values of life. The old values have been completely changed. Wealth is being accorded almost the highest respect and it is being placed on the highest pedestal. It has become a measure of prestige. Moral values are no longer held in the respect they were once held. Religion has come to be regarded as a private affair and stress is being laid on secularisation of social relationships. Importance is now given to quantity or number instead of quality. More importance is being given to external pomp and show than to contemplation and thought. The fundamental elements of culture are being disregarded in the face of ostentation and pretension. Human relations are becoming impersonal and secondary. On all sides one is confronted with 'human machines' which possess motion but not sincerity, life but not emotion, heart but not feelings. Every 'one Is running. No one has the time to look to another. But where to and in which direction? Who knows? Who should think? If asked, everyone replies why do you worry? Why should I worry? These changes in social values have been well described by Erich Fromm in his book *The Sane Society.*

Effects on Social Institutions. Technology has not spared the social institutions of its effects. Many functions of the family are being performed by other associations. Many of the family activities are being mechanically performed. As a result, the womenfolk have more spare time. Now, even outside the house, they are working at the side of the men-folk. Family control is on the decline. Signs of disintegration are also clear enough. The number of children is decreasing. Along with the family ties, the bonds of marriage are also becoming ineffective since marriage is no longer a religious ritual but a social contract which can be broken at any time. The sphere of choice in marriage has increased and more emphasis is being placed on love. The number of divorces is increasing. Religious institutions are no longer the force they were at one stage, and their authority has been considerably undermined. The governments constitute welfare states which are secular by nature. With the development of technology their area is constantly increasing and they are becoming more stable. The concept of a universal government is spreading.

Effect on Urban Life. The extent of influence which technology has had on social life can be seen most clearly in urban life because it is in the development of cities that technological factors play an important role. The following effects of technological advance upon urban social life can be clearly seen: absence of communal feeling, impersonal element in relations, increase in the number and kinds of disease, absence of family control, low level of morality, increase in the number of crimes, symptoms of social disorganisation, etc. On the other hand, the welcome effects of technology are displayed in the increase in the facilities of life, leisure, self-confidence and also in the form of the types of cultural elements and knowledge.

BARRIERS TO SOCIAL CHANGE

Barriers to social change are the obstacles in the rise and growth of social change in a society. In fact all the institutions, political, social, economic and industrial, create barriers to social change while insisting upon the perpetuation of traditions. Besides traditions, customs, usages etc. lack innovation and the inability to accept them is a serious barrier to social change. The following, in brief, are the obstacles to social change:

1. Lack of Inventions and Innovations. According to Ogbrun and Nimkoff a main obstacle and barrier in social change is the lack of inventions or innovations. In the words of Encyclopaedia Americana, "An invention is recognised to be any new or useful mechanical contrivance or article, method, discovery, composition of matter or system not previously known or used, or any improvement in any known machine, art, method or system." Thus invention is the discovery of any new object, instrument, method or system or any improvement or innovation in the existing instrument, technology or method. In both the conditions invention is novel and has utility. It is said that necessity is the mother of invention. This shows that invention is useful in some way or the other. Thus, it plays an important role in social change in human society. By means of invention human beings find out new ways and modes of adjustment with their natural and social environment. This creates far reaching changes in social relationships. It is not an exaggeration to say that man's cultural development depends upon invention. It is due to his capacity of invention that man has evolved out of the primitive stage to modern society. Inventions have not only influenced the physical but also the mental and spiritual life of human beings. New inventions are constantly made not only in human living but also in art, literature, recreation and religion. The examples of Television, Tape recorders and self-starters in motor cars are sufficient to show the far reaching influence of invention upon human relationships and social life. If inventions are slow, the pace of social change is also slow. This may be seen in the difference in the social life of developed, developing and undeveloped societies. The following are the reasons for slow rate of or absence of inventions in a society:

(*i*) In the absence of traits like mental and intellectual capacity, perseverance and sustained labour, inventions are very few and far between. Societies which show these traits in abundance have abundant inventions.

(*ii*) Inventions are proportionate to necessity and demand. If the people are anxious for change, inventions follow. On the other hand, if the people are reluctant to change, inventions are generally not welcome.

(*iii*) If the members of society are not prepared to accept inventions, these are not circulated and encouraged. Therefore, social change is not encouraged. Thus, invention itself is not a sufficient reason for social change, it should be accompanied with mental preparation in the people to welcome and accept it. In countries where inventions are opposed, progress is very slow. For example, in India people opposed Railways, fearing pollution by smoke emitted from locomotives. Similarly, where prohibition is opposed, social change is discouraged.

2. Cultural Barriers. Man is suspicious of novelty and leaves new things, methods, systems, technologies, beliefs, relationships and ways of behaviour. By nature he tends to preserve traditions, customs, usages and old ways of life. Cultural barriers restrain social change . Therefore, people resist social change unless they are educated in favour of it and against superstition. In fact, ignorance and superstitions, wrong beliefs and fanaticism are at the root of opposition to social change. These may be removed by suitable education, propaganda and communication.

3. Social Barriers. Conservatism in social institutions is a chief obstacle in social change. Institutionalization itself is the process opposed to social change. For example, in India joint family system and caste system are serious obstacles to social change. Democracy is impossible unless caste system is uprooted. Change in rituals, customs, mores and traditions is necessary before any social change is introduced.

4. Political Barriers. These include institutions such as forms of state, nature of government, power and politics etc. A change in these is necessary to welcome any far reaching social change. Feudal lords everywhere resist social change. Monarchy and Totalitarianism are against social change, while democracy is in favour of it. Socialism and communism have introduced far reaching changes on the one hand and ruthlessly opposed other social changes.

5. Economic Obstacles. Poverty, unemployment, destitution are serious impediments in social change. However, these again may lead to revolution and far reaching social changes. On the other hand conspicuous consumption also becomes a serious obstacle to social change. Rich people and capitalists are notorious for resisting and retarding the processes of social change as they fear change may be against their interests. Therefore, neither poverty nor plenty are suitable conditions of social change.

From the above elaboration it is clear that acceleration of the pace of social change presupposes abolition of the barriers or obstacles to social change. Education is the best means to achieve this objective. Propaganda and communication and advertisements are other means to change beliefs and to encourage acceptance of social change.

Is Every Change Progressive?

That social change is for the most part based on technological advance is evident from the foregoing analysis. Technological advance is constantly accompanied by changes in the social organisation. But can every change of this kind be termed progress? This is a controversial issue. Society has benefitted by many advantageous changes which result from technological development, and there has been an increase in the means of the comforts and joys of life. But as far as the human relationships are concerned this effect has been none too healthy. Thinkers of consequence, such as Aldous Huxley, Sorokin, Toynbee, Schweitzer, Berdyev, Tolstoy, Mahatma Gandhi, Sri Aurobindo and others have sketched the ill effects of technological development and have warned mankind to be beware of them. It can be definitely asserted that all change resulting from technological advance is not in the nature of progress. This blind race in technological development is fraught with possibilities of grave errors. Thoughtful people have to pause and think as to where they are going and where they are to go. Technology is a means and to treat it as an end in itself is to make a stupendous mistake. What is the end? This can be known by ethics, philosophy and religion. Technology can be employed to advantage only by knowing the end and by using technology as a means to its attainment.

QUESTIONS FOR EXERCISE

1. Define social change. Analyse any one definition.
2. Write short note on meaning of social change.
3. Analyse the phenomena of social change.
4. State the main factors of social change and explain how these are interrelated.
5. Explain the meaning of social change and discuss the main factors influencing it.
6. Define social change. Mention briefly the major factors of social change.
7. Describe the factors of social change.
8. What are the factors of social change?
9. Write short note on social change.
10. Explain the concept of social change. Discuss its main factors.
11. What are the factors of social change? Give suitable examples.
12. What is social change? Explain linear theory of social change.
13. Describe the ways in which man adapts himself to the environment.
14. Distinguish between the physical, biological and social levels of adaptation.
15. Evaluate the role of the technological factor in social change.
16. Discuss the impact of technology on society.
17. Distinguish between cultural change and social change. Explain the influence of technological factors on social change.
18. Explain barriers to social change.

Chapter 2

Theories of Social Change

In sociology important theories of social change have been classified into three categories:

1. Unilinear Theories or Deterministic Theories.
2. Cyclic Theories.
3. Evolutionary Theories.
4. Functionalist Theories.
5. Conflict Theories.

These will now be explained briefly.

1. Theory of Unilinear Change or Deterministic Theories. According to this theory social change occurs in a straight line like the flight of the bird. Society incessantly proceeds towards definite aims. These aims of social progress are predetermined. Nature, fate or God has already determined them. Though the process of change may sometimes appear to waver but society always proceeds towards them. Historical accidents are helpful in this progress. Social change theory of Karl Marx is a Unilinear deterministic theory. Contemporary thinkers do not accept determinism or Unilinear movement. The following arguments have been forwarded in this connection:

(i) Cosmic. This theory tries to explain social change on cosmic level. Therefore, though this may appear to be philosophically feasible, it cannot explain change in human society.

(ii) Oversimple. This theory suffers from the defect of oversimplification. In fact social change is a complex process which cannot be explained by some pre-determined courses. It is difficult to fix the objectives of social change.

(iii) Unscientific. There is no scientific basis to prove this theory.

(iv) Pre-deterministic. This theory assumes objectives of social change to be pre-determined though these may not be so. Even if the society is proceeding towards some fixed objectives it is not possible to determine these objectives since this will require knowledge of the outline of future development of society. It is true that future may be predicted on the basis of past but neither does the human history exhibit some definite aims nor is it logical to accept some definite and fixed objectives of social evolution.

2. Evolutionary Theories. After Charles Darwin presented his theory of evolution, thinkers tried to trace the principle of evolution in every field of life, *viz.* philosophy, literature, religion, art, politics and economics. The evolution, however, may not be linear, it may be spiral, creative and emergent. Thus, while Auguste Comte, the father of modern sociology, traced linear evolution, Lloyd Morgan presented emergent theory and Karl Marx traced dialectical process. Herbert Spencer advanced biological theory of evolution.

3. Cyclic Theories. According to these theories, as is clear by their nomenclature, social change is cyclical in nature. Examples of cyclic theories have been presented by Oswald Spengler, A.J. Toynbee, Vilfredo Pareto and P.A. Sorokin among others. According to cyclic theories social change involves repetition. Philosophers and thinkers since ancient times admitted cycles of creation and destruction. According to this theory social change proceeds like the pendulum of a clock in which various stages return again and again. Many ancient and modern thinkers have supported their theory.

According to Spengler just as in the physical world different seasons come after one another, similarly cultures pass through spring, summer, autumn and winter season one after another. According to A.J. Toynbee, the histories of great cultures show that they have passed through definite stages of rise and fall. Thus, one may find some definite pattern in social change. Great culture is born in response to some challenge. Gradually this challenge, if not successfully answered, becomes a crisis and the great culture declines. Thus, there is a predetermined rhythm in the rise and fall of culture.

Cyclic theory of social change perceives a sequence in the change in nature and society. Just as human being passes through different stages in life similarly society and culture pass through several stages. Cyclic change influences even the fields of politics and art etc. For example, in the field of art there is change from traditionalism to romanticism and again from romanticism to traditionalism. In the field of philosophy Hegel has pointed out definite stages of transition. Human history passes from thesis to antithesis and then to synthesis in every field of human achievement. The thesis again gives birth to a new thesis and the process continues. These stages may be seen not only in thought but even in literature, art and other fields of culture.

Some truth may be seen in cyclic changes in these fields but there is no dearth of exception. Cyclic change is however, but one aspect of change everywhere. In other aspects there is no repetition. In the view of Pareto history repeats itself is true but it is as much true that it does not repeat itself. In fact, it the cases of repetition one may observe even differences. Some historical incidents resemble the earlier ones but others are totally new. So many factors are active in different fields of life. Here a question arises that if there is no definite pattern in history how are predictions possible? The fact is that all predictions are mere probabilities.

No historian can claim absolute certainty for his predictions. Human intellect is very limited. Therefore, whatever sequence we may discover in some fields there in no warrant to claim certainty. The dispassionate observer should always keep his eyes upon the facts, only then alone his assertion will be reliable. The scientist, while predicting, must be flexible and modest. Hence, in the final analysis cyclic theory is one-sided and merely probable.

4. Functionalist Theories. Functionalist theories explain change in terms of function. This class includes the sociological theories which have been propounded about the constituents of society on the basis of the function of its units. Examples of such theories are those propounded by Herbert Spencer, Emile Durkheim, Vilfredo Pareto, Malinowsky, Radcliffe Brown and above all Talcott Parsons. Contemporary followers of this group emphasise the interrelationship of social structure and function. Of these, the most notable are Robert K. Merton and Talcott Parsons.

5. Conflict Theories. Conflict theories explain change in terms of conflict of individuals, groups, classes and cultures. Examples of conflict theories may be found in the views of Herbert Spencer, G.E. Sumner, Ratzenhofer, Small and Oppenheimer. The most famous theory is that of Karl Marx.

EVOLUTIONARY THEORIES

Auguste Comte is regarded to be the father of sociology. He organised and classified the social thought prevailing before his times. Comte gave birth not only to a specific methodology of studying knowledge but also analysed the evolution of human thinking and its various stages. The principle evolved by Comte in the study of human thinking presumes gradual evolution and development in human thinking and is known as the law of three stages of thinking. It is known as the law of three stages because, according to it, human thought has undergone three separate stages in its evolution and development. The main importance of this principle is that it provides the basis of sociological thinking.

According to Auguste Comte, human thinking has passed through the following three stages. There has been an evolution in the human thinking so that each succeeding stage is superior to and more evolved than the preceding stage:

1. Theological or Fictitious stage,
2. Metaphysical or Abstract stage,
3. Scientific or Positive stage.

August Comte has explained his classification of human thinking into various stages in the following words: "....that each of our leading conceptions, each branch of our knowledge, passes successively through three different theoretical conditions, the theological or fictitious, the metaphysical or abstract, and the scientific or positive." In the following pages we shall discuss these stages briefly.

1. Theological or Fictitious Stage. The first or primary stage of human thinking is theological or fictitious. This type of thinking is found among the primitive races and sometimes the thinking of children is also at this level. At this level of thinking there is marked lack of logical and orderly thinking. The primitive men and children do not have the scientific outlook. Therefore, theological thinking is characterized by non-scientific or unscientific outlook. The unusual and unintelligible events of nature tend man towards theological or fictitious interpretation of the events. Unable to discover the natural causes of the various happenings, the primitive man attributes them to imaginary or divine forces. The explanation of natural events in non-natural, divine or imaginary conditions is known as theological or fictitious thinking. For example, if we explain and understand the excess or deficiency of rain due to godly wrath, such a causal explanation would be in terms of theological or fictitious explanation. The theological thinking implies belief in an other-world wherein reside the divine forces which control the events in this world. Thus, it is clear that theological thinking implies a belief in divine and extra-terrestrial forces. Comte has classified the theological stage further into three-fold stages. These are: (1) Fetishism, (2) Polytheism and Monotheism.

(a) Fetishism. The first and primary stage in theological thinking is that of Fetishism. Fetishism is a belief that there is some living spirit in the nonliving objects. This is also known as animism. As the very term animism signifies it means that the so-called inanimate objects are not dead and lifeless but are informed by a living spirit. The example of fetishistic thinking can be seen from the widespread belief among rural people in India that some deity resides in trees. They are, therefore, seen engaged in the worship of trees etc.

(b) Polytheism. With the gradual development in human thinking there occurred a change in the form of thinking. The move evolved and developed a form other than that of Fetishism known as Polytheism. At this stage man had classified gods as well as natural and human forces. Each natural or human force had a presiding deity. Each God had some definite functions and his scope and area of action was determined.

(c) Monotheism. The last and most developed form of theological thinking is seen manifested in monotheism. As the very term monotheism implies, at this level of human thinking a belief in one God had replaced the earlier belief in many gods. The monotheistic thinking symbolizes the victory of human intellect and reason over non-intellectual and irrational thinking. In monotheism it is believed that one God is Supreme and that He is responsible for the maintenance of order and system in the world.

2. Metaphysical or Abstract Stage. The metaphysical or abstract thinking marks- the second stage in the evolution of human thinking. According to Comte each successive stage is an improvement upon the earlier stage. With the gradual improvement in human thinking the human problems also become more complex and intricate. The theological thinking was not adequate to tackle these efficiently. The appearance of conflicting and opposite forces in the world presented problems which could not be successfully tackled by monotheism. In was difficult to believe that the same God was responsible for primordial creation as well as destruction. A personal and concrete God could not account for the simultaneous creation and annihilation. In order to resolve this intellectual puzzle or riddle, metaphysical thinking was invented. Under metaphysical thinking, belief in an abstract transcendental entity or Absolute replaces the belief in personal concrete God. Under metaphysical thinking it is believed that an abstract power or force guides and determines the events in the world. Metaphysical thinking discards belief in concrete God.

3. Scientific or Positive Stage. After theological and metaphysical thinking comes the next stage known as scientific or positive stage. All metaphysical knowledge is based upon speculation and is at best inferential knowledge. There are no direct means to confirm the metaphysical knowledge. In the last analysis it is a matter of belief or temperament. The modern temper of man is such that it cannot remain satisfied with mere guesswork; it craves positive knowledge which can be scientifically confirmed. The positive or scientific knowledge is based upon facts, and these facts are gathered by observation and experience. The observation and classification of facts are the beginning of scientific knowledge. From the facts we generalize and draw conclusions. These conclusions in turn are subjected to verification and once verified these become established laws, which can be relied upon in gathering and classifying the facts. The scientific thinking is thoroughly rational and in it there is no place for any belief or superstition.

Auguste Comte is of the opinion that all human thinking before reaching the stage of positivism must have passed through the two earlier stages of theological and metaphysical thinking. Even in scientific thinking some traces of earlier types are to be usually found.

Relation of Levels of Thinking to Social Organisation

Where Comte has tried to prove that there are various levels in human thinking, he has also tried to show that each of these is linked with a particular social organisation. According to Comte social organisation in a particular society is correspondent to the stage of human thinking through which it happens to be passing. It is only with change in the level of human thinking that there occurs a change in the social organization. The types of social organizations obtaining at the various levels of human thinking are discussed briefly below:

1. Theological Stage and Social Organisation. In the theological condition of human thinking, the social organization was of a particular type. The particularity of social organization at this stage was that the social laws, political laws etc., were accepted as absolutely valid and nobody questioned their validity. The theory of divine rights of king was accepted. The king was accepted to be the representative of God; and, therefore, the laws made by him could not be wrong. Most societies in the theological stage were ruled by monarchs and in some societies king was considered to be a God on earth. The discipline was quite rigorous in these societies. The primary reason for the rigorous and martial discipline was that the laws made by the king were considered to be divine and any violation of these was considered tantamount to disobedience of God's will. Therefore, no one easily dared to oppose and flaunt the laws of the society. Superstitions were rife in these societies.

2. Metaphysical Stage and Social Organisation. Under metaphysical state of human thinking, social organization was of quite different type from the social organization under the theological stage. These societies were guided by some abstract principles. The political system also undergoes change and the power of the king becomes restricted. The constitutional system of government gets priority. The constitutional changes are gradual and there is a movement toward decentralisation of power leading ultimately to ushering in of democracy. Thus under metaphysical stage some power passes into the hands of people.

3. Scientific Stage and Social Organization. In the scientific stage the social and political laws are determined in a definite and well defined form. In these Societies industry and technology predominates. The natural resources are harnessed for human good. The superstitions are mistrusted. Reason is demanded in every matter and the fear of divine wrath no longer prevails.

EMERGENT EVOLUTION

Meaning of Emergent Evolution

In the modern times, Lloyd Morgan presented a theory of emergent evolution. In this theory, as is clear by its name, every new level is an emergent. Thus, in the sequence of evolution the higher levels are different from the lower levels, and are not mere resultants. As against emergent theory, the resultant theory believes that a new level is merely a result of former level. The resultant theory has been supported by the materialist philosophers. According to it, in the process of evolution, each new level is a result of the past level. For example, 5 and 7 make 12. There is nothing in 12 which was not already in 5 and 7. In another example, a billiard ball hits at another ball and the two move in a new direction. But this new direction is a result of the motion and direction of both the balls. The new direction can be predicted on the basis of a knowledge of the motion and direction of both balls. As against this materialistic viewpoint, according to the emergent thinkers, a new level is not merely a result of the past levels but has much novelty in it. In the words of Lloyd Morgan, "When carbon having certain properties combines with sulphur having other properties, there is formed not a mere mixture but a new compound, the properties of which are quite different from those of either component. Now the weight of the compound is the additive resultant, the sum of the weights of the components; and this could have been predicted before any molecule of carbon disulphide had been formed. One could say in advance that if carbon and sulphur shall be found to combine in any ascertainable proportions there will be such and such weight as resultant. But sundry other properties are constitutive of emergents which could not be foretold in advance of any instance of such combination.

Criticism of Materialism

As has been already pointed out, according to the emergent theory of evolution, the materialistic explanation of creation is inadequate. In the words of Lloyd Morgan, "The whole doctrine of emergence is a continued protest against mechanistic interpretation and the very anti-thesis to one that is mechanistic." The following are the main distinctions between the emergent and the materialists points of view:

1. According to the materialists, matter is the only existent eternal and basic yet it is not the only existing substance.
2. The emergent theory condemns the mechanism of materialism.
3. According to the materialists, the world is born in final shape while according to emergent theory, it is imperfect.
4. According to the materialists, there is never an evolution of a new product while according to emergent theory the novelties take birth from time to time.
5. According to the materialists, the sequence of creation is absolutely predetermined, while, according to emergent theory, it has novelty in it.
6. According to the emergent theory, as against the materialists one finds some new qualities on each level of evolution as compared to the earlier

Due to the above-mentioned distinctions between the materialists and emergent theories the two have bitterly criticized each other but because the emergent theory was developed after the materialists theory, it has avoided several mistakes of its predecessor.

Characteristics of the Emergent

According to emergent theory, each emergent displays certain new characteristics of which the main are as follows:

1. Stability. Each emergent has more stability as compared to the substance before it, in spite of the fact that its existence depends on its predecessor. For example, a social group depends on its individual members, a body on the cell, a cell on the molecules and a molecule on the atoms and yet a group is more stable than individual members, body more stable than cells, a cell more stable than the molecule and the stability of a molecule is more than that of atom. Individual members come and go and yet the social groups and associations remain in existence. Similarly, while the cells are born and die the body is kept alive. Again, this is also true in the case of the cells and molecules. Thus, the stability of an emergent is not merely equal to its predecessor, but much more. Though it is dependent on the levels preceding it yet it is also independent.

2. The Structure of Emergent is More Different, External and Additive than its Constituents. As has been pointed out earlier, the emergence can be explained by the example of a compound and not of the mixture. The structure of a compound is different from that of its constituents. It exhibits certain traits which are not found in its constituents. For example, a molecule possesses certain qualities which are visible in the atoms. It not only includes the internal relations of atoms but also mutual relations among them. It is clear that these mutual relations are not existent in individual atoms. Therefore, the structure of molecule becomes very much different from the atoms constituting it. Similarly, the structure of a living cell is very much different from that of the molecules constituting it because it not only includes the structure of the molecule but also relationships among them. Similarly, the structure of an animal body is different from that of the cells constituting it. Again, the structure of a family is different from that of the members in the family. The structure of a city is different from the structure of houses in it. Similarly, the structure of a country is different from that of the cities within the country. In ail the examples, given so far, each new emergent, while it includes its constituents, also consists of their inter-relations and therefore, its structure becomes different from that of its constituents. It should be remembered here, that if the constituents are removed the constituted remain no more and yet no structure can be completely explained in terms of the structure of its constituents. For example, while it is true to say that if all the cells die, the living body will die along with them but does it mean that a living body is merely a conglomeration of cells?

3. The Method of Functioning of the Emergent is Different from that of its Constituents. Since the emergents possess new qualities their reactions in different situations are very much different from those of their constituents, in the same situations. For example, a society performs many functions which an individual cannot do. Again, the body has the capacity of performing many actions which are not possible by the cells. Similarly, the functioning of cell is different from that of the molecules which in its turn differs from that of the atoms. It is clear that many functions cannot be performed in the absence of emergents. For example, when men could not perform certain actions individually, they combine together in groups. These groups were gradually combined to constitute communities. It goes without saying that the group cannot perform functions characteristic of the community while an individual cannot carry out functions which are peculiar to the group. Had it not been so, what was the need of individuals combining in the groups and the groups constituting a community? Therefore, it is clear that many functions that are characteristic of community were not possible in the groups and the function carried out by the group could not be done by its individual members. Thus, the performance of new functions requires the emergence of new things.

4. The Laws of Behaviour of the Emergent are Different from those of its Constituents. Every emergent exhibits laws of behaviour different from those of its constituents. Thus, the laws of communal behaviour are different from those of group behaviour while these in their turn are different from the laws of individual behaviour. Not only this but the laws of the behaviour of a body are different from those of the cells and the laws of the behaviour of cells are different from the principles of the functioning of molecule which in their turn differ from those of the atoms. Had it not been so, what was the need of the emergence of new sciences for the study of behaviour of different emergents? Thus, the laws of communal behaviour are studied in psychology. Physiology studies the laws of the behaviour of the living cells. The study of the laws of the movement in atoms is the subject matter of physics. It is clear that the explanation of the laws of the behaviour of an emergent on the basis of those of its constituents is absolutely improper. This does not lead to the conclusion that the laws of behaviour of an emergent have absolutely no connection with the laws of behaviour of its constituents. Different sciences are intimately related though this relation does not make any difference in their independence. The knowledge of the laws of the behaviour of the constituents provides a suitable background for understanding the psychological principles. For example, the knowledge of physiology is helpful in understanding the psychological principles. Similarly, a physiologist is required to know the fundamental laws of biology. Again, the biologist should be conversant with the laws of physics though biological behaviour cannot be explained on the basis of physical laws.

5. Every Emergent has Peculiar Effectiveness as Causal Agent. The structure of every organism affects the structure of its constituents and they have to do certain functions which they do not do individually. Thus, the function of organs very much depends on the structure of the organism. In other words, the emergent is not only effective but also causal agent, for certain phenomena. For example, in human society the functions of the members in different groups and associations are determined by the structure and laws peculiar to them and so long as the individual retains his membership he has to act accordingly. Similarly, the functioning of the cells is determined by the body, that of the molecules by the cells and that of the atoms by the molecules. It is clear that the emergent originates many functions which were not possible before its emergence.

Different Levels of Emergents

The philosophers advocating emergent theory of evolution differ regarding the levels and numbers of emergents. In this connection Lloyd Morgan has pointed out, 'It is beyond the wit of man to number the Instances of emergence. It is due to this difficulty that one finds so much difference of opinion among emergent philosophies in this connection. Whereas Lloyd Morgan has admitted three different levels *viz.,* mind, life and matter, Sellars has not stopped at the mind but placed society above it, Samuel Alexander substitutes God by society and considers matter to be born of space-time. It is clear that all the philosophers have equally admitted the three levels of matter, life and mind. In our own times the theory of relativity advocated by Einstein has proved that matter is the outcome of space-time. It is on the basis of this theory that Alexander has postulated the level of space-time before matter. In the pyramid of evolution, Alexander places Deity at the apex, because the mind has a spontaneous attraction towards God. In the explanation of Nature, Sellars has found no need of bringing in a God and therefore he places society at the top of the pyramid of evolution.

Causes of the Evolution of Emergents

The questions of the what how, and why are very much important in the philosophical discussion of creation. Therefore, a question arises in the emergent theory of evolution as to what is the cause of the evolution of emergents. The advocates of this theory have discussed this question. According to Lloyd Morgan and Alexander the cause at the root of emergence is the nisus towards God. Both these are theists and therefore, they consider God as the motivating force. According to Lloyd Morgan, God is the directing force inside the scheme of creation. Alexander calls it Deity. According to him, every new level acts as Deity for the level preceding it. All the limited living beings are creations of space-time in a sense. The nisus is inherent in the structure of space-time as time. Motion is created by the activity of time on space. This limited motion is re-organized in the form of some groups of motion which create matter with some fundamental qualities. When this motion becomes even more complex, primary and secondary qualities are born. Life is born out of the variety and complexity of motion in matter. In the end, mind is born of the living complex structure. But the process of evolution need not stop at the mind because there is no reason why it should be so. From mind is born Deity and Deity of Deity will evolve in future, continuing evolution indefinitely. It should be remembered that generally by Deity Alexander means the future level of evolution. Being atheistic, Sellars presents a naturalistic explanation of the evolution of the emergents. Matter itself has the tendency of organization towards higher levels. This tendency itself is the cause of evolution of the emergents and there is hardly any need to bring in a God to explain it.

Characteristics of Emergent Theory

A comparison of the different theories of emergent evolution exhibits the following characteristics of this theory:

1. Synthetic Attitude. The most important characteristic of the emergent theory is the fact that it tries to present a theory reached by synthesis of different philosophical theories and the truth discovered by sciences.

2. More Scientific than other Theories. As has been already pointed out, the advocates of emergent theory have been influenced not only by the discoveries in the field of physical sciences but also by the discoveries in the field of social sciences. Thus, their theory appears to be more scientific as compared to other theories.

3. Balanced Attitude. In the discussion of different philosophical problems the emergent theory exhibits a more balanced attitude. For example whereas these philosophers have given importance to stability and controlling power to the mind they have not committed the mistake of calling it as the only or the most superior substance. While on the one hand, they have admitted matter, they have fulfilled the demands of religion by admitting God as the moving force on the other hand. While on the one hand, they are determinists, they have everywhere admitted freedom though in a relative sense.

4. Purely Evolutionary Standpoint. The emergent theory considers evolution to be necessary and continuous on every level. This process, according to it, is always moving forward and shall be so in future as well.

5. Optimism. In spite of tracing the evolution of the universe from matter, the emergent theory has expressed faith in realization of human values. Thus, these philosophers are optimists and the optimism is a necessary characteristic of all successful philosophy.

Criticism of the Emergent Theory

Different philosophers have presented different arguments against the emergent theory of which the main are as follows:

1. Inadequate Explanation of Values. The advocates of emergent theory have explained values from a naturalistic standpoint which appears far from being adequate. According to Lloyd Morgan, the values are particularly related to the mental level and can be explained only by a mind or a soul. The values thus, become subjective while in fact they are free, unique and self-sufficient. Any psychological, biological or mechanical explanation of values is one-sided and therefore inadequate.

2. Improper Synthesis of Naturalism and Theism. In the emergent theory one finds an improper and unjustified synthesis of naturalism and theism. In Morgan's schemes, if the principle of evolution is led to its logical limits, we arrive at the idea that the matter is evolved God. On the other hand, as a naturalist, Morgan arrives on the contradictory conclusion that God is evolved matter. In Alexander's theory God has been a mere product of the mind. The explanation of matter, life and mind before God is not coherent with the creativity and nisus of God, because there can be no synthesis of naturalism and theism.

3. Absence of Explanation of the What of Evolution. In any evolutionary theory the first question which arises is about the what of evolution. The emergent theory does not give any answer to this question. If with Alexander it is believed that space-time evolves, it does not explain the different levels of evolution. If every new level is born out of the complexity of space-time, there can be no real qualitative distinction between the emergents. The conscious cannot evolve from unconscious unless it is involved in it. Therefore, if life evolves from matter and mind evolves from life, the vital principle must be present in the matter and mental element in life and finally all these must be implicit in space-time. Alexander's space-time, on the other hand, is a blank form which different qualities cannot evolve.

4. The Linear Explanation of Evolution is Inadequate. The process of evolution, according to emergent theory, is linear. However true this may be in the case of matter, it cannot explain evolution in life and mind. Evolution, on the mental level, is spiral rather than linear because it involves extension and constraint, ascent and descent.

5. Epistemological Difficulty. According to emergent theory mind is an emergent. Then, how can it know the emergents different from it? According to emergent theory, the qualities, structure and laws of functioning of every new level are different from those of earlier levels. It is clear that having different qualities, structure and laws of functioning, the mind cannot know the qualities, structure and the laws of functioning at other levels. Therefore, one arrives at a type of dualism in emergent theory which gives rise to an Epistemological problem.

6. Against the Law of Causation. In the scientific field, the law of causation is recognized by everybody. In emergent theory each emergent is not merely a resultant of the levels preceding it but something entirely new. This view is against the law of causation because according to this law whatever is an effect, must be implicit in the cause, though we may not know it and however different it might appear from the cause.

7. Subordination of Matter to Soul, Unity to Multiplicity and Higher to Lower Level. Against emanationism, the emergent theory believes that plurality is prior to unity and unity is the result of evolution from multiplicity. Similarly, the emergent theory believes the lower levels to be preceding the higher levels and the spiritual evolving out of the material. For the spiritualists and emanationists, the real process is contrary to this scheme, and in fact God is rather the creator of matter than created by it. It goes without saying that this hypothesis is more consistent with the moral, religious and spiritual demands of man as compared to the emergent theory.

8. Too Much Importance to Matter. Like naturalists the advocates of emergent theory have given too much importance to matter and conceived everything to be born out of it. This hypothesis has been rejected by the idealists, spiritualists and organist philosophers.

9. Absence of Answers to Many Evolutionary Questions. Besides the above mentioned difficulties, one finds no answer to the following questions in emergent theory:

(a) If evolution is constant, from what evolves matter and space-time? In other words, what was the level preceding space-time?

(b) If evolution is continuous, why does it not proceed beyond mental level?

HERBERT SPENCER

Herbert Spencer has put forward some original and novel ideas about social evolution. Among the theoreticians of social evolution, Spencer occupies an important place. He has put forward his views in a special and peculiar manner. He has tried to explain the phenomenon of social evolution in the background of physical and biological evolution and has based his theory on these. Therefore, in order to appreciate Spencer's theory of social evolution it is necessary to learn something about his theories of physical and biological evolution.

Theory of Physical Evolution

In presenting his theory of physical evolution, Spencer has divided the universe into two segments: Known and Unknown. The segment of Unknown relates to religion and its subject matter is God and Soul. The Unknown has nothing to do with science, it is beyond and irrelevant to science. Science pertains to the segment of Known. Science is the discovery of the causes of the Known phenomenon. Science also tries to explain the origin of the matter and understand the laws governing its evolution, growth and development. Spencer was of the view that the rules and laws governing evolution in the physical world also apply to society. Thus, in order to understand the laws of social evolution it is necessary to understand the laws of physical evolution. Below we shall discuss the laws.

Main Principles of Evolution

According to Herbert Spencer in order to understand the laws of evolution of the physical world it is essential to know the fundamental cause of physical world. Besides, we should understand the primary and secondary laws of the physical world. According to Spencer the fundamental cause of physical world is energy, but it is not possible to know the form of energy. The form of energy is Unknowable. It cannot be seen. But we can experience its manifestations. It manifests itself in two ways, in matter and in motion. As fundamental invisible energy becomes active it manifests itself as matter and motion and it is by the action of matter and motion that the evolution takes place. The evolution of matter and motion takes place according to certain specific laws. Some of these laws are more important and are called primary laws while less important laws are known as secondary. Firstly, we shall discuss the primary laws.

1. Energy or Force Tends to Persist. According to the first law of energy there is no diminution or increase in the energy in the course of evolutionary change. The quantum of energy is persistent. It undergoes no change. The energy is the cause of evolution but is itself unaffected by the evolutionary process.

2. The Matter is Indestructible. According to Spencer matter which is one form or aspect of energy is never destroyed. It may undergo formal changes but it cannot wither away or vanish from the world. The changes in the form of the matter are responsible for the evolutionary process, but the fundamental nature of matter never changes. Therefore, matter is indestructible.

3. Motion is Indestructible. The third primary law is the law of motion. Like matter, motion also is never destroyed. The motion is continuous and it is never wholly dissipated. There are of course changes in the form of motion. It is on account of these changes in form that there are stages in the evolutionary process.

Secondary Laws of Evolution

Besides the above-mentioned three primary laws of physical evolution, Spencer has enumerated four secondary laws of evolution. These are:

1. Harmony of all Laws. According to Spencer there must be harmony among the various laws of evolution. No two laws should contradict each other.

2. Principle of Formal Changes and Uniformity. According to this law neither matter nor motion is ever completely destroyed. These undergo changes in form only. Of course, even during formal change the quantum of matter of motion remains static.

3. Principle of Least Resistance or Great Attraction. According to this third laws of evolution the direction of evolution is always towards the line of least resistance or greatest attraction.

4. Principle of Gradual Motion. For evolution motion is essential, but it is not required that motion should be at one level all the time. It may speed up or slow down.

Characteristic of Evolutionary Process

Having discussed the seven laws of evolution, Spencer undertakes a discussion of the process of this evolution. According to him evolutionary process is characterized by gradual increase in the integration of matter and concomitant dissipation of motion. Spencer avers that "Evolution is the integration of matter and concomitant dissipation of motion during which matter passes from an indefinite incoherent homogeneity to a definite coherent heterogeneity."

The crux of Spencer's theory of physical evolution is that according to Spencer in the process of evolution latent becomes manifest and that indefinite passes towards definiteness and lastly homogenous mass of matter becomes more and more differentiated.

Biological Evolution

As has been referred to above the social theory of evolution of Spencer is based upon his theories of physical and biological evolution. Therefore, in order to understand Spencer's theory of social evolution it is essential to understand his theory of biological evolution. Spencer has discussed in detail various aspects of biological evolution. The biological theory of evolution of Spencer may be described thus: animal has to struggle to preserve its existence. The struggle for existence is not confined to any one aspect of life but pervades whole of life. According to Spencer strong are always victorious. Only strong creatures survive and evolve; only strong make progress. The weak is gradually eliminated. It must be emphasized here that the term "strong" has been used here in a special sense. A strong creature is one who has the ability to adjust himself with the ever changing conditions of environment. A creature unable to make adjustment with the changing circumstance is weak and is liable to perish. The weak are unable to cope with the circumstances. The gradually mounting impact of adverse circumstance wears down the creature in the long run and they perish. Herbert Spencer adapted his principle of evolution from Darwin. Later on Spencer used same principle to propound his theory of social evolution.

Theory of Social Evolution

Spencer utilized the principles of physical and biological evolution in order to elaborate and explain his theory of social evolution. The analysis of physical evolution convinced Spencer that the underlying principles of all evolution are two. These are that evolutionary movement is from simple to complex and homogenous to heterogenous. The evolution is always a movement from indefinite and incoherent situation to definite and coherent situation. Besides the underlying principles of physical evolution, namely, a movement from simple to complex and homogeneity to heterogeneity, Spencer also utilized the underlying principle of biological evolution, namely, only those creatures survive in the struggle for existence who are able to make effective adjustment with changing circumstances. Spencer utilized these two principles to propound his theory of social evolution. He put forward the theory that like physical evolution, in social evolution also there is a movement from simple to complex. The society is gradually moving from homogeneous structure to heterogeneous structure. Besides, society is also moving from indefinite state to definite state. Transporting the idea of struggle for existence from biological evolution to social evolution, Spencer proposed that only those cultures survive which are able to adjust themselves with the changing circumstances. A strong culture is that which is able to make adjustment with changing environments. If a civilization is unable to make adjustment with the changing circumstances it caves in and gradually becomes extinct.

After giving theoretical explanation of his theory of social evolution Spencer presented practical explanation of his theory. By giving historical explanation, Spencer tried to prove his theory. According to Spencer primitive society was simple. Every individual lived an individualistic life trying to do everything by himself. Everybody was quite ignorant about organized life. In this sense, the people were homogeneous. At this state there was no system, nothing definite or coherent. They formed "an indefinite, incoherent, homogeneity. But gradually with increase in their knowledge a social organization came into existence. Thus, society moved toward a state of definite, coherent heterogeneity."

ORGANISMIC THEORY OF SOCIETY

The social thought of Herbert Spencer was heavily influenced by Biology. He had sought assistance of one or the other biological principle in setting up and explaining his social principles. In order to explain social structure he employed the analogy of a living organism. The theory which tries to understand and explain the social structure on the analogy of a human organism is known in sociology as "Organismic theory of society".

Herbert Spencer believed that the social structure is a living organism. It is made up of parts which can be distinguished but which cannot survive or exist except within the framework of society. Spencer wanted to explain clearly the nature of social structure by the help of this theory. Through in line with his theory Spencer considers society to be an individual writ large, he does not let the individuals lose their identity in society. Indeed he is an individualist and is a firm advocate of the independence and right of the individual. He only tried to point out certain striking similarities between the individual living organism and society on account of which the individual may be regarded as microcosmic society and society as macrocosmic individual. In drawing analogy between the individual and society, Spencer has drawn up an exhaustive list of similarities and dissimilarities between the individual and society. These are the following.

Organism and Society

1. Both are Different from Inanimate Bodies. The first similarity between a living organism and society is their difference from inanimate bodies. None of them is inanimate. In inanimate there is no growth and development, but, on the other hand, there is continuous growth and development in both society and living organism. Thus, on account of their common difference from the inanimate bodies, society and living organism may'be regarded to be similar.

2. In Both Increase in Quantity Leads to Change in Structure. The second similarity in society and living organism is that increase of quantity in both leads to change in their structure. According to Spencer as there is increase in the quantity of living organism there is change in its structure. The primitive living organism is a unicellular creature: but with increase in the cells differentiation of organs results. At the higher levels of evolution the structure of body becomes quite complex. Similar is the case with society. In the beginning the structure of society is very simple. At this level each individual does all the works by himself and there is no differentiation of functions. Each man himself is a craftsman, hunter, sculptor etc. But with the quantitative increase in the society the structure of society becomes more and more complex and there is increasing differentiation of functions in society. Like the organs of the society the functions in society become specialized.

3. In Both Change in Structure Leads to Change in Functions. With the change in the structure, organs and communities there results a change in their function. The functions become more and more specialized. This applies to the body of a living creature. With the changes in the structure of organs, there is change in its functions.

4. In Both there is Differentiation as well as Harmony of Organs. While it is true that with the evolution there develops greater differentiation in the organs of society as also that of an individual, but side by side this differentiation there is also harmony between various organs. Each organ is complementary to the other and not opposed. This holds true both in the body of a living organism and society.

5. Loss of an Organ does not Necessarily Result in the Loss of Organism. Society as well as individual is an organism. It is a fact common to both that a loss of some organ does not necessarily result in the death of an organism. If one individual loses his hand it is not necessary that this may result in his death. Similarly, in Society loss of a particular association does not necessarily mean death of the society.

6. Processes and Methods of Organization are Similar. There is another similarity between society and the living organism. According to Spencer as there are various systems, circulatory system etc. similarly there are various systems in the social organism responsible for its efficient functioning. In society, transport system, production and distribution systems etc. fulfil their respective roles. Thus, Spencer has shown similarity between a living organism and society.

Differences

Spencer was not a one-sided thinker. He was objective in his outlook. According to him while there are striking similarities between society and a living organism, there are certain crucial differences between the two which cannot be overlooked. These are:

1. The Parts of Body are Incapable of Independent Existence but Parts of Society can Exist Independently. Explaining the difference between a living organism and society, Spencer observes that whereas the various organs of the body are incapable of independent existence same is not the case with society. The various parts of society can exist independently. Whereas the limbs of body like hand, leg etc. cannot be conceived to exist outside of body there is no such difficulty in conceiving the independent existence of family, association etc., apart from society.

2. Difference Regarding Centrality of Consciousness. There is another difference between society and a living organism. The difference pertains to consciousness. In a living organism there is one centre of consciousness which is conscious of the whole body. There is no separate consciousness and thinking power in the various parts of the body. On the other hand, in society there is no central consciousness, only individual possesses consciousness.

3. Difference Regarding Dependence of Organs on Organism. Both society and individual are organisms. The organs of society are individuals, family, group etc. and the parts of body are its various organs. According to Spencer parts of the body are dependent upon the body. Their existence is for the sake of body. On the other hand, in society its parts are more significant than the society. Indeed society exists for the good of its constituents. Spencer was a thinker, he had affinity with individualist philosophy, according to which the state and society exist for the good of the individual and not *vice versa.*

Ever since the systematic discussion of the social facts began, varying views regarding the authority of the state have been expressed. The various scholars have expressed divergent views about the necessity, non-necessity, functions and advantages of the state. As we consider these questions an important point that arises for discussion is how did the state originate and how has it evolved. Spencer has expressed original views about the origin and evolution of the state.

According to Spencer the source of the origin of the state is the fear among people. It may be pointed out here that according to Spencer the origin of religion is in the fear of the dead souls. The development of the authority of the state leads to a tyranny of strong men. The power and authority of these persons induces fear among people. The terrorized people are sapped of their moral strength and will power and the domination of strong on them becomes firm. According to Spencer there are three stages in the evolution of the state. These are: (1) Military State: (2) Industrial State, and (3) Ethical State. Now we shall discuss in brief the characteristics of each state

(1) Military State. The primary form of state, according to Herbert Spencer, was a military state. In order to explain this form of the state, Spencer has used the principle of social evolution. In the beginning the society was simple, indefinite and homogeneous. At this stage society was undeveloped and little organized. At this state no specific authority of the state had come into being. At times different communities used to indulge in war against each other. In the course of wars some persons happened to show great act of bravery and heroism and they emerged as strong men and leaders of the group. In wars they acted the roles of Commanders and their commands were acceptable to others. At this stage chances of war were rather few and therefore there used to be no permanent chief or Commander. With the passage of time, society became more complex and in complex societies the chances of war also increased. At this stage the need for a permanent chief arose. When the tradition of permanent chief came into force, the chieftainship became hereditary. Now with the death of the chief the son of the chief used to replace him. Thus, the post of chief became hereditary and this was under the framework of the patriarchal system. Gradually council of advisers to aid the chief came into being. The council of advisers was appointed by the Chief himself. Some advisers were elected and they were supposed to represent the public interest. Thus, the authority of the state came into being.

The chief function of the military state was to engage in wars of self-defence and expansion. In this state the individual has little value.

(2) Industrial State. After the fall of military states the industrial state came into being. In the military state the aim and purpose of the state was to amass the military strength. But amassing of military might and waging war do not satisfy the aspirations of people. People want industrial prosperity. To this purpose public and government give attention to the development of industry and commerce. As the industrial development picks up the structure of the state also undergoes change. In an industrial state the development and growth of industry is the aim of the state. In the industrial state the tendency to attack other states declines. Gradually the industrial development gave rise to industrial state. In the industrial state the individual enjoys much more freedom than in the military state. There is also less interference in the personal life and liberty of people. There is also some amount of attention to the welfare of people.

(3) Ethical State. The idea of an ethical state is an imaginary conception of Spencer. The military and industrial state are in existence. But the rise of an ethical state is still in the womb of future. According to Spencer as industrial progress reaches its peak the prosperity would be universal and all the conflicts would disappear. In the state of extreme industrial development, the man's selfish interests would wane and give way to altruism. When this state will be reached man would automatically follow the moral law. There will be no need for external discipline. Man would automatically obey and observe the morality. All conflicts would cease.

Herbert Spencer was a firm believer in individualism. According to him it is the individual and not society which is primary, individual is not to be sacrificed at the altar of state; rather the utility of society is valid only in so far as it subserves the interests of the individual. According to him annihilation of state does not mean the destruction of the individual. Spencer was a firm votary of individual freedom. In order to preserve the freedom of the individual he formulated a law known as Law of Equal Freedom. According to this law an individual is entitled to same amount of freedom which he is prepared to accord to others. According to Spencer, indeed, the real aim of both society and state is to secure freedom for the individual. Therefore, according to him, the functions of the state are quite limited. Spencer was of course not an anarchist, he did not want to dispense with the state altogether. Indeed the state had certain important functions to perform. Spencer has drawn up a clear-cut list of functions which as state need perform and those in which it should by no means interfere.

CYCLIC THEORIES: OSWALD SPENGLER

Oswald Spengler propounded a cyclical evolutionary theory of rise and fall of civilization. It is the best example of cyclical evolutionary perspective. Spengler rejected all previous conceptions of historical time. According to him there was not one linear time but as many times as there were historical civilizations.

Spengler identified eight great civilizations with similar development and similar destiny. To quote his words: "Every culture passes through the age- phases of the individual man. Each has its childhood, youth, manhood, and old age. It is a young and trembling soul, heavy with misgivings, that reveals itself in the morning of Romanesque and Gothic.... childhood speaks to us also — and in the same tones — out of early Homeric Doric, out of early Christian (which is really Arabian) arts. The more nearly a culture approaches the noon culmination of its being, the more virile, austere, controlled, intense the form-language it has secured for itself, the more assured its sense of its own power, the clearer its lineaments. At last, in the gray dawn of civilization, the fire in the soul dies down. The dwindling powers rise to one more half successful effort of creation and produce the classicism that is common to all dying cultures. The soul sinks once again and in Romanticism looks piteously back to its childhood; then finally, weary, reluctant, cold, it loses its desire to be and, as in imperial Rome, wishes itself out of the over-long day light and back in the darkness of proto-mysticism, in the womb of the mother, in the grave."

Thus, according to Spengler, each society has birth, adolescence, youth, maturity, decline and decay. Culture is the rising phase of the society. Civilization is the decaying or declining phase of the society. During the culture phase the society has a soul which nurtures the folk spirit. All activity occurs during this phase. As society grows to enormous size, large cities develop like cancer on its body drawing off its vigour and vitality by continuing inter-personal relationships and by over institutionalizing social network. Concerning the city's history Spengler wrote, "Growing from primitive barter center to culture city and at last to world-city, it sacrifices first the blood and soul of its creators to the needs of its majestic evolution and then the last flower of that growth to the spirit of civilization and so, doomed, moves on to final destruction."

Noting the present crisis in human civilization, Spengler interpreted it as the last gasp of a dying civilization. "The history of the megapolitan machine techniques", said Spengler, "is fast drawing to its inevitable close. It will be eaten up from within, like the grand form of any and every culture when, and in what manner, we know not." Thus, Spengler predicts the doom of the present western civilization. He is not optimistic about man's future. As a thinker of doom he is pessimistic about man's destiny. He rejects any system, value, organisation or culture in humanity. As he observe: "Mankind, however, has no idea, no plan any more than the family of butterflies or orchids. Mankind is a zoological expression of an empty world. "

ARNOLD J. TOYNBEE

We have found by observation that the most stimulating challenge is one of mean degree between an excess of severity and a deficiency of it, since a deficient challenge may fail to stimulate his challenge parity at all, while an excessive challenge may break his spirit. But what about the challenge with which he is just capable of coping? This is the most stimulating challenge, imaginable, and in the concrete instances of the Polynesians and the Eskimos and the Nomads and the Osmanlis and the Spartans, we have observed, that such challenges are apt to evoke *tour de force*. Therefore, on the longer view, we must pronounce that the evocation of the greatest immediate response is not the ultimate test of whether any given challenge is in the optimum form, the standpoint of evoking the greatest response on the whole and in the end the real optimum challenge is one which not only stimulates the challenged party to achieve a single successful response but which also stimulates him to acquire momentum that carries him a step further from achievement to a fresh struggle, from the solution of one problem to the presentation of another. The single finite movement from a disturbance to a restoration of equilibrium is not enough, its genesis is to be followed by growth. And, to convert the movement into a repetitive recurrent rhythm, there must be an *Elan Vital* (to use Bergson's term) which carries the challenged party through equilibrium into an overbalance which exposes him to a fresh challenge and thereby inspires him to make a fresh response in the form of further equilibrium ending in a further overbalance, and so on in a progression which is potentially infinite.

This plan working through a series of overbalance can be detected in the course of the evolution of civilisation from its genesis up to its zenith in the 5th century B.C.

The first challenge presented to the new born Hellenic civilisation was the challenge of chaos and ancient light. It was victoriously met, it was decided that Hellas should be a world of cities and not villages, of agriculture and not of pastures, of order and not of anarchy, yet the very success of their response to their challenge exposed the victors to a second and a Malthusian problem. The response was in terms of Hellenic expansion though impeded in the 6th century due to series of causes. Thereafter, the Hellenic society was on the defensive, assaulted by the Persians, and Carthegians. The breakdown marked by the Athteni on Peloponnesian war followed nevertheless by a fresh outburst of geographical expansion.

We will now consider whether the progressive conquest of the physical environment by improvement in technique will provide us with an adequate intention of the true growth of civilisation. Is there evidence of a positive correlation between an improvement in technique and a progress in social growth? An example of improvement in technique in a static society is the Polynesians who have excelled as navigators, the Eskimos as fishermen, the Spartans as soldiers etc. An example of the reverse is the society in Europe where the people remained content with the implements of rough workmanship, but it developed a fine aesthetic sense.

The history of development of techniques, like the history of geographical expansion, has failed to-provide us with a criterion of the growth of civilisations, but it does reveal a principle by which a technical progress is governed, which may be described as law of progressive simplification. The ponderous and baulking steam engine with its elaborate permanent way is replaced by the neat and handy combustion engine. The copernican astronomy, which has replaced the ptolemic system, presents, in far simpler geometrical terms an equally coherent explanation of a vastly wider range of movement of heavenly bodies. Simplification connotes omissions and eliminations, whereas what has happened in each of the above cases is not a diminution but an enhancement of practical efficiency or of an aesthetic satisfaction or of intellectual grasp.

Our illustration suggests that the criterion of growth and for which we are in search and which we failed to discover in the concept of the external environment either human or physical, lies rather in a progressive change of emphasis and shifting of the line of action out of this field to another. In this field challenges do not impinge from outside, but arise from within, and victorious responses do not take the form of surmounting external obstacles or of overcoming external adversary, but manifest themselves in an inward self-articulation and self-determination. In Hellenic history, for example, we have seen that the earlier challenges all emanated from outside the challenge of Barbarianism in Hellas and the Malthusian problem which were met by expansion overseas and involved as their consequences challenges of facing Carthage and Persia. However, in the later stages, Hellanic society was threatened from within and its failure to respond successfully to the new challenges from within led to its decline.

This study and conclusions about Greek society can be effectively translated to the Western world too as a series of responses to never ending challenges. Arnold Toynbee, in his concluding essay, gives the criteria of growth thus: "We conclude that a given series of successful responses to successive challenges is to be interpreted as a manifestation of growth if, as the series proceeds, the action tends to shift from the field of an external environment, physical or human, to the interior of the growing personality or civilisation. In other words, the criterion of growth is progress towards self-determination and progress towards self-determination is a prosaic formula for describing the miracle by which life enters into its kingdom."

VILFREDO PARETO

Theory of Elites

Contemporary political science finds the elite concept indispensible if only as a hypothesis to be rejected. From the Paretoian approach have sprung such radical reappraisals of democracy as that of Schumpeter for whom it is a system in which elites publicly compete for the authority to govern. The work of Aron, inter-relates elites, government and social structure. The studies of community power structure of Hunter argues for the presence of an unidentifiable elite. Dahl argues the contrary, the great programme of comparative elite studies was carried out by Basswell and his school.

Pareto has developed his idea of elites in an original way. He has in the main discussed the class of governing elites. According to Pareto all men are not equal. They differ among themselves in regard to their capacities and abilities. Some are more intelligent, efficient and capable than others. On account of this difference in regard to abilities, there is social stratification. Some belong to superior class by virtue of their higher qualifications. Defining the class of elites, Pareto says, "So let us make a class of people who have the highest indices in their branch of activity, and to that class give the name elite. The elites form the upper classes and are usually also the richest." Thus, in every sphere of social activity, there is a class of superior persons which is termed elite. Pareto has chiefly discussed the governing elite.

Classes of Elites

Pareto has distinguished two classes of elites. These are:

(a) Governing Elites. In this class are included persons who are directly or indirectly concerned with administration. These persons play highly important role and enjoy prestigious place in society.

(b) Non-Governing Elites. In this class are included persons who are not connected with administration but occupy such a place in society that they somehow influence the administration.

Bases of Elites

According to Pareto there are two fundamental features which contribute to the formation of elides. These are:

(a) Qualities. The intelligence, the mathematical ability and love of fine arts, high moral calibre are some of the qualities which make persons superior to others. These qualities also contribute to making riches and therefore we normally find that elites belong to the class of rich people.

(b) Riches. As observed above, the better class of person's are also rich. It is normal that men of superior qualities should become rich. As Pareto says, "The so-called upper classes are usually the richest." These classes represent an elite.

Basic Characteristics of Elites

(a) There are two types of elites: the The persons not-governing elites. The persons not belonging to either of the above category are called non-elite.

(b) The elite manipulate overtly or covertly the political power.

(c) The class of elite is universal. It is to be found in every society. Whatever type or method of administration may be in , bound to be a class of superior persons which indirectly concerned with it.

Circulation of Elites

In every society there are two main groups. The one is concerned with government and usually controls the means of production and is therefore rich. The other group is constituted by those who are poor and governed. This fact is expressed by saying that in every society we find upper and lower classes. The upper classes are elite and the lower are non-elite. However, the distinction of elite and non-elite is neither permanent nor fixed. There is up and down movement of members of elite and non-elite. An elite may degenerate into nonelite and a non-elite may rise to the level of elite. This exchange between class is technically known as circulation of elites. No society can maintain *status quo* indefinitely, there are bound to be changes which may adversely affect the elite and help the non-elite. Though governing class does its best to prevent the entry of the member of non-governing class into its fold, it is not always successful in this. As Pareto observes, history is a graveyard of aristocracies. They do not last long; they are doomed to disappear by thinning down of their membership.

The up-and-down movement of elite takes place in two ways. Firstly, some non-elite by their merit may rise to the level of elite and secondly by revolution the entire governing class may be reduced to the status of the governed. Indeed, in the opinion of Pareto, circulation of elite is necessary for healthy social change. A slowing down of this circulation of individuals may result in a considerable increase of the degenerate elements in the classes which still hold power, and on the other hand, in an increase of elements of superior quality in subject classes. In such a case the social equilibrium becomes unstable and the slightest shock will destroy it. A conquest or revolution produces an upheaval which brings a new elite to power and establishes a new equilibrium.

According to Pareto the circulation of elites is due to acquisition or loss of qualities or merits. The persons who acquire merit move upward and those who become degenerate lose the membership of elite class.

Following are the points of criticism of Pareto's theory:

1. Pareto has not given adequate definition of the qualities of elites. These are vague and unscientific.
2. To say that circulation of elites is due to psychological factors is not sufficient. It must be shown as to what is the nature of these factors.
3. Pareto's hypothesis is not borne out by history.
4. Pareto has failed to maintain distinction between residues and their derivations.

Theory of Residues

Residues are the most important among social factors enumerated by Pareto. In order to understand the meaning of the term residue, Pitrim Sorokin has explained the meaning of residue in the following words: "Human actions depend greatly on the character of their drives. Among these drives the especially important are those which are relatively constant." Pareto calls them residues. His residue is not an instinct, nor is it exactly a sentiment. From this explanation it is clear that residue is a sort of motivator which is more or less fixed in human behaviour. Though it bears relation to instinct and sentiment, it is none of these. According to Pareto residues are manifestations of instinct and sentiment but the manifestation is not constant. Thus, sexual instinct may manifest itself heterosexually, homosexually, auto-erotically or in some other way.

Features of Residues

(a) Residues are more or less permanent motivators of human behaviour.
(b) Residues are neither instinct nor sentiments though they bear close relation to these.
(c) Residues are not based on any reason.

Types of Residues

1. Residues of Combination. These are the motivators which combine similars or opposites. These residues combine like with like.

2. Residues of Persistence of Aggregate. These are the drives to keep persistence or perseverance of man's relations to other men or places. These are expressions of sentiments held in high esteem and handed down from generation to generation.

3. Residues of Manifestation of Sentiments through Exterior Acts. Such residues impel us to express our sentiment by external acts. Our sentiment of patriotism may manifest itself in burning the effigy of the enemy leadership.

4. Residues of Sociability. These residues make for communal living. They also impel men to conform and induce uniformity in behaviour.

5. Residues of the Integrity of Personality. These are drives which help us to integrate our personality and ward off injurious sentiments.

6. Residues of Sexuality. These are the residues concerning the sexual urges. These residues influence our outlook, attitude and thinking.

Critical Evaluation

Pareto's complete system is valuable at many points, its mechanistic and atomistic nature, its definite of what is "non-logical", its oversharp dichotomy between ends and means, its assumption that ends are random and unsusceptible to any "logic of ends" and so forth. The residue theory and derivations are the two main pillars of this theory.

The central problem in the Residue theory is whether residue is a psychic cause of overt action or merely a description of these? Pareto himself recognises both senses of the word and warns that he will use it to mean both the cause of actions and the description of them.

If we assume that the residues are psychic states and hence causes, two difficulties arise. First, Pareto himself admits that the only way he can establish the existence of the "residue-cause" is through examination and classification of overt actions, not from any other and independent source. He also admits that he infers their existence from these overt acts; he does not know it. Thus, the only evidence for the existence of the "cause" is the overt action which is alleged to be its effects. To quote Sorokin "He puts those residues into a man and later on deduces from them whatever he likes." Causal explanation such as Pareto gives may be correct but he provides no proof. In the absence of such a proof, they are merely labels.

This does not mean that they are useless to sociology. To establish that some actions form syndromes in the sense that a man who performs one is usually observed to perform the others is not a senseless exercise. At the worst, it has some predictive value; at the best it permits "typing" men according to the peculiar syndrome of actions they perform. This is precisely what underlies such conception as "introvert-extrovert" or Znanicki's, "Bohemian", "Philistine" and "Creative" types of characters, or Resiman's "tradition- directed", "inner-directed' and "other directed types".

Involved in the concept of the residues is the concept of the Derivation, and this corresponds, closely enough, with what we now conceive of as "ideologies". This aspect of Pareto's residue theory is a major contribution which has exercised on contemporary political science an influence which is direct as well as profound. Indeed, in so far as the founding fathers of Italian Fascism looked to Pareto as one of their antecedents, it can be claimed that it exercised direct influence upon contemporary political practice. The expression "ideology" first used during the Napoleonic period, owes most of its contemporary meaning to Marx. For him ideology was the "false consciousness" which sees the world upside down, unlike science (including Marxism itself) which sees it truly. Pareto widened the meaning into roughly what we mean today: a system of thought which makes and rationalises human predispositions and urges and not simply the ones that are due to their economic interest or class position. More important, however, has been the associated distinction between the inherent truth or falsity of a belief, and its social utility, for this is the key to understand the social role of beliefs. Pareto's position resembles Plato's doctrine of the "noble lie", his position was of course shared by Sorel and Mosca. Disciplines like political science and the theory of propaganda have learned to regard beliefs as objective facts in the social situation, as far as social and political action is concerned, what matters is whether and how deeply the beliefs are held.

The role of ideology and propaganda as derivations of the Residue theory cannot be underestimated. These are now the starting points in the comparative analysis of government and politics. They have enormously reinvigorated the discipline and made it far more realistic, many tributaries have fed into the general movement. But Pareto's work is the only one which incorporates the elite, residue and derivations as positional references.

P. A. SOROKIN

Every thinker accepts the proposition that there is a close and intimate relation between personality and society. Sorokin has also deliberated on this theme. Sorokin accepts the intimate relationship between personality and society. Indeed, according to him, personality is an indivisible part of society. Neither society nor individuals can survive in isolation. They are inter-dependent. Sorokin is not prepared to consider either society or individual more important than the other.

Explaining the intimacy between society and personality, Sorokin writes, "Since individuals are the indispensable components of all social and cultural systems, their personalities obviously influence the framework of the social and cultural patterns; on the other hand as we have seen, the superorganic aspect of personality is not determined by or acquired from biological heredity. It is moulded by social and cultural milieu. There is no other source for the social and cultural properties of the individual." From this quotation it is quite evident that in the opinion of Sorokin the relationship between society and personality is very intimate and close.

An individual is according to Sorokin, a multi-faceted creature. He is not only related with society but is also deeply influenced by his connections with many other associations in society. Explaining in categorical terms his point of view, Sorokin writes, "My thesis is that the individual has not one empirical soul, or self, or ego, but several; first biological and second social egos the individual has as many different social groups and strata with which he is connected." Sorokin is a pluralist thinker.

SOCIOLOGY OF REVOLUTION

Pitrim A. Sorokin was well acquainted with the circumstances and causes of the Russian revolution. Therefore, Sorokin has analyzed in detail the sociological aspects of revolution. He has tried to make clear his conception of revolution in his various writings, particularly in his book: *The Sociology of Revolution: Social and Cultural.*

What is Revolution?

Sorokin categorically terms revolution a crime. The political revolution is nothing but a crime on a large scale. Indeed there is little difference between crime in general and the crime of revolution. If a revolution is confined to narrow limits, it is regarded to be a general crime, while, on the other hand, a general crime on a large scale is regarded revolution. Thus, it is obvious that in the opinion of Sorokin revolution is nothing but criminal act. Sorokin considers revolutionary crime to be the wrath of God. Therefore, he has included revolution in the category of wrath of God such as famine, epidemic, war etc. Revolution is thus inimical to the interests of the society.

Causes of Revolution

Sorokin has described in detail the causes of revolution. According to him contrary forces are always present in a society. There is conflict among these contrary forces. If there can be no harmony among these conflicting elements, revolution results. Sorokin also explains why the harmony is not possible. Like some other psychologists Sorokin believes that the behaviour of man is guided more by sentiment than by reason and that instinct plays large part in the life of men. Now if the natural instincts become corrupted for some reason, man is inclined towards crime and anti-social activity. In this condition social harmony is lost. As soon as social harmony is destroyed there is disorganization in the society and in a disorganized society the criminal tendencies get maximum scope of expression. Once revolution comes into force in a society all old values and social laws become extinct. Anarchy rules over everything and peaceful tendencies are subdued. In place of human behaviour animal behaviour becomes the nature of man. In order to substantiate his views on revolution Sorokin has referred to a number of revolutions and by analyzing them he has shown that his observations about revolution are valid.

Revolution and State Control

The revolution is directly concerned with state control. It is in the event of insufficient state control revolutions occur. Generally, State is indifferent to the seeds of revolution and does precious little nip in bud the revolutionary tendencies in the society. The State's attitude is relaxed and flabby until there is full blown revolution. Taking advantage of the flabby attitude of state, the revolutionary tendencies gain strength. When the revolutionary become strong the state gets alerted and uses its might to curb the revolutionary tendencies. This leads to direct confrontation between the forces of state and the forces of revolution. In a decisive battle that ensues whatever forces are more strong gain ascendancy. If the revolutionary forces are strong a successful revolution takes place; otherwise the revolution is curbed.

Effects of Revolution

As is quite clear from the above discussion, all social organisation is disrupted at the time of revolution. All norms of human conduct and thought, all processes of normal life come to an end at the time of revolution. The political fall-out of revolution is that the ruling clique is thoroughly discredited and may even be divested of property or done to death. Of course the persons in the forefront of revolution try to take a lion's share of loot. They act as a rule like a band of criminals. The men of peace are at a disadvantage in revolution and anti-social elements enjoy all the benefits.

Ways of Stopping Revolution

While, on the one hand, Sorokin has analyzed the causes of revolution and their impact upon society; on the other hand, he has also suggested ways and means to stop the revolution. According to Sorokin in order to control revolution change in human nature is indicated. The selfish tendencies of man must be converted into altruistic tendencies. If altruistic tendencies in man develop, the seed of revolution would never find any suitable soil to grow. It is in the mud of gross selfishness that these seeds take root and grow. Thus, Sorokin is of the view that by modifying the emotional nature of man we can put an end to revolution.

Analysis of Culture

Sorokin has made an exhaustive analysis of the concept of culture. He has made the scientific analysis of the development and changes in culture. He has also described the various processes underlying the culture. The principle by which Sorokin has tried to understand the cultural phenomena is known as the principle of cultural integration. In order to understand Sorokin's conception of culture it is necessary to discuss the various forms of culture. According to him there are the following three types of culture;

1. Sensate Culture,
2. Ideational Culture,
3. Idealistic Culture.

1. Sensate Culture. In this culture sensuous pleasures are considered to be important and the objects of sense perception are considered real. This sensate culture is materialist in its outlook and follows the philosophy of hedonism, *i.e.*, the attainment of pleasures is considered to be the aim of life. In such a culture higher values of life are disregarded and only sensuous pleasure is considered worthy. In sensate culture there is progress in science but fine arts are neglected. The liberty and philosophic pursuits are also at discount in this culture.

2. Ideational Culture. The second type of culture is known as ideational or indirect culture. The characteristics of this culture are opposite to that to sensate culture. In ideational culture sensuous pleasures are not given primary importance. However, in this culture spiritual pursuits are also not given much importance. The aim of this culture is attainment of bliss. The truth is considered to be supersensuous and its attainment is possible by divine grace. The amount of importance which is given to science in sensate culture is paralleled by the importance given to religion in the ideational culture. In ideational culture fine arts are used as means to attainment of the supreme good. Sorokin has high regard for such a culture. It may be said that the ancient Indian culture was of this type.

3. Idealistic Culture. This idealistic culture is the mixture of the above two types of culture. This culture is the culture of transitional society wherein neither science nor fine arts are given absolute importance. There is tension between the sensate culture and ideational culture. The modern Indian culture can be considered to be of this type. There is neither an ascendancy of science nor ascendancy of religion.

Cultural Fluctuation

Pitrim A. Sorokin has not only discussed the types of culture but also discussed the internal changes taking place in the culture. Some sociologists consider the cultural changes are in one particular direction while other believe that these changes are cyclic. Sorokin agrees with neither of these views. According to him cultural change is characterized by up and down. According to him one culture reaches its acme and then falls to its nadir and other culture comes up. For example, sensate culture, on reaching its acme, may take a turn and start developing into an ideational culture. Thus cultures alternate between sensate and ideational phases. Between these are periods of relative uncertainty and a mixture of culture comes to fore. The period of mixed cultures is known as idealist phase of culture.

From the above discussion it becomes plain that in this world there is rise and fall of sensate and ideational cultures. Now the question arises as to why these changes take place. What are the causes underlying these shillings of cultures. Sorokin has explained this process in his own unique fashion. According to him these changes are natural. As from the seed of pomegranate the fruit of pomegranate results, in the same manner a culture develops out of another culture. The changes in culture are not due to any external factors but are results of an inner necessity. Sorokin has named the principle of culture change as Principle of Immanent Change. Unlike other sociologists Sorokin attaches no importance to external factors in the changes of culture. The external factors can at most speed up or slow down the rate of change but the fundamental causes of these changes lie within the culture itself; they are inherent in the culture.

TALCOTT PARSONS

Functionalist Theories

In Sociology, Talcott Parson's theory of social action has a special significance and importance. The theory of social action is the cardinal principle of Parson's sociological thought. The ideas of Parsons are quite close to behaviourism.

Therefore, in order to appreciate Parson's theory it is important to distinguish it from behaviourism.

Distinction between Theory of Social Action and Behaviourism

In Psychology the theory of Behaviourism was propounded by Watson. According to him all behaviour, whether animal or human, was fundamentally of stimulus-response pattern. For example, there is an explosion and a man is afraid. The fear of man is a response to the stimulus of explosion. According to Watson the social actions are responses to various social stimuli. Behaviourism reduces all actions to stimulus-response pattern. The view of Parsons is different. According to Parsons while animal behaviour can be explained in terms of stimulus and response, the human behaviour cannot be explained in this manner. According to Parsons in human behaviour many factors other than stimulus and response play their part. In different psychological situation, a man acts differently. The self-same stimulus may produce different response in two persons. Thus, it is clear that Parsons' theory of social action is quite different from that of behaviourism.

Subject and Situation in Social Action

The behaviour of an individual or society in a social context is called "social action". Any social action has two main aspects. Firstly, there is an actor or a subject of social action and, secondly, there is a context or situation in reference to which the actor performs a social action. Any social action presupposes the existence of both of these factors or elements. The actor performs the social action, and therefore, anyone who does the social action is called the subject or actor. A social action, however, cannot take place in a social vacuum; there must be some situation or social context under which a social action takes place. The actor and situation of social action are mutually linked; they are interdependent. The actor by his behaviour, in turn, is also affected by the situation.

The Significance of Function in Social Action. According to Parsons, the main business of sociology is to describe and explain the social action. The concourse of many individuals results in a social action. In any social action each individual performs a specific function. In the analysis of a social action, it is important to know the function of every individual.

Types of Social Action

While discussing the meaning of social action, Parsons described the various types of social action. Talcott Parsons takes motivation or orientation as the basis of distinction among the types of action. According to Parsons there are three forms of orientation:

1. Cognitive Orientation. The nature of the orientation of social action determines its type. Therefore, with the change of orientation, the type of social action changes. If a social action is dominantly rational or cognitive it is said to have cognitive orientation. In a cognitive social act, the feeling or emotion does not play any part. It is dominated by rational considerations exclusively.

2. Cathartic or Emotional Orientation. Some social actions are predominantly emotional. Their orientation is said to be cathartic or emotional. In an emotional social action the inspiration for the action comes from within the man. In an emotional social action it is emotion and not reason that plays the dominant role. For example, under the influence of the emotion of love, a man is prepared to give up all his possessions or else make some other great sacrifices. In these actions rational considerations do not count.

3. Evaluative Orientation. The system of values plays a vital role in society. The different values inspire men to act in various ways. The actions guided by values are said to have evaluative orientation.

Social System

All sociological theories of Talcott Parsons are somehow based upon his conception of social action. The overt form of social action is expressed as role or function. The role or function presents itself in various ways. When the role is performed by an individual, then it comes under the category of Personality System. On the other hand when the role is performed in the context of some cultural background, then it comes under the category of Cultural System. And if a role is being performed in certain social context or background, then it is covered by the category of Social System.

Meaning of System

Parsons has discussed the personality, the cultural and the social systems. In order to explain the meaning of the term system, Parsons points out that each individual and society have certain nature or habit. It is generally believed that each individual should act according to his nature. We expect a certain kind of behaviour from an individual having a particular habit or nature. There is a norm or standard of behaviour in respect of each individual. Generally, the behaviour of a person conforms to this norm. If an individual acts against the expected behaviour and contrary to the norms of his behaviour, he is considered to be suffering from the disorder of his personality system. For example, if a celibate person indulges in lascivious and risque acts, he is considered to be imbalanced because a celibate is not expected to indulge in sex. This fact applies not only to individuals but is equally applicable to society and culture. From every society or culture a certain standard of behaviour is expected. If the behaviour is contrary to the norm or standard, anarchy ensues. Thus, a system implies conformity to a standard or behaviour expected of an individual society or culture.

Personality System. The personality system is concerned with the social actions of an individual. The social actions of an individual can be looked upon from two points of view. The first point of view is self-regarding, that is he views his action according to the nature of his own self. The second point of view is evaluation of the actions of the individual from the viewpoint of others. The other persons have a definite idea about the nature of an individual and they expect from him a particular type of behaviour; they judge with reference to the norm of behaviour they have in mind about him. Under these conditions an individual is prepared to make some sacrifice and also fulfil his desires. If the behaviour of an individual is in accordance with his own nature and the expectations of others, he is considered to have a well-organised personality. If, on the other hand, the behaviour of an individual is in conflict with his own basic nature or the expectation of others, he is considered to have a disorganized personality. A concrete illustration of this fact can be given. Let us suppose that there is a man who considered himself an altruist and is prepared to help anyone who is in distress and other persons accept him as a social servant and a sacrificer. Now if there is flood in the area in which he lives, he is supposed to do everything to help others. If he actually behaves in this manner he has a well-organized personality; but, if on the other hand, if he does nothing to help others or indulges in unsocial activity, he will be deemed to have a disorganized personality. According to Talcott Parsons each society expects a certain standard of behaviour from its members. Those individuals who conform to these standards in their behaviour are said to have well-organized personalities and those who fail to live up to the standards of behaviour expected of them by society are disorganized. For example, in most of the societies individuals are expected to be honest and truthful and, therefore, those persons who are dishonest or lie habitually are considered to have disorganized personalities.

Cultural System. When the individual system rises to the level of culture, it is known as cultural system. The individual and society gather cultural facts. The culture is represented by certain signs or symptoms. When any action is done with reference to these cultural signs and symptoms, Parsons includes it in the category of cultural system. For example, if certain social ceremonies are deliberately performed, the cultural system comes into effect. Where the ceremonies or social formalities remain unchanged for a long time, there the cultural system is said to be well-organized. On the contrary, if the culture of society does not affect the lives of the individuals, the cultural system is then ill-organized. Thus, it is clear that a cultural system is well-organized as long as it actively influences the lives of the individuals.

Social System. A society is made up of individuals. A number of different types of individuals live in society. They may have a common culture or may belong to different sets of culture. According to Parsons if all individuals in a society belong to same culture, they form a social system. The various cultural signs or symptoms have self-same meaning for all the members of that society. For example, in a Hindu Society all individuals illuminate their homes by earthen lights, candles etc., on a particular day. If for all of them this lighting and illumination is related to the story of Rama's victorious return to Ayodhya then we can say that a social system obtains in the society. Besides commonness of culture it is necessary for a social system that the social actions of various members of a society should be well-coordinated and should not so conflict as to destroy the social harmony. In advanced society certain institutions do the work of systematization of these social actions.

Functional Pre-requisites

Talcott Parsons no doubt is the leading exponent of the concept of "social system". Despite wide usage of this concept by other sociologists, its development by Parsons on many levels of abstraction and its application by him to a wide range of human interaction not only gives him undisputed primacy in its use but also has provided a basis for extensive secondary literature.

Two basic doctrines underlie Parsons' delineation of the four categories of activity which are variously related to social systems as phases, problems and functional imperatives. He subscribes to the view that action generated within any given social system is in part directed towards its internal situation, the proportions varying with the type of system. The external-internal dichotomy is one axis. Consistent with this means-ends formulations, he also sees some activity as instrumental in that its product represents the means to a goal and not the goal itself, whereas other activity is consummatory in that the product *per se* of the activity or the activity itself represents the goal attainment. The instrument consummatory dichotomy is the 2nd axis, which upon interaction with the external-internal axis describes 4 general areas of activity as revealed in the table that follows:

		Instrumental	Consummatory	
External	A	Adaptive functions	Goal attainment functions	G
Internal		Pattern Maintenance and Tension Management functions	Integrative functions	
	L			I

The activity occurring in each social system is directed in part to all the four categories described above, although its emphasis in one of the four categories justifies its classification as primarily of one type or other. Thus the family falls into cell 'L' above but nevertheless exhibits all the four patterns.

The important sub-systems of the larger modern society are differentiated by their assumption of activity predominantly devoted to one or other of the four categories.

The execution of such activity is functional imperative, its specialized role legitimised societally by cultural evaluations. The economic producer or in more abstract terms, economy belongs to cell A, policy to cell G organizations oriented to the generation and allocation of power like government, banking etc. The Churches, the schools, the arts, and the kinship groups primarily of pattern maintenance fall in cell L. Each of the four categories possess distinctive functional problems or dimensions of social structure and process and hence give rise to differentiated organizations. According to Parsons, "a good organization for the physical production of goods at the technical level would inevitably be a bad one for the educational process."

Whatever its functional imperative, the concrete formal organisation exhibits differentiated activity levels separated from each other by observable breaking points, each level responsible to the organization for its own functional imperative in as much the same way that the organization as a sub-system is responsible to the society for a given function. A more concrete presentation is the picture of an economic organization which faces the adaptive exigencies of procurement of the factors of production, land, labour, capital and 'organization' in a competitive society. Having procured the fluid resources through the adaptive process, the organization is now faced with the necessity for providing a set of mechanisms by which these resources can be brought to bear on the actual process of goal-implementation in a changing situation. These "operative goal-attainment mechanisms" prove to be decisions operating clearly for internal integration also.

The central focus of the integrative sub-systems of a society is boundary interchanges among various sub-systems. The very pattern maintenance which gives sub-systems their cohesion can also be a centrifugal force in jeopardising cohesion of social systems at a higher level The problem of interpretation, for a given social system becomes one of extending and maintaining the range of solidarity to a point of inclusiveness more or less commensurate with the emerging from decision-making process, boundaries of the given social system. Loyalty, co-ordination, co-operation, efficiency, motivation are all terms used by Parsons in connection with internal integration.

Parsons Contribution

Talcott Parsons is no doubt the leading exponent of the concept of "Social system". Despite wide usage of the concept by other sociologists, its development by Parsons on many level of abstraction and its application by him to a wide range of human interaction not only gives him undisputed primacy in its use but also has provided a basis for an extensive secondary literature. This in turn has broadened the usage of the concept for Parson's talks about the integrative adaptive features of a social system as a functional pre-requisite. He describes the rules of "actor orientation" in a "situation" and differentiates "need" primacy from "norms" or "standard" primacy as classifications of the former.

Parsons views all the four components of organization — the cultural, social, psychological and biological, as being analytically separable and mutually reducible, each possessing unique and emergent properties which make its distinction truthful. At the same time there is a high level of inter-relatedness inter-penetration among the components of systems, a circumstance which is basic to a fundamental working assumption.

Although emphasising social system in the tradition of sociology, Parsons is always eminently concerned with the general theory of action without which, in his opinion, important boundaries of the social system with the other three systems remain unexplored. Parsons first attempts to discriminate types of social structure following, the lead from Tonnies, distinction of Gemeinschaft and

Gesellschaft and from Max Weber's refinements thereof. Gradually tie 'became convinced that although a given structure might clearly exhibit attributes suggestive of one polar type, it often possessed other attributes not necessarily represented by that same polar type. As an example he noted that Marshall was right in interpreting increasing economic rationality as an inherent tendency of human action but wrong in thinking that it is associated only with a specific type of social organization, such as free enterprise which is Gessellschaft like, and that it cannot be made compatible with another type of social organization, such as traditionalism of the Indian Caste system which is Gemeinschaft like.

Parsons treats Effectivity *Vs.* Affective neutrality, Diffuseness *Vs.* Specificity, Particularism *Vs.* Universalism, Quality *Vs.* Performance, Collectivity Orientation *Vs.* Self Orientation as Pattern Variables of a social structure.

KARL MARX

Conflict Theories

The fundamental principles of Dialectical Materialism of Karl Marx are as follows:

1. Dialectical Change. The Dialectical conception declares that the laws of reality are the laws of change. There is a constant transformation in inorganic nature as well as in the human world. There is no eternal principle. Human and moral conceptions change from one age to the next.

2. Evolution. The real world is also characterized, as it were, by a hierarchy in the species of being, a sort of qualitative progression from inorganic nature to the human world, and in the human world from the initial regimes of humanity to the regime which will mark the end of prehistory in the socialistic regime.

3. Laws of Change. Natural and social changes occur in accordance with certain abstract laws. Beyond a certain point, quantitative changes becomes qualitative. The transformations do not occur imperceptibly a little at a time, but at a given moment there is a violent, revolutionary shift. Finally, the changes seem to obey an intelligible law, the law of contradiction or, the law of negation of negation.

What is the negation of negation? According to Engels, if you negate A, you have minus A; if you multiply A by A, you have A, which is apparently the negation of negation. An example of this in the human world is the capitalistic regime which is the negation of the regime of feudal ownership. Public ownership under socialism will be the negation of negation *i.e.,* the negation of private ownership.

In the concept of dialectics, first there is the ideas of change and then the idea of the relativity of ideas or principles of circumstances. One of the dialectics that plays the greatest role in the thinking of Marx and the Marxists is precisely the possible contradiction between the forces of production and the relation of production. One of the simplest versions of the dialectics would be the following: At a certain degree of development of the forces of production, individual ownership represents an impediment to their progress. It leads to the contradiction between the full expansion of the technique of production and the preservation of individual right of ownership.

This contradiction contains, it seems to us a share of truth, but it is not relevant to the dogmatic Marxist interpretations. If we consider the great modern enterprises in France such as Citroen, Renault or Dupont or General Motors in the U.S., we can say in effect that the volume of forces of production has made it impossible to maintain individual right of ownership. For example, Dupont, General Motors etc., belong to thousands of shareholders, and while the latter and owners in the legal sense, they no longer exercise the traditional and individual right of ownership. Modern corporations are already overcoming typical capitalism and therefore it may be said that Marx was right to show the contradiction between the development of the forces of production and individual right of ownership since in the modern capitalism of the great shareholding associations, right of ownership, in a certain sense has disappeared.

On the other hand, if you believe that the great modern corporations the great shareholding associations, are the very essence of capitalism., then it is easy to demonstrate that the theoretical contradiction between forces and relations of production do not exist. The development of the forces of production, or again new forms of traditional right of ownership.

According to the second interpretation, the distribution of income determined by the individual right of ownership is such that a capitalist society is incapable of absorbing its own production. In this case, the contradiction between the forces and relation of productions affects the very functioning of the capitalist economy. The purchasing power distributed to the masses would always remain lower than the demands of the economy itself. Here a commonsense observation would be that this contradiction has been exposed for a century and a half. Meanwhile the forces of production in all capitalistic countries have undergone a prodigious development.

In other words, incapacity of the economy based on private ownership to absorb its own production was already predicted when the forces of production were fifth or tenth of what they are today, and this will still be the case when the forces are five or ten times what they are today — which would seem to indicate that the contradiction has not been clearly demonstrated. It continues to be unknown as to what point an economy in which private ownership pursuit is Incapable of absorbing its own production.

In other words, neither of the two reasons of contradiction between forces and relations of production have been demonstrated. The only version that obviously contains a share of truth is the one that does not lead to those political and messianic propositions on which the Marxists insist most strongly.

Historical Evolution

Dialectical materialism contains all the essential ideas of Marx's economic interpretation of history. The 1st and essential idea is that men enter into definite relations that are independent of their will. In other words, we can follow the movement of history by analysing the structure of societies, the forces of production, and men's ways of thinking about themselves. Secondly, in every society there can be distinguished the economy base or infrastructure as it has come to be called, and the superstructure within which figure the legal and political institutions as well as ways of thinking, ideologies and philosophies. Thirdly, the mechanism of the historical movement is the contradiction, at certain movements in evolution, between the forces and relations of production. The forces of production seem to be essentially a given society's capacity to produce, a capacity which is a function of scientific knowledge, technological equipment and the organisation of collective behaviour or labour. The relations of production which are not too precisely defined seem to be essentially distinguished by relations of property. However, relations of production need not be identified with relations of property; or at any rate relations of production may include in addition in property relations, distribution of National Income which is itself more in less strictly determined by property relations.

Class Struggle

Now it is easy to introduce the class struggle, into this contradiction between forces and relations of production although, again, Marx has not made direct reference to it. Indeed we need merely suppose that in revolutionary periods, one class is attached to the old relations of production which are becoming an obstacle to the development of the forces of production and another class, on the contrary, is progressive and represents the relations of production which, instead of being an obstacle in the way of the development of the forces, will favour the maximum growth of those forces. In a capitalistic society the bourgeoisie and the proletariat are the two forces.

Theory of Revolution

This dialectic of forces and relations of production also implies a theory of revolution. For in this vision of history, revolutions are not political accidents, but the expression of historical necessity. Revolutions perform necessary functions and they occur when conditions for them are given. Capitalistic relations of production were first developed in the womb of feudal society. The French Revolution occurred when the new capitalist relations of production had attained a certain degree of maturity. And, at least in this passage, Marx foresaw an analogous process for the transition from capitalism to socialism.

Economic Determinism

In this historical interpretation, Marx not only distinguished infrastructure and superstructure; he also opposed social reality to consciousness. It is not men's consciousness that determines reality, on the contrary, it is the social reality that determines their consciousness. Statements of this kind may provide a basis for what is referred today as sociology of knowledge.

Stages of Human History

Finally, a last theme contained in his *"The Communist Manifesto"* is the stages of human history. Just as Auguste Comte differentiated moments of human evolution on the basis of ways of thinking, so Karl Marx differentiated stages of human history on the basis of their economic regimes, and he distinguished four of these or in his terminology four modes of production which he called the Asiatic, the Ancient, the Feudal and the Bourgeoisie.

QUESTIONS FOR EXERCISE

1. Discuss August Comte's theory of gradual evolution in Human thought.
2. State and explain the theory of Emergent Evolution propounded by Lloyd Morgan.
3. Evaluate the contribution of Herbert Spencer to social evolution and social change.
4. Comment on the Organismic analogy in the sociology of Herbert Spencer.
5. Describe the gradual evolution of the state according to Spencer.
6. Discuss Oswald Spengler's theory of evolution of civilization.
7. Discuss the Significance of Toynbee's Theory of "Challenge and Response"
8. Discuss Vilfredo Pareto's Theory of Elites.
9. What does Pareto mean by 'circulation of elites'? Explain with examples.
10. Discuss Pareto's Theory of Residues.
11. Examine Pareto's Theory of Residues and Derivations.
12. Write short note on Personality and Society according to Sorokin.
13. Discuss Sorokin's views on the Sociology of revolution.
14. Critically examine Sorokin's analysis of culture.
15. Discuss Talcott Parsons' theory of social action. How far was he influenced by other social thinkers?
16. How far Talcott Parsons' theory has been influenced by Max Weber's analysis of social action?
17. What according to Parsons are the functional prerequisites of a social system?
18. Examine the concept of social system as delineated by Talcott Parsons.
19. Discuss Talcott Parsons contributions to the modern sociological thought.
20. Write an essay on Dialectical Materialism of Marx.
21. Critically examine Karl Marx's Theory of Society.

CHAPTER 3

M.K. Gandhi's Theory of Social Change: Sarvodaya

Literally speaking the Hindi term Sarvodaya is a combination of the term 'sarv' meaning all and 'udaya' meaning evolution or uprising of development. Thus Sarvodaya means total evolution or total development without leaving even the worst person outside its spheres. M. K. Gandhi developed the ideology of Sarvodaya by the influence of Ruskins' *Unto This Last*' in Gujarati language. M. K. Gandhi translated this book with the title Sarvodaya. This book emphasises the following three ideas:

1. The individual's welfare lies in the welfare of all.
2. Even the job of a Barber is as much important as the job of an advocate since all the individuals have a right to earn their living by their activities.
3. Only the life of a labourer is worth living. It was due to Ruskin's influence that M.K. Gandhi arrived at his famous trusteeship theory. He believed that the wealth, like water, must flow towards the poor. In order to propagate his views on this issue M. K. Gandhi published a monthly magazine *Sarvodaya*,

Historical Background

This does not mean that the ideal of Sarvodaya is the creation of M. K. Gandhi. The ideal of Sarvodaya has been there in India since the days of Vedas where seers have prayed for the happiness of all Similarly 2000 years back the Jain scholar Samant Bhadra said, "Sarvodaya is the destroyer of all calamities, it is my pilgrimage." The ideal of '*Sarva Bhuta Hite Ratah*' propounded by Bhagwadgita, is in fact, the ideal of Sarvodaya. Among contemporary Indian philosophers the ideal may be found in the ideals of Swami Vivekananda, Swami Dayananda, Raja Ram Mohan Rai, Keshab Chandra Sen, Annie Besant, Rabindra Nath Tagore, Bhagwan Das and Sri Aurobindo. It is not only the traditional Indian contemporary philosophers who have supported this ideal but also those contemporary Indian thinkers who were influenced by Western thoughts such as J.L. Nehru and M. N. Roy. However, M. K. Gandhi and after him Vinoba Bhave, Jaiprakash Narain and Kaka Kalelkar have the credit of conceptual formulation of the ideal, its development and its taking shape into a popular movement. Today, Sarvodaya ideology is considered as an alternative to communism, and a better alternative since it is against violence, war and class struggle. As against communism it lays emphasis upon love, humanism, peace and harmony.

Man, A Moral Being

M. K. Gandhi maintained that basically the problem of human beings is a moral problem. If a man becomes a human being in the true sense of the term there may not be anything like conflict among human beings. Therefore, every thoughtful person must follow the still small voice of reason everywhere though it is often suppressed by selfishness and the animal element in man. Long back Swami Vivekananda explained this ideal as the ideal of man-making. Therefore, Sarvodaya insists upon moral character as a solution of all evils — economic, social and political.

Thus, Sarvodaya means welfare of all and not of any particular class. This makes for the difference between Sarvodaya and communism or utilitarianism. Sarvodaya differs from Marxism though to some extent there is some agreement on some points so much so that Gandhism has been said to be communism minus violence.

SIMILARITIES BETWEEN SARVODAYA AND COMMUNISM

The following are some overt similarities between Sarvodaya and Communism:

1. Opposition of Social Injustice. Both these ideologies are dissatisfied with the present economic, social and political injustice and inequality. They oppose social injustice and wish to eliminate all sort of inequalities between human beings.

2. Stateless Society. Both Gandhi and Marx considered state as a mere means and not an end. Both called it a necessary evil which sometimes becomes an instrument of repression. M. K. Gandhi was against the violent means of the state. Therefore, both Marx and Gandhi were anarchist. However, they differed in details in their idea about state. While Karl Marx maintained that the state will wither away with the establishment of a proletarian society, M. K. Gandhi asks for decentralisation of power for the purpose. Of these two the latter idea appears to be more practical. In fact in communist countries the states have become more and more powerful.

3. Classless Society. Both Sarvodaya and communism aim at a classless society in different ways. Communism seeks to achieve the ideal by eliminating the capitalist class and even the middle class. Sarvodaya, on the other hand, seeks to achieve the ideal by realising perfect co-operation and harmony between all the classes so that there may be no class conflict.

4. Support to Repressed Class. Both the ideologies support the weaker sections or the repressed classes in society. Both insist upon provision of minimum necessities to the backward classes so that everyone should achieve opportunities for the development of the capacities. As Kishori Lal Mashruwala has pointed out, Gandhi and Marx both are worried about the repressed, meansless and ignorant, dumb and a hungary sections of society.

5. Humanism. Both Marx and Gandhi were humanist. However, while Karl Marx explained human nature through his materialist principle of economic determinism, Sarvodaya defined human nature as divine and spiritual. Therefore, while Marx presented the ideal of economic man, Gandhi's man is a moral being, first and last.

6. Emphasis upon Labour. Both communism and Sarvodaya lay emphasis upon labour. According to M. K. Gandhi everyone should earn his living and physical labour is no less valuable than the mental labour. Similarly, communism has everywhere eulogised the labour which is the factor increasing the value of the raw material and creating surplus value which is the share of the labourer. Both are against the idle middle man and the capitalist who earns without any labour on his part. Both call him an exploiter and both are against exploitation.

7. International Peace. Communism and Sarvodaya both declare elimination of war and establishment of world peace as their aim. However, it is difficult to understand how there may be a compromise between encouragement to violent revolution and realisation of world peace, both advocated by the communists.

DISSIMILARITIES BETWEEN SARVODAYA AND COMMUNISM

The above discussion shows that there is only overt similarity between communism and Sarvodaya and in fact they have more dissimilarities than similarities. Vinoba Bhave has pointed out that to say that Sarvodaya and communism differ only with reference to violence is to forget that this very difference makes the two entirely different. In fact there cannot be any compromise between the two. The following are the important distinctions.

1. Philosophical Bases. Philosophically speaking, Sarvodaya and communism are based upon totally different metaphysical background as well as epistemology and axiology. While communism is materialism, Sarvodaya is based upon a spiritual world view. While Communism is empiricism Sarvodaya is idealism. While Communism is hedonism Sarvodaya is spiritualism and even asceticism. M.K. Gandhi considered self-control and non-covetousness as necessary qualities of an aspirant after Sarvodaya. He insisted upon minimisation of needs and desires. This is in tradition with Indian philosophy and Indian psychology according to which mental control is a *sine qua non* of liberation.

2. Means end Relationship. As has been already pointed out, in our discussion of the philosophy of M. K. Gandhi, Sarvodaya believes that the means should be as good as the end. On the other hand, communist do not believe in the purity of means. For a communist revolution any means, however inhuman it may be, may be adopted to achieve the end. Therefore, while Sarvodaya insisted upon moral means, communism makes no distinction between moral and immoral means.

3. Methodology. The above two distinctions make an absolute difference between the methodology of Sarvodaya and communism. Sarvodaya permits only non-violent, human and spiritual means to achieve any social change. Evolution and not revolution is its techniques. Even where it accepts revolution, it is absolutely non-violent. M. K. Gandhi was so much against violence that he maintained that if India adopts violence he will not like to live in this country. Communism, on the other hand, directly supports encouragement to class hatred, conflict and violence. The Russian leaders, since Lenin to present day, have backed violent means to encourage communism everywhere. Communism does not believe in evolution but only in revolution.

4. Social Classes. Sarvodaya and communism are poles apart so far as the question of class conflict is concerned. Karl Marx maintained that the history of different societies is the history of conflicting classes. According to Sarvodaya world view, society is based upon co–operation rather than conflict. The communists seek to intensify class conflict, the Sarvodaya workers seek to reduce it to their minimum. Class conflict has no place in Sarvodaya. In place of conflict Sarvodaya emphasises love, sacrifice and satyagraha for bringing about co–operation and harmony between classes. M. K. Gandhi was against capitalism but not the capitalist. He maintained that the capitalists may remain if they think themselves as trustees of the public wealth and utilise it for general welfare. Communist, on the other hand, insists upon not only the elimination of capitalism but even the elimination of the capitalists and their stooges the petty bourgeois.

5. Role of Religion. M. K. Gandhi was a religious man and so were all the famous advocates of the Sarvodaya ideal. Karl Marx, on the other hand, was absolutely against religion in eveiy form and so were all the other spokesmen of communism. Communism does not believe in the existence of God. For M. K. Gandhi, as has been already pointed out, the political leader should remember God 24 hours in a day. Thus, Sarvodaya ideology believes in God and religion and also seeks to encourage it. The structure of Sarvodaya is based upon religious and spiritual foundation. The edifice of communism is based upon materialism which is against all religion as such.

6. Private Property. Karl Marx declared elimination of private property as the communist aim in his *The Communist Manifesto*. In communism the state is the sole owner of all property and the individual is not allowed any personal property to retain with himself. This has been questioned by the psychologists and sociologists alike. It has been pointed out that elimination of property is against human nature. It takes away all incentives and inspiration to work. It hits at the liberty of the individual. It retards the total development of personality Sarvodaya is against a life of luxury. However, M. K. Gandhi did not see any evil in a person having wealth and property so far as he is prepared to use his assets for public welfare and leads a life of self-control. For communist the capitalist can never change his heart, for M. K. Gandhi such change of heart was an important economic programme of Sarvodaya. Therefore, the Sarvodaya movement asks for voluntary donation of land and money for the people's cause. It supported compensation to the capitalist and the land owner if his wealth and land and money is used for the people's cause. It supported compensation to the capitalist and the land owner if his wealth and land has to be taken by the state. On this issue, thinkers have taken sides with both Sarvodaya and communism. Both the theories have advantages and disadvantages.

7. Democracy. While Sarvodaya supports democracy, communism is against it. Here communism agrees with fascism and nazism who considered parliament a talking shop and democracy a joke upon the people. The communist thinkers have rejected democracy in favour of totalitarianism though it may be the totalitarianism of the proletariat.

8. Centralisation *Versus* Decentralisation. Communism believes in centralisation in economic and political field. In the economic field it favours establishment of huge industries and centralisation of production through more and more mechanisation. In the political field it believes in centralisation of all political power in the hands of the state machinery or the communist party and finally in the hands of one person who is chief of the state or head of the communist party. Sarvodaya, on the other hand, is against economic and political centralisation. In the economic field M.K. Gandhi asked for encouragement to cottage and rural industries. He was against mechanisation and movement, in place of monopoly he supported co–operation movement. In the political field Sarvodaya seeks to decentralise political power in every village. M. K, Gandhi asked for giving all the economic, social and political powers to the village panchayat. Sarvodaya ideology aspires for making every village self-sufficient both economically and politically. It is against centralisation of political power anywhere. It cherishes the establishment of most liberal democracy in every field of life.

From the above mentioned dissimilarities between Sarvodaya and communism, Acharya Vinoba Bhave, the foremost spokesman of Sarvodaya in our time, said, "The two ideologies are face to face, each bent upon swallowing up the other." According to Vinoba Bhave the rich are degenerated and poor are fallen people. Therefore, the Sarvodaya ideal is to uplift both the rich and poor. Thus the Sarvodaya aims at economic welfare of all classes. The economic welfare in the capitalist class, requires the encouragement of the spirit of sacrifice and non-covetousness among the rich people so that they may be led to spiritual welfare. In the poor section of society, the sarvodaya ideal preaches for more and more labour in co–operation with the middle and the capitalist class. Nowhere immoral or violent means are permitted for any class.

CHARACTERISTICS OF SARVODAYA

According to M K. Gandhi, Vinoba Bhave, Jayaprakash Narain and other leaders, the following are the important characteristics of the ideal of Sarvodaya:

1. Evolution of All. On 25th December 1975, replying to a question "What is Sarvodaya?", Vinoba Bhave replied that the following are the five basis of Sarvodaya:

1. Establishment of a casteless and classless society.
2. Clear and efficient administration in public sector.
3. Decentralisation as the bases of social system.
4. The people will achieve all power.

5. The administrators will not consider themselves masters of the people but their servants. Thus Sarvodaya aims at providing happiness to all not only to the majority as aimed by other ideologies. According to Vinoba Bhave, under a good political system all the people are happy. While the utilitarianism aims at physical welfare, Sarvodaya aims at total welfare.

2. Truth and Non-violence. According to Shankar Rao Deo, the ideal of a Sarvodaya society is a society based upon non-violence and truth, casteless and classless, without any exploitation and in which every individual and every group may have opportunity and means for total development. Sarvodaya ideal is absolutely tolerant, even tolerant of the enemy. It preaches Christ's message of love in exchange of enmity.

3. Harmony. Sarvodaya aims at harmony of all. According to Dada Dharmadhikari the ideal of Sarvodaya is non-dualism and its policy is harmony. It seeks to establish a classless, casteless and egalitarian society in which every individual and group will have opportunity of total development. This is possible by revolution, non-violence and truth. Therefore, Sarvodaya supports all these. Writing about the aims of Sarvodaya J. C. Kumarappa has pointed out that the ideal of Sarvodaya represents an ideal social system based upon love. It has place for everyone without exception, may be a prince or a peasant, saint or sinner. It has no place for repression or exploitation of any individual or community. All will participate in this social system, everyone will utilise his labour, the powerful will protect the weak and act as their Guardian and everyone will for everybody's welfare.

4. Stateless Society. Politically speaking Sarvodaya is a developed version of Gandhism. M.K. Gandhi was a bitter critic of the state. According to him the greatest evil of the state is that it is based upon violence. Therefore, M. K. Gandhi considered the best society as stateless. Deriving inspiration from Gandhian philosophy, Vinoba Bhave aimed at establishment of a society free front all repression and exploitation. Sarvodaya ideal is against the present form of the state based upon repressive tendency. In an ideal society there will be no distinction between the ruler and the ruled. Jayaprakash Narain and others have even criticised a welfare state since it increases the powers and functions of the government. In practice, this criticism appears to be valid since with the advent of the concept of the welfare state the powers of state are constantly increased. Sarvodaya aims at. a society absolutely free from all authority and government. This society will not be based upon danda or the power to punish. It will be ruled by the popular opinion, though in the interim period, some sort of authority may continue.

5. Opposed to Representative Democracy and Party System. At present in most of the countries of the world, including India, Britain and USA, there is a democratic state. Sarvodaya is opposed to the democracy. According to it this democracy is not the rule of the people but the rule of the powerful political party. Therefore, democracy consists of cut-throat competition for power among political parties and no political paity is controlled by the people themselves. The party system has given totalitarian forms to democracies. After the First World War, the totalitarian government established in Italy and Germany were the result of the so-called democracy and the party sy stem. Modern democratic system is only an external show since all the issues are first decided in the meetings of the political party itself. Their presentation in the Parliament and discussion upon them is merely a formality. Therefore, in a modern democracy Parliament and legislation are a mere show. Party system leads to moral degeneration of the members of the party. They utilise all sort of good and evil means to make their party powers and to win the general elections. Even the majority party is always busy in concentrating more and more power. The single point programme of the opposition parties is to oppose the party in power without caring the least for the good of the people. Therefore, Dada Dharmadhikari, a spokesman of Sarvodaya, has clearly pointed out three evils of democracy — misuse of power, fear of strong men and corruption. Besides this the Indian democracy suffers from communalism and casteism. The politics based upon party system is full of struggle for power. Democracy is limited to ballot and vote. Therefore, Sarvodaya ideology opposes the party system. So long as it is not eliminated, it should be made more liberal.

6. Decentralisation of Political Power. Sarvodaya stands for decentralisation of political power. This will be done by establishment of what Vinoba Bhave called basic democracy. This will be established in every village in which the village panchayat will be elected through direct election and everybody will participate in its functioning. To achieve this purpose the election of members of panchayat should be free from the party system. It should be an open election. The village should be made the primary unit of society. The citizens should know each other. According to Sarvodaya scheme, the village panchayat will elect members of Tehsil panchayat who in their turn, will elect members of district panchayats. The district panchayats will elect panchayats of the state and the state panchayats will elect the central government. This will require a total revolution in the present system. In this system the elections above the village panchayat will be indirect. Every voter and every representative will have to devote some hours everyday to physical labour, M. K. Gandhi maintained that in order to have the right to vote the qualification will not be wealth or post but physical labour. The condition of literacy or property has proved to be useless. The physical labour gives opportunity to all those who wish to participate administration in the interest of the state. According to Vinoba Bhave, this provision of physical labour will help in removing corruption from the political field.

7. Economic Decentralisation and Equality. The decentralisation suggested by Sarodaya is not merely political but also economic. This is contradictory to the communist proposal. M.K. Gandhi was against heavy industries. The Sarvodaya leaders argue that industrialisation leads to centralisation of wealth and political power which increase exploitation. Machines take the place of human beings and increase unemployment. The creative and artistic capacities are destroyed and human values degenerate. Therefore, Sarvodaya is against mechanisation. Economic decentralisation not only means small industries or cottage industries but its necessary condition is the right of the producers. For example, the land should belong to him who actually cultivates it. The property right should be vested in the actual user of the land or the factory. The Sarvodaya ideology seeks to bring about equality of property but not by repression. It is against the law of the forest. It does not utilise even the law of the legislature. It is based upon the law of love and love is higher than law. It has no place for profiteering, earning interest or rent. Everything will be done with the sentiment of the general good. Each will act according to his capacity and needs.

8. Faith in People's Power. As against *Rajniti,* Sarvodaya believes in *lokniti.* Pointing out the distinction between these two concepts, K.D. Bhatt has maintained that while administration is the main element of politics, discipline is important in *lokniti.* Power is the centre of politics and freedom is the locus of *lokniti.* Control is rampent in politics and freedom is the locus of *lokniti.* While politics involves competition of power and right, *lokniti* is based upon performing the duties. Thus the Sarvodaya sequence of progress is from administration to discipline, power to liberty, control to self-restraint and competition of rights to performance of duties. *Lokniti* is based upon people's power. The government cannot do anything about it. While the people constitute the well the government is only a bucket. If the well has no water, from where will the bucket get it? Therefore Sarvodyaya goes direct to the people. What the government cannot do is done by the people.

Sarvodyaya ideology is not limited to any state or nation. It is cosmopolitan. It aims at internationalism and world brotherhood. It is based upon the ancient Indian ideal that the whole world is one like a family. The Sarvodaya society will not have national state. It has a world-wide vision and every individual is a citizen of the whole world. The boundaries of the national state will be broken and the whole world will become one family. In this process the leaders of Sarvodaya have rejected the Varna system which was appreciated by M.K. Gandhi. Dada Dharmadhikari and Kaka Kalelkar have asked for elimination of Varna system since it is based upon the distinction. Sarvodaya, however, supports the ashram system for spiritual development. In the social life the competition should be substituted by an urge for constant progress. Sarvodaya programme aims at making every village self-sufficient, developing cottage industries and establishing the superiority of labour and the equality of male and female. In the humanitarian ideology virtues occupy the highest place. It seeks to establish the human values through change of heart.

QUESTIONS FOR EXERCISE

1. Define Sarvodaya and discuss its historical background.
2. Explain similarities and dissimilarities between Sarvodaya and Communism.
3. Outline chief characteristics of Sarvodaya.

CHAPTER 4

Demographic Theories of Social Change

Since the early part of the 19th century, the problem of rapid population growth has been a curse in our country. Galbraith rightly opines that before 1880 the problem as we see today was not present in any form because of no rapid increase rates as we have been observing since then. The year 1930 has been described in economic chronology as one of great Divide because of the fact that India has witnessed increasing growth rate since that year without at any time reaching a lower level. With regard to population studies it has to be borne in mind that there is no definite 'trend' as such in birth and death rates which are composite factors in a population study. There are serious fluctuations during the periods with severe anomalies in question too.

CAUSES OF RAPID POPULATION GROWTH

1. Illiteracy. Various factors have in combination resulted in rapid growth of population. Illiteracy of the masses is to begin with the cause of many other sub-causes. India is a country with perhaps the lowest rate of literacy among the developing countries. In a country where almost 71% of the population is illiterate there can be nothing but a population growth which is appaling to economists all around. Illiteracy is a curse on any population and the social standard of such a composition can be in no terms regular. The masses are not aware of the advances in other countries and the advantages of a small family in the role of progress. They are not aware of the advantages thrown open to a small family by way of better standards of living, less mortality, better social amenities like education, quality of upbringing etc. because of their basic no-knowledge situation.

2. Agriculture. India is primarily an agricultural country and people have landed property. Agriculture being an extensive operation requires a large number of "farm hands" to work on it successfully. Hence, more number of children would necessarily mean more hands to look to for labour. The availability of farm hands is ensured to each landed family if the family be large, hence more children ensure a better source of labour.

3. Faith in Large Families. Traditional beliefs and customs rule the Indian lives. It is common knowledge that India's population being concentrated upto 80% in the rural areas, the rule of customs and beliefs cannot be ignored. People are bred by the culture set up with folkways and mores of doing and believing things, ideas etc. In such a context it is only apparent that in a culture which believes strongly in large families, the people welcome every additional child in the family. The strength of numbers is vouched by customary beliefs. The average Indian family is believed to have five to six children which is largely due to the traditional faith in large families.

4. Cultural Taboos. Coupled with these beliefs, we have socially speaking what are known as cultural taboos. India's culture, be it in a Hindu or Muslim set up, has strong restrictions on the social life of the people. The culture places severe taboos on any practice that is detrimental to the set pattern of the culture. Any effort to violate these patterns is severely curbed and individuals are ostracised by the society. Hence, the propagation of "small family" norm or the practice of it deliberately tends to face anything but disapproval.

5. Importance of Sons. Traditional beliefs not only emphasise the need for large families but the importance of having sons is given more emphasis. Sons are sure assets to a family, hence families are large either because of the late arrival of male children, or due to a craving for more male children.

6. Security for Old Age. The Indian has all through the ages placed undue importance on the security necessary during old age. More children means more security during old age, hence the average family in our country tends to be large, though it is economically not beneficial.

7. Lack of Education. Lack of general education about the economic implications of large family among the masses is a chief reason for our rapid population growth. People here are not aware of the small-family norm which has resulted in the social betterment of people in other countries.

Lack of adequate knowledge about the strides that other countries have made chiefly because of viable population is one of the primary reasons why India is facing the population problem. Demographic studies clearly reveal the ignorance of the people about the economic and social advantages of a limited family. Also lack of knowledge about how to curb population growth adds to the immensity of the problem. Control measures to be adopted by each family by which rapid increase in the total population is to be checked, are not known to the masses. Educating the couples about the various birth control measures which could be safely adopted, should be our primary aim. Lack of knowledge about birth control measures as well as lack of confidence in the administering doctors can be the primary reason for unchecked births in any country.

POPULATION EXPLOSION

Malthus theory of population envisaged a "population explosion" for any country where birth rate is far more than the death rate. In other words due to scientific advances the death rate has been brought down from its original level but the birth rate seems to continue to grow due to various factors operating in combination upon the economy. In India we are now in the final stage of Demographic transition propounded by Robert Malthus with an explosion impending.

Various measures of population control have to be adopted if explosion is to be stopped efficiently. Precautionary measures include use of contraceptives, abstinence and conscious check on family growth. Precaution has to be taken through aids like condoms, I U D etc., to curtail family growth. Sterilization compulsory or otherwise would be necessary to solve this problem.

Nature occasionally answers this problem as a result of floods, famines and droughts. These natural occurrences prevent population growth and hence are referred to by Malthus as preventive measures in population growth. However, these types of checks are only nature's choice and not the result of man's manipulations.

If the rapid fluctuation in population level is to be checked, adequate steps have to be taken to educate the masses about the impact of real population increases in terms of poverty, lack of enough food supply, economic dependence etc. Also publishing methods of birth control could affect real birth rates in our country. The obsolete traditional belief in large-family should be nullified as "more mouths to feed" and not more "farm hands" to depend on because of the changed social set-up.

POPULATION AND SOCIAL CHANGE

Population is a significant factor in social change. This fact can be clearly understood and its importance realized if we study the consequences of population growth on society. A steep rise in the population in any country gives rise to various social problems. Many a change in the society is due mainly to population increase. For example if there is such a rise in the population that male population outnumbers the female population, the value of women will rise. If the female population outnumbers the male, sexual promiscuity is likely. As a result of war in the past there used to be sharp decline in young and healthy males, and this used to result in widespread prostitution and lesbianism. This was the case in the post-war Germany. In social change, the increase in population has the following effects:

1. Increase in Poverty. This point hardly needs labouring. We are witnessing this phenomenon in India these days. As observed by Malthus the population increases in geometric progression while the economic sources increase in arithmetic progression. Thus, we find that the pace of growth in the economic resources is very slow and gradual. Accordingly, any sharp increase in the population is bound to put extra pressure on the available resources and this in turn will lead to impoverishment.

2. Famine. As noted above, according to Malthus, the natural resources fall much behind the increase of population. Unless a new technology intervenes to boost the production or war occurs to destroy considerable number of people, the conditions of famine are likely to occur. As we know there were so many famines in India and other parts of the world. In the famine of 1896-97, 75 lakh people died and crores were affected. Three years later another famine occurred in India. The famine of 1899-1900 took the toll of 12 lakhs human lives and affected crores of people.

3. Fall in the Living Standards. This fact is a corollary of the above facts. If as a result of population rise there is general impoverishment of people, the cost of living is bound to rise and the capacity for purchase reduced. Thus, it is likely that the money now will be less than it used to. This means people will be buying less goods now than before and this means fall of living standards. The population rise means more pressure on space and therefore, housing problem becomes acute. In the past two decades though there has been 2 to 4 times increase in the wages the cost of living has gone up 10 times or more in India. Naturally the living standards have declined by 100% or more.

4. Decline in Health. More population means more pollution and more disease. The slums grow rapidly and morals loosen. Prostitution for livelihood becomes a feature of crowded living conditions. What is more, unhygienic conditions prevail. Health declines and diseases become rampant.

It has been calculated that in India the number of people dying of various diseases every year is as follows:

TB	5 lakhs
Cholera	2 lakhs
Small pox	71 thousand
Plague	25 thousand.

5. Distribution of Agricultural Holdings. The increase in population leads to distribution of agricultural holdings and ultimately they become uneconomic. This can be illustrated by a model. Suppose A has 10 acres of land. At his death this is distributed among his five children. Each gets 2 acres. Now, if these persons have their children, say 4 each. At the time of their death their children will receive 54 acre of land each, which is wholly uneconomic.

6. Dissolution of Family. When people suffer from want and disease, they are unhappy, morose and bitter. They are liable to blame others for their ills and this means tension and bitterness in family will grow. This tenets to assume proportions where divorces, suicides and other ills abound. All this leads to break-down of family. As noted above slums conditions breed corruption and prostitution. There are slums in India and abroad in which prostitution is so common that family has become a farce.

7. Personal Disintegration. Poverty is the chief breeder of crimes and when criminal tendencies are fanned in individuals the personality of the concerned individuals is adversely affected. It is a common knowledge that juvenile delinquents come from poor families and crowded slums. In an overcrowded home children have no separate rooms for study and no indoor games to keep them engaged. This sends them to streets where they roam like vagabonds and develop criminal tendencies. Naturally, they fail to develop constructive personalities. Besides, early exposure to sex makes them take to homosexuality, prostitution and promiscuous sexuality. These factors naturally distort the personality. Another effect of poverty is that children growing up in rural surroundings when become adults feel compelled to move to cities for employment. The drastic change from rural environs to urban environs makes them prey to multiple vices and diseases. This complicates the problem still further. This gives rise to all sorts of mental and physical ills which in turn, leads to disintegration of the personality.

8. Marital Disintegration. Indirectly, the cudgel of poverty, falls rather heavily on the stability of marriage. As population rises the disintegration of marriage sets in. The population rise leads to poverty and poverty gives rise to tension of all sorts. Due to stress and strain husband may take to liquor and wife to vagrancy. All this leads to marital disintegration.

9. Social Disintegration. The disintegration of family, personal and marital disintegration leads to social disintegration. The traditions and mores loosen their holds fast. People become selfish, tense, anxious and bitter and become misfits. They are unable to carry out their work efficiently. With the rise in urban population the feeling of communal togetherness declines and with rise in the rural population the exodus to cities begins.

All the above mentioned social effects of population rise can be observed in modern India. This is the main reason why government is propagating family planning so lavishly. According to some scholars the population rise affects even the form of the government.

MALTHUSIAN THEORY

The most important theory in the history of demography was presented by Thomas Robert Malthus (1766-1834). Among his most important works was his famous Essay on Population entitled: *An Essay on the Principle of Population as it Affects the Future Improvement of Society, With Remarks on the Speculations of Mr. Godwin M. Condorcet and others.* This essay was published anonymously. It, however, became one of the most controversial books of modern times, and brought both honour and criticism to the author. Its importance as a landmark in the history of population can be judged by the fact that the year of its publication is reckoned as the base year for the study of population doctrines.

As is clear by the title of the Essay, it was mainly directed against the optimistic views of William Godwin, an English philosopher and Marie Jean Antonie Condorcet, a French mathematician, economist and philosopher. Therefore, it is necessary to understand the view of these two persons before understanding Malthusian theory. According to Condorcet, "All inequalities of wealth, of education, of opportunity, of sex, would soon disappear. Animosities between nations and races would be no more. All persons would speak the same language. The earth would be bountiful, without stint. All diseases would be conquered, and if man did not become immortal, the span of his life would have no assignable upper limit. The question whether production would always suffice to satisfy the people's wants could not be answered, for the problem would not have to be faced for ages to corne, by which time man would have acquired new types of now still unimagined knowledge. In the rational age to come, men would recognise their obligations to those not yet born and to the general well-being both of their society and of all humanity and ... not to the pure idea of filling the earth with useless and unhappy beings. At that time, a limit could be set to the population other than by premature death of a portion of those born."

William Godwin published his book *Enquiry Concerning Political Justice,* in 1793, which presented a Utopian ideal of perfect society. In this society, according to him, "There will be no war, no crimes, no administration of justice as it is called, and no government." Besides this, there will be neither disease, anguish, melancholy nor resentment. Every man will see with ineffable ardour the good of all.

This Utopian thesis was challenged by Malthus. He pointed out that the tendency of the population to grow faster than the means of subsistence gradually leads to human misery and creates impediments in the path of progress. He laid more emphasis on criticism of the Poor Laws in the 2nd edition of his *Essay* published in 1803. This edition contained substantial statistical data in support of arguments. It proposed moral constraints as a preventive against rapid growth of population. Next five years in the life of Malthus were devoted to collection of further statistical data and study of the writings of other authors. In 1826 was published the 6th edition of the work of Malthus now entitled: *An Essay on the Principle of Population or a View of its Past and Present Effects on Human Happiness, with an Inquiry into our Prospects Respecting the Future Removal or Mitigation of the Evils which it Occasions.* In 1872 was published the 7th edition of the Essay.

The Central Theme

Malthus started his Essay by laying down two postulates: "First, that food is necessary to the existence of man." "Secondly, the passion between the sexes is necessary and will remain nearly in its present state ." He argued, "Assuming then my postulate as granted, say that the power of population is definitely greater than the power in the earth to produce subsistence for men. Population, when unchecked increases in a geometrical ratio. Subsistence increases only in an arithmetical ratio. A slight acquaintance with numbers will show the immensity of the first power in comparison with the second. The following propositions were put forth by Malthus, to establish his theory: "(1) Population is necessarily limited by the means of subsistence; (2) Population invariably increases where the means of subsistence increase unless prevented by some very powerful and obvious checks; (3) These checks, and the checks which repress the superior power of population and its effects on a level with the means of subsistence, are all resolvable into moral restraint, vice and misery." Therefore, Malthus concluded, "Taking the whole earth, the human species would increase as the numbers 1, 2, 4, 8,16, 32, 64,128, 256 and the subsistence as numbers 1, 2, 3, 4, 5, 6, 7, 8, 9. In two centuries, the population would be to the means of subsistence as 256 to

8 ... " Malthus recognised that the growth of population does not go unchecked. Pointing out powerful checks on the growth of population, he said, "The first of these checks may, with propriety, be called the preventive checks to population, and the absolute necessity of their operation in the case supposed is as certain and obvious as that man cannot live without food." Now in order to check the preventive checks such as epidemics, wars and famines, Malthus suggested moral restraints as the best preventive check. He described it as, "Abstinence from marriage, either for a time or permanently, from prudential consideration, with a strictly moral conduct towards the sex in the interval. And this is the only mode of keeping population on a level with the means of subsistence which is perfectly consistent with virtue and happiness." Vice was described as, "a sort of intercourse which renders some of the women of large towns unprolific," such as prostitution and extra-marital sexual relations. The preventive checks were necessary in order to avoid positive checks which tended to shorten human life. These positive checks have been described by Malthus: "Such as unwholesome occupations — severe labour and exposure to the seasons — bad and insufficient food and clothing arising from poverty — bad nursing of children — excesses of all kinds — great towns and manufactories — the whole train of common diseases and epidemics — wars, infanticide, plague, famine." Malthus was against Poor Laws since he considered poverty as an evil. He classified positive checks also into two categories: "The first were those brought about by natural causes and labelled as 'Exclusively misery', such as epidemics, famines etc., the other positive checks were those which mankind brought upon itself by itself such as wars and all types of excesses which could have been avoided."

Evaluation of the Theory

Malthusian Theory, as we have already pointed out, has been acclaimed as epoch-making theory. It was a landmark in the history of population which divided the history into two periods: before it and after it. Though some of the ideas were known earlier, Malthus presented them in a large framework. He examined the inter-relationship between population growth and economic and political developments. His style of writing was polished and authoritative with a philosophical touch. He never claimed originality but only more systematisation. According to Kenneth Smith, the success of Malthus may be attributed to the opportune circumstances and the political climate prevailing in his time. Disillusioned by the French revolution, the intellectuals of his time supported his theory. His economic message was welcomed. The optimism of his predecessors paled before his realistic pessimism. According to Kenneth Smith, "Malthus offered a scientific pessimism which, gloomy and fatalistic though it was towards the hopes of the working classes, absolved the ruling classes from the need to make futile efforts on their behalf." His plea for the abolition of poor laws naturally appealed to many persons. His doctrines were convenient to the rulers who were always afraid of the growing poverty.

Criticism

However, the theory of Malthus was subjected to harsh criticism as well. Kautsky, one of his bitterest critics, accused him of plagiarism and said, "It was as correct to name the new population theory after Malthus as to name America after Amerigo Vespucci. Both did no more than to spread the news of what others had discovered." It is undeniable that many of the ideas put forward by Malthus were already anticipated by Macchiavelli, Sir Walter Raleigh, Francis Bacon, John Graunt, William Petty, Sir Matthew Hale, Benjamin Franklin, Saxe, Joseph Townsend, Sussmilch, Sir James Stuart, Hume, Robert Wallace, Arthur Young Archdeacon, Paley and others. Some writers even used abusive language and bitter criticisms. While criticising Malthus very harshly, Karl Marx referred to him as one who, "have taken the monastic vow of celibacy." It may be noted in this connection that Malthus was married and had three children. The criticism such as this were obviously based upon misconceptions and ignorance. However, the weakest point in the theory of Malthus was the ratio between the arithmetical and the geometrical progressions. According to Kenneth Smith this ratio was never really proved. It was pointed out that the theory that the population would double in a period of 25 years was based upon the evidence of doubtful American statistics in which the role of immigration in the North population was completely rejected. According to E.P. Hutchinson the idea of arithmetical ratio concerning the growth of the means of subsistence was unanimously rejected by scholars. As a general rule the following points were raised as criticism against Malthusian theory:

1. As has been already pointed out, the ratio of arithmetical progression of means of subsistence and the geometrical progression of population growth was never proved.
2. In so many cases the theory of the growth of the means of subsistence in arithmetical ratio was not proved.
3. Malthus did not clearly distinguish between fecundity and fertility or the physiological capacity to reproduce and the actual reproductive performance.
4. The classification of checks on population growth as preventive and positive were cited as example of poor classification, since they were not independent categories.
5. Malthus did not succeed in connecting positive and preventive checks with his theory.
6. Malthus placed undue emphasis on the limitation of the supply of land. Agricultural production tremendously increased through agricultural revolution in the 19th century.
7. Malthus painted a too gloomy picture of the future growth of population. According to Ralph Thomlinson, his predictions did not come out to be true due to agricultural revolution.
8. Malthus underestimated the importance of industrial development in increasing means of subsistence.

9. The religious belief of Malthus, according to Ralph Thomlinson prevented him from understanding the possibility of the widespread use of contraceptives.
10. According to Eversley, Malthus did not utilise the 1831 census data of England. According to him Malthus did not make any significant contribution to social thought.
11. One finds a contradiction in the twin role of Malthus as a scientist and a moralist. His role as a scientist was vitiated by his attempts of opposing birth control.
12. He favoured postponement of marriage and even total abstinence.

In spite of the above mentioned criticism, Kingsley Davis has rightly maintained that though not empirically valid Malthusian theory was theoretically significant. His name occupies an important place in the history of population thought. He was the first thinker who systematically and thoroughly applied inductive method to social science. Though by 1900 his main thesis was almost completely rejected, it was revived in the second decade of the 20th century. The wave subsided by 1934 but again revived after the 2nd World War. In evaluating the status of Malthusian theory in the history of demography it will be best to conclude with Charles Emil Stangeland, who remarked: "Malthus's work was a great one written in an opportune time, and though it cannot lay claim to any considerable originality as far as the theories presented are concerned, it was successful in that it showed more fully, perhaps more clearly, and certainly more effectively than had any previous attempt, that population depends on subsistence and its increase is checked by want, vice and disease as well as by more restraint or prudence."

NEO-MALTHUSIANISM

Neo-Malthusians are the successors of Malthus, They were keen supporters of family planning movement. According to them Malthus was the first thinker who established that uncontrolled increase of population will lead to poverty and therefore birth control must be popularised. Among the most important neo-Malthusian thinkers may be mentioned Mary Stopes of Great Britain and Margaret Senger of U.S.A., besides so many supporters in Western Europe. These people popularised chemical and mechanical methods of birth control. The family planning movement gradually extended not only to the entire Western World but also to the countries of Asia and Africa continents.

According to Neo-Malthusianism, Malthus did not distinguish between sex desire and desire for children. Both these are fulfilled by the same physical organs. The sex desire also involves desire for reproduction. Neo-Malthusians however, do not accept this view. They reject the Malthusian theory that sex desire is identical with the desire for children. According to them sex desire is a natural and biological desire. It is the most powerful physical and psychological desire among the adults. Its repression leads to so many mental and physical evils. Desire for children, on the other hand, particularly depends upon social, moral and cultural values. It is not inherent but a product of socio-economic conditions. Fulfilment of sex desire is a must for normal and healthy life. The desire for children however, should be adjusted according to favourable or unfavourable circumstances. Only that woman should reproduce who is physically and mentally fit for the purpose. Males and females should be allowed to satisfy their sex desire without procreation There is no moral evil in using chemical or mechanical means of birth control to satisfy sex desire.

Neo-Malthusians acclaimed Malthus as their leader in family planning movement. However, the Freeh economists did not agree with this idea. They pointed out that Malthus would have called modern means of birth control, "Unmitigated conjugal fraud". He would have declared them as anti-Christian and un-Godly. In his *Essay on Population* Malthus has pointed out that artificial means of birth control are much inferior as compared to natural restrictions such as self-control. The Neo-Malthusians, on the other hand, maintain that in the second edition of his Essay, Malthus concluded that population cannot be controlled by moral restraint alone. Moral restraint is a means which cannot be expected to be practised by ordinary people. Therefore in spite of himself Malthus was prepared to allow artificial means of birth control. The Neo-Malthusians have advanced the following arguments in favour of their artificial birth control movement:

1. Birth control is necessary to limit the family size in the context of available economic means, otherwise the standard of living will fall down considerably. Without limiting the family, it is impossible to bring up children properly and pay attention to their physical, mental and moral development.
2. Birth control is equally necessary to limit the burden on world economy. This has already reached its saturation point. Therefore, it has no more capacity to feed the additional growing number of world population.
3. Birth control is necessary on the ground of health and medical care as well.
4. Those who oppose the Neo-Maithusian approach maintained that birth control is unnatural. It is an undesirable interference in the working of the natural process. The sexual intercourse aims at child birth. Restriction upon child birth will therefore restrict the very aim of marriage. In answer to this objection Neo-Malthusians point out that if birth control is unnatural, the same can be said about wearing clothes since man is born nude and that is his natural condition. Then, why do we wear clothes? On the same grounds artificial birth control may be supported.
5. Another argument advanced against birth control is that it is immoral. To this Neo-Malthusians point out that morality is a relative concept. Ethics is man-made. Human principles are never categorical and fixed. If a principle is useful from the social viewpoint, it may be accepted from the moral viewpoint as well. Birth control is today a social necessity. It should be accepted as desirable without any stigma of immorality.

History records that in spite of criticism and vehement opposition to the Neo-Malthusian theory of birth control, the message gradually spread in the West and also in the East. When Mary Stopes declared in England that women have a right to enjoy sex without child birth, she was threatened by the English Lords for what they called the misguiding of their women. Mary Stopes however, won her point. The feminist movement started by her not only spread over the entire British Island but also in Europe. Today, there is no controversy about the use of artificial birth control to check population growth. On the other hand, most of the governments in developing countries like India are doing everything within their means to popularise the methods of artificial birth control. The feminist movement, spread all over the world, has also encouraged artificial birth control.

THE CLASSICAL SCHOOL

The classical theory of population was based upon the idea that the production, consumption and distribution of wealth are determined by economic laws. This school was founded by Adam Smith, followed by David Ricardo, Thomas Malthus, Nassau Senior, John Stuart Mill and J.B. Say. They were political economists and believed that economics functions better under a free and private initiative with keen competitions.

NEO-CLASSICAL SCHOOL

This school of thought placed more emphasis on mathematical economics and the analysis of the psychological background and consumer demands, decisions and actions. It was founded by William Jensons, Carl Menger and Leon Walrus. Among its notable leaders were Alfred Marshall, John Bates, Clark, Irving Fisher and Vilfredo Pareto.

Both the classical and neo-classical schools were concerned with an examination of the inter-relationships between population and production. This was a serious point of discussion. While according to some, increasing population resulted in increasing production, others maintained the opposite view. None of these views was conclusively proved due to lack of empirical and theoretical evidence. The issue appeared to be resolved by the formation of the economic principle of diminishing returns in the second decade of the 19th century. This principle supported Malthusian theory. The classical economist accepted it as a natural law. In 19th century it was observed that the general being of the people and the population growth went hand in hand. This was contrary to Malthusian theory and the principle of diminishing return. John Stuart Mill and Henery Sidgwick pointed out that many countries would be better off with smaller numbers since their population had already reached the point of diminishing return. The economists Gray, Chambers, Burn and Wirth pointed out that increasing number of people stimulate production. Godwin, Ravenstone, Sadler, Almond, Scrope and Ricardo disproved the principle of diminishing return. According to Marshal, a neo-classical economist, this law was applicable particularly to agriculture and not to industry. It was realised that the total and the per capita production not only depend upon population but also upon resources, labour, capital and technology. It was pointed out that per capita income was inversely related to the number of population. It was the factor of capital which influenced the size and growth of the population. Thus, by the end of the 19th century, it was concluded that population variable is only one variable in the total economic system. The importance of population growth was therefore considerably diminished. It was even ignored by some writers. Economic growth in the West kept pace with the population growth, negating the gloomy picture painted by Malthus. In this ferment of thinking about the relationship of population and production, the following points emerged:

1. Population is only one of the several factors affecting production, distribution and other human affairs.
2. The socio-economic phenomena in general and the effect of population phenomena in particular are far from simple.
3. A more cautious appraisal of the socio-economic role of population is required. It has been recognised that productivity is affected by so many factors depending on the stage of economic development and the demographic situation.
4. The law of diminishing returns is applicable more to agricultural production and seldom to industrial production.
5. The population question cannot be considered only in relation to economics. It is also influenced by cultural factors. Therefore, it is a dependent variable, a product of so many influences.
6. The theory of optimum population has resolved the old debate about the consequences of large and growing population.

OPTIMUM POPULATION THEORY

The optimum population theory had its beginnings in the writing of Karl Winkelblech (1810-1865), a German Professor who classified nations into three categories according to the size of their population:

1. Under-populated nations, 2. Over-populated nations, and 3. Normal populated nations. It was Edwin Carman (1861-1935), an English economist, who used the concept "optimum population", as synonymous with the test possible population. According to him, "at any given time, the population which can exist on a given extent of land, consistent with the greatest productiveness of industry at that time, is definite." United Nations have defined the concept of optimum population, "to mean the size of the population which results in the highest per capita income, the highest productivity as measured in different manners, or the highest level of other less well-defined economic indicators, such as economic welfare, level of living, real income and, in some cases, employment." While some writers have considered the concept too restrictive, most of the writers have accepted the idea. However, later development provoked a critical re-examination of this theory. This theory implied that the growth of population was beneficial upto a certain point, after which it becomes harmful. The following criticisms were levelled against this theory:

1. It is doubtful that the optimum point in the growth of population can ever be determined. The demographers have never agreed over this point.

2. The concept of optimum population is essentially a static concept, based upon the assumption that there is an optimum limit of technology, resources, foreign trade and social structure.

This theory was very popular in the second and third decades of the present century. It has been rightly concluded by Sauvey that this theory may be accepted not as an absolute theoretical concept but as a convenient tool.

MARXIST SOCIALIST THEORY OF POPULATION

As has been already pointed out, Karl Marx completely rejected Malthusian theory, as it did not fit in a socialist society. According to Karl Marx there can be no natural or universal law of population. According to him, "An abstract law of population exists for plants and animals only, and only in so far as man has not interfered with them." Again, "Every special historic mode of production has its own special laws of population, historically valid, within its limit alone." Thus, the population theory is peculiar to the capitalist system of production. It is inherent in the capitalist system and not in production. Engels maintained that under the capitalist system surplus population was linked with surplus capital. This state of affairs, according to socialist view, can be changed by social reorganisation. *Communist Manifesto* laid down the fundamentals of a socialist society. *Origin of the Family* emphasized the need for emancipation of women. The need of conscious control was emphasized. It was maintained that due to the superior status of women there will be slower growth of population in a socialist society. Later socialists however, supported responsible parenthood. According to them reproductive behaviour should be based upon complete harmony between the individual and the society. Since birth control contributes to the emancipation of women, it is accepted. Even abortions are permitted. The Marxist socialist theory of population is applicable to modern socialist countries of Europe where it is being practised and supported. Criticism of this view have been obviously advanced by the thinkers' of the capitalist society since in the capitalist countries the views of Marx and Lenin are not accepted.

BIOLOGICAL THEORIES OF POPULATION

1. The Density Principle. This principle was laid down by Michael Thomas Sadler (1730-1835), an English political economist in his work entitled *The Law of Population.* This book presented the principle that fertility varies inversely with the density of population. The contradiction found in countries like Netherlands, where both fertility and density were high, was explained by Sadler by pointing out a direct relationship between fertility and mortality. According to him, increasing fertility increases mortality which in turn decreases fertility. This principle, however, has not been accepted by most of the demographers.

2. The Diet Principle. This was propounded by Thomas Doubleday (1790- 1870) an English political economist in 1841, in his essay *The True Law of Population Shown to be Connected with the Food of People.* According to Doubleday poverty stimulates population growth since the diet of the poor is inadequate. On the other hand if the diet is sufficient one finds less fertility. It was pointed out that due to this principle one finds high fertility among Chinese, Irish and the Scotch and low fertility in France. Similar conclusions were reached by Josue de Castro in his book, *Geography of Hunger* in 1952, based upon the negative correlation between the protein content of the diet and the birth rate in a country. Most of the demographers however, rejected this theory. Thomlinson remarked about Castro, "He might as well have considered the correlation between national fertility and consumption of ice cream, soda, use of washing machine or watching of television."

3. Theory of Herbert Spencer. Herbert Spencer presented a theory of population on biological basis, in 1880. He pointed out that fertility increases in response to the progress of society. It is a great agency for the advancement of mankind. However, when population becomes excessive, it threatens the very existence of the human species. This requires control of population.

4. Theory of Corrado Gini. The Italian biologist Corrado Gini has recently presented a biological theory of population, known as the cyclical theory. According to Gini the population tends to follow an evolution similar to the life cycle of the individual. As the individual passes through the successive stages of development, maturation and involution, similar is the case with the evolution of the human being. The biological theories have not been accepted as sufficient explanations of population since, as has been pointed out by social and cultural theories, social and cultural factors are equally important in the growth of population. Fertility is not a mere biological phenomena but very much influenced by social and cultural factors.

THEORY OF DEMOGRAPHIC TRANSITION

Demographic transition means the progress from one demographic condition to a different stage, for example, in Western countries it was found that the population moved from a condition of high mortality and high fertility to conditions of low mortality and low fertility. Thus, the stage of high expansion of population itself leads to the stationary stage and *vice versa.* Several demographers such as Landry in 1909 and Warren Thompson in 1929 attempted to construct a typology to describe demographic transition from conditions of high mortality and high fertility to the conditions of low mortality and low fertility. None of these demographers, however, made an attempt to explain these changes. In 1947 C.P. Blacker identified five phases of the demographic transition as follows:

1. The high stationary stage characterised by high birth rates and high death rates.
2. The early expanding stage with falling birth rates but rapidly decreasing mortality.
3. The late expanding stage with falling birth rates but rapidly decreasing mortality.
4. The low stationary stage with low birth rates balanced by equally low mortality.
5. The declining stage with low mortality and deaths exceeding births.

It was Frank W. Notestein who, for the first time presented an explanation for the changes in fertility. John Caldwell has therefore credited Notestein with expounding the theory of demographic transition. According to Notestein, the rapid growth of population during the past three centuries was particularly due to the decline in the death rate, this decline resulted from the process of modernization. Modernization involved high standard of living, high incomes and advanced level of sanitation and medical knowledge, with the result that fertility registered a decline. By the middle of 1930 birth rates reached very low levels in Western countries. This was the result of widespread acceptance of contraceptive methods due to the ideal of small family prevalent in urban industrialized society. According to the stage of demographic evolution the population in different countries may be characterised into the following three types:

1. Incipient Decline. In this stage fertility falls below replacement level. This stage could be seen in populations of Europe, the United States, Australia and New Zealand.

2. Transitional Growth. Notestein has explained this stage where, "Birth and death rates are still high and growth is rapid, but the decline of the birth rate is well established."

3. High Growth Potentials. Notestein has defined this stage of population in these words: "Mortality is high and variable and is the chief determinant of growth, while fertility is high and thus far has shown no evidence of a downward trend. In these populations, rapid growth is to be expected just as soon as technical developments make possible a decline in mortality." Examples of this stage of population were pointed out in most of the countries of Asia, Africa and Latin America. According to George J. Stoinitz, "All nations in the modern era, which have moved from a traditional, agrarian-based economic system to a largely industrial, urbanised base, have, also moved from a condition of high mortality and fertility to low mortality and fertility."

Demographic transition has been also studied from the point of view of economic development. According to Ansley J. Coale and Edger M. Hoover, the agrarian peasant economy is generally characterized by high death rate and high birth rate. The death rates fluctuate according to the variations in harvests and the incidents of epidemics. Due to poor diet, lack of sanitation and medical and public health programmes, the death rates are usually high in peasant societies. On the other hand, the birth rate is high due to the prevalent ideals of prolific fertility reinforced by the economic advantages of having a large number of children. As the agrarian economy changes into industrial economy, level of production and urbanisation rise, with the result that death rate falls due to better diet and medical care. Due to the acceptance of the ideal of small family in urban society the birth rates fall. This decline occurs after a time lag to the decline in the death rate. The birth and the death rates pursue a parallel downward course, though the decline of birth rate lags behind. As further deductions in the death rate are difficult to achieve, the birth rate again approaches the level of the death rate with the result that population grows slowly. While the death rates do not fluctuate, the birth rates fluctuate due to social and cultural reasons.

Some other thinkers have pointed out different stages in demographic transition. According to Donald Oien Cogwill, the population passes through the five stages known as: Primitive Cycle, Modern Cycle, Future Cycle or Baby Boom period, Probable Cycle and Population Cycle in the long run. According to this view population increases in S-Curve. Karl Sax has categorised the above mentioned stages into four stages only. According to him the second and the third stages in population growth are the stages in Population Explosion. Landry has divided demographic changes into three demographic regimes on the basis of the theory of Cantillon: A Primitive Regime, An Intermediate Demographic Regime, and A Modern Epoch.

Criticism of the Transition Theory

Generally speaking, the following criticisms have been advanced against the theory of demographic transition:

1. This theory was based on the experience of population changes in Western countries. But since the population growth in different countries does not follow identical patterns, therefore no theory can explain population growth everywhere. One finds so many exceptions to the rule. Thus, this theory is only a broad generalisation.
2. This theory fails to explain the phenomenon of 'The Baby Boom' in Western countries after the Second World War.
3. This theory does not provide a theoretical explanation of fertility as a force in demographic transition.
4. In fact this theory cannot be called a theory in the real sense since it neither extracts fundamental processes from a phenomenon nor identifies crucial variables.
5. This theory does not provide explanation of fertility decline nor does it identify crucial variables in it. Therefore, it has no predictive values.
6. This theory cannot be applied to developing countries since the demographic stages in the Western countries are not necessarily explicit in the population growth in developing countries.

In the face of the above mentioned criticism, it may be concluded that the demographic transition theory at the best provides a framework and means for wider empirical generalisations. It cannot be considered a theory in the strict sense of the term, particularly for the explanation of the demographic growth in the developing countries.

SOCIAL THEORIES OF POPULATION CHANGE

The social theories of population, as is clear by the title, explain population growth on the basis of social factors. The most important among the theories was the theory of Karl Marx.

1. Theory of Single Tax. This theory was presented by the American Economist Henry John. According to him, "The law of population accords with and is subordinate to the law of intellectual developments and any danger that human beings may be brought into a world where they cannot be provided for arises not from the ordinances of nature, but from the social maladjustments that in the midst of wealth condemn men to want." Therefore, the principle of population is subordinate to the principle of mental growth. Fecundity and fertility decrease with mental growth. There is no contradiction in the growth of population and the means of subsistence, provided the latter are controlled by the state. Therefore, the government should directly charge single tax from the users of land.

2. Theory of Social Capillarity. This theory was presented by Dumont (1849-1902) on the basis of his study of the growth of French population. According to Dumont, "The development of number in a nation is in inverse ratio to the development of individual." In other words as the individual develops, birth rate decreases. Dumont has called it theory of social capillarity since capillarity means the will for social progress. According to Dumont this theory of population applies to a well developed society based on rational thinking and idealism. He says, "From the moment when the imagination and the attraction of the ideal enter the scene, we find ourselves in the presence of a new principle of population." Thus, a theory of population is directly related to the stage of growth of a society. Malthusian theory of population applies only to undeveloped and primitive societies. There is an inverse relationship in social capillarity and rate of birth. Since this force is inactive due to caste system in India, the birth rate is high. In France, on the other hand, due to political freedom and democracy, the birth rate is low. According to Dumont, "Just as a column of liquid must be thin in order to rise under the force of capillarity so must a family be small to rise in the social scale." The birth rate, due to the same reasons, is high in the villages and low in the cities. According to Dumont this theory does not apply to India where capillary power is inactive due to caste system. Thus, a rigid social structure retards social progress. Birth rate in the cities is always less than that in the villages. The reason of this distinction is the urban urge for a high standard of living. The thinking and conduct of urban people is more rational since they have better knowledge. Other factors influencing lower birth rate in the urban areas include: democracy, middle class, will to progress and higher standard of living. On the other hand, the factors leading to higher birth rate in the rural areas include casteism, old style thinking, illiteracy, ignorance and poverty, etc. According to Dumont this theory is not applicable to the societies having socialistic economy since in it an individual has limited scope of rising high. "The socialist principle of equality of function, if entirely applied, would necessarily imply the destruction of social capillarity and cause a high birth rate."

The theory of population advanced by Dumont was an improvement upon Spencer's theory. However, the rise of a society does not depend upon merely on lower birth rate but also upon so many social, economic and political factors. Therefore, Dumont's principle cannot be accepted as a rule.

3. Theory of Voluntarism. This theory was presented by Frank Fatlar in the end of the 19th century. According to Fatlar, the main defect of Malthusian theory was its being confined to sex motive among human being. Man, on the other hand, is a complex being very much influenced by ideals, experiences, ambitions and desires, etc. Therefore, the behaviour of a group is influenced by so many factors. Hence, no theory of population explains all the social phenomena. The demographic changes should be explained on the basis of factors influencing society. Several psychological tendencies influence man's reproductive behaviour. Different classes exhibit different types of family environment. The poor do not pay much attention to restrict reproduction since the additional child will rather add to the family income. On the other hand, the rich do not want such increase since it will further divide the family income and property with the result that the standard of living will fall down. Therefore, Fatlar concludes that economic progress retards birth rate since the incentive shall be considerably less. Voluntarism seek to remove lack of farsight and economy. Similar theories had been presented in U.S.A. by Arthur Hadley in 1796 and Weber in 1899. According to Arthur Twinning Hadley, "Intellectual man is more capable of birth control than emotional person. He can exercise more self-restraint."

4. Principle of Individuality. This theory was advanced by the Italian economist Francesco S. Nitti in his book *Population and the Social System.* Nitti pointed out defects of other demographic theories including that of Malthus, Spender, Marx and Dumont. According to him demographic progress has also led to the progress of civilization. Pointing out the factors influencing growth of population he said, "The influences of the psychical moral order and the influences of the political order, are but slight compared to influences of an economic kind. But for a true understanding of the law of population the biological factors play important parts."

5. Theory of Increasing Prosperity and Pleasure. This theory was presented by Brenton. According to this theory the ideal of human life is pleasure. Reproduction rate increases among persons who have better means of pleasure. The poor class does not have so many options in pleasure seeking. They have no access to books, art and spiritual pleasures. Therefore, the only means of pleasure accessible to them is sexual intercourse. Consequently, they reproduce more children. On the other hand, since the rich have so many options to enjoy pleasure, therefore, birth rate among them is lower.

6. Theory of Rationalism. This theory was presented by Ungem-Stemberg. He, for the first time, admitted that birth rate may be lower even among poor. The real cause of birth rate, according to him is not biological but psychological. As he pointed out, "The women too become masculinized (when infected by the capitalist mentality) in their search for equality. Love relationship becomes business-like and matter of fact." Advancing examples from Norway, Finland, etc., he maintained that the wealth or poverty itself is not the factor determining birth rate nor is it urban or rural environment. The real factor determining birth rate is mental, it may be both among males and females. There is a correlation between economic development and lower birth rate. It is the capitalist mentality that induces low fertility. This, however, may be equally found in rural areas. Therefore, rural or urban rich or poor do not necessarily determine birth rate.

QUESTIONS FOR EXERCISE

1. Account for the rapid growth of Indian population and suggest the measures of population control.
2. Discuss the role of demographic factor in social change.
3. Critically discuss Malthusian Theory of Population.
4. Write short none on — Neo-Malthusianism.
5. Write short note on — Neo-Classical School of Demographic changes.
6. Explain Optimum Population Theory.
7. Write short note on — Marxist Socialist Theory of Population.
8. Evaluate biological theories of population change.
9. Discuss Theory of Demographic Transition.
10. Discuss Social Theories of Population Change.

Chapter 5

Social Development

Until not long ago — and this view tends to persist — the term development was used to refer to economic growth. But the importance of non-economic dimensions of development, political, social, cultural and human, is being increasingly realised now. Although economists themselves were the first to recognise the importance of human factors in economic development, it was sociologists who brought into focus the social dimensions of development. To begin with, sociologists devoted their attention to the social determinants and consequences of economic development. For works on a sociological approach to economic development, one may refer to B.F. Hoselitz, *Sociological Aspects of Economic Growth*, S.N. Eisenstadt, *Essays on Sociological Aspects of Political and Economic Development,* Neil J. Smelser, *The Sociology of Economic Life,* Herbert R. Barringer, G.l. Blanksten, and R.W. Mack, *Social Change in Developing Areas.* Only from their sustained interest in the sociological bearings of economic development did they derive the notion of social development.

This is not to deny the concerns of early social philosophers with social progress. To be sure, the idea of social progress held almost the same appeal to social philosophers in the late seventeenth and early eighteenth centuries as the idea of development today. But it could not last long, for it was perceived as a philosophy inimical to Christian tradition. This was so because the myth of progress implied belief in man's rationality and his ability to construct his own history which was at odds with the tradition of Christianity which lacked such a belief. In his paper Berger maintains that 'Christianity has always been pessimistic both about man and about his ability to construct his own history, and the (literally) godless optimism of the myth of progress clashed directly with the root proclamations of the Christian tradition. So intense was the ! antagonism between them that if Voltaire, a major apostle of progress, saw the church as a formidable obstacle to the rational salvation of man, the Church consigned Voltaire's works to the category of prohibited literature.

Once again the same concern for social development appeared in the nineteenth century when Schmoller pleaded for the use of social sciences for social engineering. But it was muffled by Weber's powerful doctrine of value free social science which is why sociologists have been loath to question development until recently, leaving the floor entirely to economists. But the hold of the doctrine seems to be slackening now with the result that sociologists have started confronting the question of social development in right earnest.

Economic and Social Development

The rise of the sociological perspective on development has led to several significant questions about the relationship between economic development and social development: (1) Whether social development accelerates economic development, or, is it economic development that leads to social development? (2) Whether the relationships between the two is that of primacy of one over the other or of simultaneity? Is it possible to have the one without the other? The answers to these questions are not in short supply, even if they are preconceived (if not really misconceived). Take, for instance, the first question. There is sometimes a tendency towards a kind of vulgar Marxist assumption that economic growth is the determinative factor of social development, for the latter belongs to the category of superstructure. On the other hand, there is a tendency towards a kind of Western academic sophistry which implies that if the underdeveloped countries of Asia, Africa and Latin America are to develop they must adopt social institutions, social forms and social values resembling those of the West. Similarly, the answers to the second question regarding primacy or simultaneity tend to vary according to the ideological predilection of the scholars. As to the third question, it is possible to have economic development without social development just as it is possible to have social development without economic growth. The validity of these answers depend as much on the definitions of the terms 'economic development' and 'social development' as on the evidence of historical cases. Hence, the need for clarity about the concept of social development.

The emergence of the category of social development notwithstanding the concept of social development is yet to acquire an identity independent of economic development. This is so partly because of a tendency to so stretch the meaning of economic development as to include within its scope the components of social development, and partly because of the economic bias of the existing definitions of social development.

Broad Meaning of Economic Development

The meaning of economic development has broadened over the years, as is evident from the following conceptions, which have emerged in that order: economic development as economic growth; economic development as change in the social and political structures accompanying economic growth; economic development as a trinity of economic growth, economic equity and economic self-reliance. Until recently, Western economists tended to identify economic development with economic growth, as measured by the rate of increase of per capita income or product. This view fell into disrepute because of the common criticism of GNP statistics, *e.g.*, lack of coverage, rough methods of estimation involving arbitrary assumptions, etc., than because of the experience of poor countries in the post-War II period when their leaders became conscious of the inadequacy of economic growth as a measure of economic development. Accordingly, economic development came to mean long-term changes in GNP together with complementary changes in social and political structures. With the growing evidence of divergence between GNP and welfare during the first Development Decade of the 1960s, even this view lost much of its currency more recently, the concept of economic development has been further enlarged to refer to economic equity and self-reliance along with economic growth. This clearly reflects a tendency to stretch the meaning of economic development beyond its conventional usage. Or, perhaps this indicates that development implies much that cannot be specified in purely economic terms.

The existing conceptions of social development are derived from the same paradigms as economic development — functionalist and Marxist. The term social is so defined in the existing conceptions as to reflect largely the material concerns, signifying thereby the hegemony of the economic dimension over the social. Little is it realised that beyond a certain point, economic growth begins to erode social bonds, which means that economic overdevelopment is accompanied by social maldevelopment.

Development analysis has taken rapid strides in recent decades. In the fifties and sixties it was under the heavy influence of functionalism. The seventies have witnessed the upsurge of a dialectical perspective in development theory. From these two theoretical perspectives have emerged two alternate conceptions of development alongwith their respective development paths and strategies.

FUNCTIONALIST PERSPECTIVE

According to the functionalist perspective, development is defined as a movement in the 'upward and forward' direction. Following a neo-evolutionary stance, functionalists such as Parsons, Smelser, Eisenstadt, to mention only a few pioneering names, tend to view development as a process of social differentiation, integration and adaptive upgrading. Such a view of development has proliferated in the current themes of modernisation all of which share at least one attribute in common, *i.e.,* European ethnocentrism. Taking economic growth as the key feature of development, the functionalist perspective seeks to explain underdevelopment as a state of non-development caused and perpetuated by sheer ignorance and inaction rooted in traditionalism. At any rate, the underdevelopment of some countries is not to be attributed to the high development of other countries. This argument is most succinctly presented by Aron when he says that: 'The high development of the some countries is neither a cause nor a condition of the underdevelopment of other countries. Accordingly, the prescribed strategy of development is to get aid and technical assistance from developed countries and emulate them as a model of development.

DIALECTICAL PERSPECTIVE

With the rise of the dialectical perspective in development analysis, the above view of development has been challenged and an alternative philosophy of development had appeared. Rather than viewing development as an evolutionary process, the new philosophy emphasises, in contrast, the development of underdevelopment as a remarkable fact of recent centuries. It envisages a dialectical relationship between development and underdevelopment and contends that underdevelopment of the Third World is a result of the development of the First World. Following a Marxist historical interpretation, many scholars including Lenin, Paul Baran, Andre Gunder Frank and Samir Amin have variously elaborated the above thesis by tracing the dialectics of development and underdevelopment from the period of merchant capitalism through colonialism to neo-colonialism. In consequence, the dialectical analysis has parented what has come to be known as theories of liberation reflected in the works of radicals such as Illich. Goulet and Rodney the dependency of the Third World on the First World, implying thereby a rejection of aid, technical assistance and model emulation as a strategy of development. Instead, it suggests the importance of the 'original' path of development with technical co–operation as its strategy.

Criticism

Both the above delineated conceptions of development has been criticised as much for their logical imperfections as for their empirical distortions, aparts from their ideological predilections, and attempts have also been made to reconcile the two perspectives. But given their diverge premises and contradictory dominant assumptions, such efforts have borne little fruits.

SOCIOLOGICAL CONCEPT

At the outset, it may be noted that there are two types of conceptions of social development: evolutionary and normative. The history of sociology is replete with evolutionary conceptions which are not what we are concerned with here. One has only to think of Comte's law of the three stages — Spencer's theory of social evolution from simple to complex, Durkheim's scheme of social development from mechanical to organic solidarity, and Marx's delineation of the history of human society from the stage of primitive communism through modern socialism, to reckon the evolutionary concept of social development. There are many other formulations regarding the evolutionary course of social development. Some of them even recent. In fact, how it has come to be accepted on all hands that development is essentially a normative concept. As Sears rightly observes, 'Development is inevitably treated as a normative concept, as almost a synonym for improvement. To pretend otherwise is just to hide one's value judgements. A glance at the existing literature on social development as a normative category reveals two broad conceptions: social development as increase in the life chances of people and social development as egalitarian alteration of 'society' resource allocation or distribution, A brief survey of each follows along with a critique.

Social Development as Increase in Life Chances

At a rudimentary level, the current usage of the term social development connotes as move towards a better social life. As Streeten aptly puts it: development is 'change towards a social state judged desirable'. If this is too general, one might turn to Warner who observes: 'societal development, then, refers to an increase in the life chances of people in society. A similar view is advanced in a publication of the United Nations: 'As the ultimate purpose of development is to provide increasing opportunities to all people for a better life, it is essential to expand and improve facilities for education, health, nutrition, housing, social welfare, and to safeguard the environment.' In short, comments Baster, development is synonymous with 'improvement in the level of living'. All the points to a welfare based conception of social development, with its stress on the ever-increasing scale of social services to be organised by the state.

While the above conception of social development is the most common kind, it is problematic on several counts. First, it reduces a better quality of life to a better standard of living. No doubt a better standard of living is an essential ingredient of a better quality of life, but a better quality of social life implies much more than mere increase in life chances. If increase in life chances alone were sufficient for social development, then the affluent societies of the world would also have been the socially most accomplished societies, which they are not. If anything, they tend to show signs of social retrogression. Take for example, the capitalist countries of the West which take pride in their higher levels of living. There seems to be something basically wrong with the model of social life that they have evolved. Nowhere does one find as high an incidence of the so-called 'civilisation disease' — mental illness, heart trouble, cancer, etc. — as in these societies. Nowhere have freak cultures such as Hippie and Beatnik grown as much as in these countries. Nowhere has the sense of community been undermined to quite the same extent as in these nations. Maybe, overabundance tends to breed psycho-social pathologies, as there is a surfeit of both in the affluent countries of the West. At any rate, this shows the vulnerability of the utilitarian conception of social development. Secondly, insofar as this conception of social development implies that it is the duty of the state to provide necessary social services, to the same extent it blunts an individual's sense of responsibility for the good of other individuals. What is more, in a highly developed society 'the ruthless pursuit of self-interest without regard to the welfare of others is fully sanctioned,' says Hosditz. Above all, there is the problem of limited resources with the state, particularly in the Third World, to provide these services to all their peoples. While the economically prosperous nations of the capitalist West can afford to extend these services with their existing arrangements, the same seems to be unrealizable in the economically underdeveloped societies unless their economic and power relations are altogether restructured.

Social development as Alteration of Resource Allocation

Here social development is defined as that type of structural change which involves alteration of a society's resource allocation or distribution. The sharpest formulation of this view has been advanced by Kim. Treating societal development as a value concept, Kim identifies the following as the core development values of all human societies: social and economic justice, economic prosperity, political freedom, health and education. Following a structural perspective, he proposes the concept of 'structural flexibility' as a measure of societal development. Structural flexibility refers to 'the degree to which the structure of society allows the deprived and alienated majority not only to demand their just (or equal, ideally if possible) share of resources, but also to actually obtain such goals.' Thus, as long as 'the structure of society changes in the direction that enhances the opportunity for the deprived mass to obtain a greater share of resources, that structure is in the process of development.'

Evidently this is an egalitarian conception of social development. The goal of social development here is to create a just and non-exploitative social order rather than a mass consumption society. It is valuable insofar as it champions the cause of the underdog, but it is vulnerable in that its core development values are not self-consistent. In reality, the above outlined core development values lack internal consistency If anything, a certain amount of strain inheres in their inter-relations with the result that pursuit of one may impede the realisation of another. Take, for example, the problem of compatibility between national sovereignty *versus* individual autonomy, or for that matter, between freedom and justice. These are not contrived value dilemmas but genuine problems of coherence between development values.

Furthermore, if one looks at the experience of socialist societies, which are implied in this conception as models of developed societies, one cannot help noting that while they put a premium on equality, freedom is at a discount there, especially, formal freedoms such as the right to express, to vote and to worship. What use are formal freedom, socialist thinkers, may ask if the people, especially the poor and downtrodden, have no real freedom to survive, let along forge their destiny? To this critics like Aron would say that the totalitarian regime itself may be experienced by individuals not as the forger of to total liberation but as the author of total servitude. Those who regard freedom as a life-fulfilling value and there are many who hold this view — consider it too great a price to be paid for development. They would rather have no such development than have it at the expense of freedom.

Lack of freedom apart, there is the additional charge of political repression in socialist states. Given the centralised political power, any dissent may be an invitation to trouble, if not always to torture. That is the reason why even M.N. Roy, who participated in the socialist revolutions of as many as four countries, describes the political machinery in socialist states as 'dictatorial.' In any case, socialist states are for most part dominated by what Rene Dumont calls the 'proto-socialisms' of the national bureaucracies.

OPERATIONAL INDICATORS

Attempts have teen made to devise operational indicators for both the conceptions of social development — utilitarian and egalitarian. Whichever the conception to be operationalised, it cannot escape the issue of contextuality, the question of a place-time dimension. As is often the case with such issues, scholarly opinion is divided on this matter too. If some stipulate a uniform set of indicators which is supposed to be universally applicable, others plead for a relativistic set which is of necessity country-specific. On the one hand, we have Seers who postulates 'the realisation of the potential of human personality' as a 'universally accepted aim' of social development and spells out its 'necessary conditions'. On the other hand, we have Mukherjee who maintains that 'at the present state of our knowledge in the social sciences, we are not in a position to standardise the concept of social development and evolve 'universally' applicable social indicators on that basis.' Under the circumstances we will do well to consider the parameters of social development from both the unifomitarian and the relativistic perspectives.

Uniformitarian Sets

Following a uniformitarian approach to social development, various sets of operational indicators have been constructed in recent years, some of which pertain to a welfare-based conception of development while others to an egalitarian conception. Notable among the attempts to operationalise a welfare-based conception of development are those of Drewnowski (1967), Seers (1972) and McGranahan (1972). Drewnowski, for instance, has focused on such components as: nutrition, shelter, health, education, leisure, security and environment. Specifying the conditions for the realisation of the potential of the human personality, which he regards as the universally accepted aim of development, Seers has, in the first instance, underlined the importance of enough food or adequate income, jobs or employment, and freedom from 'repressive sexual codes', from noise and pollution, etc. In a work edited by McGranahan for the United Nations Research Institute for Social Development the following set of a 'highly-correlated core' of 17 variables has teen offered: (1) expectation of life at birth; (2) percentage population in localities of 20,000 and over; (3) consumption of animal protein per capita per day; (4) combined primary and secondary enrolment; (5) vocational enrolment ratio; (6) average number of persons per room; (7) newspaper circulation per 1000 population; (8) telephones per 1,00,000 population; (9) percentage E.A.P. (Economically Active Population) in electricity, gas, water, etc.; (10) agricultural production per male agricultural worker; (11) percentage of adult male labour in agriculture; (12) electricity consumption Kwh, per capita; (13) steel consumption; (14) kilograms of coal per capita; (15) per cent of GDP derived from manufacturing; (16) foreign trade per capita in I960 U.S. dollars; (17) per cent salaried and wage earners to total E.A.P.

Egalitarian Conception

Turning to the attributes and indicators of the egalitarian conception of social development, it will be appropriate to begin with Marx. The attributes of social development according to Marx, as can be inferred from his works and from the works of Engels, are: absence of the institution of private property, liquidation of the class structure — 'from each according to his capacity to each according to his needs' — and the withering away of state power (the last one remaining yet a remote possibility in practically all the contemporary socialist states).

One of the most systematic formulations of the indicators of an egalitarian conception of development has been advanced by Weisskopf. He groups the major development objectives into three categories: growth, equity and self-reliance. The principal indicators of economic growth, according to him, are the rates of increase of GNP and per capita GNP together with separate estimates of the rates of growth of the two major goods-producing sectors: agriculture and industry. The equity objective is held to comprise equality of current income, employment, welfare and opportunity with their indicators as follows: (a) the degree of equality in the overall distribution of income class; (b) the differential between average levels of living in urban and rural areas; (c) the dispersion of average levels of living among the different regions of a country; and (d) the range of incomes accruing to people working within an economic enterprise, from the Mghest paid executive or manager to the lowest paid worker; (e) the extent to which employment opportunities are available to the (potentially) working population as well as the adequacy of provisions made for the unemployed and the underemployed; (f) the extent to which health care is available to all members of a society; (g) the extent to which literacy and primary education have been made accessible to the whole population and (h) the degree of social mobility within society. Finally, the indicators of self-reliance of a country are: (a) the extent to which the control of productive enterprise is exercised by nationals; (b) the extent to which the country has remained free of foreign exchange problems and foreign debt; (c) the extent to which the country has been able to do without foreign aid; and (d) the extent to which the country has developed an independent technological base for economic activity.

Relativistic sets

As noted before, relativistic sets of operational indicators have to do either with a particular country or with a group of analogous countries that have common characteristics. The attempt made by Mukherjee to formulate some relevant attributes of development for India, derived from the documents on the development goal, strategy and priorities, as envisaged by the five political parties, is an example of the first category, while Myrdai's delineation of 'modernisation ideals' for Asia is an example of the second category.

QUESTIONS FOR EXERCISE

1. Is development synonymous to economic growth? Discuss.
2. Discuss functionalist and dialectical perspectives of development.
3. Discuss the prevailing sociological conceptions of development.
4. Discuss various operational indicators of development.

CHAPTER 6

Social Evolution and Social Revolution

What is Social Evolution?

According to Herbert Spencer, "Evolution is an integration of matter and concomitant dissipation of motion, during which the matter passes from a relatively indefinite, incoherent homogeneity to a relatively definite, coherent heterogeneity and during which the retained motion undergoes a parallel transformation."[1] Social evolution means social progress from an indefinite, incoherent homogeneity to a definite, coherent heterogeneity. Three facts are fairly evident in this process. Firstly, in social evolution indefinite associations, communities, institutions, etc., assume definite forms. Secondly, the process of adjustment or synthesis operates in social evolution and the various parts of society are continuously adjusted. Thus, social evolution is not merely change. Thirdly, social evolution is accompanied by increasing heterogeneity in society, meaning that newer associations, community, institutions, etc., are ever coming into being.

CHARACTERISTICS OF SOCIAL EVOLUTION

Herbert Spencer has prescribed four important principles of evolution. These principles are: (1) Social evolution is one cultural or human aspect of the law of change of cosmic evolution. (2) Hence, social evolution takes place in the same way at all places and progresses through some definite and inevitable stages, (3) Social evolution is gradual. (4) Social evolution is progressive. In addition to these four characteristics, three other features of social evolution are clearly evident from its foregoing definition.

(a) Social evolution takes place through the process of differentiation. In order to understand this, just study the history of a society over a long period of time, and you will find that its associations, institutions, etc., are constantly evolving or developing. In social evolution new and ever newer circumstances and problems are constantly appearing and in order to cope with them new associations and institutions are evolved. Take for example, the community in a town. Previously, when the town had been a small community Its management was the responsibility

1. Herbert Spencer, *Principles of Sociology*, Vol. V.

of a panchayat or a town area committee. Now that the town has become a big commercial centre, its management was in the hands of a dozen different committees. One of them looked after the educational facilities; another after sanitation, a third was deputed to look after the octroi while a fourth managed the markets, and so on. In this way, this differentiation increased with the evolution of the town.

(b) But without integration this differentiation cannot take one anywhere. Hence, synthesis, along with differentiation, is necessary. In cities while one will find sectarian associations such as Brahmin society, South Indian Association based on various caste and class distinctions. Today, while new nations are coming into being in the human society, equally strong efforts are being made to create a world society by uniting these nations.

(c) By virtue of this double process of differentiation and integration the efficiency of society is being constantly increased. Division of labour is the keyword of modern economic evolution. By an increase in the number of associations and institutions in society, work in various spheres is performed more successfully and because of the process of synthesis various spheres take advantage of each other's efficiency also.

In the theory of social evolution, the naturalists apply the biological principles of survival of the fittest and struggle for existence to society. Many scientists have found this theory tenable and have offered their explanations of it. Hobhouse has written, "By evolution I mean any sort of growth, by social progress the growth of social life in respect of those qualities to which human beings can attach or can rationally attach values." The principle of social evolution maintains that there is lineal progress in society, but all scientists do not accept social evolution as a linear process. Some scholars believe it to be unilineal while others consider it to be cyclical. According to Morgan, Haddon and Engels, the evolution of every society passes through the three following stages: (1) Savagery, (2) Barbarism, and (3) Civilizations. In the same way these scholars have held that there are four stages in the economic development of every society: (1) Hunting, (2) Pastoral, (3) Agricultural, and (4) Industrial stage. According to the evolutionary principle, there are three recognized stages in the development of technology: (1) Stone Age, (2) Bronze Age, and (3) Iron Age. In the same way, the evolutionists have attempted to show that there are stages of development in the various institutions of human society, such as marriage, family, religion, property, law, government, etc.

But some scholars have indulged in the bitter criticism of the evolutionist opinion. Goldenwesier who has written *The History and Prospects of the Social Sciences*, has staunchly advocated this viewpoint. According to these scholars it is fallacious to conceive of evolution in the social sphere. The description of the stages of the development of society is no more than a flight of imagination. There is no historical evidence supporting description of these stages of technological, economic and cultural development. And it is entirely wrong to believe that there occurs orderly progress of the same type, in every society because each society has its own peculiar circumstances and any changes that occur in it concur with its conditions. These conditions are always changing and this change also is not orderly and uniform.

REALITY OF SOCIAL EVOLUTION

In his famous hook ***Society*** MacIver supports the principle of social evolution. According to Maciver, evolution is the process whereby all that is implicit is made manifest successively or slowly. Direct increase is not called evolution. In evolution the structure of an object changes along with an increase in its size. It is that incessant and unwavering process of quantitative and qualitative change by which the internal characters of an object appear and become distinct and clear. Thus, the fundamental characteristic of evolution is differentiation which comprehends the sense of unification. In society differentiation is usually evinced if the division of labour increases in the number and varieties of active associations and greater variation and excellence in the means of social communication (particularly language). Maciver has strongly criticized the practice of believing social evolution to be imaginary.

What is the reality behind social evolution? In order to reach some definite conclusion in this connection it would be useful to acquaint oneself with the arguments given by sociologists in favour of the reality of social evolution. Roughly speaking, these arguments are as follows:

1. The variety and difference to be seen between primitive and civilized societies is also to be seen between the different kinds of animals in animal society. Thus, if the principle of evolution can be applied to animals, why can it not be applied in the sphere of human society? Hence, from the variety in human society it cannot be concluded that there is no reality in the principle of evolution.

2. The existence in social life, of the process of differentiation is a proof of there being evolution in society. Actually, as has been stated earlier, it is MacIver's contention that this activity of differentiation is in itself a fundamental characteristic of social evolution. Hence, MacIver holds that if evolution, in the form of unilineal evolution, is to be so interpreted as to mean that some specific institutions of society, after passing through many stages in a definite order, become the special circumstances of developed societies, then the reality of evolution cannot be accepted. The reality of evolution is in the process of differentiation. It is only due to this process that in every society, as time passes, new associations, systems, groups and institutions develop to perform different functions. In this way, all the various groups — political, economic, religious and cultural — are continuously developed History tells us that, in the beginning there was no differentiation of institutions within human society for the performance of diverse functions. This differentiation was introduced later as culture and civilization progressed and it is even now increasing. This historical fact is an evidence of tne extent and element of reality in the principle of social evolution.

3. This reality of social evolution is even better evinced in the composition of modern nations including primitive societies. In primitive societies every family

or at the most one kin group collectively performs all the activities such as farming, hunting, fighting, etc. Neither are there any classes as there are in modern societies, nor any specific associations for the performance of particular functions. Even the religious, cultural and educational institutions are not distinct. On the contrary, in modern societies, one finds differentiation in the religious, economic, cultural, verily all spheres. It is evident that this difference between primitive and modern societies is due to the reality of social evolution. Only one example in support of the reality of social evolution would suffice. In order to clarify the reality of evolution, MacIver has utilised the evolution of religion as an example. According to him the evolution of religion passed through the following stages:

1. The Fusion of Religious and other Cultural Elements. In the primitive religion the religious element is fused with other cultural elements. Actually, at one time, religion was the method of the primitive man's meditation on the important matters. It was a kind of mental approach which was active in all the major occurrences in life. In this way, birth, death, famine, the sudden manifestation of various natural forces, social customs, crops, seasons, the institution of leader and everything else was interpreted and understood on the basis of religion. Primitive man did not learn to distinguish between natural and intellectual powers.

2. Cult and Magic. Religion progressed from this chaotic stage to the stage of cult and magic. In this stage, the unknown powers began to be adorned with definite forms and the mystery sense was attributed to some specific objects. The society had now started accepting these forces as having definite forms and to them were attached particular rites, folk-lores and beliefs. In this way cults were born. Earth, sky, storm and the forces related to the objects of nature now became separate and specific existence. Particular methods were evolved to propitiate them. The priest, as one who knew these methods, came into existence. Along with him, magicians were also recognized in society. In this way religion assumed the form of institution and became limited to a definite aspect of life. In this stage no distinctions between body and soul, social and spiritual elements, magic and religion had been made.

3. The Formation of Specifically Religious Institutions. The third stage was that of the formation of specifically religious institutions. In this stage, the goodness and evil of the world was recognized and their supra-mundane causes, gods and devils, were imagined. In this stage the two following stages are important:

(a) Communal deities. Religion, having assumed an institutional form, began to be treated as the possession of the entire society or race. As a result of this the real or imagined ancestors and sages, and sometimes even existing kings, were deified. In this way polytheism spread and was succeeded a tendency towards monotheism.

(b) The emergence of the sacred and the profane. Along with the introduction of communal deities, religion became a separate institution and at the same time particular religious rituals, methods and priests also came into existence. Then all objects related to them began to be considered to be sacred, while all objects contradicting them termed profane.

4. From Religious Institutions to Specific Associations. In the fourth stage of religion, religious associations appeared. With the introdution of association, following religion or rejecting it one's wish. This is the existing state of religion. But in the development of religion from the stage of institution to many million human beings have had to struggle hard. In medieval Europe the people everywhere had to accept the religion of their kind. A tremendous struggle raged for years in order to put an end to this custom. Now in most civilized societies the government and religion have been recognized as separate institutions. Membership of religion is voluntary, not compulsory.

The above example of religion, in connection with social evolution, presents only a rough outline of evolution as well as opportunity for different scholars, to express differing opinions, but such differences are natural, and this example does not fail to convey that the principle of social evolution is no sandy edifice. At least this much is conceded, even by the most vehement critics, that the evolutionary point of view throws a new light upon the study of social institutions and associations. It is difficult to conceive of a state in which everyone will accept the reality of social evolution sincfe it s understanding depends very much upon the viewpoint of the particular scholar, and yet at least this much is evident that the evolutionary studies of various institutions and associations of society in the present time and in immediate past, are not only interesting but also suggestive.

SOCIAL REVOLUTION

The meaning of the term revolution is clarified and explained by the distinction drawn between it and the process of evolution. The word 'revolution' is employed in three specific senses. When some people or a large group of people revolt against the existing government and completely change the governmental organization, it is called 'political revolution'. Political revolutions and uprisings are common and almost normal incidents in the histories of most nations since revolutions of this kind keep taking place from time to time. Revolution denotes the sudden and abrupt change in the customs, behavioural patterns, values, etc., of a society. In this process the beliefs, attitudes and habits of the general public are completely changed. Cultural revolution comprehends religious and economic revolutionary process but the most comprehensive is the social revolution in which process the entire social structure or organization undergoes very considerable change and modification as a result of which the patterns of social institutions, classes, status, action, etc., are suddenly and greatly changed. Although social revolution is the most comprehensive process yet the most popular form of revolution is the political. As Kimball Young has written in his work, A Handbook of Social Psychology, "For our purposes, we define revolution as an abrupt shift to new forms of power or authority within a nation state."[2]

2. Young, K., *A Handbook of Social Psychology*, p. 57.

The Psychology of Revolution

Revolution has its various aspects such as political, economic, social and others, yet fundamentally it is a psychological process. It is this psychological aspect and nature that is analysed and studied by social psychology. According to this science, the following are the main psychological factors at the root of revolution:

1. Explosion of Repressed Drives. In the opinion of many psychologists, revolution is the explosion or collective outburst of repressed drives. Most of the modern psychologists hold that the desires and tendencies that the individual represses or suppresses are not completely eliminated from the mind but they rather manifest themselves even more violently as a violent reaction when the right opportunity presents itself. When, in a country, various kinds of desires and tendencies of the people are repressed and are not allowed the change to manifest and extend themselves, then in most people some sort of reaction takes place. And it is this same reaction that in collective form assumes the proportion of revolution. It is Freud who has specifically explained the reaction of repressed desires. In his book *The Sociology of Revolution* Sorokin has written, "The immediate cause of revolution is always the growth of 'repression' of the main instincts of majority society, and the impossibility of obtaining for these instincts the necessary minimum of satisfaction."[3] Then the necessary instincts of majority of the population remain dissatisfied, or satisfaction becomes impossible, and repression increases, then the reaction to this suppression itself is in the form of revolution.

2. Expression of Unconscious and Lowly Passions. In order to explain revolution Lebon has adduced the simile of mob behaviour or crowd behaviour. Just as in crowd behaviour the unconscious and lowly passions of the people find expression, in the same manner revolution is caused by the same factors. It is often seen that in times of revolution the behaviour of the people is just as excited, irrational and emotional as is the case with a crowd. The major constituents of the revolution are derived from the suppressed, tortured and frustrated morass of humanity that form the masses. In a revolution they turn a deaf ear to every one and are prepared to do practically anything. And hence one comes across actions done by people which cannot be equalled by any human being possessing his faculties. During the French Revolution even the women murdered people and sucked their blood. In this way, in a revolution, extreme cruelty is witnessed and most of the people behave like animals, as if they were reluctant to forget their origin.

3. Expression of Unconscious Desires. According to Sigmund Freud, the exploited and tortured beings in society foster feelings of hatred and animosity towards the administrators and upper classes in their unconscious minds. In his infancy the individual hates his father because of latter's tyrannical and strict administration and later on in life this hatred is transferred to the administration and power. In a revolution it is this same hatred that is collectively manifested and expressed and efforts are made to destroy the power and its representatives.

---

3. Sorokin, P.A., *op. cit*, p. 383.

It is evident from the foregoing description of the various opinions concerning the psychological factors in revolution that the psychological foundations of revolution are formed, particularly of repressed desires and instincts. As L. P. Edwards has written, "People come to feel that their legitimate aspirations and ideals are being repressed or perverted that their entirely proper desires and ambitions are being hindered and thwarted."[4] What must be kept clearly in view is the fact that psychological causes are not the momentary or immediate causes of revolution but are rather the fundamental causes. In other words, the psychological factors create a readiness in the individual for revolution. In the absence of this readiness or psychological preparedness, there can be no revolution because, be the political, social and economic conditions what they will, they are not sufficient to induce the group to take any positive action. In the words of Kimball Young, "We may say in fact that no revolution is possible until the psychological moment has arrived. There must be a definite 'readiness' for revolutionary behaviour."[5]

Cultural Cause of Revolution

As has been indicated at an earlier juncture, revolution is caused by factors other than the purely psychological ones. In addition to the psychological factors there are some cultural factors that help to precipitate a revolution. These factors are also important contributory factors of circumstances in the final result. Ogbum and Nimkoff have written, "Revolution is a rapid change of some magnitude in culture."[6] As and when the existing and traditional institutions, dogmas, customs, mores and traditions, etc., become continuously less capable of satisfying the needs of the people, the society becomes marked with unrest and perturbation and disturbance. The people revolt. And the residents of urban districts have a particular role in this revolt. Because of the more facile availability of the means of suggestions and propaganda in the urban areas in comparison with the rural areas, revolutionary ideas circulate more rapidly among the urban population than they do among the rural population. And even otherwise the urban population on the whole is more in favour of progress and novelty and opposed to tradition and stagnation. And it is in this class that the revolutionary spark finds the most respective substance and it easily produces a conflagration. If new nations and thoughts, inventions and novel things find their place in society easily and without resistance and as a matter of course, then the necessity of revolution is avoided. But this does not happen because there are many individuals in society who are opposed to change which adversely affects their vested interests. Hence, revolution becomes necessary and is inevitable. Myth, emotional symbols, legends and stereotypes also have a hand in this. It is the change in them that induced revolution. Kimball Young writes, "The rise of a new social myth means that the

4. Edwards, L.P., *The Natural History of Revolution*, p. 30.

5. Young, K., *A Handbook of Social Psychology*, p. 568.

6. Ogburn and Nimkoff, *A Handbook of Sociology*, p. 616.

desires, beliefs, attitudes and habits of the people have been altered. The new myth is the promise of a new heaven and a new earth."[7]

Economic Causes of Revolution

In addition to the cultural causes of revolution there are some economic factors that are important in this connection. In the opinion of the famous revolutionist, Karl Marx, the main causes of revolution are of an economic nature. According to him, the increase of the disparity between the various social classes and the exploitation of the power by the richer class in society leads to a situation in which revolution becomes inevitable because the exploiters are not prepared to voluntarily relinquish their power. According to Marxist thinking the main factor at the root of revolution is class struggle which is caused by the exploitation of the labourers and the farmers and agriculturists at the hands of the rich classes. The leaders of revolution are these exploited farmers and labourers. What must be kept in view here is that it is not possible to say definitely in exactly which economic condition will a revolution be necessary. Actually, it sometimes happens that a revolution does not take place in a comparatively richer community. For example, in India the labourers and agriculturists have never revolted despite their having been subjected to extreme exploitation and continuous poverty and hardship. On the other hand in 1918, when the German agriculturists revolted against Kaiser though their economic condition was not very poor. Similarly, in the 1917 American revolution the economic condition of that country was fairly good. The fact of the matter is that even at the root of economic causes, it is the psychological factor that is at work. Whatever may be the condition of economy in the country the people will revolt if they have come to believe that it is necessary to improve their economic condition since such a belief leads to an increase in the dissatisfaction that is inherent in life. It is not the extent to which the agriculturist and the labourer is exploited that is a determining factor of whether a revolution will take place. It is not the decisive factor. What is also needed is hatred and disgust for the moneyed class and the landlords in the hearts of those who serve them. It is only when these strong emotions are aroused that the revolution can take actual shape. It is for this reason that the revolutionaries pay particular attention to arousing and inflaming these feelings.

And, finally, we come to another important aspect of the causes of revolution, the political causes of this phenomenon. In different countries there is continuous conflict between various political parties and leaders for political power. Taking advantage of the opportunities that present themselves, they do their best to persuade the public opinion to support them and to encourage it to denounce their political rival. For example, the communist party always aims at arousing and engaging the labourers and agriculturists in order that the party may be able to gain power. In this manner, revolutions happen and are caused for political interests.

---

7. Young, K., *A Handbook of Social Psychology*, p. 525.

QUESTIONS FOR EXERCISE

1. What is the reality about Social Evolution? Explain the concept with special reference to any one example.
2. Discuss MacIver's concept of Social Evolution.
3. Write an essay on Social Evolution.
4. Distinguish between Social Evolution and Social Progress.
5. Describe the various stages of change from primitive to civilized society.
6. Write short note on — Language and Social Control.
7. Write short note on — Revolution.

CHAPTER 7

Psychological Factors of Social Change: Fashion, Style, Fad and Craze

The reader would have often heard of people talking of a particular thing being in fashion in a particular field or of the fashion of a particular thing having been ousted from a particular sphere. Young men and women almost never tire of talking of fashion irrespective of the place in which they are and are always desirous of appearing the most fashionable among their friends. It is not unusual for women of a neighbourhood to go stampeding to buy a new sari if one of the women among them has bought a new one. Previously, the men used to wear trousers which were open at the bottom but now they have reverted to the use of what is known in knowledgeable circles as a drainpipe. Fashion is not limited merely to the sphere of clothes but extends to practically every field such as jewellery, modes of behaviour, conversation and thought, etc. And yet this does not mean that the field of fashion is all comprehending. Despite its appearing to comprehend a very large part of life, fashion influences only those spheres concerning which we are indifferent. For example, the legs of a salvar can be either wide or narrow. And as one cannot turn to a specialist when one wants to sew a salvar as to how should its legs be fashioned the mode in the fashion at the moment is chosen. On the other hand, the modes of behaviour in the relationship between men and women, particularly in the case of the marital relation, are not governed by fashion because this is one sphere in which we are indifferent but tend to conform to some specific traditions. In this way, the sphere of fashion increases with an increase in the field of indifference. For example, if there are no definite traditions or well defined modes of mutual address between husband and wife in some society then fashion takes command of this sphere as well.

FASHION

What is Fashion

As is evident from the foregoing description, there is an intimate relationship between fashion, custom, ettiquete, usage, convention and tradition. Before proceeding to describe this relationship it would be better to know what fashion, scientifically considered. Generally, People take fashion to mean personal choice or the choice of the majority or the choice of the leading people but such an indistinct definition cannot serve the purpose of scientific study. Hence, it must be defined more precisely.

Defining fashion in his book *Social Psychology*, Ross writes "Fashion is a series of recurring changes in the choices of a group of people which though they may be accompanied by utility, are not determined by it."[1] This particular definition of fashion stresses the following four facts:

1. Fashion is a Change in the Choice of some Group. Fashion is related to the choice of the liking of a group of people. Fashion transforms this choice. For example, in India previously the number of people who wore bushshirts was very small but now even the most ordinary individual can be seen wearing it because its fashion has spread to every class in society.

2. Fashion is a Chain of Recurring Modification. Fashion is constantly changing and the effect of this invariable variation is that some object goes out of fashion at one particular time but it stands a chance of being included in the fashion parade at a later date. For example, there was a time in India when the educated and literate individuals sported the buttoned up coat. Then, for some time this particular article of dress lost its charm and became outmoded and now once again it is considered a very fashionable dress. In this way fashion is a dynamic process. It is a series or chain of recurring variations and changes.

3. Fashion can be Related to Utility. Many fashions also have much utility. For example, the bushshirt is a very comfortable article of the gent's wardrobe, particularly in the warm climate of India. In this way it is both fashionable and comfortable to wear bushshirt.

4. Fashion is not Determined by Utility. But utility is not the determinant of fashion. Many objects and articles become fashionable without having any utility whatsoever, such as ties, broaches, jewellery, etc.

Nature of Fashion

The nature of fashion is brought to light in some detail from the preceding analysis of the definition of fashion given by Ross. Accordingly, it was seen that fashion causes a change in the choice of individuals. In their book Society, MacIver and Page write, "By fashion we mean the, socially approved sequence of variation on a customary theme."[2] In this sequence it is not essential that either our contemporaries or our predecessors must be copied and imitated. Further, it is not of essence to fashion that either the higher social classes or the lower classes must be emulated. Fashion can be any one of these, %s MacIver has indicated in the definition that he has given of fashion, fashion is neither a contradiction of custom nor is it outside custom. It functions in the field of custom. For example, the Indian dress is determined to a large extent by tradition and custom but minor changes and variations in this dress are governed by fashion. Most Indian ladies

1. Ross, E. A., *Social* Psychology, p. 47.

2. MacIver and Page, *Society*, p. 181.

wear the sari by custom but the colour, design, border, etc., of the sari are a matter of fashion and contemporary convention.

Psychological bases of Fashion

The power of suggestion or the attraction that characterizes fashion are adequately explained by psychology. At the root of fashion are present two psychological but mutually contradictory desires — those of novelty and of conformity. The individual on the one hand wants to appear distinct and distinguished from the multitude, and for this he indulges in all sorts of eccentricities of dress, behavioural modes, conduct, mode of life, etc., while on the other hand, he resorts to the socially accepted and acceptable patterns of behaviour, dress, diet, etc., in order that he may not appear different from the others and may conform to the general standard of his own class. Fashion satisfies and satiates the demand of both these desires. E. Sapir, in his essay entitled Fashion published in the Encyclopaedia of Social Science writes, "The slight changes from the established norms in dress or other forms of behaviour seem for the moment to give the victory to the individual, while the fact that one's fellow revolt in the same direction gives one a feeling of adventurous safety."[3] In this way, fashion is the contradiction of tradition but it itself gradually becomes the convention. Once it has become the common convention it is in time replaced by another fashion and thus a change occurs and this chain progresses in this manner, continuing all the time. There is imitation in fashion but this imitation is not one of object but of style and even in imitation every individual has his own style. In this manner then whereas fashion introduces an element of conformity yet it simultaneously provides ample scope for individual nuances and idiosyncrasies.

Fashion and Imitation

It is certain and indisputable that imitation has an important role in fashion. Fashion spreads in society only by means of the process of imitation but is worth thinking over as fire problem of who imitates whom. Psychological analysis of this human phenomenon reveals that imitation takes place according to some well defined laws. These laws are the following:

1. Imitation of Person on Higher Level. It is generally recognized that everyone wants to attain to a higher social level. Thus, everyone is usually seen imitating the habits, decorations, conduct, etc., that are recognized as fashionable in the higher groups. No one imitates the fashions belonging to a lower social level than his own class. And if he does it, he loses his social prestige and renders himself open to ridicule.

2. Imitation of the Rich. In this way, then people usually imitate those richer than themselves. The middle class people want to copy the richer people and thus win admiration and respect of the society.

3. Sapir, E., in his article *Fashion,* in Encyclopaedia of Social Science, New York (1935), pp. 139-144.

3. Imitation of the Powerful People Influence Everyone. The power possessed by the powerful can be of any kind such as beauty, energy, intellect, wealth, office, etc. There is attraction in power. Hence, everyone imitates the powerful.

4. Imitation of the Leaders. In this way, the population possesses a tendency for imitating the leaders, this tendency being particularly evident, in the field of politics.

5. Imitations of the Successful. There is a saying, "nothing succeeds like success." Successful people win the admiration and respect of everyone. Hence, one often comes across people who are trying to imitate them in order to appear as successful as them.

6. Imitation of the Citizen. From the viewpoint of types of community life, the town presents behavioural and fashion patterns to the village. Fashions proceed from the big cities to the smaller towns and villages. For example, the people living in Bombay and Delhi are believed to be the leaders in matters of fashion.

7. Imitation of the Personalities. Now-a-days, the films have a powerful influence upon the people in practically all countries. At almost all places it is the actors and actresses who determine fashions in matters of dress and hairstyles, etc. For example, this influence can be seen only too clearly on the younger generation in the towns of India.

Fashion and Custom

Comparing custom and fashion, Kimball Young has written, "If we consider custom as a stable and persistent phase of social behaviour, fashion may be thought of as variation permissible within this general acceptance."[4] In this way, fashions are more unstable than customs and they progress by causing change in the sphere of custom. For example, it is custom among the Indian women to wear a sari and blouse. But there are many things concerning the sari and the blouse, such as the colour of the sari, the style of tying it, the design of its border, the arms of the blouse, the shape of its neck, its colour matching or differing from the colour of sari etc. that are determined by fashion and not by custom. In this way, then fashion' tends to increase the variety in society whereas custom tends to hurry the society on its way to a static and homogeneous condition. Then, in addition to this, there are some spheres of life in which there are no customs and the only determinant of the individual's behaviour is the fashion that is prevailing. For example, art, the decoration of hair, conversation, pronunciation, etc., are some spheres in which there are no definite customs that may guide conduct and for this reason the common individual imitates the fashion in these fields. Further, the changes that take place in these spheres also occur comparatively faster than in other spheres. While, on the one hand, custom has the advantage of saving the individual a lot of mental exercise by obviating the necessity of thinking originally on every problem, it, on the other hand, also satisfies the sense of self-expression

4. Young, K., *Handbook of Social Psychology* (1951), p. 411.

of the individual. It is of course not inevitable that fashion has some utility. It is sometimes adopted by the individual in order that he may appear distinct from the crowd and may become the cynosure of all eyes. Distinguishing between custom and fashion, Tarde has written that fashion is the imitation of the contemporaries, whereas custom is the imitation of the ancestors. Custom proceeds through the ages and the person who upholds custom and tradition acts as those who have acted before him. On the other hand, the fashionable men and women do just what has not been done before but they resort to doing what is being done all around them in order to appear the most up-to-date and latest in their dress, mode of life, behaviour, etc. The rapid change that is discernible in the young men and women of India today, in matters of dress is the outcome not of custom but of fashion. In the words of Ross, "If we figure the life of a society as a flowing stream then we think of one (custom) as down imitation, the other (fashion) as cross imitation."[5] This statement by Ross also points to the same fact that has been mentioned before, *viz.*, that custom is the imitation of ancestors, their thoughts and activities, whereas fashion is the imitation of contemporary thoughts and actions.

Cycle of Fashion

Describing the cycle of fashion, G. Simmel has written, "The very character of fashion demands that it should be exercised at one time only by a portion of the given group, the great majority being merely on the road to adopting it. As soon as an example has been universally adopted, that is, as soon as anything that was originally done only by a few has really come to be practised by all as is the case in certain portions of our apparel and in various forms of social conduct we no longer speak of fashion. As fashion spreads, it gradually goes to its doom."[6] In this way, fashion moves in cyclical order in society. For example, in ancient India, the women were accustomed to wearing very brief blouses that looked more like cholis. They covered only a small portion of the stomach and were also fairly low in the neck. Then, as almost everyone turned to this particular form of the blouse, people who were the very personification of fashion proceeded to wear more elaborate blouses. Following this, the fashionable women once more reverted to the brief blouse as a result of the influence of Western fashions. In a slow but steady process the blouses proceeded upwards from the stomach and downwards from the neck. It would be a matter of little surprise if they were soon to assume the form of the ancient cholis which are known for their brevity and economy of cloth. But when this fashion also becomes universally accepted it too will inevitably be outmoded and rejected and it would occasion little surprise if the women again wore the elaborate and sleeved blouse. Similar fashion cycles can also be seen in other fashions. Fashion cycles are set in motion by the inability of the old fashions to satisfy the psychological elements. They do not possess the characteristic of self-exhibition and they are devoid of any attraction or special feature. Some people are often heard holding

5. Ross, E. A., *Social Psychology*, p. 196.

6. Simmel, G., *Fashion, International Quarterly* (1904-5), pp. 137-38.

forth on the subject of fashion clothes and saying that they are so much in vogue that even the scum of the earth are wearing them, how can they be expected to wear them, as if one of the intentions of wearing the clothes is to distinguish them from what they are prone to call the scum of the earth. On the other hand, the people belonging to the lower strata of society start imitating the fashions that prevail in the higher strata. In the urban communities of India people of even the lowest strata of society like to be called mummy and papa by their children. What is the surprise if the people belonging to the higher strata of society prefer to be called by the old ancient names characteristic of Indian affection such as bapu and maan when these Westernized names become the custom? Park is definitely right when he says that some of us can stay behind fashion but none of us can be ahead of fashion. And how can we do it? The moment one has the originality to suggest something new, it is immediately imitated by the others and it becomes the fashion. The only condition that is necessary for this to happen is that the idea should have the fundamental qualities such as self-expression, sexual attraction, uniqueness, etc. In this cycle of fashion those who set the pace are the people who occupy high posts or the rich men of society. Leaders, cinema actors and actresses are all included in this group. Kimball Young has written, "Reputability is essential to the adoption of a fad or fashion." Respected people occupy the place of honour among those who set the direction of fashion. The main cause of this is that they are the ideals of the people, each in his own particular sphere. Hence, the people start imitating every aspect of their lives. In America it is the wife of the President and in England it is the Queen who guide women in their quest for the most fashionable and the fashions that they create very quickly take the shape of craze. In this cycle of fashion, the time that the lower strata of society takes to adopt the fashions of the higher strata is sufficient for the higher strata to change its fashion and once again a degree of distinction and in this manner the cycle of fashion continues to progress.

Fashion and Sexual Attraction

One main cause of why the cycle of fashion exists in group behaviour is that fashion is a means to sexual attraction. Almost everyone is aware of the fact that with the introduction of co-education in India fashion has also rapidly changed. In the present age, no man or woman wants to be left behind the other in matters of ostentation. Most of the young men and women of the new generation want to prove themselves to be the most fashionable, modern and progressive by whatever means that they can employ or are available to them, and this is done with a view to impressing themselves upon individuals of the other sex.

Contemporary thoughts and ideas also influence fashion. Kimball Young has written, "Our contemporary ideology of the equality of the sexes is doubtless influencing the direction of fashion: Women attempt to prove their equality with them by adopting the manners, dress and habits of men."[7] One example of this fact

7. *Ibid.*, p. 420.

is that the number of girls with their hair cut and the number of boys with long hair is now very much on the increase. Even the clothing of the boys and girls is marked by increasing similarity.

Motivating causes of Fashion

In analysing the motivating causes of fashion, Estelle Barr[8] has mentioned the following as the important factors among them — (1) Sense of individuality, (2)Desire for conformity, (3) Desire for comfort, (4) Consciousness of one's physical form, (5) Desire to be beautiful, (6) Desire to manifest the personality, (7) Desire to appear different and distinguished, (8) Desire to conceal physical deformities.

All the above mentioned factors can be seen in the group behaviour of both sexes in as much as it pertains to the nature of fashion. As Hurlock has written, "One of the chief values of clothing is that it enables people to advertise themselves in a way that will win the attention and admiration of others. Many who lack any ability and could not hope to rise above the 'average' on their merits alone, find a satisfactory outlet for this desire for recognition through the medium of dress.[9] One needs only to glance at the men and women, boys and girls, in particular belonging to the new generation, around one in order to see the justification for this statement on the part of Hurlock.

As has been mentioned at an earlier juncture, fashion is of great importance for commerce even though fashions are not utilitarian and are sometimes even considered immoral. In 1929, Stewart Chase[10] made a study of the amount of money spent on fashion by the citizens of The United State of America and came to the conclusion that one-third of all expenditure incurred by the people is an object of fashion. In 1938 also much the same sort of observation concerning expenditure of this nature was made by Elizabeth Hawes.[11] This is not true of only a prosperous nation like America but even in a country like India where the economic development is nothing to be happy about, people spend a large part of their income on objects of fashion. In particular the tendency towards fashionability is most prominent in men and women of the middle class even though because of such action they have considerable difficulty in giving balanced look to their family budget Exploiting this tendency towards fashion, traders and manufacturers are always engaged in making articles of fashion. Fashion is of particular importance in the field of dress and in this sphere it also changes very rapidly. To begin with cotton saris were fashionable, to be replaced by silk which in its turn gave way to nylon and now the people of upper strata have again returned to cotton saris while the middle classes have gone over to terylene saris. In this way, with the return to the cotton sari, the cycle has been completed.

8. Estelle de Young Barr, *Psychological Analysis of Fashion Motivation,* Archives of Psychology (1934), No. 171.
9. Hurlock, E., The Psychology of Dress; An Analysis of Fashion (1929), pp. 27-28.
10. Chase, S., *Tragedy of Waste* (1926).
11. Hawes, E., *Fashion is Spinach* (1938), p. 4.

FASHION AND STYLE

Concerning style, Kimball Young has written, 'The term style is often associated with fashion and fashion change, but it is a vague concept."[12] Style and fashion are mutually related in a profound relationship. But nevertheless it is important to understand the difference between them. Fashion, in accordance with custom, is a change in behaviour concurring to the contemporary tendency. Style is the term employed to indicate minor variations in this same fashion. For example, it is a matter of fashion whether one grows a beard or not. But the type of beard that one would grow — the French cut, the Muslim style or the type sported by the Rajputs — is a matter of style. Similarly, smoking cigarettes may be a matter of fashion but there can be many styles in this fashion. The well known Indian film personalities Dev Anand and Ashok Kumar are both seen addicted to cigarette smoking but the difference in the styles they employ in doing this are well known to their fans. One sees marked differences in the styles of cigarette smoking employed by the older and younger generations. The villain of the Indian screen Fran has his own way of making whorls with the cigarettes.

FASHION, FAD AND CRAZE

Two other words are related with fashion. They are fad and craze. Both of these words are related with the mobility and speed of fashion. When fashion becomes extremely fast and spreads almost as fast as a contagious disease it comes to be known as a craze. Fad is the stage between craze and fashion. Fad becomes a craze when the former becomes very mobile and extensive and comprehends a very large field. Once the field increases and the fashion attains some degree of constancy it becomes a fad. According to Kimball Young, fad is related to insignificant things such as clothes, jewellery, etc., and mostly dogmatic people are apt to find interest in it. When the fad becomes a craze it spreads as much as does a contagious disease with the one difference that there is inoculation against it. Almost every individual is seen running after it, and in this too it differs from a contagious disease because people usually run away from it. Objects sell like cheese when they assume the form of craze. If it is an activity that becomes the craze then everybody does it. In this way, fad is more permanent than fashion while craze spreads faster than fad. People who want greater novelty discard a fashion as quickly as they adopt it.

The main factors that assist the fashion in progressing to the stage of fad are novelty, propaganda, advertisement, concurrence with time and interest of the objects, etc. In this way, effective propaganda can be utilised to change fashion into fad and fad into craze. Actually, craze is a form of fad. Fad is of two kinds — of the kind of religious group or of the craze kind. Fad of the religious kind is of a more permanent nature and people obey it with religious faith. On the other hand, craze spreads at a extremely rapid pace but at the same time it lacks permanence. Skillful traders and producers not only try to make their products acceptable to the fashion minded but also try to create a fad or craze for them. Many things rapidly assume the form of fad and carze in the fields of arts, specific and folk

12. Young, K., *Handbook of Social Psychology* (1951), p. 411.

art. For example, in the near past rock and roll had become a craze. It is a dance form. Presently, the dance form rapidly assuming the form of craze is the 'twist'. Fashions take a comparatively long time to spread in India and it is only rarely that they succeed in reaching the stage of fad or craze. There are many causes of this reticence. In comparison with their Western counterparts, the Indians are more dogmatic, satisfied, introverted, religious and at the same time poor. The means of transport and communications are not as well developed in our country as they are in the West. The ideals of the Indian women are also different from the ideals of the Western women. In view of all these and some other causes, the mobility of fashion is not as great in India as it is in the Western societies. Nevertheless, this mobility is increasing along with the increase in the influence of Western culture and modern education. And the most important contribution to this mobility can be said to be proceeding from the cinema.

QUESTIONS FOR EXERCISE

1. What do you understand by Fashion? Discuss its psychological bases.
2. Write a short note on — Fashion.
3. How will you account for the love of fashion in a person? What are the social forces behind changes of fashion?
4. Write a short note on — Limits of fashion.
5. Comment on fashion as a form of social norm.
6. Write short note on — Fashion and Custom.
7. Discuss fully the significance of custom and fashion.
8. Distinguish between fashion, fad and craze. Discuss the psychological laws operating in the frequent changes of fashion
9. What are fads and fashions? What do the changes in fashion indicate?
10. Write a short note on — Fad.

Chapter 8

Social Change Through Education

Whatever is acquired in human life is the result of formal or informal education. When the child is born, he has no knowledge of his surroundings. Gradually he comes to recognize his environment by using his sense organs and by coming in contact with other people. Many ideas and habits he learns merely by observing others. But in no civilized society it is believed possible for an individual to be fit for adult life if he does not have some degree of formal education. For this reason, one finds arrangements for education everywhere. Not only in civilized societies, but even in primitive societies the adults try to educate adolescents in the ways of adult life. Among the tribals of India, this social education of the young girls and boys takes place at the dormitories. To put it briefly, the individual's character, personality, culture, thinking, commonsense, skills, habits and even the other less significant things of life depend upon education. The importance of education in human life is thus evident.

FUNCTIONS OF EDUCATION

This importance is further clarified if we look at the following functions of education:

1. Development of Natural Abilities. When the child is born, he is already possessed of many kinds of natural abilities. As the body grows the mind also grows, but the innate abilities and qualities do not develop quite so naturally and without aid. It is often said that if the mind is not exercised its abilities cannot be developed. Hence, the first aim of education is to try to develop such abilities as power of imagination of thinking etc., by providing appropriate opportunities and stimuli. It is for this reason that, as a part of child education, one of the first steps is to put various kinds of instruments and apparata before the child so that he can learn to use his sense organs. This is called education of senses. The child is also made to improve his power of thinking by presenting many different kinds of problems. His imagination is allowed to develop through the medium of various arts and skills. He is taught to concentrate by using many kinds of techniques to attract his attention. The various methods of learning are brought to his notice by letting him know different kinds of work. He is also taught to make adequate use of the different parts of his body by various games and sports. Such basic requirements of life as eating, sleeping, sitting and walking, moving around are taught to the child by the family itself. All these activities are part of the child's early education.

2. Character-building. Psychologists contend that the foundation of the child's character is laid in the first few years of his life. The impressions about behaviour and conduct that fall upon the infant's mind are later exhibited in the form of his character. The importance of character is hardly a subject to be discussed. It is developed by education, mainly informal education. Putting it differently, the infant's character is built up not so much by lectures and lessons as by the examples presented to him in the family, school, neighbourhood, group, etc. Character is the organisation of various sentiments. The focus of this organisation is the sentiment of self-regard. And it is upto the teacher and the child's parents to develop this sentiment of self-regard in the child. Once this is developed, the child can then move further on the road of self-development. Education is of particular significance in the development of a moral character because the child is not naturally endowed with the power to distinguish between the right and the wrong. The difference between right and wrong is taught by adults. Socialization is an important factor in the development of a moral character. This is aided by story telling, setting good examples and providing education of social life. In fact, many educationists believe that the aim of education is to develop a moral character. As Herbert has expressed it, the development of a good moral character amounts to education.

3. Development of a Personality. The patterns of behaviour that a child chooses in his adjustment with the individuals and objects in his environment depend upon his personality. It is the development of personality which leads to a development of individuality, which is an inevitable characteristic of an educated individual. The informal development of the personality takes place through his family, neighbourhood, the condition of work, etc., but educationists believe that one important objective of education is to develop personality. Hence, the child is given opportunities of performing different kinds of work so that his personality may develop. Games play an important role in personality development. His personality achieves integration and strength in facing the many kinds of problems which make up a game. The social aspect of his personality is developed in the communal life of the school. Social customs, traditions, the forms of social control, cultural elements etc., also play an important part in developing the personality. It is for this reason that distinct differences can be seen in the personalities of individuals belonging to different cultures and -societies. The first and most permanent influence upon the child's personality development is the family. Such things as his order of birth in the family, his place among his brothers and sisters, the social and economic status of the family, the parent's behaviour towards the child, the mutual behaviour of the parents themselves, their profession, influence his personality. It is said that parental education plays a large part in building the personality of great men. Apart from this, the child's personality is influenced by many kinds of literature such as biographies of great men, stories, novels, essays, etc. It is believed that it is the duty of the teacher to prevent his wards from developing bad habits and also to see if the wards are developing balanced personalities. The teacher can take the assistance of the psychologist and also of the parents in ensuring a healthy development of personality. If the child does not develop a balanced personality, it can be said that his education is incomplete.

4. Preparation for Adult Life. Livelihood is believed to be the aim of education. Economic factors controlling life in the present day world have become so complex that no one who is not properly educated can hope to successfully earn his living. In the past, most people pursued agriculture, which does not demand such a high degree of specialization. For them education was not so essential. But the recent developments in science and the increasing specialization of all professions has made it impossible for one individual to perform any job without previous training and education. As a general rule, highly paid jobs require specialized training of a very high calibre. The ability to earn enough is not the only factor to be considered in the preparation for adult life. Earning money is one of the aspects of adult life, another is marriage and children. Once this stage is reached, the individual has to face all the attendant responsibilities. Education aims at training the individual to earn his livelihood, to marry, to bring forth children, to fulfil his duties towards other individuals and society in general. In fact, if the child is helped to develop a balanced personality and a good character, there can be no better preparation for adult life. If education can perform his task, then men and women become highly responsible and useful citizens.

5. Control and Sublimation of Basic Instinct. Every living being is born into the world possessed of certain basic instincts. There may be difference of opinion about the instincts that the child is born with, but there can be no doubt about the presence of some instincts. The child's mind is not a blank tablet on which anything can be written. Psychologists have demonstrated that not only does the human infant possess some instincts, but also that there are individual differences in respect of these instincts. If a human being lives alone, he can give expression to his instincts in any manner that he likes. But human beings live in groups, and hence it becomes necessary for them to control some instincts and to change the mode of expression of other instincts in such a manner that they do not injure other people. Besides, there are certain instincts which can be fulfilled only with the co-operation of another human being. Sex is one such instinct. Since, from the moral standpoint, the individuality and the humanity of every individual must be respected, it becomes necessary for people to control their instincts in all forms of communal life, such as marriage. Civilised life would become completely impossible if such instincts as aggressiveness and sex are not sublimated. Education helps in the control, sublimation and change of instincts. Various kinds of arts are used as medium of sublimation. Education in social life helps the child to learn how to control his instincts. The same end is served through the system of reward and punishment found in the family, college or society at large. Rules of administration and the means of social control also help in this work.

6. Creation of Useful Citizens. Although many thinkers have dreamt of a society without government, in actual fact no such society exists. Individuals who have been deprived of their citizenship or have never been granted this, make all kinds of efforts to get the citizenship of one nation or another. If they cannot obtain it, they have to face all kinds of difficulties. Hence, the relationship between the individual and the state is universal. In this relationship, the status of individual is called the status of citizenship. Hence, it is desirable that the individual should be trained in behaving as a citizen so that he can fulfil his duties to the state. In the present age, this function of education is emphasized very much because most states themselves are responsible for providing education. In democratic system, the public also plays a hand in guiding the educational systems. But in communist countries, the state has complete control of the educational system. Despite this, it is believed that education must provide capable citizens, because in the absence of such citizens the adjustment between the individual and the state would suffer. The thinkers of ancient Greece believed that this is the most important function of education. Now-a-days almost all thinkers agree that true democracy in any country is possible only when almost all its citizens are properly educated. Education in responsible citizenship is also given through the medium of political parties, radio, television, newspapers, magazines, etc.

7. Development of a Sense of Community. The statement that man is a social animal means no more than that he lives in society. It does not imply that the human child is possessed of social qualities at birth. These social qualities are acquired and taught. One major objective of education, therefore, is the teaching of social qualities and development of a sense of community. This community feeling urges the child to co-operate with his fellows, to make sacrifices if they become necessary, to rise above the considerations of caste and creed and develop a sense of oneness with the nation, etc. The development of this feeling depends upon opportunities provided in family life, play groups and schools and colleges. For this reason educational institutions play particular role in this. The student is given the opportunity of collectively running the administration, of organising extra-curricular programmes, of devising constructive programmes which help in developing this sense of community. This feeling is the basis of national unity. The efforts being made in India today to evolve an emotional unity are in fact efforts to develop this feeling of community.

8. Protection and Increase of Culture and Civilization. As compared to Other animals, man has progressed more because human society has succeeded in protecting its knowledge and conveying it to future generations. This has been through the medium of culture and civilization. A child born in the present time does not think of everything from the beginning. His thinking and modes of behaviour are determined by customs, traditions and social institutions, which are repositories of the experience and thinking of his ancestors. For this reason, societies which have a more ancient culture show signs of greater organisation and systematization, greater stability. Hence, it is now universally accepted that culture and civilization should be protected and allowed to grow through new developments. This is mainly achieved through education. The child receives the social heritage in the form of education. Then, through education the child develops his own knowledge, character and personality thus becoming capable of contributing to the literary, cultural and social life of his society. In this manner he helps to maintain his own culture and to add to it. Developments in the arts, literature, the sciences etc., are all the efforts of educated people. Their efforts are collected in the forms of books and objects in libraries, museums, etc., and thus passed on as social heritage to the coming generations. For this reason many contemporary thinkers in India have suggested that teaching of Indian culture should be made compulsory in all universities.

9. Encouragement to Social Welfare. Both formal and informal education helps the individual to evolve a critical attitude which helps him to analyse everything presented to him. If he finds any faults in it, he exercises his mind to find some ways of removing the faults. In this manner education has been the basis of all social welfare programmes. When English education was introduced in India, it brought along with it the western tendencies of individualism, rationalism, etc. As a consequence all educated people in the county were impelled to re-examine ancient Indian traditions and institutions. This led to the development of such institutions as the Brahmo Samaj, Arya Samaj, Prarthana Samaj, Theosophical Society. Each one aimed at social welfare. And the inspiration for each of these institutions came from highly educated individuals. Education thus leads to continuous analysis of the various constituents of society, its institutions, modes of social control, etc., and inspires efforts to make improvements where they are needed.

10. National Development. The overall development of all national groups is essential for the development and progress of human society, but this is not possible without universal education. It is for this reason that the U.N.O. is making efforts to provide education to the backward countries. In every country, efforts are made to develop a feeling of belonging among its citizens, the sense of nationality. It helps to induce the individual to do his best for the nation. Besides, almost every nation has its own plan of national education which seeks to fulfil the aims of that nation.

11. Use of Leisure. One of the main aims of education is to teach an individual to make the best use of leisure. Using leisure time in educational activities is itself useful. On the other hand, education itself guides the individual to utilize his leisure time properly. Educated people can use their leisure time effectively by devoting themselves to books, magazines, arts. Even the standard of their normal conversation, discussions etc., is higher than that of the uneducated person. Education helps to develop various kinds of interests so that leisure itself does not become a burden.

12. Increasing Consciousness of other Cultures. In countries in which many different cultural groups co-exist, education helps to increase consciousness of these other cultures and of cultural exchange. This helps individuals to understand each other, thus increasing national unity. There are many different cultures in the world today. As long as education cannot create a feeling of co–operation and of mutual love, the ideal of a unified world cannot be realized.

13. Improving Emotional Unity. At the present time, many disintegrating forces such as regionalism, casteism, communalism, linguism, etc., are working towards a complete disintegration of the country. If the nation is to be saved from complete fragmentation it is necessary to generate a sense of emotional unity in all men and women. The individuals can be expected to feel that they are members of the same nation and to behave in the interests of the nation. Education can help to create this emotional unity. Many educationists have given valuable suggestions for achieving this.

14. Developing an International Feeling. As a result of the unprecedented improvements in the means of transport and communications, people of different nations are constantly coming into contact with each other. All kinds of people are also realizing the importance of internationalism, after having witnessed the havoc caused by the two recent world wars. All contemporary educationists in India, including Sri Aurobindo, Rabindra Nath, Vivekanand, have stressed the importance of creating this feeling of internationalism in all educands. In the present context, therefore, one of the main tasks of education is to generate this feeling in the student community. From the foregoing description of the functions of education in human life, it is evident that the functions of education are the same as its objectives. To put it differently, the objectives which have been assigned to education by various thinkers are the tasks it has to do. It needs hardly be stressed that the functions of education change when ideals governing it undergo changes. Nevertheless, the fundamental elements of human life are the same today as they were in Plato's and Aristotle's times. Hence, such aims of education as character-building, development of personality, social welfare, proper use of leisure, protection of culture and civilization, development of communal feeling, creating able citizens, preparation for adult life, development of innate qualities, etc., are permanent objectives which will remain the same in future also.

CHANGE IN NATIONAL LIFE THROUGH EDUCATION

The functions of education in national life differ somewhat from its functions in normal life because human life is possible even without a nation. Primitive societies still do not possess any kind of sentiment of nation. Nations are found in more civilized societies. Before examining the role of education in national life, it is necessary to discover the nature of a nation. Nation is a group of human beings which lives in a country delimited by geographical boundaries. This group is possessed of a desire to be bound by common traditions, common interests, similar political ambitions and political unity. The important aspects of national life can be understood from this description. For national life to be possible, it is essential that its members should have common traditions, interests, sentiments and political ambitions, and an emotional unity. Education aims at creating and maintaining all these various elements, and thus it contributes to National life. The following points are to be considered in this connection:

1. Maintaining Communal Interests and Traditions. The main objective in applying a uniform system of education to an entire nation is that a similarity of interests and traditions may be generated among the people. For India, this is of even greater importance because the nation is composed of many different cultural and linguistic groups. Education achieves this similarity and identity through its prescribed syllabi and various kinds of extra-curricular programmes.

2. Similarity of Political Ambitions. If different groups within a single nation are found to possess various and contradictory political ambitions, it becomes difficult to maintain that nation's independence and unity. One chief objective of education, thus, is to propagate similar political ambitions among all classes and groups of people. In India, young men and women who received English education studied the history of Western nations and concluded that India must also win its freedom. Once this political awakening spread among the educated classes and led to similarity of political ambitions, national movements took shape and the demand for a free India was put forward. In the more recent context, education should aim at creating a desire for complete and comprehensive development of the nation so that people may rise above their own narrow interests and work in the interests of the nation as a whole.

3. Diffusion of Emotional Unity. It is obvious that one task of education is to diffuse a feeling of emotional unity in the younger generation so that all its members may feel identified with the nation and be inspired to work for its improvement. Such forces of disintegration as communalism, casteism, liguism, regionalism, etc., can be countered only when emotional unity is increased. For this the educational programme should insist on the teaching of the same history, same cultural heritage, etc. Sense of community is an essential part of nationalism and the foundations of the sense of belonging to a community are laid in schools. Hence, efforts should be made to create such an atmosphere in schools and colleges that the students may have a sense of belonging, not of alienation.

4. Development of a National Language. Although the development of many different languages and the common use of them does not hinder national unity in any way, the absence of a single common language hinders it considerably since language is the medium through which thoughts and emotions are expressed. Just as thoughts and languages are intimately connected, nationalism and language are also intimately related to each other. Hence, one objective of education is the development of a national language. In India, the Constitution has laid down Hindi as the national language and it has been accepted in principle that this language must be spread over the entire country. But it is regrettable that the work of giving this status to Hindi is not progressing as fast as is desirable. If greater efforts are not made in this direction, it may create a danger to national unity in the country.

Hence, it is desirable that the teaching of Hindi should be compulsory at all stages of education.

5. Respect to All Religions. India is a secular state in that it grants equal status and importance to every religion, and refuse to discriminate between citizens on the basis of their religious beliefs. But despite this provision of the Constitution, the poison of communalism is found in greater abundance in the country, and it has been impossible to remove it despite the greatest efforts. One way of achieving this is to indoctrinate the children through education that every religion deserves equal respect and that one's own religion is not necessarily the best. Education must seek to eliminate all such prejudices. Hence, in a country like India, one task of education is to generate respect for all religions.

6. Training for Leadership. Proper development in any sphere can be achieved only if there is adequate leadership. A country can progress only if it has able leaders in the social, economic, political, literary, cultural, artistic, industrial and moral fields. Education can provide such leaders. Hence, one of the objectives of education is to bring forth leaders in various spheres and to train them to perform their tasks efficiently. This can be done by encouraging student participation in various kinds of extra-curricular programmes in the college so that the student's capabilities can find expression. This also helps to aid him in leadership.

7. Fulfilling the Need for Skilled Workers. In addition to leaders, every sphere needs the dedication and co–operation of skilled and efficient workers. Such workers are required not only in industry and commerce, but also in the social and political spheres. This need can be fulfilled by education. During the process of education it is possible to discover the sphere for which a particular individual is best suited. Once this has been found out, he can then be trained in this particular profession.

8. Consciousness of Duties. If a nation is to progress, it is essential that its citizens should be aware of their duties and responsibilities. Education can spread this awareness among the people. In schools the students are told of their duties and they are also taught how they can fulfil these duties. This role of education is of greatest importance in democratic states.

9. Evolution of a National Feeling. The strength of national feeling in an individual is judged by the extent to which he can subjugate his personal and narrow class interests in favour of the wider national interests and the extent to which he is prepared to work for the national interests. For this it is essential that the individual should be conscious of his duties to the nation as well as capable of rising above narrow interests of regionalism, communalism, casteism, etc. Both these can be made possible through education. National feeling is generated among the students in the colleges through various extra-curricular programmes and syllabi. But, in fact the informal modes of education, such as family, newspapers, magazines, radio, television, etc., play an important role in generating a national feeling. National education programmes should pay particular attention to these and to the creation of a national literature.

It is evident from the work of education in national life that the members of the nation should be educated in such a way, through the teaching of national history, the national language, different kinds of programmes, etc., that a national sentiment should be created in them. They should begin to consider national interests as higher than any other interest, and they should be prepared to make any sacrifice for the nation. It is education which provides efficient leadership in the various spheres of national endeavour, and it is education which maintains the nation's heritage and hands it over to the future generations.

STATE AND EDUCATION

Though some anarchist and individualist thinkers may oppose state control of education but there is no denying the fact that people cannot successfully put into effect a complete educational programme. Raymont presents a balanced view when he comments, "We observe that education, like the other beneficial influences at work in a civilised community, may be conducted by all or any, of the three means, first by voluntary effort with a view to profit; secondly by voluntary effort arising from philanthropic or religious motives; thirdly, by the agency of the state."

Having accepted that the state must exercise control over the educational system, it becomes necessary to determine the extent to which this control should be exercised. Historically viewed, education has been carried on in every state through a variety of means and agencies. On the one hand, one finds colleges and schools run by individuals for profit while on the other one runs across institutions created by religious groups or philanthropists who have collected funds from private individuals for this purpose. In addition, one finds state-aided institutions in every country. Even J. S. Mill, who objects to state control of education, has admitted that the state should establish some ideal education institutions which should serve as models and which should inspire the people to create similar institutions. Mill objects to the state control of education on the ground that the state tries to educate the people along lines which support its own ideology and thus it controls the ideas of the people. This belief is not completely without logic and supporting evidence, because communist states do try to control the thinking of the younger generations by intellectually feeding them on communist literature. It amounts to slow brainwashing. Much the same tendency has been seen in the past in totalitarian states which also tries to control the thinking of the people by making educational institutions the centres of state propaganda. This is unfair and improper. In fact, state control in education is exercised with the sole purpose of preventing encroachment upon the political and social independence and freedom of the people, because this is essential for a proper development of personality. In the second place, the state has at its disposal unlimited means and resources which enable it to arrange for education on a large scale, something which is beyond the reach of private individual and groups of individuals. Briefly speaking, it is desirable that state control of education should be guided by the principle of the least possible infringement of the liberties of the people. The welfare state provides for education on precisely this principle. With the establishment of democratic governments, the sphere of education is widening rapidly with the result that the responsibilities of the state are increasing. The state imposes taxes on the people in order to finance education and then compels people to send their children to schools and colleges. It also supervises educational arrangements in institutions not controlled by it to ensure uniform standards, also provides financial aid to them.

Explaining the functions of the state, MacIver and Page have pointed out that there are certain functions which the state alone can perform, others which can be performed by others but not so efficiently as by the state, and yet others which are best left to other agencies, apart from those which the state does not have the ability to perform. The provision of education falls into the first and second of the above four categories, because not only is the state the best equipped for this task, it is in fact the only agency capable of coping with the educational problems of populations of remarkable size. The state alone can provide universal education to such a large number of people.

Functions of State

The functions of the state in the sphere of education can be summed up as follows:

1. Provision of Proper Schools. The state should establish different kinds of schools — primary, secondary, higher learning and professional colleges — so that the local requirement of the people can be fulfilled. In addition to this, the state must also correlate these various institutions in such a way that effort at education is not wasted.

2. Making Primary Education Compulsory. At least at the primary stage, the state should make all education compulsory, free and universal. This kind of education, at least the elementary education, is absolutely necessary for the mental development of the people. Hence, the state should compel parents to send their children to school.

3. Providing Finances for Education. The state must plan for and provide the finances required for education. Some people have advanced the argument that the provision of free and compulsory primary education will reduce its value in the eyes of the people. While this may be true, the same is faced with the necessity of doing so, because the private sector has failed to provide primary education for the masses. It is now accepted that every modern state must provide free and compulsory education to all children in the country. Apart from primary education, it has been experienced that private resources are never sufficient to provide proper secondary and higher education to adequate numbers of students. Even here institutions have to seek the assistance of the Mate. In addition to the creation of primary and secondary schools and universities and professional colleges for higher learning the state helps the cause of education by providing scholarships and financial help in different forms to poor but brilliant students. In many Western countries the number of students receiving state aid in one form or the other frequently rises to fifty per cent of the total number enrolled in the university. In India, this stage has not been achieved, and consequently many brilliant students are deprived of the opportunity to study.

4. General Control and Guidance. One important aspect of state functioning in the sphere of education is control, inspection and guidance of individual institutions. The state government officials plan syllabi for various levels of education, with the help of educationists and other learned people. In the same manner, the state does not take independent decisions about educational matters, but seeks the advice and guidance of experts. The state should normally not interfere in the teaching methods, but leave it to experienced teachers, researchers and scholars. Besides, the state can also not profitably guide the techniques of evaluating educational ability. This, too, is the task of the teacher and the educationist. All that the state can lay down, in the way of guidance, is that some method of evaluating educational ability must be introduced at each level of education. The state may also require this method to be so accurate, dependable and valid that it may serve as a basis for evaluating the individual's fitness for various tasks.

5. Providing Skilled Educators. It is clear from the preceding paragraph that there is little the state can do in the absence of skilled educators. Hence, it is a major responsibility of the state to provide such educators. Even if the national educational policy has been created by brilliant thinkers and incalculable effort has gone into its creations, it will fail to achieve anything if there is no skilled educators to implement it. The responsibility of the state does not end with putting up buildings for schools, filling such schools with educands and making arrangements for the administration of the institution. As Raymont has pointed out, "Educational salvation lies not in bricks and mortar, nor in sumptuous equipment, nor in paper curricula, nor in elaborate machinery of whatever kind, but in the subtle influence of informed men and women upon the pupils committed to their care. A good teacher, in sympathy with his work, and doing it under reasonably liberal condition of service will achieve better things in a barn than a bad or dissatisfied one will achieve under the best of external circumstances." Hence, it is desirable that the state should take upon itself the responsibility of providing trained and qualified teachers, and of seeing that their conditions of service create the satisfaction so necessary for the job. The educand's mental health depends very greatly upon the mental health of his educator. More often than not, in most non-governmental educational institutions one finds conditions of work which are not at ail conducive to mental balance, for example, varying scales of pay, physical conditions of work, absence of opportunity to progress, etc. The state should investigate all such conditions and improve them, and also enact legislation which secures the rights of people working in private institutions.

6. Training in Citizenship. In the sphere of education, one important function of the state is to train young men and women in citizenship. For this, the state must create institutions for training in science, industry, agriculture, etc. The cultural training and advancement of the people can be provided for by creating art galleries, cultural committees, means of recreation etc. Nowadays, states send cultural delegations to other countries. Another way in which the state can help in improving cultural standards is by facilitating the international exchange of teachers and students. In a democratic society it is necessary for the state to maintain a healthy level of social living, by creating conditions conducive to the physical and mental development of its people, and by assisting all private agencies engaged in similar work. Political training is also essential in a democratic country, because political awareness must be created if proper leadership is to emerge. It is for the state to exploit all means of communications — newspaper, radio, television, cinema, etc., — in order to acquaint every individual with the latest in political, economic and social thinking, and also to inform him of all economic and industrial progress taking place within the country. In this way, it can be seen that the political education of people living in a democratic country depends entirely upon the co–operation of the state.

QUESTIONS FOR EXERCISE

1. Indicate the major functions of education in society.
2. Discuss Education as a social institution. What are the functions expected of it in organised society?
3. Describe the meaning of socialisation. What is the significance of family and educational institution in the socialisation of individuals?

CHAPTER 9

Social Change Through Culture and Civilization

In common parlance the word 'culture' is understood to mean beautiful, refined or interesting but this interpretation does not constitute its scientific definition. It is wrong to explain cultural growth in terms of only one set of factors with possible neglect of the rest.[1] Culture displays a large complexity, multidimensional activity and polymorphous relations. Therefore, it cannot be explained by only functional factors. Pointing out this difficulty, A. J. Toynbee has said. "The riddle of the relation between God's law and human soul's freedom is the last, the most difficult and the most crucial of all questions on our agenda."[2] However, in order to understand culture, it is necessary to be definite about its meaning and components. Toynbee has made a successful attempt to show that one may observe some regularity in cultural processes.

MEANING OF CULTURE

In common parlance the word 'culture' is understood to mean beautiful, refined or interesting but this interpretation does not constitute its adequate definition. Some of the more popular definitions of culture are as follows:

1. *E. B. Taylor*. "Culture is that complex whole which includes knowledge, belief, art, morals, law, custom and any other capabilities and habits acquired by man as a member of society."[3]
2. *R. Redfield*. "Culture is the organised body of conventional understanding manifest in art and artifact which persisting through tradition, characterises human group."[4]
3. *Joseph Pieper*. "Culture is the quintessence of all natural goods of the world, and those gifts and qualities which, while belonging to man, lie beyond the immediate sphere of his needs and wants."[5]

---

1. Sorokin, P. A., *Social and Cultural Dynamics,* Vol. I, Introduction, pp. 45, 51, 53.
2. Toynbee, A. J., *A Study of History,* Vol. IX, p. 219.
3. Tylor, E. B., *Primitive Culture*, p. 1.
4. Redfild, R, "Unpublished Lectures *Social Science,* University of Chicago.
5. Joseph Pieper, *Leisure, the Basis of Culture* (1920), p. 20.

4. *L. A. White.* "Culture is a symbolic, continuous, cumulative and progressive process."[6]

5. *MacIver and Page.* "This is the realm of styles, of values, of emotional attachments, of intellectual adventures. Culture, then, is the antithesis of civilization. It is the expression of our nature, in our modes of living and thinking, in our everyday intercourse, in art, literature, in recreation and enjoyment."[7]

6. *Hobbs and Blank.* "Culture refers to those ways of thinking, feeling and behaving that are socially transmitted from one generation to the next."[8]

7. *P. David.* "The system of values and meanings shared by a group or society, including the embodiment of those values and meanings and the material objects."[9]

8. *T. S. Eliot.* "It is the product of a variety of more or less harmonious activities each pursued for its own sake, the artist must concentrate upon his canvas, the poet upon his typewriter, the civil servant upon the just settlement of particular problems as they present themselves upon his desk, each according to the situation in which he finds himself."[10]

The above-mentioned definitions, except the last one, are those advanced by anthropologists and sociologists. These are functional in nature. According to functional view, "culture is an external combination of independent activities."[11]

Characteristics of Cultures

The essential characteristics depicting the nature of culture may be summed up as follows:

1. Culture is inclusive of those elements which man has created and in which he can make improvements.
2. The introduction of novel elements increases the complexity and qualities of culture.
3. It is communicated from one generation to another generation in a psychic form.
4. Culture is found only in human society.

NATURE OF CULTURE

The above-mentioned characteristics of culture throw light upon its nature. Important facts concerning the nature of culture are as follows:

1. Culture is an Acquired Quality. Culture is not innate. Traits learned through socialization, habits and thoughts are what is called culture. Man exhibits cultural behaviour because he has capacity of symbolic communication.

---

6. White, L. A., *American Sociological Review* (Dec. 1947).

7. MacIver, R. M. and Page, C. H., *Society : An Introductory Analysis*, p. 499.

8. Hobbs, D. A. and Blank, S. J., *Sociology and the Human Experience*. John Wiley, New York, 1978, p. 447.

9. David, P., *Sociology*, Prentice-Hall, New Jersey, 1977, p. 566,

10. Eliot, T. S., *Notes Towards the Definition of Culture*, p. 19.

11. See Malinowski: *Scientific Concept of Culture* and Ruth Benedict, *Patterns of Culture*.

2. Culture is Communicative. In this way, culture is communicated from one generation to the next. As a result of this, culture is constantly accumulating. The new generation benefits by the experience of the earlier generation through the communicability of culture. In this way, culture becomes semi-temporary and remains unaffected by the extinction of a group or an individual.

3. Culture is Social, not Individual. Every individual takes some part in the transmission and communication of culture, but culture is social rather than individual. It is inclusive of the expectations of the members of groups. Man cannot create culture while existing apart from the groups.

4. Culture is Idealistic. In culture are included those ideal patterns and norms of behaviour according to which the members of society attempt to conduct themselves. Society accepts these ideals, norms and patterns.

5. Culture Fulfils some Needs. Culture fulfils those ethical and social needs which are ends in themselves. Social habits are included in culture. Habits can be formed of those activities only which tend to fulfil some needs. Without fulfilling these needs, culture cannot exist.

6. Culture has the Characteristic of Adaptation. Culture is constantly undergoing change in concurring to the environment, and, due to this transformation, it is constantly being adapted to external forces, but once it is developed, the influence of the natural environment begins to decrease. Besides, the various aspects of culture are also undergoing development and some internal adaptation among them consequently is being necessitated.

7. Culture has the Quality of becoming Integrated. Culture possesses an order and a system. Its various parts are integrated with each other and any new element which is introduced is also integrated. Those cultures which are more open to external influence are comparatively more heterogeneous but nevertheless some degree of integration is evident in all cultures.

In this way, culture is social, idealistic and acquired and fulfils many of man's needs. It possesses the characteristics of communication, adaptation and integration. It is a special quality of man. It is the evidence of his social heritage.

COMPONENTS OF CULTURE

According to Clark Wissler the universal components of culture include: (1) language, (2) concrete apparatuses like food, house, means of conveyance, dress, weapons, utensils, arms, industries and occupations, (3) arts, (4) legendary and scientific knowledge, (5) rituals and blind beliefs, (6) family and marriage, social control, games and other social institutions of the kind, (7) property value, exchange and trade, (8) government and law, (9) war.

These universal components are found in all cultures but their forms are different. Thus, the components of culture are what is known as non-material culture in sociological studies which include abstract things, such as different customs, conventions, methods, arts, knowledge, religion of a society, etc.

Some Terms Connected with the Concept of Culture[12]

1. Cultural Diffusion. The process by which cultural traits spread from one group or society to another.

2. Cultural Integration. The fitting together of cultural units into a cohesive whole.

3. Cultural Lag. A theory which holds that most changes occur first in the material aspects of culture, and that non-material cultural change lags behind material change.

4. Cultural Pluralism. The pattern of partial assimilation in which the dominant society allows minorities to achieve full participation, yet at the same time permits them to maintain many of their cultural and social differences.

5. Cultural Relativity. The principle that a culture must be understood and judged on its own terms without reference to the values of another culture.

6. Cultural Survival. A culture trait that has survived after its original function has disappeared.

7. Cultural Complexes. Clusters of inter-related culture traits that function as distinct and separable units in a society.

8. Cultural Shock. The psychological stress caused when a person faces rapid cultural change.[13]

The bewilderment, frustration and disorientation that immersion in a different culture has upon the unprepared visitor. Culture shock is evidence of the uniqueness of human groupings.[14]

9. Cultural Assimilation. A sub-process of assimilation that refers to the extent to which an ethnic or minority group adopts and internalizes the cultural patterns of the larger society.[15]

10. Cultural Trait. The simplest unit or element of a culture.[16]

NATURE OF CIVILIZATION

In contrast to the non-material nature of culture, civilization is material. It includes material or concrete things used by man, such as house, household commodities, different kinds of apparatus, instruments, weapons, pots and means of conveyance etc. According to J.L. Gillin, and J.P. Gillin civilization is a more complex, and evolved form of culture. A.W. Green has written, "A culture becomes a civilization only when it possesses written language, science, philosophy, a specialized division of labour and a complex technology and political system." Ancient cultures did not possess all these elements and would consequently be considered as having no civilization. Franz Boas, Ogbum and Nimkoff also treat civilization as a state which follows culture. Ogbum has written that "Civilization may be defined as the

12. Popertoe David, *Sociology*, Prentice-Hall, New Jersey, 1977.

13. *Ibid.*

14. Hobbs, D. A. and Blank, S. X, *Sociology and the Human Experience*, John Wiley, New York, **1978**, p. 447.

15. *Ibid*

16. Propenoe, David, *Sociology*, Prentice-Hall, New Jersey, 1977, p. 566.

latter phase of super organic culture." According to Weber, civilization includes usefull material objects and the methods of producing and using them whereas culture consists of the ideals, values and the mental and emotional aspects of a group. Merton, Richard Thumwald and many other sociologists have subscribed to this opinion. P.A. Sorokin has opposed it. But this is the opinion most widely prevalent among the sociologists today.

Components of Civilization

Thus the components of civilization are generally physical, biological and technological. Technique is a part of civilization, Civilization attempts at attaining physical adjustment with the environment. It represents the external structure. It involves techniques of human adjustment with nature. It is the result of processes of natural selection and social selection. The components of civilization are thus external and objective. The study of a civilization includes the study of housing, means of communication, dress, industries, weapons, etc.

Relation of Culture and Civilization

While studying a group, modern anthropologists and sociologists study both the material civilization and non-material culture, since the two are closely related. Both have been developed by the same human processes. Both are complimentary to each other. Culture needs civilization for further growth, civilization needs a culture even for its vital force and survival. The two are therefore interdependent. Life is the most severe and most necessary test of the superiority of a culture. Existence Is the first law of human life. A civilization cannot survive without strong stimulus and motive, however high may be its achievements in science. Man is still a struggling unsuccessful hero in this world. A culture which claims any greatness should help man in this upward effort. It should inspire the terrestrial endeavours of man.

DIFFERENCE BETWEEN CULTURE AND CIVILIZATION

In spite of the above close relationship between culture and civilization, the two are very much different. This difference has been particularly pointed out in the field of literature and philosophy. The definition of culture given by T.S. Eliot, at the beginning of this chapter, shows those characteristics of it which are not found in civilization. Culture, as Sorokin aptly calls it, is a "Causal Meaningful System."[17] Civilization, on the other hand, involves techniques. Techniques are differentiations of instinctive behaviour utilized to answer the challenge of Nature. Most of the scientific growth is the growth of technology aimed at achieving man's adjustment with the environment. However, as A. L. Kroeber has pointed out, "Culture is different from mere physical equilibrium, it is a higher unity which should not be subjected to the categories of the inconscient."[18] Thus, civilization implies animal adjustment while culture has much more high orientation. Thus,

17. Sorokin, P.A, *Social Philosophies in an Age of Crisis*, p. 277.

18. Kroeber A. L., *Nature of Culture*, pp. 112-114.

while technology may be a condition of the advancement of culture it is not its fulfilment. Civilization is concerned with the physical and external equipment of a community to ensure physical requirements. Culture, on the other hand, is concerned with internal growth. While civilization is external and objective, culture is internal and subjective. It is not mere stimulus-response. It is an expression of creativity of an individual or a group. This distinction between culture and civilization can be summed up in the explanation of culture richness given by Toynbee: "In other words, the process which we are examining involves not merely a simplification of apparatus but a consequent transfer of energy or shift or emphasis, from some lower sphere of being or sphere of action to a higher sphere. Perhaps we shall be describing it in a more illuminating way if we call it not simplification but etherealization."[19] Thus, cultures are born by spiritual necessities, the challenges of circumstances. Therefore, culture is particularly spiritual in nature. Civilization, on the other hand, is particularly physical, based upon science and technology. While civilization involves the efforts of the masses, cultural advance is the function of a creative minority of artists, poets, philosophers, etc. In the words of MacIver and Page, civilization includes all those things by means of which some other objective is attained, such as typewriter, press, lathes, motor, etc. In civilization are included both basic technology which means the authority' of men over natural phenomena as well as special technology or modes which control man's behaviour. On the other hand, culture comprehends such elements as religion, art, philosophy, literature, music, etc. which bring satisfaction and pleasure to man.

Thus, culture and civilization differ in the following respects:

1. Civilization has a Precise Standard of Measurement but not Culture. The universal standard of civilization is utility because civilization is a means. Culture has no similar qualitative or quantitative standard of measurement because culture is an end in itself. The elements, ideals, values and thoughts, etc., of culture change in accordance with the time and place.

2. Civilization is Always Advancing, but not Culture. The various constituents of civilization, e.g. machines, means of transportation and communication, etc., are constantly progressing. But concerning culture, it cannot be asserted that art, literature, thoughts or ideals of today are superior to those of the past.

3. Civilization is Transmitted without Efforts, but not Culture. Objects comprehended by civilization have utility and are connected with the external life of man. Hence, they can be easily adapted from one generation to another or from one country to another but culture is not communicated and adapted with equal facility because it is related to an inner tendency and can be adapted only after the appropriate inner development. It is communicated only to the like-minded. One cannot appreciate art without the quality of an artist nor can any one enjoy music without the quality of an artist nor can any one enjoy music without the sensitivity of a musician. In contrast to culture, civilization does not make any such demand.

19. Toynbee, *A Study of History*, Vol. 3, p. 183.

One may enjoy the products of civilization without sharing the capacity which creates them. Civilization may be adopted without efforts. The adoption of culture depends upon personality and nature.

4. Civilization is Borrowed without Change or Loss, but not Culture. Why civilization is borrowed by a country or a generation other than its originator, it does not suffer any deterioration, loss or change, Railway, motor cars, aeroplanes, machines, etc., are borrowed as they are, but the elements of culture such as religion, art, literature, thought, ideals, etc., can never be borrowed in their original character. For example, the Indian Christians are found to possess many elements, borrowed from the Hindu and Muslim religions, which are not to be found in their Western counterparts.

5. Culture is Internal and an end While Civilization is External and a Means. Civilization is inclusive of external things, culture is related to internal thoughts, feelings, ideals, values, etc. Civilization is the means for the expression and manifestation of culture. It is the body while culture is the soul.

CULTURAL GROWTH

The development of culture is a continuous process. In this process while the experiences of the proponents of one culture are accumulated and handed down from one generation to another on the one hand, new elements from other cultures are introduced through accommodation, cross fertilization and diffusion, on the other hand culture progresses as a result of their unification. The existing developed culture of any country is a result of these processes carried out over a period of hundreds and thousands of years. In this development the rate of progress is not uniform. At times it is slow while at other times it is relatively fast, sometimes it is moving towards progress at others towards deterioration.

In order to understand cultural growth properly, it is necessary to understand those processes of cultural growth which were mentioned above. Briefly, these processes are the following:

1. Accumulation. To begin with, an individual experiments with an object about which he knows virtually nothing. Of the various experiments he makes, he discards those which have proved fruitless and adopts for subsequent application those which have been successful. In this way, the experience gained in this experimentation is accumulated and passed on by one generation to its successor as social heritage. The development of language has been of tremendous value in this accumulation. New experiments continue to be made, in addition to these experiences. Inventions increase along with the increase in needs. It has been said that necessity is the mother of invention. In this way, both the material and non-material aspects of culture progress through such accumulation. The accumulation continues uninterrupted.

2. Diffusion. Cultural growth results not merely from accumulation but also by the adoption of novel concepts from other cultures. Accordingly, diffusion applies to the adoption of new ideas by one individual or society from another individual or society. Almost all the cultures of the world are adopting innumerable new ideas and things from the modern Western culture through diffusion.

3. Accommodation. The new ideas which have been acquired through diffusion have to be accommodated with the other features of the culture. It is only through having accommodated themselves with Indian culture that the numerous objects and various elements of Western culture which have been acquired and adopted in India have become a part of its life and have added to its progress.

4. Cross Fertilization. The conjunction of two cultures is beneficial to both since it does not happen that one should borrow the other exclusively. This process of mutual give and take is called cross-fertilization. Due to this, culture retains its vitality and life.

5. Acculturation. When such a conjunction of two cultures occurs, causing cultural growth, and they are intimately related rather than identified, the process is called acculturation. Sometimes a process called the process of contraculturation, also sets in. It is the opposite of the process of acculturation. For example, many English things were adopted in India but the Swadeshi movement and the development of nationalism abolished and condemned many things of Western origin.

6. Assimilation. In this process of cultural conjunction, when one culture becomes so intimate with another as to lose its individuality, it is called assimilation.

It would have become apparent from the preceding description that the process of cultural growth is not simple, but complex. Many processes are involved in it. In the process of such interaction many cultures have become completely extinct and are only mentioned in history. Great cultures are invariably progressive. This is the secret of their life force. Indian culture is one such example.

THEORIES OF CULTURAL GROWTH

The growth of culture has been a significant subject of research for anthropologists. In this connection the following questions have been particularly raised:

1. How are cultures born?
2. Why the cultural traits and cultural complexes in different cultures are generally similar? This is sometimes known as the study of cultural parallels. The question is raised about the reason or theory of the formation of cultural parallels. This question has been answered by the anthropologists by means of the following theories.

    1. Evolutionism.
    2. Diffusionism.
    3. Acculturation.

EVOLUTIONISM

Evolutionism in the field of culture was born when Darwins' theory of evolution was most popular. Therefore, this theory has been immensely influenced by Darwin's theory. Some thinkers have, however, pointed out that cultural evolutionism has not been influenced by biological evolution. Of these, the name of Taggart is the most important. He has tried to point out that books on evolutionism in cultural growth were published side-by-side with the publication of Darwin's famous book The Origin of Species in 1859. Most of the books on evolutionism in cultural growth were published between 1859 and 1865. Of these the important works were presented by Bachofen, Bastain Maine, Mclennan and Tylor. According to Taggart in the 19th century no significant influence of Darwin's theory upon evolutionism in cultural growth can be observed. It is generally believed that while Darwin was conducting the researches and propounding theories, the anthropologists were independently working upon evolutionary theory of culture. However, it must be conceded that Drawin's theory definitely influenced evolutionary theory of culture. According to Dr. S.C. Dubey, the theories of evolution in culture were clearly influenced by Darwinian thought, it will not be proper to say that these theories are Darwinian theories. In 1877 Louis H. Morgan, in his book *Primitive Society* pointed out evolution in human institutions. At the same time Tylor presented his works Primitive Culture. These two works are the foundation stones of the evolutionary theory of culture.

Salient Points of Evolutionism

According to evolutionary theory, cultural growth follows Unilinear Sequence. It passes through definite stages which were studied by comparative method. All the societies passed through these cultural stages. In its higher stage of a culture some residues of the primitive stage can be observed. These ate known as survivals. They remind us about the earlier stages of the culture. The most important points in the evolutionary theory of culture are as follows:

1. Human culture, particularly social institutions and social thought evolve in unilinear sequence.
2. By the study of cultural elements in different societies through comparative method the above fact has been proved.
3. More developed and higher traditions stay longer in society.

Unilinear Evolution

Morgan, in his book *Primitive Society*, has considered social evolution as unilinear. According to him, societies have passed through the following cultural stages:

1. Savagery,
2. Barbarism,
3. Civilization.

According to Morgan's scheme, the lower status of savagery was the infancy of human evolution. In middle savagery human beings knew about the use of fire and generally depended upon fishing. In upper savagery bow and arrows were generally used. In the first stage earthen wares were invented. In middle stage animal husbandry was developed. In the stage known as upper barbarism iron was used for making different types of implements. Civilization started with the development of alphabet. This theory advanced by Morgan has been supported by

Tylor. According to Tylor, "Simply placing civilized nations at one end of the social series and savage tribes at the other, arranging the rest of mankind between these limits... ethnographers are able to set up at least a rough scale of civilization...a transition from the savage state to our own."[20]

Morgan has maintained unilinear evolution in the institution of marriage as well. According to him, the first stage in the evolution of marriage was known as promiscuity or sex communism. Marriage institution further passed through the stages of group marriage, Polyandry, Polygyny and Monogamy. This theory has been also supported by other anthropologists through their studies of other human institutions. For example, Tylor studied the evolution of religion in which the first stage was termed as Animistic Polytheism, the second stage as higher polytheistic ideology and the next stage as Monotheism. Similarly, Haddon studied evolution in the field of art. Levy Bruhl studied evolution in the field of Logic. Thus propounders of evolutionary theory tried to find out the origin of different cultural elements. For example, The Golden Bough, published in 13 volumes by Sir James Frazer traces the nature and evolution of religion.

Unilinear theory of evolution has been widely criticized. Due to these criticisms, some important modifications have been made in it, ultimately leading to some sort of multilinear theory of evolution.

Multilinear Evolution

This theory was supported by Julian Steward. According to it the various stages in the evolution of different cultures were not uniform throughout the world. However, some stages can be identified in cultural evolution. Steward made a comparative study of parallel cultural evolution of cultures of Peru, Mesopotamia, U.S.A. and China and pointed out different stages of evolution. Thus he not only carried the evolutionary theory forward but also gave it new direction.

PARABOLIC CURVE

According to some anthropologists social institutions developed in parabolic curves. First of all, a social institution is born in a specific form, then it develops an entirely different form and evolves it. For example, the institution of property born in the form of communal ownership is again evolving in the form of communism. Same can be said about the human dresses. In the beginning there was a shortage of cloth, therefore not many men used much cloth. In the middle ages dressing of the whole body was considered as a necessary sign of civilization. In modern times the physical culture movement is again leading to nudism. Similar evolution can be traced in the field of sex-behaviour. Sex- behaviour almost everywhere started in the form of sex-communism or promiscuity. Gradually this developed into polygamy and polyandry, etc. Finally, with the further growth of cultural values in the field of male-female relationships monogamy was evolved. Most recently the bonds of monogamy are breaking and sex-mores are again becoming more and more loose and permissive. This is particularly true of the Western countries. But

20. Tylor, *Primitive Culture* (1871), pp. 26-27.

societies in the East will also follow suit. However, the sex-mores will again harden and the cycle will go on.

In 1945 the famous American anthropologist Leslie White again raised the discussion of evolution in culture. He maintained that culture grows according to the growth of human capacities. The theory of evolution has been rightly discussed and criticized. It cannot be rejected as absolutely imaginary. The proper viewpoint is perhaps in between these two extremes.

DIFFUSIONISM

Evolution of culture is a gradual process. In this process, whereas on one side the experiences of the followers of single culture accumulate and are handed down from one generation to the other, on the other side new elements keep coming into the culture from other cultures through organization, acculturation and diffusion, etc. and the culture grows through their assimilation. The present evolution of culture of any country is the result of these processes carried on through hundreds and thousands of years. The speed of growth in this evolution is not always the same. Sometimes it is fast and at other times it is slow, sometimes towards improvement and sometimes towards a decline.

What is Diffusion?

Cultural diffusion is one of the processes of cultural evolution. Adoption, of new things by one individual or society from another individual or society is called diffusion. Almost all the cultures of the world are adopting new things every day through the diffusion, e.g., the influence of the culture evolving at the banks of Nile river reached India; Indian modes of thought reached China and played an important part in the growth of Western culture. It was again due to diffusion that the cultures of Mycene, Crete and Egypt influenced the Greek culture. In the same way, modern cultures also keep on influencing other cultures through diffusion. Ogbum and Nimkoff, while defining diffusion, have written that a transmission of culture traits from one area to another and from one culture to another is called diffusion. Railway trains, motor cars, aeroplanes, cinemas, tanks, telephone, telegraph and television, etc., and thousands of other things seen in the modern world today are examples of such a transmission. Not only instruments and machines but even ideas keep moving from one country to another. Religion of Buddha spread from India to China, Japan, Burma and other countries. Communism from Russia went to other countries. Indian decimal system crossed to Arabia and Europe. The following factors help in diffusion:

(a) Contact and communication, (b) the desire and needs of new traits, (c) competition with old traits and their opposition, (d) respect for those who invent or bring in new traits.

Diffusion is possible among different societies and even in one and the same society; unprecedented development of the means of conveyance and communication have been the cause of high speed of diffusion in the present century. The German scholars, Graebner, Ankerman and Schmidt have done important work in the establishment and spread of diffusion theory. Their ideology is called *Culture Historicheschule.* According to this ideology similarity in two cultures cannot be regarded as a result of diffusion so long as historical evidences affecting their mutual contacts are not given.

R. Linton, in his book *The Study of Man* has given in detail the influence of diffusion in American life. For example, the bed which an American leaves in the morning, was invented in the near East and was reformed in Europe, the curtains which he removes are made of the cotton which was first grown in India, If the curtains are made of silk, they were invented in the near East. If they are made of linen, they were discovered in China. The soft leather moccasin shoes, which he puts on after leaving his ted were made by Red Indians of North America. The bath room which he enters after this, is the result of modern European and American inventions. The trousers which he puts on were first made in India. The soap which he uses in cleaning his hands was first made by the people of ancient Gal. After this, the razor which he uses in shaving was made in Sumer of Egypt. In the same way, among so many other things of his use, neck-tie is the residual of the shawl used by Croatian people on their shoulders in the 17th century. The felt of his cap is the invention of Asian Steppes. The umbrella used in rains is a discovery of South-east Asia, and the rubber of the shoes he puts on is the invention of the primitive inhabitants of America. Among his utensils, plate is an invention of China, his knife is made of steel invented in South India, his fork is the invention of Italy in the middle period and his spoon is the invention of ancient Rome. Among the articles of food, orange is the discovery of Mediterranean countries, coffee of Abyssinia, tea of China and sugar of India. The pipe, which he smokes, has been taken from the natives of Virginia and the cigarette that he smokes has come from Mexico. The tobacco used in both these things was first grown in Brazil. If he uses cigar, it is the origin of Antelesc of Western Indian archipelago. If he reads a newspaper, it is the product of the printing system invented in Germany. It appears from this long statement of R. Linton that the modern American culture is the result of diffusion from so many other cultures. It shows the importance of diffusion in the evolution of culture.

Diffusional anthropologists disapprove the claim of evolutionists that the similarities found in different cultures of the world are evolved not because of diffusion, but because of separate evolution of similar traits in different cultures, not because of free reciprocal adaptability but because of free evolution. But the fact, that many other different traits of culture change places only through diffusion, cannot be ignored. The claim of evolutionists that evolution is the only cause of cultural similarities is therefore altogether unscientific. On the other hand, their statement that cultures, in their order of evolution, have passed through similar situations everywhere in the world, is also incorrect. That people's culture of one place is undoubtedly influenced by the other reaching there from a superior is a matter of common experience. A mutual exchange of culture does take place among the people living close to one another. For example, people who live close to one another and speaking can be possible only when they understand and adopt some words from the language of one another. Then, when they begin to speak, a change in their wearing apparel, ornaments, utensils and even in outside life through mutual cultural influence can be observed. Diffusion in cultures coming in close contact with one another is thus unavoidable. Migrating individuals carry culture traits from one place to another and diffuse them into people of the place where they reach. Thus diffusion-is one of the causes of finding similar cultural traits among different culture groups.

German Diffusionists

Among the modern diffusionists who have laid stress on the importance of diffusion in the growth of culture, there are two classes in Europe, German diffusionists and British diffusionists. In the beginning of the 20th century, Graebner, Ankermann and Schmidt presented in Germany the theory of diffusion in culture and since then their disciples have been regularly advocating the theory. These diffusionists believed that a diffusion of different cultural traits took place in the world in different places and periods and these cultural traits later spread to other parts of the world through diffusion. The cultural traits which thus spread through diffusion can be clearly identified in culture. This class of German diffusionists is known as Culture Historiche Schule, because it has shown the contribution of diffusion in particular culture by sketching its historical evolution. These scholars exemplify diffusion mostly through material culture and do not give evidence from diffusion of social institutions. But Graebner's contribution to the study of culture, in establishing criteria of quantity and form of diffusion, was very important. He stressed the point that in the absence of historical evidence, it cannot be said on the basis of outward similarity alone that similar traits appear in two cultures due to cultural diffusions. The evidence of diffusion will be accepted only when, along with similarity of form, there appears similarity of number and the arrangement of constituent elements of cultural traits.

Culture Area Approach

German diffusionists presented the view of culture area in order to define diffusion. When Graebner and other thinkers were engaged in search of facts to prove the example of diffusion, Franz Boas raised the question why diffusion, after all, took place. Boas classified the study of diffusion into different stages. According to him, facts about different situations should be described first. After that, proceeding from particular to general, analytic study should be done wherein, before talking about continents and the world, a factual distribution of special culture traits need be given. According to Boas the root causes of diffusion lie in the psychic make up of an individual.

What Boas meant by restricted area was called cultural area by Clark Wissler. Wissler pointed out that narrowing down the diffusion area was necessary. He showed how no culture trait, specially if it is non-material, can migrate to distant areas without undergoing a change in transit. It loses some of its specialities in the process of diffusion and picks up from other cultures some such traits which it did not possess in the beginning. According to Wissler there is a central point of diffusion in every culture area and the limits of diffusion are fixed. The forms of culture traits continuously keep changing in proceeding from central point to their limits and their traits become indistinct. Material obstacles in the diffusion of culture provide the cause of the change. Mountains, oceans, deserts and distances cause obstacles in the process of diffusion. Besides this the areas, through which the traits of any culture are diffused, break its adjustment and it is not diffused as it is. To prove his theory, Wissler sketched many different American cultures and described the technological, artistic and institutional traits of every area. He showed that many particular human societies can be found in one and the same cultural area. Some people live in the boundary limits of two cultural areas and are found to possess traits of both these cultures. These areas can be railed boundary areas.

British Diffusionists

As has been said before, besides the Culture Historiche Schule, the names of British diffusionists are included among the scholars who examined cultural diffusion. In fact, British scholar, Tylor, talked about cultural diffusion much earlier than German and American diffusionists. He had written that culture was like a plant which is diffused from one place lo another much more rapidly than its free growth. He had drawn a map of the diffusion of many culture traits which can be known, not from the name of British diffusionist, Tylor, but from the name of E.W. Smith, W.J. Perry and their disciples. They came among the diffusionists first, but were also the first in losing their names. They are also called Egyptologists because they have regarded Egypt as a centre of world culture. E. Smith and Perry stressed the point that evolution of culture everywhere in the world originated through diffusion from Egypt, but their theory has not been proved in figures. They have given a strange argument to prove their viewpoint. They said that people greatly lacked in their imaginative and inventive capacities. They said that people invented only through excitements created by very favourable environment and that a favourable environment of kind was available only in ancient Egypt. Thus, they maintained that human culture originated first among Egyptians whom Perry has called the Progeny of the Sun and that it was from there that cultural institutions were diffused everywhere in the world.

There were many such errors in the theory of British diffusionists because of which it was greatly criticized. Hutton pointed out that many culture traits originated generally in different areas due to different causes. Hutton gave many examples to prove it, such as fire piston, he said, was invented independently in Asia and France. Magic, medicine and many other technological apparatus were similarly invented separately in different areas of the world. Perry tried to give a counter reply to this criticism of Hutton. It is true that just as the evolution of similar culture traits in different places alone is not enough to declare the diffusion theory to be incorrect, in the same way, it would not on the other hand appear correct to say that culture traits have been diffused from one place to everywhere on earth. The truth is that there cannot be only one reason of sameness of culture traits. If one culture trait is the outcome of free evolution in cultures existing separately, the other culture trait reaches other places through diffusions from the place of its origin. It is not correct to say that human being is quite unimaginative and uninventive, and to say that evolution of culture has passed through similar situations everywhere in the world would be equally incorrect. No culture evolution can be shown in one straight line. The fact is that the very question whether a particular culture came into existence through evolution or diffusion is wrong, because, as a matter of fact, both of these processes are responsible for the growth of culture. A particular or a similar culture trait can be caused by evolution or diffusion, and which of these is the real cause cannot be ascertained by any pre-established theory. It can be decided only after studying actual facts related to it.

ACCULTURATION

Whenever culture traits or culture complexes spread from one culture to another, it is called diffusion. When the whole system of life in a culture begins to change under the influence of any other culture, it is the process of acculturation or contra-culturation. Linton, Redffeld, Herskovits, Hoizer and Beals have given many examples to define the process of contra-culturation. According to Herskovits, when a child learns to obey its cultural traditions in the process of development, it is called acculturation. When there is an exchange of culture traits and culture complexes between two cultures, it is transculturation, but when in place of one system of life in any culture, another system is established, it is contra-culturation. An assimilation may take place in this, but often it does not happen. What happens is that the afflicted culture first disintegrates and next, when improvement in it begins anew, its individuality is lost and it takes a new form. Such a process can be called contra-culturation. For example, among the tribals of Chota Nagpur in India, individuality had ended at first under the exploitation and poverty in which they lived for centuries, but, when the country became free, their insistence on cultural, social, economic and political freedom developed in them in the shape of Jharkhand movement under various political influences, but it was not their previous original form. Scholars, who illustrated this process of contra-culturation, say that no culture of the world today possesses its unadulterated form, which means that every culture has taken a lot from other cultures. They also insist that it is not enough to say, as diffusionists do, that different cultures have taken a lot from one another through diffusion. It is also necessary to say what and how they took from it.

THEORIES OF CULTURAL INTEGRATION

Various theories have been presented to define integration of culture in the modern age. The main theories among them are given below:

1. Functionalist Theory
2. Theory of Patterns of Culture
3. Theory of Themes
4. Theory of Style of Life.

A detailed description of these theories is given below:

1. Functionalist Theory. Great emphasis has been laid on the functional view in anthropology According to this view, every culture trait and culture complex in culture has some special work to do and it exists for its aim to do it. When its work is done, it ends. Thus no cultural trait has any importance without work. Nothing is unnecessary in culture. Whatever and whenever it becomes unnecessary, it ceases to exist. In this way, every culture is found to be internally complete; its every part is closely related to the other and no part can be known by separating it from other parts. Every culture trait can be defined with reference to other traits. In other words, functionalists lay stress on completeness of culture. The culture traits, which appear to be unimportant and useless when examined separately, begin to appear important when referred to other culture traits.

Functionalists define the internal structure of culture. Various kinds of social, mental and material factors are included in culture. What is the relation among these factors which makes them meaningful? Functionalists answer this very question. They maintain that there is an internal co-ordination among the factors. This co-ordination makes every culture in integrated whole. The question, why is it so, has not been answered by functionalists in one and the same manner. According to Malinowski, culture is the means of keeping man's biopsychic identity intact. It helps man in keeping his mental and literary existence high. In this way, every aspect of culture, may it be economic organization or social organization, may it be religion or language, depends on human needs. Now, since these needs are related among them, the various aspects of culture are also related among them. No culture trait is separate from this integrated whole. In this way functionalists reject the view of evolutionists that there are some functionless traits also in culture Functionalists say that these traits are called functionless because evolutionists are not capable of defining them. According, to Malinowski, all culture traits are related among them and every trait can be defined with reference to the whole.

Malinowski defines cultural diffusion in a new way. According to him, culture trait can retain its original form even after diffusion, but it will do only that work in a new culture which it can possibly do. It is only due to a close relation among the various factors of culture that, whenever there is a change in some new factor, some change can be perceived in the whole culture.

According to Malinowski, every culture is born to supply the bio-psychic needs of the local people and it should therefore be defined in that form. In this way, all the cultures of the world cannot be learnt by similar original causes.

Culture does not depend on any impartial or full values. It supplies the local wants. In this way, Malinowski establishes cultural pluralism. But where Malinowski regards the various factors of culture as part of one integrated whole, there he fails to show the relations among human inspirations which are satisfied by these factors. In his concept of a human being, man is only a collection of various wants and tendencies.

Besides Malinowski, Radcliffe-Browm also has accepted the functional theory of culture. According to him, the purpose of integration of culture is not only to maintain the existence of an individual but is also to maintain the existence of the society as well. Integration of culture is both idealistic and factual. If integration is lost, the society too will come to an end. Every institution of culture helps in this work of culture. Its aim is not to supply a particular need. It is to maintain the existence of the whole human society in total culture.

Malinowski and Radcliffe-Brown have both viewed cultural integration in the form of culture content. According to D.N. Majumdar, both these viewpoints are partial. The claim of Malinowski that form depends on function is wrong. According to Majumdar, the form has its own independent existence and integration depends on it.

2. Theory of Patterns of Culture. This theory of cultural integration was presented by Ruth Benedict. Ruth Benedict took inspiration from the field of art and aesthetics. According to her, integration in any culture is due to the arrangement of its content in a temporary or a permanent style. This arrangement is called pattern by Benedict. There is a particular style in every part of a culture and these separate styles combine together and present a grand design of the culture as a whole. This is the configuration of culture. The production of this re-union in culture is due to the common tendency seen in all the aspects of culture. This main tendency is called a special genius of culture by Ruth Benedict. It is this genius of a culture that brings about its integration. This alone is the basis of the integration of form. According to Benedict, there are two kinds of this genius found in human society: one is Apollonian and the other is Dionysian. The word "Apollonian" is made by a Greek word "Apollo" which means peaceful sun deity. Apollonian genius is found in those cultures which have peace and tranquility as their main qualities; and this same is the cause of their integration, an example of which can be found in the Pueblos of New Mexico. The word 'Dionysian' is derived from the name of a Greek god Dionysius who appears to be connected with drinking and a luxurious life. In this way, dionysian genius is found in a culture in which a great deal of storms and changes are experienced, an example of which can be found in Dobu and Kwakiutl cultures on the northwest coast of America. According to Dr. D.N. Majumdar, an integration of the theories advocated by Malinowski, Radcliffe-Brown and Ruth Benedict is necessary to reach a better theory of cultural integration.

3. Theory of Themes. M. E. Opler presented the theory of themes in order to define cultural integration. Themes mean those common inspirations which create various types of behaviours in a culture. According to Opler, Benedict's theory limits the genius of the people's attempt of self-fulfilment in a culture. On the other hand, in Opler's theory of themes, integration is not tied down to any special kind of behaviour. Opler leaves an investigator free in every field to discover the basis of integration. His theory of cultural integration is thus far more elastic than that of Benedict. Specific expressions of cultural integration in each individual case can be found out through any theme. Opler has applied the theory of themes in describing the culture of a race known by the name of 'Apache'. Like the theory of Ruth Benedict, Opler's theory is also a key to the specific structure of the mode of life of any kind.

4. Theory of Style of Life. The latest theory to define cultural integration is the theory of style of life. Style of life does not include only culture but it includes the most fundamental and permanent elements. It includes the means of livelihood only to the extent to which they can he helpful in giving a practical shape to the conception of good life. Style of life includes explicit and implicit judgements about right conduct. It also includes comparatively less important elements which explain the individual character of some group. Redfield, who presented the theory of the style of life, regards the style of life like the concept of manners, Lionel Trilling includes explicit and implicit expressions of values in manners. But as D.N. Majumdar has stated, Redfield only tells where the principle of integration can be found located, but he himself does not present any principle of integration.

From the above description of various theories of cultural integration, it is clear that none of these theories is sufficient in this respect. The best thing here would be to make use of the universal viewpoint which wilt include specifications of all the theories.

CULTURAL LAG

The word lag connotes crippled movement. Hence, cultural lag means the faltering of one aspect of culture behind another. For example, if either the material or the non-material aspect of culture were to stay behind the other, it would be a case of cultural lag. It is generally observed that material culture progresses faster in comparison with non-material culture.

Ogburn's Theory

The term cultural lag originated in a famous sociologist W.F. Ogburn's treatise entitled Social Change. The term was coined by Ogburn. According to him, culture has two aspects, one material and the other non-material. The material aspect, as compared with the non-material, tends to progress rapidly. Thus the non-material part lags behind. It is this faltering action which is termed cultural lag. Defining cultural lag in their work, Handbook of Sociology, Ogburn and Nimkoff have written that "the strain that exists between two correlated parts of culture that change at unequal rates of speed may be interpreted as a lag in the part that is changing at the slower rate for the one lags behind the other." Citing an example of cultural lag in his Social Characteristics of Cities, Ogburn has stated that the number of policemen per 10,000 residents is less in towns in which the population is increasing than the towns in which it is decreasing. This situation Ogbum has represented diagrammatically, thus:

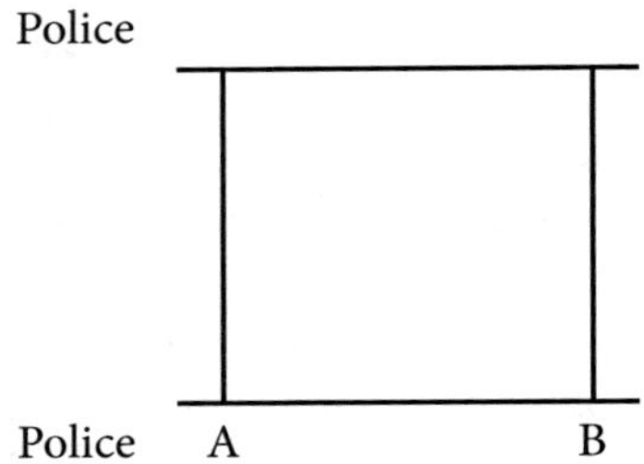

In this diagram, the line above represents the increase in population while the one below shows the increase in the police force. It has been assumed that at the point A the police force was adequate for a town. The population of the town increased rapidly but the police force did not expand till population had reached the point B. In this way, the difference between 'A' and 'B' indicates that while the population increased continually, expansion in the police force lagged behind. Similarly, presenting another example of cultural lag Ogburn has stated that the advent of the motor car was disastrous for railway companies as many became bankrupt as a result of their inability to compete with motor trucks for hauling material over short distances.

Some Examples from Indian Conditions

In Indian conditions one comes across many forms of cultural lag. During the last two hundred years much has been borrowed from the West in India's material culture and such towns as Delhi, Calcutta and Bombay are in no way inferior to the Western towns in respect of superficial gaudiness. But in spite of having borrowed so much from the West in its material culture, Indian culture has undergone very limited changes in the sphere of non-material culture. In this way, so far as the question of borrowing from the West in education is concerned, a tremendous lagging behind from material culture is evident in India's non-material culture. Another example of cultural lag can be found in the condition of Indian women. In India women share equal rights with men in receiving education, casting votes, taking equal part in the social, political and religious life, and they are progressing in this direction. And yet how different is an Indian woman from her Western counterpart in her sentiments, feelings, thoughts and ideals! The fact of the matter is that whereas the Indian woman owes much to the Western in one direction, she is still much the same as she was in another. It is not true that there has been no transformation or change in this direction but rather it is a fact that the change is very little compared with the change that has occurred in the other directions.

Culture is changing very rapidly in the sphere of fashion, dress, artificial beautification, art, recreation etc., but the change in the sphere of religious notions is comparatively very slow. The present age is called the age of science and rationalism and the West is considered the most advanced in this respect but how scientific and rational is the Christian outlook, both medieval and modern, concerning beliefs, rituals etc.? Actually, we are seeing newer and newer superstitions in the age of science. In this way, in the modern age, cultural lag in the various elements of culture is evident in all cultures, be it Indian, Japanese, English or any other. Lumley has written correctly that it seems as if many pedestrian soldiers or a complete army are marching out of step or as if some of the performers of an orchestra are playing this year's music on their instruments while others are playing last year's music and still others last century's music or even more ancient music at the same time. Such music would not be particularly musical or melodious. But this is the picture of every culture.

Causes of Cultural Lag

What is the cause of this cultural lag? The main cause is that the various elements of culture possess varying degrees of changeability, As has been said before, changes in religious opinions are slow and few. It is doubtful whether the major religions, Christianity, Islam, Buddhism and Hinduism, have undergone any change in the last few hundred years although major changes in the dress, standard of living, methods and even the values of life, of their respective followers are only too apparent. The same slow speed of change is true not only of the major religions but also of the religions of ancient people. For example, in America, the Red Indians have changed enormously in their methods of obtaining food, of fighting and of using the gun and the horse, but their religion is still more or less intact. Similar to religion the speed of the change in law is also slow though not quite as slow as the changes in religion. A major cause contributing to the slow speed of change in law is that traditions are deeply respected in law. In many countries particularly in England, traditions are valued very much. The judges dispense justice on the basis of precedents. New laws are enacted only when extreme difficulty is experienced in some spheres due to their absence. It is evident that laws change after other changes have taken place. For example, in the earliest days of the Industrial Revolution the number of factories increased rapidly and they employed women and children in addition to the men. There was no law pertaining to the hours of work of these labourers, their wages and working conditions, hence the capitalists, taking advantage of their helpless conditions, exploited the labourers causing widespread dissatisfaction. Only then did the government wake to this predicament, and the labour laws came into existence. Even now many examples can be cited of cases where changing conditions have necessitated newer and more adequate legislation which has not been enacted or implemented. In India, the question of coloration of hydrogenated vegetable oil is a case in point. Like the labourers, the women had to launch movements for a long period before they could manage to have laws concerning their rights. Technology progresses at a faster rate than does non-material culture. But even in technology, the rate of change is not uniform everywhere. For example, at present the speed of change in chemistry and electrical science is faster than the speed of change in power production.

Similarly, culture lag is responsible, in the main, for the existing international tension. Science has made the world a small one. The discovery of atomic power has precipitated a stage in which there should be a solid organization of the human race on an international scale so that conflagration destructive of the entire world may be avoided even if there is a spark. But the hearts of men are as yet unprepared for such a change. Narrow nationalism has not yet vanished, but is assuming aggressive forms in some spheres. In addition to the difference In the rate of change of the various elements of culture, one major cause of cultural lag is man's psychological dogmatism, Man commonly respects old concepts and dogmas or mores. He finds it convenient to follow the path of his ancestors. In such spheres as religion, novelty is not only objected to but also regarded as a sign of depravity.

Criticism

Many sociologists have indulged in biller criticism of Ogburn's theory of cultural lag. According to Mueller, cultural lag is artificial and imaginary. Some other scholars regard it as a very simple background of the understanding of social change. James W. Woodard and R.M. MacIver, have put forward the following objections to Ogburn's theory of cultural lag:

1. Ogburn's distinction between material and non-material culture is not clear. Again, it is not necessary that non-material culture should invariably lag behind material culture.
2. A major defect of Ogburn's theory lies in the fact that the same term cultural lag has been employed for all disequilibriums occurring in the process of social change. MacIver has in this connection, suggested the use of many terms for the various types of disequilibriums and conflicts, such as technological lag, technological restraint, cultural clash, cultural ambivalence, etc.
3. According to the theory of cultural lag, one thing progresses forward while another lags or restricts. Hence, this word should not be used in the context of those objects in whose case the encouraging as well as the restraining objects are similar and possess a common standard of evolution.

CULTURAL COMPLEX

The simple unit of culture is the cultural trait. These cultural traits develop concurrently and collect together like a bunch of flowers and gain in their importance in terms of the degree of significance they have for the behaviour of human beings. This bunch of collected traits is called a culture complex. These culture complexes are formed according to the various needs of life. In this way culture complexes concerning food habits, the different occupations, etc., can be seen in different cultures. Examples of culture complexes found in Indian culture are in the form of the caste system, joint family system, the principle of karma etc. Metallic utensils are indicative of the culture complex concerning food habits in Indian culture. Among these culture complexes some develop more than the others and become more influential and effective. But in any one culture, these culture complexes exhibit a high degree of concurrence among themselves. Cultural patterns, which are representative of the unique nature of any culture are formed by them.

TECHNOLOGICAL LAG

The word lag connotes a tendency to hesitate or falter behind. Hence, the term technological lag is indicative of a condition of technological progress in which the various interdependent elements loose their suite of balanced progress and cease to exist in a state of equilibrium. As a result of this imbalance, the entire process of production is slowed and sometimes even completely stopped, Ogburn has given a beautiful example in this context. The importance of forests in preventing soil erosion through rain and in preventing the spread of deserts is a matter of common knowledge. In order to get the benefit of these functions, both protection of forests and afforestation are essential, and all countries make efforts in this direction. On the other hand, many forests are destroyed because wood is needed for fuel, furniture and many industries. In this situation it is essential to strike an adequate balance between the growth and destruction of forests. An equilibrium can be maintained only when the number of trees cut and the number planted afresh is equal. If the number of trees cut exceed the corresponding number of those planted afresh, the balance is disturbed and in consequence, the rainfall is decreased, the desert encroaches upon cultivable land and agriculture suffers. This imbalance is an example of technological lag. If no consideration is directed to a state of technological lag, the organization of industries is disturbed and can result in loss.

CULTURE AND PERSONALITY

In the modern age, many anthropological studies of personality in primitive cultures have shown intimate relation of personality and culture. These studies have shown that man is a far more cultural being than imagined by the psychologists. In this connection, the discoveries by Ralph Linton and Abram Kardiner are notable. These anthropologists found that in every culture there is a basic personality type which is an outcome of cultural influences on the individual. As these cultural influences change so also change the basic personality types. About the Alorese of Indonesia, Kardiner has written that in their society the basic personality type is a dubious, quarrelling, cowardly and parasitic person, whereas in our society, such a person will be considered as psychopathic and abnormal. According to Ralph Linton, in certain Islands of the pacific the same anxiety, rituals, customs and taboos are found about food as about sexual behaviour in our society. These studies prove that every society has a particular culture which profoundly influences the personality of its members.

The British anthropologist Malinowski has presented functional approach to culture. According to him, culture should be studied with a view to find out what it does for him. Ruth Benedict has presented important discoveries regarding national character. She studied Zuni Indians of New Mexico, Dobu tribe of Malanesia and the Kwakiutl tribe of Vancouver Island. These studies showed many such motives to be acquired which were formerly considered to be hereditary.

The members of Zuni tribe use rituals and magic to fulfil their aims and purposes. Their religious practices show complex traits. Ritualistic activities take a major part of their time. They have a keen memory regarding the details of rituals. Ruth Benedict found imitative magic among them. For example, they rolled big stones down the slopes in order to bring rains on the faith that the thunderous sound made by the stones will make the clouds thunder and rain. Thus, among them religion was mixed with magic. Competition and conflict is comparatively rarer. They are non-violent and do not like change in daily routines. Their example shows that man is not aggressive by nature. Competitions, conflict and aggression are results of cultural influences.

The Dobu tribe of Malanesia are exactly a contrast to Zuni in temperament and personality. In them one finds abundance of conflict, competition, combat and violence. In Dobus also religion is mixed with magic but this magic is used to bring harm to others or to defend oneself against others. Most of the individuals in this tribe are deceivers. They scarcely care of promises and compromises. In their society, the promises are normally broken. They do not think it to be wrong as it is in other cultures. This difference in the personality traits of Dobu and Zuni individuals is due to the difference in their cultures.

The Kwakiutl tribe, as against Zunis, does not believe in religious practices. They are materialist. In their society, wealth determines status and social prestige. Hence, everyone is seen busy in earning money by hook or crook. Those who have less money feel ashamed on account of it. The tendency of self-assertion is fairly clear, self-assertion is exhibited in a strange custom known as potlatch. In this the rich person destroys his wealth before others to show that he can destroy even more than they have.

All the above mentioned studies of personality type in primitive cultures show how personality traits differ in different cultures. Culture determines methods of child beaming, form of social control, mores, customs, rituals, myths, legends, and ways of thinking and living. All these influence personality. Culture determines the standard of normality in a society. Thus, what appears normal personality in a culture may appear abnormal in another. Thus, culture determines personality.

PRIMITIVE AND MODERN SOCIAL GROUP

Differentiation between primitive and civilized society has been made in various ways. According to Durkheim and some other thinkers, there is a great difference between a primitive and a civilized society in that there is greater division of labour in a civilized society than in a primitive society. Division of labour in human society goes on increasing along with increase in the evolution of civilization.

There is very little division of labour in a primitive society. The necessary things for the family members are produced in the family itself. Every work, from cutting wood, weaving of cloth and building of houses to the task of cultivation is done by every family separately. On the other hand, in a civilized society, the work of weaving cloth is done by weavers or in a cloth factory; the work of building houses is done by masons and labourers; the work of cutting the wood is done by wood-cutters or in a mill raised for that purpose. Not only this, but in modern and huge factories, one labourer makes only one part of an article and, in this way thousands of labourers are engaged in making separate parts of one and the same thing. In a civilized society there is a marked specialization in social, economic, political and business matters; in matters concerning health and medicine and, in brief, in every aspect of life.

Relation between Useful and Cultural Activities

According to MacIver, a great difference between primitive and civilized society lies in the fact that there is no difference between the cultural and the useful in a primitive society. In the words of MacIver, in a primitive society, "the means of living are not, as so often with us, detached from the end of living." In the civilized society of today one person is found turning files for eight hours in the office, the other is engaged in making a motor car; one waves a green flag to the railway engine and the other is busy in performing a juggler's show. Do all these bring them food or do they satisfy their need? Do these roles satisfy the physical, mental and spiritual needs of the clerk? The answer is 'no[5]. Why then does he go on turning them the whole day? The reason is quite plain. He does all that because he gets money out of it to help him in buying things which will ultimately satisfy his needs. In this way, these efforts of the clerk, bus driver, railway guard and the juggler are only the means but not the ends. They do not satisfy the needs of their lives. They are only useful for the satisfaction of their wants. In the same way, the importance of factories, shops, cloth mills and the like consists in their being useful. People do not get pleasure from them and nor do they live for them. Life is not in them and nor is it for them, but they are all for life. The individual of a civilized society does not keep an eye on life nor on pleasure but on the usefulness or the gain. They try to do their work with steadiness, laboriousness and cleverness, so that they may have maximum benefit from them. They do it all like a machine. It has no cultural importance. On the other hand, every work of an individual in a primitive society, may it be fishing, hunting, cultivating or building a house, has a cultural importance. They have traditions, festivals and fables connected to them. They dance, sing and make merriment after a hunting expedition. The work, instead of being the means, becomes an end in itself. They take joy in it and it is their life.

But it does not mean that every work in a primitive society has purely a cultural importance. Along with its being cultural every work is useful as well. As a matter of fact, a primitive man makes no difference between cultural and useful. For him, art for art and art for life are not two opposite views. Their art is both useful and cultural. Baskets, mats, lances, bows and arrows and such other things have their cultural values along with their being useful as well. In a primitive society, useful and cultural are similar things. Malinowski has written, "The meagre furniture, the hearth, the sleeping links, the mats and pegs of a native hut, show a simplicity, even poverty of form, which, however, become immensely significant through the depth and range of sociological and spiritual association." In this way, speed of change, in primitive society, is not so fast that the means of production may be separated from their cultural background. There is not too much and varied specialization in works. Sentiments are connected even with the things of daily use. In this way, there appears a mixture of the useful and cultural in every aspect of life in a primitive society. MacIver bas written that "Ritual is as important as craftsmanship in the making of a canoe or in the cultivation of the soil. Prayers are as important as arms in the conduct of war. Religion is compounded with magic and cannot be divorced from the business of living. The dance is as much a means of warding off evil spirits or of inducing fertility as it is a mode of social recreation. The success of a fishing expedition is as much endangered by a woman's touching a fishing tackle as by unfavourable weather, sickness comes from spells and the breaking of taboos. The people are bound in spirit to the soil, the home of their ancestors and their gods. Everything in nature is instinct with social meaning and enshrined in social ceremony. Culture, technique, authority, people and land are subjectively unified."

Importance of Basic Personality Type

It reveals one more distinction between primitive and civilized societies. Because of this mixture of the useful and cultural, some individual qualities of the people of every primitive society are also common. Kardiner has called it basic personality structure. This basic structure is commonly found in all the individuals of a primitive society, although there are individual dissimilarities also in them besides this basic structure. In this way, the inhabitants of Samoa Island take pleasure in life and are jovial. The inhabitants of Admiralty island are suspicious and comparatively less serious. This similarity of viewpoints and attitudes is not visible in any group of civilized societies. Civilization and culture are found more mixed in primitive societies than in civilized societies. This does not mean that there is no similarity and unity of any kind among the people of civilized societies, The difference is only this, that unity and organization in primitive societies is all-inclusive; whereas in civilized societies it is visible only in some aspects of life. The personality of a person in a primitive society is formed by social rules, traditions, methods, festivals and religion etc. Environments in a civilized society are more complicated and a person is more free. In this way there are more varieties in a civilized society than a primitive society.

Relation of Culture with Soil and Consanguinity

Another difference between primitive and civilized societies is this that in primitive societies culture is bound to soil and consanguinity or blood groups, whereas in civilized societies, various cultures are seen on one and the same ground and one and the same culture is seen in many countries. For example, one and the same culture is found in different countries of Europe; whereas in India there are many cultures in on and the same country. The reason of this difference is that philosophy, art, literature and science are so much improved today that they cannot be fastened to the boundaries of any one country. In the same way, religion in a primitive society is tied to the local boundaries. Deities in tribes are their own deities just as their festivals are their own festivals. The religious importance of a particular thing in a tribe increases with the increase of its usefulness. In this way, the people of a tribe, living in a bamboo forest, make their houses, weapons and utensils of bamboos and even make cloth from bamboos. Not only this, they also regard the bamboo to be something sacred and their deities live in bamboos. Thus the local mountains, rivers, trees and the like are given religious importance. In civilized societies, where religion, on the one hand, is their own, it is not, on the other hand, so much limited by the boundaries of the country.

The difference between primitive and civilized society, as given above, is a relative difference, because primitive and civilized societies are two stages of one and the same form of evolution. Evolution is an upward process from a relative, uncertain and a matchless homogeneity to a relatively certain and a synthesized non-homogeneity. Religion, culture and economic organization of a primitive society are the starting steps in the cultural evolution of man.

QUESTIONS FOR EXERCISE

1. Define culture and distinguish between material and non-material culture.
2. Write an essay on Culture and Civilization.
3. Give a comparative account of culture and civilization.
4. Write short note on Cultural Lag.
5. Explain Ogburn's theory of cultural lag. What objections have been raised against this theory?
6. Write short note on Cultural Change.
7. What do you understand by Cultural Lag?
8. Write short note on Cultural Complex.
9. Write short note on the following:
   (a) Technological Lag
   (b) Cultural Growth.
10. Define Acculturation. Give examples.
11. Write a short note on Diffusion of Culture.

Chapter 10

Social Progress

The literal meaning of the word progress is moving forward towards some objective or, simply 'moving forward'. But moving forward or backward, progress or regress, are relative terms. If it be remarked that such and such country has progressed, no meaningful information can be extracted from such a statement unless the direction be known towards which progress has been made. In this way, progress is not mere change. It is change in a particular direction. To quote Lumely, "Progress is a narrower concept. It is change but it is change in a desired or approved direction, not any direction."[1] The word progress cannot be appended to change in every direction. For example, if the condition of agriculture in a particular country worsens and a famine results, it is undeniably change, but it will not be called progress. Progress means moving forward in the direction and achievement of some aim. In this way, its connotation is less comprehensive than that of evolution. As a general statement, the definition by Park and Burgess can suffice. According to it, "Any change or adaptation to an existent environment that makes it easier for a person or a group of persons or other organised form of life to live may be said to represent progress."[2] In this way, progress can roughly be descriptive of any change that assists in the life of an individual, group or institution because, even though not an ultimate value, 'to live' is certainly a primary and indispensable value. Thus, any change desirous of being dignified by the name of progress should at least be life giving.

CHARACTERISTICS OF PROGRESS

The concept of progress will be clarified by a knowledge of its characteristics. The following are its main general characteristics:

1. There is Change in Progress. Progress is change or motion in some direction. Hence, change is its first essential characteristic.

2. In Progress, the Desired Aim is Achieved. But mere change cannot be called progress. It can be called progress only when it fulfils the desired aim. Whatever this desired objective may be, it must be beneficial and pertain to welfare since no one desires his own ill-being.

---

1. Lumley, *Principles of Sociology*, p. 387.

2. Park and Burgess, *An Introduction to Science of Sociology*, p. 382.

3. Progress is Communal. Progress, in its ethical and certain other meanings, is also personal but in sociology this meaning of progress is not accepted since sociology is the science of society and in it the individual is taken into consideration only as a part of society. Thus, progress, according to sociological viewpoint, is communal, or, in other words, in progress the entire group moves ahead in some desired direction.

4. Both Loss and Gain are Possible in Progress. It is not that there is only gain and no loss in progress, although ultimately, of course, there is more gain than loss. In case the loss is greater than gain, the social change involved cannot be called progress. In social progress the community has to suffer hardships and make sacrifices. In gaining its independence what hardship India did not suffer and what sacrifices she was not compelled to make? But nevertheless in the history of independence every struggle was a step towards progress.

5. Progress is Voluntary. Progress does not come about involuntarily. Desire and volition are needed for progress. It is an uphill task. Efforts have to be made and when these efforts are successful it is called progress. It must be remembered that every effort is not progress since efforts are also wasted and despite the most desperate endeavour one makes no headway whatsoever.

6. Concept of Progress is Variable. The concept of progress does not remain constant in all times and at all places. That which is today considered the symbol of progress may tomorrow be considered and treated as a sign of regress. In India a particular fact may be interpreted as an indication of regress whereas the same fact may, in the West, symbolise progress.

INFLUENCE OF SOCIAL VALUES ON PROGRESS

Progress is the process of the realisation of our social values. In this way progress is determined by social values. The concept of progress will concur with the social values of the time and place to which it belongs. Now, before studying the effect of social values on progress it would be better to understand the exact connotation of the word 'value' as it is interpreted in sociology. In sociology, the word, 'value' carries a very special significance. In their book Patterns of Culture, Gillin and Gillin have written, "The value of a thing is its worth or desirability as compared with something else. Value clusters around (1) activities and attitudes which serve needs of the group, or a large or dominant portion of the group, or (2) about ways of life which have become habitual or customary and therefore require little conscious adjustment from day-to-day or they are (3) so intertwined with other elements in the culture that disturbance of one part of the complex threatens others." In this way the desirable or desired is value of valuable. It is based on those actions or ideas that fulfil the needs of the communal life. Value is related to those facts which have become habits and have been absorbed into the culture. In this way, it is apparent that values are social and the individuals want their increase or that society has need for an increase in them. Hence, the more the social values are achieved the farther shall society progress in the desired direction. It is clear that progress is based on social values. Whether any change shall be considered progress or regress depends upon the social values which are constantly changing. Thus, there is no object which may be uniformly or eternally considered valuable, irrespective of time and place. In this way the concept of progress changes colours like a chameleon. Here some people may argue to the contrary by citing the uniformly and constant nature of concepts of abstaining from theft, killing, exploitation, etc. But a careful and minute observation will make it apparent that these words have different meanings in different times and at different places. For example, the Jain religion looks down upon the killing of even mosquitoes and flies whereas in the political sphere even the elimination of an enemy does not count as a killing. Similarly, there was a time when even the practice of slavery was not considered to be exploitation. And even today the word exploitation has different meanings in the communistic and capitalistic contexts. In this way, the meaning of progress depends upon specific social values. This changeability of values does not mean that the concept of progress is not definite. All that it means is that progress does not have precisely the same meanings at all times and places, and that it is dependent upon and is determined by social values. These social values change but at a very slow rate and many values suffer very insignificant variation even over considerably long periods. Hence, upto this limit the concept of progress remains constant. Thus, it is evident that the concept of progress depends upon social values.

Just as the concept of social progress is based upon social values, in much the same way, the conditions conducive to social progress also are not the same in all times and at all places. Besides, the conditions conducive to social progress will vary with the different spheres of progress. Conditions conducive to progress in various countries vary according to their respective stages of progress. To take an example, the provision of education, means of livelihood, foodgrains, etc., in India would be conditions which would conduce to progress in this country. These commodities are essential for every society but where these are available at the outset, progress would take place in spheres other than these. Hence, it would stand in need of different conditions. Programmes of cultural development may be conducive to progress in the country in which the population is universally and properly fed. Such programmes would be a waste of effort and time in country in which the people do not have enough to eat. In this way, it is not possible to prescribe such conditions conducive to social progress that would hold true for and be applicable to all times and places. Keeping in mind their essentially relative nature, the following can be said to be the major general conditions of progress:

1. Physical and Mental Health. A healthy mind and body are the first requisites of progress in any direction. Only this can ensure a healthy future generation and a bright future for the country.

2. Collection of Physical Objects. Besides having health, it is also essential to get rid of poverty. Health can hardly be exported to be good in conditions of poverty and starvation. Hence, the acquisition of objects necessary for life is an essential condition of progress.

3. Universal Education. In addition to the appropriate physical means, a universal education is also necessary. Without this science and technology would remain undeveloped, and physical resources cannot be fully utilised.

4. Social Security. Another important condition which conduces to progress is the provision of social security in the form of insurance against disease, accident, old age, unemployment, etc.

5. Liberty and Equality. Without liberty and equality, people cannot enthusiastically work towards progress. Both of these render much assistance in progress.

6. Faith in the Possibility of Progress. People should have faith in the possibility of progress and should be free from any fear on this account. But, on the other hand, progress should not seem to be inevitable for people would then cease their efforts in this direction.

7. Minimum Obstacles. It is encouraging to be faced with a minimum of obstacles in one's movements, behaviour and paths to progress in life. This helps progress. Man should have maximum freedom in his work.

It need hardly be said that the foregoing description of conditions conducive to progress is both brief as well as incomplete. According to their time and place or their context these conditions can be elucidated. This description comprehends only those fundamental conditions which are indispensable to progress.

CRITERIA OF PROGRESS

As in the case of conditions for progress it is difficult to explain or describe the criteria of progress which also are relative to their spatio-temporal context Social values are the criteria of progress, and social values change with time and place. Hence, it is difficult to formulate a universally acceptable criterion of progress. But nevertheless, the following can be tentatively suggested.

According to their time and place or their context these conditions can be elucidated. This description comprehends only those fundamental conditions which are indispensable to progress.

Bogardus Views

According to Bogrdus, progress has the following 14 conditions on the basis of which it can be determined whether progress is taking place or not:

1. Utilization of natural wealth in the public interest.
2. Increase in number of people healthy both in body and mind
3. Increase in a healthy environment.
4. Increase in useful entertainments or means thereto.
5. Increase in organised families.
6. Opportunities for creative work open to the maximum number of people.
7. Increase in social insurance against accidents, disease, deaths, unemployment, etc.
8. Increase in the democratization or nationalization of industries and trades.

9. Improvement in the standard of living of the majority of people.
10. Increase in co-operation with government.
11. Propagation of arts as far as possible.
12. Development of religious and spiritual aspects of human nature.
13. Propagation of technical, vocational and welfare education.
14. Increase in co-operative life.

In compiling these conditions of social progress, effort has been made to give a place to material, physical, intellectual, spiritual, and all kinds of values. Hence, as a temporary measure, these criteria of social progress can be accepted.

Lumley's Opinion

Lumley has prescribed only eight conditions of progress. These bases he has termed the directions of human progress. These eight directions are the following:

1. The first condition of progress is the belief that conflict and struggle will lead to the desired aim. Such a belief will lead them to an effort for change and modification. In its absence the possibility of change and consequently the possibility of progress is reduced.

2. The second condition of progress is the belief among the people that progress is not inevitable, or that progress is not self-caused. Belief in progress as a doubtful proposition if left to itself will lead people to make effort, the absence of which deprives the people of their incentive to act and achieve.

3. The third condition of progress is the belief of the people in its possibility. It makes progress seem a live position, not of course in the Jamesian fashion, but as a distinct possibility. If there is no such belief, one can rely on the people to become fatalists on this subject.

4. The fourth condition of progress is that there should not be any fear among people. If fear be instilled in their minds then they will shrink from instituting some changes, and this will hinder progress. The absence of such hindering due to fear will lead them to continuous experimentation and inventions.

5. The fifth condition of progress is the accumulation and use of physical materials in the right quantity. Progress however, consists not merely in the accumulation of material comforts and goods but also in their complete and equitable distribution among the maximum number of people.

6. The sixth condition of progress is the universal and diversified propagation of education in order that the greatest number of people may be benefitted by it.

7. The seventh condition of social progress is the continuous decrease in the number of people who inherit defective characteristics, both physical and mental. Such a reduction will lead to a tremendous conservation of the resources and wealth at the disposal of society which can then be used for more constructive and creative efforts.

8. The eighth and final condition of progress is the granting of freedom to the individual to travel the world at large without restriction. This will lead to better

contact and communication between individuals of different societies. This will be of benefit also on the individual level since it will help in widening the mental horizon of the people.

In fact, it is evident from the foregoing account that these conditions are no criteria of determining progress but rather conditions under which any society can justifiably progress. Again these eight conditions of social progress do not exhaust all the conditions that are essential for progress, since there can be many more conditions that are indispensable to progress and it is also possible that progress may not take place even when these eight conditions exist.

Hart's Opinion

Hamel Hart has accepted three fundamental conditions of social progress:
(1) Being advanced in years;
(2) Mental health;
(3) Considerable leisure.

Of course, these three conditions are essential to social progress but this list does not exhaust the conditions without which social progress remains only a chimera. Consequently, it must be pronounced without reservation that Hart's opinion is one-sided and incomplete.

Devine's View

E.T. Devine has prescribed the following criteria as determinants of social progress:
(1) The protection of natural resources and their proper utilisations for the benefit of the many rather than of the intelligent and shrewd few.
(2) Comparatively more healthy, mental and physical heredity, and comparative reduction in the number of degenerate offspring from moronic, alcoholic or otherwise defective parents.
(3) Conditions more conducive to healthy living and the absence of injurious domestic construction, improper sanitary conditions and the elimination of contagious diseases.
(4) Increase in healthy entertainment and a decrease in entertainment that feeds upon health as well as in the speed of life that saps the energy of urban life.
(5) Increase in the number of healthy and wealthy parents and educated children, decrease in children who are hated and resented by their parents, as also the injustices that had meted out to poor children employed in industrial concerns.
(6) Opportunities for a comparatively greater number of people to indulge in creative activity, increase in the number of individuals who perform their function with honesty and do not waste their time concurring with a decrease in the number of people who lose their efficiency and will to work in the afternoon of life.
(7) Greater democratization and nationalization of trade and industry. In this, the labourers, capitalists and the public who are in control of the industry or trade should have equally important functions, with a corresponding increase in the

number of workers, engineers and employers who are more concerned with the welfare of others than their own benefit.

(8) Increase in social insurance that covers accidents, disease, old age, death and unemployment etc.

(9) Improvement in a comparatively greater number of individuals regarding higher standard of living, involving nutritious food, refreshing entertainments and opportunities for creative activity.

(10) A situation in which the individual is less concerned with what he can coax the government to give to him than with what he can actually do for the government and give to the government. Greater interest in good music, painting and drawing, poetry, sculpture and other arts.

(11) Propagation of technical, vocational and welfare education.

(12) A comparatively greater development of the intellectual and spiritual aspects of a comparatively greater number of people.

In this way, social progress is a relative change. If the change in the direction of some desirable objective compares more favourably than with the change in the past, progress can be presumed to have taken place. Evidently, then, this progress never ends. Social progress is no predetermined status or level the attainment of which automatically precludes the possibility of any future progress. In fact, progress itself is not more than travel, a journey rather than a destination. It consists in the constant progress towards and effort in the attainment of predetermined and desirable ends and objects. The change in this journey towards these desirable ends is progress. In this way, the method for determining whether a particular society has progressed or not is to compare its present condition with that of the immediately preceding period of time. The total quantum of progress achieved is a matter for more detailed consideration but the fact of change, whatever and however it may be, is an evidence that progress has been made.

In view of the various opinions that have been canvassed on the subject of the various criteria of social progress, it may be said that it is a subject on which there can be more than one opinion, the diversity being all the more justified because of its numerous aspects. The different definitions themselves bear testimony to the diversity and complexity of the subject. Society is the organization or system of social relationships. These social relations are more than merely physical or material in as much as they are also intellectual and spiritual. These social relationships do not exist in a vacuum. They are subject to the social continuity in which they exist and are always susceptible to direct and indirect influences that have their origin in political, economic and other conditions that constitute the social flux. Hence, in social progress it is of the essence that some progress must also be made in these spheres. This is an outlook that smells of synthesis and complete comprehension, a broad mental outlook. It has been indicated earlier also that this should accord adequate importance to all values: biological, intellectual and spiritual. And yet, it is not possible to fully determine the various criteria of social progress because as man develops intellectually and spiritually, his concepts of social progress are addressed with even greater insight. This will have the effect of rendering progress a concept which is itself liable to change and progress, thereby rendered impermanent. Secondly, the positive determination of social progress itself is no simple matter. Is a particular society progressing or has a human society on the whole progressed or is it involved in a process of regression? This is a question that is very difficult to answer with complete assurance as to its validity. The determination of social progress necessitates the presentation of a detailed picture of every sphere of human endeavour and society. This in itself might defy all efforts and render them ineffective and abortive, but even if the magnitude of the problem is successfully harnessed or coped with, it will appear on close examination that progress in all spheres is neither universal nor uniform. While one sphere of society will evince a desirable progress another will show progress in a direction that is far from desirable. In such a state, and it is a very natural condition, it will be difficult to decide finally whether the society has progressed or regressed. In social, economic and technological fields one finds that while some factors show progress, there are other factors that move backwards. All these considerations make the determination of social progress a difficult task. As Farts has said, "The difficulty in demonstrating the fact of progress has become very real as the problem is presented to modern minds. It is possible to prove that the world has become more complex. It is hardly possible to prove that it has become better and quite impossible to prove that it will continue to do so."[3] This assertion by Fans does contain this element of truth that it is difficult to determine in a final form and in a completely satisfying and ultimate manner whether human society has progressed or not, but if the gradation or order of social values be kept in mind, then in any specific small society it is always possible to find out the direction in which change is gravitating. Another important factor is the difference of opinion regarding the criteria of social progress is that all thinkers are not agreed and unanimous regarding the aims and objects of progress. Some regard it as economic, while others aim at intellectual progress only to be outdone by those who would have society aim at the emancipation of religion but only if they convince some who deprive religion of any value and meaning whatsoever. In this controversy it is not possible to put forward any unifying principle that can be hoped to win the applause of everyone, nor does it appear to be very desirable to do so. Values are ideally determined, hence, it is only natural that there should be difference of opinion in this regard. But if attention is paid and the matter carefully looked into it will appear that the controversy is not so great and not so pointed as to render the various points of view contradictory. It can be generally acknowledged that social progress involves the overall progress of society in all its spheres and that in this overall progress the various aspects of society have not an equal but a proportionate importance.

PRINCIPLES OF SOCIAL PROGRESS

In the context of opinions upon social progress and its various conditions, it is possible to discuss some of the prevalent theories regarding the principles of social progress.

3. Quoted by Park and Burgess in, *An Introduction to the Science of Sociology*, p. 916.

1. Karl Marx's Theory. The most important principle regarding social progress was laid down by the famous economist Karl Marx. Marx has put forward the economic interpretation of human history. According to him, the aims of human society are essentially economic and a perusal of these economic aims can lead to a definite idea whether society is progressing or not. According to Marx, the different aspects of social life are fashioned by economic factors. The form and kind of production and distribution determine the nature of social organisation, structure and social institutions. In this way, according to Karl Marx, human civilization can be elaborated upon in economic terms.

This principle enunciated by Karl Marx contains the truth that social progress is impossible without economic progress. But then economic progress itself is not the end. Economic development is only a means in the life of both the society and the individual and its end is intellectual and spiritual development of both. It cannot be denied that economic factors exert considerable influence upon human life but then it is equally true that psychological factors have even more influence upon human life than the economic factors. Hence, Karl Marx's theory proves to be one-sided when applied to social progress.

2. Anthropological-geographical Theory. The second important theory regarding social progress is the anthropological-geographical theory. According to Buckle, two factors predominantly help in social progress, one of which is the external or geographical factor while the other is the international or related to human beings. Both these factors have shared much of the burden of mail. Great civilizations have come into being only because of man's progress and intellectual superiority and nature's generosity. This theory propounded by Buckle gives a good semblance of truth but it falls short due to its failure to prescribe the criteria whereby social progress is determined. It does no more than describe the conditions of social progress or the circumstances in which social progress is likely to occur, and even in this, the theory fails to account for all the factors that contribute to social progress. Human society is so complex and the history of human civilization has emphasized the importance of so many varied factors that its division into two factors in this manner or its being attributed to two causes smells of oversimplification.

3. Psychological Theory. Another principle that explains social conduct is called the psychological theory. Exponents of this theory emphasize the role played by psychological factors in social progress. According to this theory, sentiments have made an important contribution to the development of social life. The present progress of human society is the outcome of man's superior intellectual capacities. It is through the use of his intellectual capabilities that he has discovered the secrets of nature and has employed this knowledge for his own development and progress. According to this theory, the psychological factors are the predominant factors that fashion the shape and direction of social progress while natural causes are only of secondary importance.

The comments made in connection with the two previously described theories or principles of social progress apply also to the psychological principles. This principle is not wrong but it, too, is one-sided and inadequate. It achieves no more than pointing out some of the conditions of social progress, failing to enumerate a number of other conditions that are of vital importance. Secondly, it fails to afford any insight into social aims and objects.

4. Psycho-sociological Theory. Yet another theory concerned with the principles of social progress is adorned with the name of psycho-sociological theory. Its name bears testimony to the fact that this theory co-ordinates the sociological and the psychological viewpoints. This theory describes many factors as of vital importance where social progress is concerned. It includes all factors, be they geographical, economic or biological.

QUESTIONS FOR EXERCISE

1. Define social progress and bring out clearly its main aspects.
2. Indicate the main lines of Human Progress.
3. What is social progress? Indicate the criteria adopted to assess social progress.
4. What do you understand by social progress? Distinguish it from social evolution.

CHAPTER 11

Social Interactions and Social Processes

What is Social Interaction?

Society is a web of social relationships. Social relations are established through mutual behaviour of and intercourse between the various members of society, males and females, children, old men and young juveniles. The behaviour takes the form of mutual activity. In this way, social relationships depend upon the social interaction of the constituent members of society. Some or the other kind of social interaction is set into motion whenever two of its members come into contact. When a man and woman come into contact there may be attraction or repulsion, co-operation or conflict. The various groups in society are always undergoing strains of mutual conflict, competition, co-operation and synthesis or other activity. All these are social interactions.

Society is a web of social relationships. The term social interaction is applicable only to the action which produces some definite influence upon social relations that exist among human beings. Hence, social interaction serves to establish mental relation among persons. Individuals tend to be influenced by the ideas, achievements and emotions of other people. Thus, social interaction Is the reciprocal influence mutually exerted by human beings through interstimulation and mutual response. Man lives in a social environment. It is only natural to him to have some relations with his fellow members of society. It is equally essential for him to have mental as well as physical contacts with such people. Every person influences other people according to his status in society and the role which is assigned to him. These activities on contact and communication are given the name of social interaction. Social interaction is communicative interaction. Interaction is the simplest form of social process. In any society, all the constituents, be they individuals or groups of individuals, are perpetually engaged in solving problems and attaining some predetermined ends. In the process of performing both these functions they also influence each other. This influence is social interaction. The name social Interaction can be applied to all those actions that either serve to establish some social relationships or to Introduce some change and modification in the existing social relationship. Some of the more important definitions of social interaction are as follows:

1. *Gist* "Social interaction is the reciprocal influence that human beings exert on each other through interstimulation and response."

2. *A. W. Green*. "By social interaction is meant the mutual influence that individuals and groups have upon one another in their attempts to solve problems and in their striving towards goals."

3. *Gillin and Gillin*. "By social interaction we refer to social relations of all sort in function — dynamic social relations of all kinds — whether such relations exist between individual and individual, between group and group, and group and individual as the case may be."

4. *Eldredge and Merril*. "Social interaction is thus the general process whereby two or more persons are in meaningful contact as a result of which their behaviour is modified, however slightly."

BASIC CONDITIONS OF SOCIAL INTERACTIONS

It would be evident from the above account of social interaction that there are two basic conditions of social interaction — Social contact and Communication. There can be no social interaction between human individuals in the absence of contact and communication.

Social Contact

Social contact differs from physical or bodily contact, bodily contact being unnecessary for social contact. Social contact can be established through the medium of radio, letters, telephone, telegraphic contact and other media of communication even between people who are separated by thousands of miles of land and water. But social contacts are strengthened by physical contact. While physical contact in the various forms such as hand shaking, embracing, kissing, etc., increases social contact, it also, on the other hand, symbolises the permanence and strength of these social relations. Social contact has its origin in the mutual response between various groups or individuals. It is social contact that is the beginning point of social interaction.

Social contacts can be positive as well as negative. Positive social contacts tend to precipitate matters towards benevolence, co-operation, mutual understanding and assimilation. Negative social contacts create hatred, disregard of each other and conflict. Similarly, when there is direct personal contact between the various parties it is called primary contact. But when this contact takes on an impersonal air and is achieved through the mediation of some or the other agency or individual, it is called secondary. In addition to this simple classification, another sub-division of social contact is the one into the temporary contacts that tend to remain for a short time and into the relatively permanent contacts that are established for a long time and continue to wield their influence.

Communication

Social contacts are always established through the medium of some sense organ. And an object can be perceived by the sense organ only when that object causes communication within that sense organ. Hence, the means of communication are essential adjuncts of social contact. The more important means of communication are the sense organs of man, language, script, gestures, symbols, radio, television, post and telegraph services, newspapers, television, etc. In fact, society cannot even be conceived without communication.

Importance of the Study of Social Interaction

The very roots of society are based upon social interactions. Hence, the study of social interactions is not only important but. actually inevitable or essential for the sociologists. Social interaction is the basis of not only society but of culture as well. Both culture and society are the products of social interaction. Thus, society has risen out of social interactions. Its very existence is impossible without social interactions. They form the ground on which culture arises and thus ensure its continued existence. Hence, the study of social interactions should in fact be the first step to the study of society itself. An understanding of social interactions is an essential prerequisite for the understanding of social relations.

Forms of Social Interaction

Different thinkers differ in their opinion regarding the number of forms. that social interactions take. Some go so far as to count no more than two forms of social interactions — conjunctive and disjunctive. Most of the sociologists have accepted the following major forms of social interaction:

1. Competition
2. Conflict
3. Accommodation
4. Assimilation
5. Co-operation

Of these, the first two are disjunctive while the last three are conjunctive. Now these various forms of social interaction may be individually studied.

DISJUNCTIVE PROCESSES

Conflict and Competition

Both conflict and competition are basic social processes that are disintegrative in nature. Both are forms of non-cooperation and opposition. But they also differ from each other in considerable respects. The fundamental differences between conflict and competition can be understood from the following table:

Competition	*Conflict*
1. Continuous process.	1. Intermittent process.
2. Impersonal.	2. Personal.
3. Unconscious.	3. Conscious.
4. Based on non-violence.	4. Violence employed.
5. Both combatants gain.	5. Both combatants suffer loss.
6. Productive.	6. Non-productive.
7. Encourages hard work.	7. Discourages efforts.
8. Separates into very small division.	8. Divides into large divisions.
9. Observes social laws.	9. Disregards social laws.
10. Achievement of aim the primary object.	10. Prevention of damage the prime consideration.
11. The aim is self-interest.	11. The aim is self-interest with loss to opponent.

COMPETITION

What is Competition?

According to Biesanz and Biesanz competition is a striving of two or more persons for the same goal. Bogardus has maintained that competition is a contest to obtain something which does not exist in a quantity sufficient to meet the demand of everyone. It is an impersonal, unconscious, and continuous struggle between individuals or groups for things which are limited in supply. There can be no competition in getting air and water. The following characteristics determine the nature of competition:

1. Competition is an Unconscious Action. Competition is concerned with the subject and not the individuals. Therefore, besides the knowledge of the subject, it is an unconscious action.

2. Competition is an Impersonal Action. The difference between competition and struggle is that the competition is always impersonal whereas struggle is personal.

3. Competition is a Continuous Activity. Competition never ends. It always tends to increase, *e.g.*, competition in the acquisition of wealth.

4. Competition is a Universal Action. Competition is found in each society as people everywhere wish to procure things which are limited in supply. Moreover, competition is found in every class of people, *viz.*, students, producers, labourers, artists, etc. It enables the development of both the individual and the nation.

Forms of Competition

Competition takes four main forms, *viz.*, economic, cultural, social and racial. In addition to these there is one more form of competition, *i.e.*, political which is nevertheless important.

1. Economic Competition. It is found in production, exchange and distribution as well as consumption in the field of economic activities.

2. Cultural Competition. Cultural competition is found among different cultures. Taking the history of any country, it can be seen that there has always been a great difference in the cultures of the natives and the invaders.

3. Social Competition. To get a high status in society, everybody seems to be engaged in competitive activity.

4. Racial Competition. In South Africa, there was an intense competition between the black and white races.

5. Political Competition. In all countries competition is obvious between the various political parties, and even between the different members of a political party to obtain political power. Similarly, in the international circle too, there is always diplomatic competition between different nations.

In addition to the above mentioned forms, there are two other forms of competition, the personal and the impersonal. Personal competition is often termed rivalry while impersonal competition is found to occur between groups and not individual members.

Importance of Competition

Competition plays an important role in the life of persons, society and other groups. It increases efficiency. While co–operation helps to do things, competition assures that they will be done well. Social status and competition are very closely associated. In fact, competition has an important hand in causing a rapid development in individual and society, as its chief aim is to move towards progress. It aims largely towards the goal of preserving or improving their status. But however advantageous it may be, it should not be left uncontrolled, because then its disadvantages will overcome the advantages and the result will be harmful to the society.

CONFLICT

What is Conflict?

Competition gradually changes into rivalry which in turn changes into conflict. Thus, conflict is a modified form of struggle. The basic difference between competition and conflict has already been discussed earlier in this chapter. Conflict comprehends a desire for violence, a desire for revenge. It is a deliberate attempt to oppose, resist or coerce the will of the opponent. Some of the more popular definitions of conflict are as follows:

1. *Gillin and Gillin.* "Conflict is the social process in which individuals or groups seek their ends by directly challenging the antagonist by violence or the threat of violence."

2. *A. W. Green.* "Conflict is the deliberate attempt to oppose, resist or coerce the will of another or others."

3. *Park and Burgess.* "Conflict evokes the deepest emotions and strongest passions and enlists the greatest concentration of attention and of efforts.

As a process conflict is the very antithesis of co-operation. The functions of a person or a group of persons are hindered due to conflict. Sometimes, individuals try to destroy their opponents by resorting to means of violent action. But it is not essential that violent actions should always be associated with conflict. Sometimes, the conflict carries a legal sanction and occurs peacefully. For example, the Indian National Army employed violent measures to fight against the British Government, under the guidance and leadership of Netaji. In elections, the various candidates contesting the elections apply legal measures, but sometimes, they violate the constitutional rights of others and for doing so they resort to violent means. Conflict arises due to contradictory aims. For example, the primary aim of Indians was to strengthen the country while the British people were exploiting the Indians when India was under their rule. So naturally there arose a conflict. Contradictory methods also lead to conflict. One party dislikes the method of the other party. But the goals of different parties approximate to each other since all the parties are trying to gain ascendency over the other.

Briefly, the following characteristics of conflict are particularly important:

1. Conflict is a Conscious Action. In conflict, the competitors try to defeat each other consciously. It evokes the deepest emotions and strongest passions and results into great concentration of attention and effort.

2. Conflict is a Personal Activity. Conflict is raised to defeat the antagonist and not to achieve any particular goal. The chief means of conflict is to cause harm or serve loss to the antagonist.

3. Conflict Lacks Continuity. Conflict is not a continuous process, it occurs intermittently.

4. Conflict is Universal. Conflict is found in each and every part of human society.

Forms of Conflict

Conflict is a universal process. Broadly speaking its chief forms are the following:

1. Personal Conflict. In it the conflict arises between different ideas and aims. For example, there arises conflict when two professors of a college contest with each other to get into the Principal's chair which is not large enough to hold both at the same time.

2. Class Conflict. Conflict arises between the classes having different interests. For example, Marx rightly said that a conflict is inevitable between the labourers and the capitalists.

3. Caste Conflict. Superiority complex has caused a conflict between different castes in India and this process is still continuing.

4. Racial Conflict. Sometimes, a particular race somehow manages to acquire the notion that it is the best fitted of all human races to dominate and govern the world and that this would do the world a lot of good. Others, particularly the governed, usually do not feel inclined to accept this notion and the result is the inevitable conflict. For example, the notion of Nordicism led to a prolonged conflict between the Germans and the Jews, much to the detriment of the latter.

5. Group Conflict. In politics, the different groups having different interests and motives try to fulfil their own interests and this leads to conflict. In this way, group conflict can arise anywhere.

6. International Conflict. Sometimes there occurs serious international conflict when a nation tries to suppress the other to fulfil some particular aim.

In economic field, there is always a conflict between the labourers and the mill-owners and further even between the mill owners themselves. In this way, there may be a conflict among the persons engaged in the same field of activity and between individuals engaged in various different activities.

Why is Conflict Universal?

Thus, conflict is universal. But why is it so? Different thinkers have given different reasons. According to Malthus, while the means of subsistence increase in arithmetical progression, the population increases in geometrical progression. This results in the scarcity of means of subsistence in even the most prosperous countries. And then, if the population is not reduced by some natural cause such as floods, pestilences, etc., the wars and conflicts generally occur as the country tries to fulfil its immediate purpose of feeding all the people that it shelters. According to Darwin and his followers, the biological principles of snuggle for existence and survival of the fittest, are the main causes which lead to conflicts. Freud and some other psychologists believe that the innate instinct for aggression in human beings is the main cause of conflicts. Gandhiji and some other religious thinkers are not inclined to believe that man is a lover of conflict by nature but rather prefer to attribute it to selfishness. In fact, each of these various views of the universality of conflict involves a grain of truth, yet each of them fails to comprehend the entire truth. A reduced supply of the means of subsistence will naturally lead to some or the other effort to bridge this gap between supply and demand, and this in turn may lead to conflict, but then conflict may also arise due to ambition, selfishness and a tendency towards aggression. Man by nature may or may not be of a violent turn of mind, but he does necessarily possess the aggressive instinct. But does it mean that as among animals, conflict is essential among human beings as well? If it is so, then one day the human race will completely disappear from the face of the earth because now in the shape of nuclear bombs mankind has got hold of weapons of great destructive potential which are sufficient of destroy the entire human race. If world war breaks out, only a few will survive, and this small number too, will be mostly comprised of disabled individuals.

But the future of mankind is not quite so dark. Both the psychologists and religious thinkers believe that the aggressive tendencies of the human animal can be sublimated through sport and cultural competition etc. It this way, no doubt, conflict cannot be eliminated completely from human life, but it may be changed into a harmless process by way of games and sports which can be used for the emancipation of the human race.

Importance of Conflict

Conflict is very important for both the individuals and society. It needs struggle to solve the social as well as the personal problems. No person can rise without struggling and the higher a person rises, the greater he struggles for it. People have to struggle hard to establish and run the associations, to increase the production of the country, to retain the freedom of the nation and to progress in any sphere of activity. Class conflicts are the chief characteristics of all societies now-a-days. In addition to political conflicts, caste conflicts, racial conflicts, international conflicts, religious conflicts, community conflicts, family conflicts, business conflicts, wars etc., are well-known to everyone. These conflicts should be put under some control otherwise it will be very difficult for the individuals and the society to progress. Now, with the help of science, human race has reached a stage where it is possible for it to achieve a complete destruction of forms of life on earth whenever any strong conflict breaks out. In fact, for the progress and development of the human race, the conflicts are essential, but they should be to eliminate the bad elements in mankind. Co-existence is not enough to check conflicts, what is actually needed is active co-operation.

CONTRAVENTION

What is Contravention?

While discussing the disjunctive social interactions, it is also relevant to say something about contravention. Contravention comes in between competition and conflict, being an intermediate stage. Contravention is characterised by two chief features, the state of bewilderment and covert hatred. For example, sometimes one dislikes a particular person as one does not consider him good, but nevertheless one cannot declare him bad because one lacks the reason and evidence for so drastic an action. In such a situation one is usually bewildered and confused, a feeling of covert hatred arises in him and he makes efforts to avoid others. In this way, contravention, too, is a disjunctive action, though it is not as obvious as conflict and as unconscious as competition.

Forms of Contravention

Normally, there are three forms of contravention — Contravention of generations, Contravention of sex and Parliamentary contravention. The contravention of generations refers to the contravention that is found to exist between any two generations. It is often seen that the young display dislike for the views of their elders who reciprocate the feeling with equal enthusiasm. The contravention of sexes expresses the tendency of regarding members of the other sex with mistrust and suspicion. Parliamentary contravention refers to the contraventions between the majority and the minority opinions in Parliament.

CONJUNCTIVE PROCESSES: ACCOMMODATION

What is Accommodation?

Accommodation is the first step from conflict to reconciliation and co-operation. Man cannot always remain conflicting with and struggling against his environment and all the people who surround him. Even if he sometimes fails to agree with them, he usually has to tolerate or to suffer them. One has to come to some sort of understanding with life. Without it, life is no path strewn with rose petals. Coming to an understanding or common agreement is accommodation. This is an unconscious process that is forever active in some or the other spheres of life. The life of the adolescent in the family is an interesting and instructive example of accommodation. The adolescent does harbour feelings and sentiments that are at variance with those of his parents, yet he chooses to mould himself after their fashion. He obeys them. He offers them his respect even if his heart rebels at the very thought of doing so. Another interesting and probably even more suggestive case is that of accommodation that a newly wed bride has to achieve when she has to adjust to an entire set of people unknown to her who constitute her new family immediately after her marriage. She must forbear from making any remarks that may plunge the family into strife and grief. It is only natural that she should feel irritated by the constant attentions of all those around her but she has no choice but to come to an understanding and the terms with them in order that conflict and struggle may be avoided. Accommodation is the art of living harmoniously. Among living beings, man possesses the ability of accommodation in the highest degree. It is this that accounts for his now being the most powerful being on this earth. This process of accommodation is to be seen in every sphere of human life. The people from the rural areas accommodate themselves when placed in an urban situation, A person must accommodate himself in every new situation in which he may happen to find himself, be it a new country, a new society, new caste, social circle, neighbourhood, or any other sphere. Accommodation is also a condition. It is a condition or state of mental and social understanding and peace. Every individual is born under a particular set of circumstances some of which are good and some bad. The individual must accommodate himself to them otherwise he forfeits his right of life. Whatever the energy of which he may be possessed, he cannot change all circumstances. There are some that will force him to bow down and change himself. He does not run from conflict but only delays it so that life may continue and that he may retain his own existence. In brief, accommodation consists in the avoiding and delaying of conflict with disagreeable circumstances. In this process there is neither complete conformity with the circumstances nor any conflict. The contending forces are adjusted to balance. In this way, it is the very foundation of a social organisation. In its absence, society cannot maintain its balance, Some of the more popular definitions of accommodation are as follows:

1. *Reuter and Hart.* "As a process, accommodation is the sequence of steps by which persons are reconciled to changed conditions of life through the formation of habits and attitudes made necessary by the changed conditions themselves."

2. *Biesanz and Biesanz.* "In one sense, accommodation is the basis of all formal social organisation."

3. *M. E. Johnes.* "In one sense, accommodation may be said to be an agreement to disagree."

4. *MacIver and Page.* "The term accommodation refers particularly to the process in which man attains a sense of harmony with his environment."

5. *Park and Burgess.* "Accommodation is the natural issue of conflict. In an accommodation the antagonism of the hostile elements is, for the time being, regulated and conflict disappears as overt action, although it remains latent as a potential force."

Accommodation and Adjustment

Accommodation is not adjustment. The two processes differ in the following respects:

Accommodation	*Adjustment*
1. Unconscious activity. 2. Both external and internal. 3. Is a later stage after adjustment.	1. Conscious activity. 2. Only external. 3. Is the first step towards accommodation.

To illustrate, if a nation is attacked by some other nation which has aggressive designs upon it, it first repels the attack vigorously but when it is faced with investable defeat it adjusts to these circumstances. This adjustment then leads to gradual accommodation and toleration between the victor and the vanquished.

Accommodation and Adaptation

Adaptation is concerned with the principle of natural selection which has resulted in significant changes in man and animals.

Accommodation and adaptation differ from each other on the following grounds:

1. While accommodation is a social process, adaptation is a biological process.
2. While accommodation is an outcome of conflict adaptation is the natural result of competition.
3. While accommodation is a process of learning, adaptation is the ultimate result of the process of biological evolution.

The nature of accommodation would be fairly obvious from the foregoing description of it. It has the following characteristics:

1. Accommodation is the Natural Result of Conflict. Accommodation arises out of conflict and keeps it from being actually put into practice. If there is no conflict, there can be no question of any accommodation.

2. Accommodation is Mainly an Unconscious Activity. The process of accommodation continues to act in an unconscious condition. Man's social environment is constantly changing and it also continually influences the individual since an individual is constantly engaged in accommodation himself consciously and subconsciously to new circumstances as they occur.

3. Accommodation is a Universal Activity. The process of all, accommodation is forever active everywhere in human society.

4. Accommodation is a Mixture of Love and Hatred. Love leads to co-operation while hatred leads to conflict. Both love and hatred are constituents of accommodation.

5. Accommodation is a Continuous Process. The process of accommodation is forever active in the individual's life and every sphere of society.

Methods of Accommodation

The following are the main methods of accommodation:

1. Yielding to Coercion. When forced by the use of physical or other power, most individuals or groups yield and accommodate.

2. Compromise. In the case of compromise, groups or individuals who wield equal power are persuaded to sacrifice some of their interests and to coexist in peace in order to avoid conflict.

3. Arbitration and Conciliation. Arbitration is employed when two groups are bent on conflict but can be dissuaded from their evil designs by the interference of a third party not concerned with either of the two contestants. The decisions of this third party are binding on both the others. In the case of conciliation, the third party does not put forward any decisions but some suggestions aiming at the avoidance of conflict. To accept these suggestions is at the discretion of the two parties. It does not carry the compulsion that arbitration carries.

4. Toleration. Toleration is the method of accommodation in which the two contesting parties view the stand of the other party with sympathy and try to understand the other's viewpoint and patiently bear the differences that exist between them. This is one of the important methods of accommodation.

5. Conversion. When any individual or group fails to come to terms with some specific circumstance, then accommodation can also be achieved by changing his own situation according to his own inclinations. In this way, when some Hindus could not suffer the restrictions of caste, they thought it fit to quit the religion and to adopt the Muslim or Christian religion. This change gave them an opportunity to do what they wished in their new circumstances.

6. Sublimation. In this method, the conflicting groups give vent to their tendencies of aggression and conflict in a manner that is harmless to anyone else and also obviates conflict.

7. Rationalisation. When any individual wants to avoid conflict with the antagonistic force and to retain its own interest and objectives, then instead of deciding to fulfil these objectives immediately or to postpone them to the future the individual or the group devises ways and means to understand the existing conditions better. In this manner people try to validate their own conduct and methods. People reconcile themselves to their poverty by attributing it to God's will. The student who fails in the examination finds it more pleasing to find fault with the examiner's evaluation of his performance rather than with his own effort.

Accommodation is very important in modern society. Information, education, propaganda, political and constitutional pressure, various organisations and cultural relations; organisations for mutual exchange between various castes, races, nations, religions, etc., law courts, police, state, organisational committees social workers, psychiatrists and psycho-analysts, etc., all play important parts in the process of accommadation. All of these have served to make accommodation simple but the process of accommodation is highly complex.

ASSIMILATION

What is Assimilation?

Assimilation is a form of social adjustment. In this process the individual or group begins to absorb slowly and gradually, somewhat unconsciously, the new circumstances in which it finds itself. It results in the modification of social attitudes. For example, in many parts of India, the Hindus and Muslims have become so intimate and well acquainted with each other that they have assimilated many points of each other's culture into their own and have made them integral part of their own social conduct. Modern American society is a poignant example of the assimilation of different cultures and societies. The very process of assimilation has become immeasurably more comprehensive with an unusual spurt in the development and invention of the means of transportation and communication whose direct impact is felt in increased social contact and considerable propagation of ideas and thoughts, both of which are essential for assimilation. Assimilation is both a process and a state. It is a cultural process. When different cultures come into contact, originally it is the sentiment of mutual conflict that is most prominent but when they gradually assimilate elements from each other, they develop a more tolerant approach towards each other. This is the process of assimilation. When different cultures get the opportunity of combining with each other promoted by feelings of kindness and tolerance of each other, each absorbs many features of the other within itself. In this, the process of assimilation is set into motion. A similar process of assimilation is evident in the relations between individual and society, husband and wife, members of the family, social institutions, associations and communities, etc. Some of the more important definitions of assimilation are as follows:

1. *Bogardus.* Assimilation is a process whereby attitudes of many persons are united and thus develop into a unified group."
2. *Biesanz and Biesanz.* "Assimilation is the social process whereby individuals and groups come to share the same sentiments, values and goals."

3. *Park and Burgess.* "Assimilation is a process of interpenetration and fusion in which persons and groups acquire the memories, sentiments and attitudes of other persons or groups and, by sharing their experience and history, are incorporated in a common cultural life."

4. *Ogburn and Nimkoff.* "Assimilation is the process whereby individuals or groups once dissimilar become similar, that is, become identified in their interests and outlook."

In terms of culture, assimilation denotes conformity and uniformity in respect of culture. It is a process of interpenetration and fusion of memories, sentiments, and attitudes of persons or groups by sharing each other's experience and history. It is the process by which dissimilar individuals or groups become similar. It is a process in which attitudes of many persons are united to form a unified group. Like socialization it, too, is a process of learning but it takes place when the individual comes into contact with other cultures outside his own family. The process of socialization, on the other hand, is usually limited to the family and the school. In the same way, assimilation differs from amalgamation, which is a physiological and biological process that results in a hybrid. Assimilation is a social and psychological process which results in the promotion of cultural unity. It helps in creating basic changes in the viewpoint and personality of the individual or group. Perfect assimilation results in complete social integration.

Factors Promoting Assimilation

The following factors promote assimilation:

1. Toleration. Intimate and close social relations are essential for assimilation to occur and these are impossible if there is no tolerance. It is only when people who believe in one culture are prepared to tolerate the proximate existence of people who uphold the cause of a different culture that they can be influenced by the culture that the other upholds. It is here that the process of assimilation finds its root.

2. Intimate Social Relationships. The next factor after toleration that helps the process of assimilation is intimate and close social relationships and contacts. The process of assimilation progresses in direct proportion to the growth of social relationships.

3. Amalgamation. Assimilation is farther encouraged by amalgamation, since amalgamation leads to the creation of blood relationships. Blood being thicker than water, these relationships are more intimate and strong and they wield their influence upon people by making them impress each other, thus accelerating the process of assimilation.

4. Cultural Similarity. If two cultures resemble each other in some vital respects, then the intimacy and toleration between their members for each other is of a higher order. This, too, encourages assimilation.

5. Equality of Opportunity of Economic Progress. Economic inequality leads to jealousy, hatred and conflict. If people get the same opportunities for economic progress as their neighbours, social intimacy increases and assimilation progresses.

Factors Hindering Assimilation

The following factors counteract assimilation and hinder its progress:

1. Strong Feelings of Superiority and Inferiority. People have nothing but hatred and disgust for each other if they harbour strong feelings of superiority and inferiority. They even decline to establish any relationship among themselves. The outcome of this is that they learn little if anything from each other, avoiding mutual contact and influence, as, they do. This naturally hinders assimilation.

2. Isolation. Just as intimacy helps to promote assimilation, isolation tends to hinder it. Living in isolation prevents the formation of social contacts and relations. Hence, the very question of mutual influence is precluded from the field of practice.

3. Difference of Colour and Physiological Characteristics. People distinguish between themselves on the basis of the colour of their skins and their physiological characteristics. One can see differences and discrimination between the white and the black or negro races almost everywhere in the world. There are very few occasions for mutual contact between the whites and negroes. The discrimination leads to the whites considering themselves somehow superior to the black people and looking upon all social contacts with them as degrading. This naturally becomes an obstacle to assimilation.

4. Cultural Difference. Just as cultural similarity promotes assimilation, cultural dissimilarity tends to hinder the process of assimilation.

5. Domination and Subordination. If some people manage to dominate others, they come to think themselves superior to the people they dominate and do not consider any reason for establishing social relationships with them on an equal footing. The Atyans who came to India as victors looked upon the native races as inferior, whom they abhorred. In this way, when people lose their independence and become slaves, their thoughts naturally turn to independence, and a corollary of this is hatred for their persecutors and rulers. Thus, social relations do not grow in either condition, and assimilation becomes difficult.

6. Social Persecution. Social persecution, exploitation and injustice only lead to increased conflict between the exploiters and the exploited. Whatever the justification for this conflict, it prevents the growth of social intimacy and consequently that of assimilation.

Co-operation

What is Co-operation?

Co-operation is the form of social interaction in which two or more persons work for the achievement of a common end. For example, the aim of all the teachers in a college is the maintenance of a high standard of education and creating and maintaining a respectable position of the college in social circles. Hence, they all co-operate with each other. If a teacher does not care for maintaining a high level of education in the college or to increase its honour and respect in society and desires to cause indiscipline and disorder in the institution then he does not co-operate with the other teachers. The government of state runs successfully only when the administrator and the administered extend their full co-operation to each other. If the administered choose to change the administrators, they withdraw their co–operation. It was the same process that led the Indians, under the guidance of Mahatma Gandhi, to refuse to co-operate with the British government. Thus, the process of co-operation involves two elements, those of common end and organised efforts. For example, the teachers in an educational institution combine and organise their effort to maintain both a high level of education within the institution and its respected place in society outside. Some of the more popular definitions of co-operation are as follows:

1. *Merrill and Eldrege.* "Co-operation thus may be defined as a form of social interaction wherein two or more persons work together to gain a common end."
2. *Fairchild.* "Co-operation is the process by which individuals or groups combine their efforts, in a more or less organised way, for the attainment of common objectives."

Importance of Co-operation

The importance of co-operation is made abundantly clear by the simple reflection that the very existence of society depends upon the mutual co-operation between the male and female of the species. It is by mutual co-operation that men and women procreate and bring up their offspring. The co-operation of the members of a family is essential for the socialization of the child and the development of his various potential capacities. Outside the family, the child is influenced by his contacts with his teachers and his colleagues at school. After completing his education when the individual enters upon some profession for life he has numerous occasions for co-operating with his fellow beings, and when he enters the holy wedded state, his entire life after it is one long tale of co-operation and mutual agreements, without which a happy marital life is impossible both for the husband and for the wife. The physiological, mental and even the spiritual needs of the individual remain unsatisfied if he does not agree to co-operate with his fellow members of society. Conflict leads to progress but progress is granted permanence only by co-operation. Conflict inspires the individual to progress, but he does so only if he gets co-operation.

Kinds of Co-operation

Most of the sociologists have accepted the following three kinds of co–operation:

1. Primary. Primary co-operation is that which is found in evidence in primary groups such as the family. In this, there is an identity of interests between the individual and the group. The achievement of the interests of the group includes the attainment of the individual interests. In this way, in the co–operation with primary groups, there is no distinction between the aims and the means used for their achievement. Every member considers co-operation essential in each and every condition.

2. Secondary. Secondary form of co-operation is found in secondary groups, whence it derives its name. One finds co-operation among economic, political, social and religious groups, factories, governments and societies and religious associations because of an identity of interests. These interests cannot be achieved if the individual strives for them in his individual capacity. Hence, secondary co-operation is considered essential.

3. Tertiary. Primary and secondary co-operation is characteristic of individual person, while tertiary co-operation characterises the social interaction between various big and small social groups. This co-operation leads to the mutual adjustment and adaptation of these groups to each other. In this way, all these three kinds of co-operation are essential for society.

Distinction has also been made between direct and indirect co-operation. This distinction is as follows.

1. Direct. In this, two or more people together pursue the same kind of activity. For example, the harvesting of a crop involves the direct co-operation of many people.

2. Indirect. In this, some people work individually for the attainment of a common end. The various functionaries of a bank, for example, all perform various differing functions, but the total functioning of the bank is made possible only by the performance of these functions, and the co-operation implicit in proper functioning of the bank.

The above mentioned description of the various kinds of co-operation makes it abundantly clear that it is essential for every individual member and group in society. Just as co-operation between individual members of society is very essential so is the co-operation between various groups in society. Of course, this does not imply that there is no place for the other methods of conflict and competition and other equivalent social interactions. Much importance is attached to competition in some gypsy societies, but even in such societies no functioning is possible in the absence of co-operation. In fact, both competition and conflict, besides co-operation, are essential for the progress of society. In peace time, it is only healthy competition that lends an incentive to the people and groups to progress further and to approach new vista. But in war time all individuals and groups of an integrated society become united in their common stand against the enemy and co-operate with each other to victory over it.

INTEGRATION

What is Social Integration?

Society is a dynamic organisation. It is a web of social relationships. Hence, its integration depends upon the organisation of these social relations. Social integration is the harmonizing or unifying of social relations. This does not involve similarity of various elements. What is essential for it is the proper organisation of those elements. The various constituents of society are customs, traditions, ideals, groups, classes, etc. Hence, for these to be social organisation it is essential for these to be organised. But it is not essential that the pattern of this organisation should be uniform and common in every society. Different societies exist in differing geographical environments and undergo different historical incidents with the result that their culture differs from that of other societies. Social organisation differs when culture differs. It is the culture that determines the specific patterns of social organisation within its own societies. In this way, social integration consists in the organisation of the various constituents of society on the basis of specific cultural patterns.

Major Characteristics of Social Integration

The foregoing description offers a glimpse of the major characteristics of social integration which are as follows:

1. Socialization. Socialization is no static condition but a dynamic process. The main characteristics and the most important medium of this dynamic process is the socialization of the individuals in society. Socialization helps the individuals to acquire and develop social qualities and the patterns of social life. This creates a harmony and synthesis in their mutual relationships.

2. Common Aim. The second characteristic of social integration is the general or mutual synthesis of the aims, and objectives of the individuals in society. The bond that ties the members of society together is no other than that of common aims and aspirations.

3. Active Relations between Cultural Elements. As has been pointed out earlier, social integration is based upon the organisation of the elements of culture. Hence, the active relationship between the various cultural elements is an important characteristic of social integration.

Social Integration in a Multicaste and Multilingual Society

Homogeneity is no essential requirement of social integration. Thus, while social integration is difficult in a multi-caste society, it is by no means impossible. What is required is that the social structure of ascending and descending between these castes should be given the form of a dynamic system. Individuals should not experience any obstacle in moving up or down the social scale of caste, despite the fact that the roles of various castes be determined along with their respective social status.

Social integration is the process of organising social relationships. And what is really essential for organising social relations is that the mutual behaviour of individuals should be harmonized and synthesized. Similarity of language is a very great advantage in achieving this harmony of behaviour. Hence, the presence of more than one language in a society will naturally hinder social integration. But the attainment of social integration does not require the elimination of all languages save one. Rather it requires the development of one common language apart from and in addition to these various languages.

QUESTIONS FOR EXERCISE

1. Explain what is social interaction, giving examples.
2. What do you understand by social interaction? Explain with examples.
3. Explain the concept of social process. Analyse the social processes of co–operation and conflict.
4. Describe the nature and importance of social interaction.
5. Describe the main social processes.
6. Explain the meaning of social process. Are both the processes of co–operation and conflict found together in society ?
7. Distinguish between associative and dissociative processes.
8. What are the associative and dissociative interactions? Explain each.
9. Discuss in detail the associative and dissociative processes.
10. Discuss the significance of the process of competition in society.

PART II

SOCIAL CONTROL

CHAPTER 1

Social Organization, Status and Role

Social organization is the organization of society. Society is a web of social relationships. In this way social organization is a system of social relationships. Social relationships are complex. They are composed into numerous small groups. In these groups are individuals. The mutual relationships between individuals are controlled and regulated by institutions and associations. Hence, institutions and associations, along with individuals and groups, form a part of the social organization. Social organisation means the sum total of cultural institutions and their inter-relationships including the body of the unorganised activities characteristic of the group. Thus, the social organisation includes and comprehends the cultural institutions and their inter-relationships in addition to the unorganised activities of the group. To quote Reuter and Hart, "By social organisation is meant the totality of cultural institutions and their inter-relationships together with the body of the unorganized activities."[1]

Society is a vast system. The organisation of this system is the interrelationship of its constituents. The constituents of society are institutions, associations and groups. A society can be described as organised only when all these various organs function smoothly and without friction, and adequately perform their function. In this way, besides being a condition, social organisation is a process as well. In its structure a society is not unlike an organism in which the different parts are so constructed as to coordinate and synchronise with each other in the performance of their respective functions. In much the same way, in an organised society, the various parts function systematically. When the social organisation is disturbed this adjustment is marred and lost. Thus, organisation is the system which meaningfully relates the parts of society to each other and to the whole society. It is social organisation that maintains an active synthesis between the mutual activities of the various units of society.[2] Society has some implicit and explicit objectives for the attainment of which its parts function. Social organisation is

1. Reuter and Hart, *Introduction of Sociology*, McGraw Hill Book Co., Inc., New York, Second Edition, 9th impression (1935), p. 143.
2. "Social organisation is the system by which the parts of society are related to each other and to the whole society in a meaningful way."

—E. Jones, *Basic Sociological Principles* (1949), p. 195.

the system which maintains this activity in its proper form. To quote Elliot and Merrill, "Social organisation is a state of being, a condition in which the various institutions in a society are functioning in accordance with their recognised or implied purposes."[3]

SOCIAL ORGANISATION AND SOCIAL GROUPS

In social organisation the processes of integration and differentiation always continue actively as a result of which large groups are constantly being disintegrated and divided into smaller ones while the smaller ones are integrated into big groups. These are the processes of social organisation. Social organisation is the net result of the interaction of these two forces within social groups. In this way social organisation is based upon social groups. The social group is a part of the social organisation. Social organisation is the organisation in small groups, particularly in those groups which are based on age, blood relationship, occupation, habitation, ownership of property and status. Actually, social organisation can be said to be the pattern of inter-group relationships. The form of mutual relationships of various groups in any society depends upon its social organisation. In this way there is a very intimate relation between social group and social organisation.

CHARACTERISTICS OF SOCIAL ORGANISATION

What are the characteristics or essential elements of social organisation? Much has been said on this subject in sociological circles. The chief characteristics of social organisation may be briefly stated as follows:

1. Unanimity among the Members of Society. The existence of unanimity among the members of society is a feature of social organisation. In its absence conflict will arise between them and social disorganisation will set in. For example, in ancient India the difference between the status of the Brahmins, Kshatriyas and Vaishyas, and the Shudras was very great. The activities of these groups also differed and the ones undertaken by the Shudras were worse than those of the other castes. But this system was unanimously accepted by all and sundry, and hence the social organisation remained impregnable. Later on, when the Brahmins abused their privileged position to the detriment of Shudras whose status deteriorated further, the unanimity of opinion in favour of this system was destroyed and this resulted in the introduction of a note of chaos and disorder into Hindu community.

2. Promptness in Accepting Status and Roles. Unanimity among members of a society can be maintained only so long as people are prompt and ready to accept their status and respective roles within the social organisation. In society it is not possible to apportion roles to all individuals in such a way that everyone gets same and equal work. Just as every cog and wheel has its own position and function in a machine, so are divided the functions of people in society. A body can function only as long as all its various organs perform their respective functions. Much the same can be said of society. In society one comes across differences in the social

---

3. Elliot and Marrill, *Social Disorganisation,* Harper and Bros., New York (1950), p. 4.

status of different individuals who differ in respect of their sex, age, status, physical capability, skill and duties. The roles of individuals are determined on the basis of the social status and role is a feature of social organisation.

3. Control of Society on the Activities of the Individuals. The members of society will be prompt in accepting their status and role only when society has control over them. Society exercises this control through the media of habits, customs, traditions, mores, rituals and institutions. It is this which creates unanimity in society. Social disorganisation starts the moment this control of society is lifted from upon the members.

In this way, unanimity among members, prompt acceptance of their respective roles and status on their part and the control of society upon them are characteristic features of the social organisation.

SOCIAL ORGANISATION AND SOCIAL DISORGANISATION

What is Social Disorganisation?

Society is a web of social relationships. In an organised society these relationships remain organised. In a disorganised society these social relationships exhibit a lack of organisation. The process whereby social relationships become disorganised is known as social disorganisation. Social organisation is inclusive of habits, institutions, associations, etc. In the process of social disorganisation all these become disorganised. In every society each individual has a definite status to which some specific roles attach. When each individual satisfactorily performs the roles which attach to his particular status in society, the society retains its organised character. A society becomes disorganised when these roles become disorderly. In this way, in a state of social disorganisation people forget their duties, the control of social laws diminishes, the balance between the various parts of society is disturbed, social ideals become degenerate and the entire social structure progresses towards a chaotic-state.

Social Organisation and Social Disorganisation

In this way, social disorganisation is the process opposed to social organisation. In an organised society there is a consensus of opinion among members regarding status and roles just as in ancient Hindu society the status and functions of the four varnas — Brahmin, Kshatriya, Vaishya and Shudra — were defined by the varna system and were accepted by everybody. But with the continued disorganisation of Hindu society this common acceptance is disintegrating and only very few are to be seen obeying the varna system. In an organised society all its various parts are in equilibrium and its members derive satisfaction from this condition. In a disorganised society this system is disrupted and one encounters hardship all-round. Explaining the meaning of social disorganisation by comparing it with social organisation Queen, Bodenhafer and Harper have written, "If social organisation means the development of relationships which persons and groups find mutually satisfactory, then disorganisation means their replacement by relationships which bring disappointment, thwarted wishes, Irritation and unhappiness."[4]

Difference between Social Organisation and Disorganisation

Social Organisation	*Social Disorganisation*
1. Unanimity.	1. Multiplicity of opinions.
2. Homogeneity of population.	2. Heterogeneity of population.
3. Mutual faith.	3. Mutual distrust.
4. Similarity in interests and attitudes.	4. Individuality and variety in interests and attitudes.
5. Intelligent behaviour.	5. Hedonistic behaviour.
6. Emphasis on duties.	6. Emphasis on rights.
7. Protection of sacred elements.	7. Degeneration of sacred elements.
8. Sincerity.	8. Ostentation.
9. Peace and happiness.	9. Disturbance and pain.
10. Synthesis between status and functions.	10. Contradiction between status and functions.
11. Clarity of situation and activities.	11. Lack of clarity of situation and activities.
12. Synthesis of mores.	12. Conflict of mores.
13. Synthesis between institutions	13. Conflict between institutions.
14. System in the symbols and tools of relationships.	14. Disorder in tools and symbols.
15. Strong social control.	15. Absence of social control
16. Adjustment between society and individual.	16. Conflict between society and individual.
17. Respect of social laws.	17. Disregard of social laws.
18. Adjustment between the various parts of society.	18. Conflict between the various part of society.

In this way, the process of social disorganisation is completely opposed to the process of social organisation. Social organisation is a tool. Social disorganisation is the disintegration of this tool.

WHAT IS STATUS?

Social organisation consists of status and roles. Most people are accustomed to talking in terms of 'status' while referring to various particular people and qualifying this term by the more common words such as higher and lower. One

4. Queen, Bodenhafer and Harper, *Social Organisation and Social Disorganisation,* Thomas Y. Crowell Co., New York (1935), p. 53.

often hears of an improvement in the status of women, of Shudras, of the Brahmins in Hindu society and of the white and black skinned men and women in Western countries. Now, what is this status? As indicated by the term itself, it implies the status or place of an individual in society. And, what is society? It is a web of social relationships. Hence, social status is the position of an individual within social relationships. As is evident, this can be both high as well as low. Hence, there is an order of social status in society. In Hindu society, Brahmins are much respected and considered superior to other castes besides being awarded many special privileges. Thus, their social status is high. On the other hand, the so-called untouchable castes of Hindu society are given less respect than the Brahmins and have fewer rights. Hence, their low social status.

In Hindu society, the status of the Brahmin is at a higher level than that of the Shudra. The leader is at the top in a group. This status will be his ranking in relation to other positions and will be called high or low accordingly. Social status is to be recognised by a pattern of prestige symbols and actions. For example, within the same college the status of the Principal and the teachers are different. How is this difference in status expressed? All the teaching staff ostensibly respects him and he is greeted wherever he may happen to go. In his presence the teachers leave their chairs and address him in the most respectful terms. This is an example of prestige symbols. Now, consider the pattern of functions. The Principal keeps an eye on the work of each of the teachers, maintains order among them and directs them from time to time, There is a distinct pattern of prestige symbols related to the Principal's status. This pattern differs from the pattern of prestige symbols and actions related to the teachers. Difference in the status of both is evident from this difference in their respective patterns. Some proportion of an individual's respect, prestige and influences is determined by his social status. In a family, the social status of the husband and wife can be gauged from the influence which one has on the other as well as from the prestige or respect that one of them receives from the other. According to this one can measure the difference in the social status of husband and wife that exists in different societies. In the villages of India the status of the Sarpanch is the highest. He is greeted with respect wherever he may chance to wander. In the meetings of the village, he is seated upon the highest pedestal. He mediates in the mutual quarrels of the villagers, who respect his decisions and judgements. In this way, the social status of an individual is that particular position in his relations with other individuals by virtue of which he is the recipient of respect and prestige, and wields influence and which can be recognised by symbols of prestige accruing to him and his actions.

DETERMINATION OF STATUS

How is this status determined? Before going into a detailed discussion of this, it is necessary to know that there are two types of status. Some status are due to office or title such as the post of a college Principal or a village Sarpanch. In the case of such posts, the social status is determined by the office occupied or held, just as the person who occupies the chair of the Principal is accorded the respect in accordance with his position. The rights and duties of a District Magistrate do not change with every new magistrate because these duties, rights and symbols of respect are related to the magistrate's chair or office and are inherent therein. Besides these, some status derive from the family, physical capability, knowledge or skill, etc., of the individual. For example, some roles and respect symbols are related to the post of the country's Prime Minister. But the social status which Mr. Nehru had in India was not due entirely to his occupying the post of Prime Minister but rather to the qualities of his character, patriotism, knowledge and skill. The social status of Dara Singh is due to his skill in wrestling, that of Vinobaji due to social services rendered by him while the social status of Tenzing is due to his having conquered Everest. In this way, physical beauty or prowess, skill in music, scientific knowledge, cultural excellence, etc., or other special qualities attainable by human beings raise the status of an individual. The social status of film actresses is due mainly to their physical charms. When a poor boy studies hard and qualifies for the I. A. S., the status of his family is raised at the same time as his own. The daughter of a rich man loses her status when she is married into a poor family. But factors and causes which determine status change according to the time and place to which they belong. In ancient India it was the varna which determined the social status. In some primitive societies, the social status of an individual bears a direct and proportionate relation to the number of wives he has. The more wives he has, the better is his social status. In some tribes, the social status of woman increases with every new divorce that she gets. According to some the determinant of social status of an individual is his financial condition. This theory is completely one-sided. In India the social status enjoyed by Gandhi, Dayanand, Sri Aurobindo, Rabindranath Tagore, Premchand and others was not due to their economic conditions.

IMPORTANCE OF SOCIAL STATUS

This social status is of much importance for the individual. Marriages in almost every society depend upon social status. It is common knowledge and an everyday occurrence that many marriages are not contracted simply because of differences in the social status or in the financial condition of the parents of the boy and the girl. Everyone wants to marry his sons and daughters into a family on an equal or better footing in society. An individual wins respect in society by virtue of his social status. Every social status is recognisable from symbols of respect. These symbols of respect change along with changes in social status. An increase in the individual's social status entitles him to more respect than before irrespective of whether this increase or improvement is due to marriage, or the acquisition of skill in some art or knowledge or due to his having moved into some higher office. The roles of an individual also change along with his social status. Different roles are conjoined to different social status. Actually, the very object in having differences in the status within society is to facilitate the division of work among people according to their ability. Kingsley Davis correctly observes, "Social inequality is thus an unconsciously evolved device by which societies insure that the most important positions are conscientiously filled by the most qualified persons. Hence, every society, no matter how simple, or complex, must differentiate persons in terms of both prestige and esteem." At some places social status grants prerogatives even in the eyes of the law. For example, in England no one can file a suit against the royal family and in case some involvement does occur, the member of the royal family is always above the commoner. In ancient India the same crimes were punished differently, depending upon the caste of the criminal, in this way, the individual gets many direct and indirect advantages from social status. This constitutes the importance of status as the basis of social organisation.

THE CONCEPT OF ROLE

Historically speaking, the concept of role was first introduced by Pareto in 1916. It was he who first recognized sociological significance of the labels such as lawyers, physicians, engineers artists, etc., which indicate their roles. For Pareto the recognition of labels was a step in the special analysis of social elites. In 1920 Max Weber more generally and explicitly analysed the methodological issues involved in the classification of human beings. He pointed out that the understanding of the origin of a society must be preceded by a functionally-oriented investigation. It is necessary to know as to what kind of typical action leads to such classification. From 1925 onwards the term role was more and more used by the American sociologists such as W. I. Thomas, E. W. Burgess and others. The first explicit formulation of the term role was advanced by George Mead in his book Mind, Self and Society published in 1934. Ralph Linton formulated the concept in anthropology in his book The Study of Man, in 1936. Since then the term role is being widely used by anthropologists, sociologists and psychologists. A most systematic treatment of this concept has been presented by Talcott Parsons, Shils and Balesand in their work Working Paper in the Theory of Action, published in 1953. Though some psychologists have demanded the invention of a better term in place of the concept of role, it has not been actually done so far. According to T.M. Newcomb, "The concept of role is not very suitable because of its dramatic and literary connotation and the figure-of-speech use it encourages."[5] S. F. Nadel shares Newcomb's misgiving about the loose and confused use of the term role. He, therefore, devotes himself to the analysis of the problems of role analysis.

Definition of Role

1. *Hobbs and Blank.* "Social roles are part and parcel of an individual's behaviour when interacting with other people in various situations. Every social situation has a role expectancy for us to fulfil."[6]

2. *D. Popenoe.* "Role is a set of expectations and behaviours associated with a specific position in a social system."[7]

5. R. H. Roher and Muzafer Sherif (Eds.) *Social Psychology at the Crossroads,* 1961, Article by T. M. Newcomb, p. 39.

6. Donald A. Hobbs and Stuart J. Blank, *Sociology and the Human Experience,* New York, John Wiley, 1978, p. 58.

7. Popenoe, D., *Sociology,* Prentice Hall, 1977, New Jersey, p. 507.

3. *Ralph Linton.* "A role represents the dynamic aspect of a status...When he puts the rights and duties which constitute the status into effect, he is performing a role. Role and status are quite inseparable, and the distinction between them is only academic interest."[8]

4. *S.F. Nadel.* "As already indicated, the role concept is basically a type of class concept. Like the class concept of Logic it labels and brings together numbers of individuals, human beings in our case — in virtue of certain properties they have in common."[9]

5. *Ex-definitions.* "The role concept has to do with behaviour or differential behaviour, and the characteristics constituted by it."[10]

6. *S. Talcott Parsons.* "The role is status translated into action, the role being the processal aspect of status, as status is the positional aspect of the role."[11]

Problems of Role Analysis

Explaining the importance of the concept of role, S.F. Nadel has pointed out, "Its usefulness, in simplest terms, lies in the fact that it provides a concept intermediary between 'society' and 'individual'. It operates in that strategic area where individual behaviour becomes social conduct, and where the qualities and inclinations distributed over a population are translated into differential attributes required by or exemplifying the obtaining social norms."[12] Thus, role provides a strategic area, an intermediary concept. Societies rest on rules or norms. Thus, they depend upon what Nadel calls, "constancies of behaviour" These constancies of behaviour are known as institutions and groupings. These again, can be further analyzed into constituents such as castes, goals, expectations, rights and duties; etc. The concept of role bridges the gap between society and individuals. It refers to individuals seen as bundles of qualities. The bundle corresponds to a class or type concept. Although the concept of role has been criticized by some scholars, no better substitute has been provided.

According to Nadel the role concept is basically a tyre of class concept. It labels and brings together a number of individuals. It always refers to existing real human beings. These human beings are classified broadly according to two types of properties: (1) Contingent properties which include physiological characteristics over which the individual has no control, such as sex, age, physiological characteristics, etc. (2) Achievement properties which the individual is free to assume and aim at, such as interests, attitudes, proficiencies, etc.

The Role Versus the Class

S. F. Nadel has pointed out the following distinctions between the concept of role and the concept of class:

---

8. Ralph Union in Marcelbw Truzzi, (Ed.) *Sociology : The Classic Statements,* New York, Random House, 1971, p. 92.

9. Ralph Linton, *The Study of Man,* p. 114.

10. Nadel, S. F., *The Theory of Social Structure,* Cohn and West Ltd., London 1969, p. 22.

11. Talcott Parsons, *The Social System,* p. 25.

12. Nadel, S. F., *The Theory of Structure,* Cohen and West Ltd. London, 1969, p. 20.

1. The role concept has to do with differential behaviour and the characteristics constituted by it. The classification in various classes depends upon contingent properties.

2. Roles materialize only in an interaction schedule. Their behavioural characteristics appear both in the active and passive voice. The class characteristics, on the other hand, are generally passive.

3. Role is purposive, repetitive and constant. This condition does not apply to classes. In the words of Nadel, "But while the class concept refers merely to accidental just so likenesses which however constant, could be quite otherwise, the role concept refers essentially to a lawful or normative conformity, in the sense that the shared attributes exhibited by individuals are understood to follow from the rules of the society or to involve them in some manner."[13]

4. The class concept requires the respective individuals to share only one property which serves as the differential. The role concept requires the presence of a series of interconnected characteristics.

Methods of Defining the Roles[14]

According to Nadel there are three interconnected methods being used for defining the rules or norms underlying a particular role. These methods are used by anthropologists and sociologists, in the investigation of social norms:

1. The first method, then, is concerned with establishing the frequency and regularity with which the attributes assumed to make up the role appear together in fact, the result being the statistical 'normality' of the role series.

2. The second method is concerned with the explicit statements and assertions of the people (made with a given degree of consensus and authoritativeness) as to the conduct appropriate to given roles, these are all value judgements, indicating the believed in or desired 'normality', and hence the normality codified.

3. Thirdly, the existing role norms are also demonstrated by what we may call the maintenance machineries of the society, that is, by the sanctions, of whatever kind, which forestall or follow deviant behaviour.

Pointing out the interconnection between these three methods, Nadel remarks, "Let us note that the first and third methods involve the piecing together of the role, while the second may furnish us with the total picture."[15] Thus, these three methods do not always give the same results.

While the class concept has the implication of further characteristics, the role concept refers to whole series of characteristics and never to one only. This series may be determined by the norms of the society. This is, however, conventional and arbitrary. The separation of entitlement and conduct which is possible in role, is not possible in class. Thus, class concepts are broader and looser than role concepts. This, of course, is a matter of degree. Exceptions might be available here and there.

---

13. *Ibid.* p. 24.

14. *Ibid.* p. 25.

15. *Ibid.*

Role and Status

A role must have a halo effect, without it is reduced to a label or category. An example of this halo effect in a role is the concept of bureaucrat. This is true about a role in the full sense of the term. However, certain terms bearing the label of roles might be in fact what Nadel calls, "Non-roles or near-roles or quasi-roles." These have been further defined by him. As he points out, quasi-roles may be named as status. Thus, status can be elaborated into roles and roles have a foundation in status. Most of the writers have accepted that roles and status are interdependent. Role behaviour is something translated into action. This translation, however, is not all at once, or in a piece. Rather, roles are enacted face by face, occasion by occasion, in a process extending over time. It is translated attribute by attribute. Role behaviour is materialized in interaction settings or situations. Thus, explaining the relationship of role and situations, Nadel concludes: "Thus the relation between role attributes and situations may be of a 'one-in-all' or of a 'one-to-one' kind. But the same role may include both kinds of attributes: nor does this distinction seem to be relevant in any other respect apart from its bearing on role perception."[16]

Attributes Concerning Role

The attributes describe the internal structure of roles. Different attributes are not equivalent. The attributes concerning roles, according to Nadel, may be classified into the following three main grades:

1. Peripheral Attributes. These are the attributes whose variation or absence does not affect the perception or effectiveness of the role. Thus, they are optional and admit alternatives.

2. Sufficiently Relevant. These attributes are firmly entailed in the roles. Their variation or absence makes difference to the perception or effectiveness of the role by making it imperfect or incomplete.

3. Basic or Pivotal Attributes. The absence or variation of these attributes changes the whole identity of the role and the interaction it would normally provoke. Thus, "The basic or pivotal attribute is simply the attribute expected to entail the rest of the series." In its absence other attributes appear as illegitimate, unexplained or different in meaning.

Role Name

The analysis of attributes in a role explains the difference between a true role and a quasi-role or mere status. In the latter, one finds a disproportionate number of optional attributes reducing the relevant attributes to a few. The ordering of the attributes in a given role creates the problems of scaling or ranking. Nadel points out to the necessity of a criteria for identifying pivotal characteristics of a role. His own method of doing it is to refer to the semantic content of the conventional role name. The semantic approach is based upon the fact that role names are

16. *Ibid.*, p. 13.

shorthand symbols for the array of properties which the entity name is presumed to possess. Thus, the role name is prescribed. However, this approach is workable only when the linguistic usages are unambiguous agreed and consistent with the social practice. In certain cases the semantic structure of the role name itself seems to indicate the basic attribute. Secondly, in the analysis of attributes one should look for the governing properties.

Occupational Roles

Some social psychologists, however, define roles as 'patterns of behaviour' (or of relationships or 'expectancies') applying to persons 'occupying specific positions' or 'fulfilling definable functions' in the society.[17] According to Nadel this viewpoint is legitimate in social psychology but not for the anthropologists and sociologists. To quote his own words, "Since, as an anthropologist, I view roles as, modes of acting 'allotted individuals' by the norms of the society. I am concerned also with this very allocation and the principles on which it is based, which means that my definition and analysis of roles must include their 'basis', the conditions entailing the 'further characteristics', as much as these characteristics themselves."

Recruitment vs. Achievement Roles

This entailment can be of two kinds:[18]

1. Recruitment Role. In the first type of role, then, the governing property is an inevitable or fortuitous state in which individuals find themselves; it then entails the further characteristic — all the other attributes in the series — as consequences or concomitants (as when mature age carries with it such and such privileges or responsibilities).

2. Achievement Role. In the second type of role, where the governing property is a behavioural attribute, active or passive, which individuals are free to choose as a goal or objective, the 'further characteristics' are entailed either as necessary preconditions or again as consequences and concomitants (as when priesthood requires celibacy and a decorous life, and promises an elevated status).

Thus, the recruitment role is identified by a governing property which indicates the method of recruitment. The achievement role, on the other hand, is based upon the precondition. The preconditions, however, belong to the prehistory of the role and not to in actual performance. The prehistory of the role, however, is important in the phases of role performance. Roles having relevant prehistory have two instead of one basic attribute, of which while one refers to the conditions of recruitment, the other is crucial in the role. In a recruitment role, the individual is forced or compelled into the given role with restricted choice. In achievement roles he embraces the role for its desirability, voluntarily committing himself to its various implications. According to Nadel, "Achievement roles mean much the

17. E. L. and R. E. Hartley, *Fundamentals of Social Psychology*, 1952, p. 486; T. M. Newcomb, in *For a Science of Social Man*, ed. John Gillin 1954, p. 252; Muzafar Sherif, in *Social Psychology at the Crossroads*, 1951, p. 25.

18. Nadel, S.F., *The Theory of Social Structure*, Cohen and West Ltd., London, 1969, p. 36.

same as achieved status ignoring the looser meaning of 'status'.[19] The recruitment roles, on the other hand, are connected with what Is known as ascribed status. The concept of ascription however, does not cover all the recruitment roles. The principle of allocation in recruitment roles depends upon the process of accommodation in society. In achievement roles the principle of allocation is the desirability. To think of roles in terms of allocation is to think of them in economic terms. This economic aspect of role system was first expressed by Pareto in his book Mind and Society. Nadel, however, calls it one-sided and points out that desirability must be supplemented by the principle of accommodation. Some roles however may not fit in any category on the grounds of allocation. Then, some roles may be viewed both as recruited or achieved such as kinship roles of father, mother, husband, but then the element of compulsion enters into the desirable role. The element of compulsion, again, varies in different cultures. The ascriptive role ascribed statuses are concealed and attenuated recruitment roles. Their names identify them with achievement roles but they include compulsive characteristics of recruitment roles. The achievement itself has a wide and flexible meaning in different cultures and in the same culture in different situations.

Role vs. Game

Thus, according to Nadel, role assumptions may be compared with a set of rules or rules of game. The role behaviour exhibits the following features like the rules of a game.[20]

1. The rules of the game have a given attitude, allowing certain options and disallowing others, with varying degrees of strictness; some 'moves' are altogether excluded since they would simply change or deny the identity of the game which is the exact counterpart of our 'hierarchy of relevance'.
2. The overall firmness with which the whole set of rules applies corresponds to the institutionalization of the roles in the social system; and as in all institutionalizations, the respective expectations are diffused through the society.
3. Finally, as in many games played according to rules, the moves open to the players, that is, the attributes they are expected to require or display, will follow a, more or less, rigorous sequences, so that a particular attribute must not appear or will not be effective unless some other specified attribute is already present.

Asymmetrical Roles

Besides recruitment roles and achievement roles Nadel admits a third type of roles which "have no precise hierarchy, there being no definite focus or pivot in the series."[21] Examples of such roles are friend, enemy, lover, patriot. These role names have no reference to any governing attribute. They indicate the role character by generalizing in a summary fashion.

---

19. *Ibid.*, p. 37.

20. *Ibid*, p. 42.

21. *Ibid.*, p. 42.

Conformity and Deviance of Roles

W.J.H Sprott has rightly pointed out that, "one of the features of our own time is the indeterminancy and rapid changing of roles."[22] Thus one finds in modern society, so many changes and disintegrating roles. While observation of the rules of the game of role may be called conformity, the non-observance is known as deviance. In the words of Nadel. "The deviancy role, we might say, is a role with a negative coefficient."[23] Every role performance has a built in element of self-regulation. This is governed by the system of rewards and punishments in society. While conformity is rewarded, deviance is punished. Thus, one notices positive and negative feedback in rules of performance as conformity and deviance. This dyadic model governs the role performance in society. The mutual steering built-in to processes of interaction in a society functions only in as much as the persons involved in it acknowledge each other's role and have congruent assumptions about them. This steering process is not necessarily held up until the sanctions are actually encountered. Secondly, the role behaviour is not corrected only by this mutual steering in the course of normal role interpretation. Thus, according to Nadel, "the roles linked in the mutual steering process posit or implicate one another."[24]

This mutual implication may be of the following two types:

1. Interactive Types. When roles are designed to meet in direct interplay, each role having a given efficiency (or responsiveness) vis-a-vis another.

2. Distributive Type. This is only indirectly interactive, representing the corollary of the basic fact about all roles, that they are differential modes of behaviour.

The above mutual implication of roles signifies division of labour in a society. It is what Talcott Parsons calls the role inventory of any society as a role system.

THE COHERENCE OF ROLE SYSTEM

Most of the roles in a society are heterogeneous without a common logical locus, incapable of inter-relation and thus incapable of yielding a coherent embarrassing structure. The following roles are, however, exceptions:

1. **Leadership or Authority Role**. These always imply, as part of the influence vested in them, the supervision of all or numerous other roles in society, disparity and mutual inclusiveness notwithstanding.

2. Expressive Roles. The name is meant to indicate that there the actors' task is the communication of ideas and emotional experience through manipulating, applying, and perhaps creatively adding to the expressive symbols current in the society.

3. Service Roles or Occupational Roles. Roles which imply the rendering of services to others and involve that kind of contractual relationship.

---

22. W. J. H. Sprott, *Social Psychology*' 1952, p. 156.

23. Nadel, S. F., *The Theory of Social Structure*, p. 50.

24. *Ibid.*, p. 57.

Dependent vs. Independent Roles

Among the logically related roles, Nadel distinguishes between dependent and independent roles. As he puts it, "To turn to logically related roles, we shall see that they form a continuum between two extremes. One is constituted by roles in the case of which the logical relation also implies, with logical compulsion, a relationship between the respective actors. In other words, a given role is so conceived that, by its character it requires to be enacted vis-a-vis another counterpart or correlative role. The second extreme is constituted by roles in the case of which the logical relation merely means that actual relationships between the actors are possible, not in any logical sense necessary. For reasons which will become clear presently I will call the first type of roles dependent, and the second, independent roles. It seems convenient, to start with the latter."[25]

While the dependent and independent roles represent only extremes, there are roles in between these extremes. In this connection Nadel has pointed out the following three types of roles:

1. Service and Expressive Rotes. These require a 'public' more or less specified in role terms, with counterpart roles such as 'patients', 'customers', an 'audience', a 'congregation'.

2. Authority or Leadership Rotes. These roles have a weaker counterpart. Their counterpart roles may be synonymous with that widest public, the 'rest of society' (the 'subjects' of a ruler, the 'followers' of a leader).

3. Distributive Roles. In these roles the correlative aspect is the weakest and independence of the role the strongest. In the words of Nadel, "This category includes roles named on the basis of belief, ethnic origin, age, residence, personality or somatic characteristics, and similar autonomous differentia...[26]

Some Terms Connected with Role

In the analysis of the concept of social role it is necessary to define certain other terms applicable to the explanations of actual functioning of roles in society. These terms include role conflict, role set, role exception, role strain and role performance. The following are some of the more popular definitions of these terms.

1. Role Conflict: (i) Incompatibility between two or more roles that an individual is expected to play.[27]

(ii) Incompatibility between two or more roles that an individual is expected to perform simultaneously. The existence of mutually exclusive expectations for behaviour.[28]

2. Role Expectation. All the expectations that specify proper and improper behaviour for an individual occupying a given position. What one is expected to do while playing a specific role.[29]

25. *Ibid*, pp. 79-80.

26. Ibid., *p.* 86.

27. Popenoe, David, *Sociology*, Prentice Hall, New Jersey, 1977, p, 570.

28. Hobbs, D. A. and Blank, S. J., *Sociology and the Human Experiences*, John Wiley, New York, 1978, p. 461.

29. *Ibid.*

3. Role Performance. The degree to which an individual acts in accordance with the expectation of a given role. Role performance is our behaviour that more or less fulfils role expectation"[30]

4. Role Set. The set of roles associated with a single status.[31]

5. Role Strain. Conflict or stress caused by the incompatible demands of a single role."[32]

TYPES OF ROLE DIFFERENTIATION

Role refers to the part played by an actor in a particular context. In drama we speak of the role of a king, servant, etc. In life also we have to play different parts in our relations to society. Thus, we are fathers, mothers, sons, teachers, employers, etc. A person may have to play several roles at the same in his day-to-day dealings in society such as of a father, son, employer, buyer, etc.

The structure of role differentiation in any society is concerned with the structure of distribution of the members of the system among the various positions and activities in the system. A minimum number of role differentiation is a prerequisite for any society's survival because there are activities in a society which must be performed by certain designated members at a time.

There are nine types of role differentiation in any society. They are:

1. Role Differentiation on the Basis of Age. Differences in age are relevant to differences in biological capabilities of persons. This refers to the biological life spans of an individual. On the basis of absolute age, individuals are classified into infants, children, adults and old people. While infants and old people are totally dependent upon other members of the society, children may partially support themselves while adults may support the other age groups. Relative age refers to the relative differences in years between two individuals. For example, brothers have role differentiation on the basis of their comparative age. Roles are differentiated on the basis of relative age because of the different capabilities of individuals according to their age.

2. Role Differentiation on the Basis of Generation. By generation we mean an individual's position relative to other individuals in order of birth in his direct biological line of descent. Role differentiation on this basis refers to the role of father, son, grand children, grand parents, etc. The functional explanation for type of role differentiation lies in the requisite of sexual recruitment and its implications and general differentiation on this basis rests on the recognition of a kinship structure.

3. Role Differentiation on the Basis of Sex. This distinction is between males and females. In physiological terms the sexes are differentiated in terms of the roles which members of each of these two types are capable of performing in the production of new members of the species.

30. *Ibid*

31. Popenoe, David, *Society*, Prentice-Hall, New Jersey, 1977, p. 60.

32. *Ibid.*

4. Role Differentiation on the Basis of Economic Allocation. Economic allocation refers to the distribution of goods and services among the various members of a society. The structure of production includes all structures from whose operation goods and services accrue to the society. The structure of consumption includes all structures from which operation of goods and services are allocated to the various members. The functional requisite for role differentiations of this type lies in the functional necessity of providing for the physiological adjustment of members of a unit. This includes the provision of food, clothing and shelter. The economic role differentiation is vast and varied. Mainly, it consists of the roles of producer, distributor and consumer.

5. Role Differentiation on the Basis of Political Allocation. Political allocation refers to the distribution of power over and responsibility for the actions of the various members of the society involving, on the one hand, the use of coercive sanctions including force. Power is the ability to exercise authority and control over the actions of others. Responsibility is the accountability of an individual for his own acts and acts of others. The functional requisite for political allocation is to effectively control disruptive behaviour. It is possible for a relationship to have mutually equal power and responsibility. Roles on the basis of political allocation refer to those of the governors and the governed, ruler and citizens, etc. or power holders and responsibility bearers.

6. Role Differentiation on the Basis of Religion. Religion refers to the aspects of action directly oriented to ultimate ends: The functional requisite rests on a discussion of a shared and articulated set of goals. Religious roles refer to those of initiators, the initiated, priest and worshipper, preacher and disciple, etc.

7. Role Differentiation on the Basis of Cognition. Cognition refers to the knowledge or understanding of a situation or phenomenon. The functional requisite of cognition rests on the requisite basis for cognitive structures. Role differentiation on this basis rests on several bases. The most obvious is the fact that new recruits for a society must be taught the various types of cognition necessary to operate in a society. This requires the roles of teacher and student. Cognitive differentiation includes the differentiation of technological roles and those dealing with value standards such as that of priest or mother and that of the expert.

8. Role Differentiation on the Basis of Non-human Environment. Features of the non-human environment of a society such as seasonal, topographical and other factors are subject to extremely wide variations. Therefore, seasonal bases for role differentiation must exist. The functional requisite is the provision of physiological adjustment.

9. Role Differentiation on the Basis of Solidarity. The structure of solidarity is a structure in terms of which relationships among the members of a society are allocated according to the content, strength and intensity of the relationship. This involves all types of intimate relations.

QUESTIONS FOR EXERCISE

1. What do you mean by organisation? Mention briefly the different factors involved in it.
2. Discuss in detail the concepts of social status and role.
3. Define and explain with examples: status and role.
4. Write short note on Relationship of Status with Role.
5. Define status and role. Discuss the various forms of status and roles.
6. What do you understand by status and role? What are the essential elements of status and role?

CHAPTER 2

Individual, Society and Socialization

A big controversy has developed among social thinkers on the question of the mutual relation between individual and society, but none challenges the view that this relation is an intimate and close one. Actually, the society precedes the individual because society is not an exclusive characteristic of human beings but also found among animals. Its life is longer than that of the individuals and while the latter may come and go, it goes on continually. But on the other hand, society has no existence in the absence of individuals, of which it is formed. Individuals constitute society. Individuals influence the society. It is society that makes individuals cultured. The child's personality depends to a large extent upon his social environment. Almost everything that he learns is acquired from society. Only the capacity of learning is his own. It is in society that his self or ego develops whereby he is called a human being. Every society has its Individual organisation. Each exercises control over the individual in a variety of ways. In this sway, in a sense, the individual and society appear to be two independent units. But nevertheless, the existence and development of both depend on each other.

SOCIAL CONTRACT THEORY

Among the many theories concerning the relationship between the individual and the society one of the most important is the social contract theory. In the 17th century, Thomas Hobbes, writing in his famous book Leviathan, maintained that society was conceived to protect man from his irresponsible, animal as well as egoistic tendencies. According to Adam Smith and his followers, society is an artificial device created to foster a mutual economy. In the 18th century the French philosopher Rousseau supported the theory that Individuals came to an understanding and formed society deliberately. Among the other supporters of this theory were John Locke (1632-1704) and Hobhouse (1588-1679). According to this theory in nature all men were born free and equal. Individual precedes society. He has some rights even outside society. Individuals made a mutual agreement and created society, giving it certain rights and authority. In this way, society is an artificial creation and it has no right to dispossess the individual of his fundamental rights. Society can exercise control over the rights of the individual only to the extent to which it has been granted rights to the extent to which authority has been vested in it.

MacIver and other modern sociologists look upon the social contract theory as illusory. The theory is based neither on historical facts nor on logical ground, its occupation of the individual apart from society does not seem to be correct. Again, its concept of the individual as preceding the formation of society is also incorrect because socialization is a necessary condition for the development of personality. As a matter of fact, the question of society or individual being before or after does not arise. Both have been together from the very beginning since, without individual, the inception of society is impossible and, without society, the individual cannot develop. Wherever man has had to exist outside human society, he has never been able to develop. This fact is proved by the condition of children nursed by wolves. In the same way conception of the individual preceding the formation of society is false. The existence of individual and society cannot remain separate.

ORGANIC THEORY OF SOCIETY

According to organic theory of society, society is an organism whose structure and functioning resemble those of the human being and which also develops according to the same laws. The cells of this organism are individuals. Association and institutions, etc., are its arteries. In the words of Spencer, "Social structure can be compared to an animal body whose system of nutrition has its counterpart in society in the industrial and agricultural systems; the circulatory systems with the heart arteries, and veins, correspond to the communication and transport systems of nation, the nervous system to the government, and so on.

The main defect of the organic theory of society lies in its reducing the relation of individual and society to the relation between the cell and the body. The two relations do not permit of analogy since there are clear differences between them. The individual is a conscious being. He has his own brain, and he himself thinks and contemplates. On the other hand, the cells have no consciousness of their own. They have no individual existence apart from the body. It is only in the sense of the interests, hopes and fears of the individuals that one may assign any function and goal to society. When one speaks of the group interest one means the interest in the members of the group.

GROUP MIND THEORY

The protagonists of the Idealistic and group mind theories look upon society as a mind. In the words of Plato, "Civil Society is a mind writ large." According to Hegel, Society as manifested in the state, is a natural organism representing a phase of the historical world process or Absolute. The state, not the individual, is the real person. The individual has reality only in so far as he is a member of the state. Among others this school of thought has been upheld by Green, Bradley and Bosanquet in England, Emerson in America and Wagner and Wundt in

Germany. To quote Durkheim, "Social mind is an existence distinct (not apart) from the minds of the individuals, and is superior to them. This mind or collective consciousness is the higher form of psychic life. It tends to absorb the individual mind from which it differs not only in the richness of content but also in kind."

Sociologists and psychologists have, at present, refuted the theory of group mind. The social contract and organic theories contradict each other. According to the first theory there is no synthesis between society and individual and according to the second there is no difference between the two. All these theories bear witness to the intimate relation between society and the individual but apart from this each is one-sided. In the words of MacIver and Page, "No one can really be an absolute individualist, any more than anyone can be an absolute socialist, for the individual and society interact on one another and depend on one another."[1]

SOCIALIZATION

Socialization is the process whereby an individual learns to behave in accordance with social traditions and mores. The human child possesses a tendency towards imitation. The child develops according to the environment in which he lives. The individual tries to win the praise of the group in which he lives. Man is a social being. He, by his very nature, tries to adopt the culture of society. Man becomes what he is by socialization and it is by virtue of this that he is believed to be superior to animals. Socialization brings balance to his personality because the social aspect of personality is very important. Through socialization the individual learns to control himself in the interest of society and realizes his responsibility towards others. Socialization develops in him the community feeling and he learns to cooperate with others.

Individuals influence each other by means of imitation, suggestion and sympathy. In addition to these, social institution and association also carry out the individual's socialization. The individual is influenced by many processes in society, praise and blame, co–operation and conflict, submission and ascendency. These help to form his personality and individuality. Education is the most prominent means to socialization.

SOCIALIZATION IN THE FAMILY

The family plays perhaps the most dominant role in the individual's socialization. The child finds much to learn in the behaviour of his family members, parents, relatives and friends. He imitates them in the mannerisms, behaviour, cliches, etc. He tries to avoid such activities which result in punishment or which are considered bad in the family. It is the family environment which forms his good habits and it is in the family that he acquires criminal tendencies. In the book *New Light on Delinquency and its Treatment*, Healy and Brenner, have pointed out that juvenile delinquents mostly hail from families which at one time or another, have suffered some restriction in the fulfilment of social relations. Psychoanalysts, prominent among them are Freud and Adler, have proved that a man behaves in

1. MacIver, R. M., and Page, C. H., *Society: An introductory Analysts,* p. 55.

society according to whatever he has become in the family. Termann, the author of *Psychological Factors in Marital Happiness*, has maintained that only those individuals can make marriage a success whose parents were contented. The preface writer of *Women of the Street*, a searching book on London prostitutes, has stated that the problem of prostitution is the problem of the parent-child relationships. Boys and girls are spoiled when family contentments and peace are lacking. Many similar circumstances give birth to many thieves, murderers and prostitutes.

In infancy, the mind of the child is very flexible and impressionable. He is very deeply and seriously influenced by any and every incident and occurrence, the behaviour of the parents towards the child as well as upon its development. Too much affection and display of excessive love spoils the child but if a child is almost completely deprived of love and affection emotional complexes are formed in the child's personality. The child is also susceptible to the influence of his relatives' behaviour towards it. The importance of the birth order in the family for the development of the child's personality has been emphasized by Alfred Adler. Whether the child is the youngest or the oldest among his brothers and sisters, whether he has or not any other brother or sister; when it is a male child and when it is a female child influences the development of its personality. Almost all the great men of the world have acknowledged the influence of their female parent. It is often seen that people make guesses as to the personality of a woman's marriageable daughter by judging her personality and in a majority of cases, the guess is fairly correct. In questions of marriage, the senile folk worry as much about the family as the girl, the family undoubtedly influences the character and personality to a considerable extent. If the progenitors themselves cannot boast of any character then the possibility of their offspring possessing any balanced traits is rather remote. Personality is further subject to influence emanating from the economic and social position of the family.

The influence of the family does not cease when the child crosses the portals of adolescence. It continues even in the twilight of life. Absence of family control tends to create situations in which young boys and girls are apt to stray from the straight and narrow path of virtuous life. On the other hand, domination in the name of family control is likely to leave indelible marks on their personalities in the form of undeveloped and repressed personality. A balanced and sane family control helps the development of personality. Having grown up, the erstwhile child emulates his predecessors, marries and has children of his own. At this stage of his life, his personality is influenced by the nature and personality of his better half. The personality is always susceptible to influences of a direct or indirect sort, such as day incidents, the number of children if any, their being good looking or physically handicapped or healthy, the health, nature, character, physique of the partner, economic situation, and a million other things small and big. In fact, much ink has been spilled in considering the effect that the family has upon the personality, the important contributions to this study having come from psychologists and anthropologists rather than sociologists.

SOCIALISATION IN THE SCHOOL

The institution that influences the child after he escapes from the family is the school. For the child the school is society and it is within its boundary that he is socialized, his abilities find expression and he gets the opportunities of developing his personality. The personality and character of the teacher are ever present before him as ideals that continuously influence his own personality. This influence extends even to actions such as speaking, thinking, meditating, moving etc. This influence is not identical in the case of all teachers. Some teachers do not succeed in creating faith and affection in the child's mind as a consequence of which the child both consciously and unconsciously contradicts him in everything. Other teachers are more successful in winning the affection and admiration of the children they teach and they are idolized by their disciples. The child then modulates his own life and personality in order to win their praise and adulation, he imitates them and wants to emulate them in his life. His colleagues also get the opportunity of influencing the personality of the child. The role and status that the child occupies among them is an important factor in determining the status that he is to adopt and the role that he is to play in later life in society. Co-education too, has an important influence upon his personality. The child's personality develops when boys and girls sit together, converse and play together, study together, and co-operate with each other in their child's play. In the school, the child unconsciously or consciously admits of government and administration. He accepts the rules of his world in school or pays the penalty for disobeying them. This lends temperance to his personality and gives it balance. If the discipline of the school is unnecessarily strict then the personality is likely to be repressed and narrow, and may even lead to developing criminal tendencies in the child. The complete absence of any control may also give the child a truant disposition but it may also engender independence in him. The cultural programmes of the school help to refine the mental tendencies of the child.

In this way, both the school and family have a very important influence upon the personality of men. Of the two, the influence caused by the family occupies a greater period of time and hence is more comprehensive in its application. In this way, an 'understanding of an individual's circumstances is essential to an understanding of his personality.

OTHER INFLUENCES IN SOCIALIZATION

But it is incorrect to believe socialization to be dependent exclusively on the family, Other institutions and associations outside the family also wield influence on the development of man. When the child has grown a bit, he leaves the sanctity and protection of his home to go out and play. At this stage lie is very susceptible to the influence of his playmates. In addition to the effect of education, the child in the school is vulnerable to the influences exerted by the personalities of his teachers and friends. In much the same way, young men and women leant to conduct themselves and to give expression to their views, such a process being an outcome of education and constant association with teachers, the unique environment, fellow collegiates, etc. Following college education the individual's occupations and marriage are also important factors of socialization. Both men and women are strongly influenced by the personality of their life partner, and their future depends upon this to a large extent. In this way, the child in the family becomes successively the protector, husband and father. These new responsibilities and rights teach him very much. In brief, socialization is a process which begins at birth and continues unceasingly until the death of the individual. Like education it too is an incessant process.

NEED FOR SOCIALIZATION

The question why is socialization necessary for the development of the individual is best answered by the examples of human beings, who were, for some reason, nurtured outside human society. Some human beings of this kind have been described by Gesell in his work *Wolf Children and Human Child*, and by Davis in several essays. In 1920, in India, two children were found in a wolfs den, of which one was eight years old and the other a couple of years younger. The second died after the lapse of only a few months while the first continued to live for six years. He was named Kamla. This girl was completely innocent of the modes or ways of human behaviour. She walked on all fours, growled like a wolf and could not speak. She became nervous at the sight of human beings as undomesticated animals are wont to do. In this way, due to the absence of socialization she possessed none of the characteristics of human beings save for her bodily structure. She was taught to speak, wear clothes and eat. In this way she could team some human behaviour due to the influence of socialization after a period of some years.

Socialization is not the exclusive but a prominent source of individual's development, because heredity also has its importance. Without the diffusion of culture through socialization, the development of the individual is impossible. The self of the individual develops only due to socialization. Every social relationship of the individual contributes to this process of socialization. The problem of man's socialization is very complex and it has not yet been completely solved in any human society. In the words of Davis, "The improvement of socialization offers one of the greatest possibilities for the future alteration of human nature and human society."

QUESTIONS FOR EXERCISE

1. Write a short note on The Individual and Society.
2. Define the term socialization. Discuss the various forms of Status and Roles.
3. Explain the relationship between Socialization and Social Control.
4. What do you understand by socialization? Clarify the factors helpful in the socialization of the individual.

5. Briefly describe the various levels of socialization.
6. What do you understand by socialization? Describe its main conditions.
7. Explain J. H. Mead's theory of socialization.
8. Define socialization. Clarify the role of family in socialization.
9. Explain Cooley's theory of socialization.
10. Explain the Freudian theory of socialization.
11. Discuss the chief factors of socialization in the context of family.

CHAPTER 3

Suggestion, Imitation and Sympathy

The word suggestion does not imply precisely the sense in which it is usually employed in colloquial usage. Suggestion is a mental process in which the thoughts or thought processes of one individual influence and mould those of another. To take a common example, many people will attack an individual if they see a crowd attacking him even if they are unaware of their animosity towards the individual. If two bulls happen to fight in the middle of the road, or if a baton charge is made or even if some people happen to run in some direction without any particular cause they are soon emulated. The main cause at the root of such behaviour is suggestion. The most startlingly apparent and direct example of suggestion is hypnosis. In the Sir J. K. Hall of Bombay a hypnotist called some people to the stage, all of whom were fairly intelligent and skilled individuals and none of them could have been expected to indulge in irrational behaviour. But showing his skill and influence the hypnotist requested the selected persons to drink water from the tumbler in his hand. In fact there was neither any tumbler nor any water but nevertheless these persons carried out all the motions of drinking water. Some time later, the hypnotist pointed out to these persons that dinner had been served. These persons settled down on the stage, following which shoes and slippers were placed in front of them. Considering them to be food stuffs, they went through all the motions of eating them and the audience laughed and was surprised. This was the influence of the power of hypnotism. Hypnotism acts through suggestion.

SUGGESTION

At this stage it is necessary to turn to define suggestion in order that it may be understood more completely and precisely. As has been pointed out in the foregoing example of hypnotism, there is no logical ground for accepting the suggestion given, concerning the drinking of water and taking of dinner at the time they were not present. And yet the persons casually accepted the suggestions and even implemented them. "The word suggestion is now commonly used for the process by which an attitude towards a system of ideas is communicated from one person to another, by a process other than that of rational persuasion."[1]

1. Thouless R. H., *General and Social Psychology* (1951), p. 247.

In the crowd that is motivated by fear most people are seen running about worriedly and anxiously even when they are not aware of the reason for this anxiety. The reason for this is suggestion inherent in the mob behaviour. Suggestion is a process of communicating information. The hypnotist employs this power to communicate his idea to others and in the manner that he wishes. The utterances of the great leaders and the militarists have the same power of suggestion and the person who hears them finds it beyond his control to resist them. Thus, Mcdougall has rightly written, "Suggestion is a process of communication resulting in the acceptance with conviction of the communicated proposition in the absence of logically adequate grounds for its acceptance."[2] Like Mcdougall, Young has also placed emphasis on the fact that the communicated suggestion has no logical or self-evident basis. To quote him, "We may define suggestion as a form of symbol, communicated by words, pictures or some similar medium for including acceptance of the symbol without any self-evident or logical ground for its acceptance."

Characteristics of Suggestion

The foregoing explanation of suggestion points to the following characteristics that are to be found in its process:

(1) Through the medium of suggestion, some idea is communicated from one individual to another.

(2) There is no evidence or logic to support suggestion.

(3) Suggestion may be conveyed through any symbolical medium such as language, picture, etc.

(4) Suggestion involves mental images.

In defining suggestion, in view of its forementioned characteristics, it may be said that suggestion is a mental process in which an idea, which does not have any evidence or logical basis, is conveyed from one person to another through any symbolical medium such as words, pictures, etc.

Suggestibility

The most peculiar and notable feature of the process of suggestion is that it finds acceptance among individuals even though it is not logical and does not have any proof to validate it. Of course, it is not true that people accept suggestions without making any response of a negative nature. People resist suggestion to a greater or lesser degree but if the suggestion carries much weight, then their resistance will inevitably crumble and they will accept it. The person accepting the suggestion accepts it because he takes it to be a form of truth. Evidently then, his prudence and reason, in addition to his mental stability, do not function at the time when he is accepting a suggestion, and hence he is not capable of criticising the suggestion. He cannot also analyse the propriety or otherwise of the suggestion. In this way, the cause at the root of the power of suggestion is the suggestibility of the subject itself. Here, it is necessary to bear clearly in mind the fact that the word suggestion

2. Mcdougall, *An Introduction to Social Psychology*, p. 83.

is used to indicate two senses. Firstly, some people consider suggestion to be a complete mental process. Secondly, some people, on the other hand, use the term to indicate the effect of some stimuli upon the individual. In this connection a third alternative could be the possibility of looking upon suggestion as a special kind of stimuli. But, whatever the sense in which the term is interpreted, there is a clear distinction between suggestion and suggestibility. Suggestibility indicates the extent to which any individual can accept suggestions. It is indicated in terms of percentages. In order to obtain this percentage, the number of suggestions accepted is divided by the number of suggestions given to him and the quotient multiplied by a hundred. In this way, then the suggestibility of any individual can be measured by the following formula:

$$\text{Suggestibility} = \frac{\text{Number of suggestions accepted}}{\text{Number of suggestions give in all}} \times 100$$

As a general rule, those individuals who possess an independent decision and are of a high level of intelligence do not fall easy prey to the suggestions of others. The suggestibility of an individual decreases in a group situation because the level of Intelligence is considerably lowered.

Kinds of Suggestions

Many functions are performed in communal life because of suggestibility. If we glance at all the occurrences that take place all around us, we shall visualise the importance of suggestion. In social life. Suggestion influences not only behaviour with others but also one's own private and individual behaviour. Some people are conversely affected by suggestion, *i.e.*, they act in contradiction to the suggestion that is conveyed to them. Suggestion is sometimes direct and sometimes indirect. In the first case the individual is aware of the fact that a suggestion is being made to him while in the second case there is no such awareness. In addition to these, in society one finds the Influence of prestige suggestions almost everywhere. The behaviour of the individual in a mob situation is an example of collective suggestion. It would be of help to glance individually at the various forms of suggestion in social life, the main among which are the following:

1. Direct Suggestion
2. Indirect Suggestion
3. Positive Suggestion
4. Negative Suggestion
5. Contra Suggestion
6. Prestige Suggestion
7. Auto Suggestion
8. Mass Suggestion
9. Ideo-Motor Suggestion.

1. Direct Suggestions. Some suggestions are of a direct nature, *i.e.*, the individual who is accepting the suggestion is aware that a suggestion is being made to him. A skilled shopkeeper does not abstain from displaying the latest model wares to any customer whom he knows to be rich and susceptible to suggestion. A successful businessman persuades you to buy commodities even though you have no desire to do so. In this process he employs suggestions. You may also be aware that he is using suggestion to overcome your hesitation, and you may also feel angry and sorry at having purchased it but you cannot resist the suggestions that are put forward by the businessman. The moment you enter his shop the shopkeeper will inform you that he has just received a consignment of the latest fashioned readymade shirts which he would like to show to you. You reason that he is not asking you to purchase them, so you permit him to show the shirts to you. The shopkeeper praises the merits of a particular shirt and then asks you to buy it while he makes you the concession of accepting deferred payment. At that stage you do realise that the shopkeeper is selling a shirt to you and in spite of the fact that you stand in no particular need of one, you buy the shirt.

2. Indirect Suggestions. But some suggestions are not quite so apparent and bizarre, and the intention of the person suggesting it is concealed. He puts forward his suggestions but he does not indicate his intention in doing it. Suggestions of this kind make a greater impression upon the educated and the intelligent people. These are indirect suggestions.

3. Positive Suggestions. The suggestions that are made for the implementation of some order or for accepting some statement are said to be positive.

4. Negative Suggestions. The suggestions that are made for rejecting some idea or for abstaining from some particular course of action are said to be negative.

5. Contra Suggestions. It is often seen that people will indulge in the very activity that they have been warned against. This is particularly true of children who will inevitably touch anything that they have been ordered to stay away from. In other words, the order of abstaining from touching the object gives a contra-suggestion.

6. Prestige Suggestions. A book of a famous author sells easily even if it is not particularly good. The ideas expressed by famous political leaders are casually and uncritically accepted by the populace. In political discussion if any person mentions the name of Pandit Jawaharlal Nehru or of Mahatma Gandhi as supporting the contention that he has put forward, then in all probability his view is accepted by many without further preamble. People tend to use the commodities that are used by film idols. For this reason many commodities of common use are advertised to be the favourites of film people and their patronage is solicited. In much the same manner, the advice of individuals is accepted in the field in which they are considered to be specialists. It happened once that a particular gentleman went to have a suit stitched in Bombay. He was struck dumb with astonishment when the tailor demanded no less than ₹ 250 for the work, and in all likelihood he would have gone to some other tailor. But the cunning tailor realised his vacillation and clinched the matter by remarking, almost casually, that Manoj

Kumar, a well known India's film star had only just got his suit stitched by him. This suggestion was quite enough and the person did not hesitate in leaving his cloth with the tailor in spite of the exorbitant rate that he had quoted. The mere mention of the actor's name was enough to recommend the work of the tailor. All these are examples of prestige suggestion. An experiment was conducted by P. A. Sorokin and J. W. Bodyreff in connection with the effect of prestige suggestion. In this experiment 1484 high school students formed the audience for two recorded songs, one of which was said to be the work of a great artist while the singer of the second was said to be a commonplace artist whereas in fact both the songs had been sung by good artists. Because of the prestige suggestion inherent in the name, 96 per cent students pronounced the first song to be good while the second they unanimously rejected as second rate. After this, the examiner pointed out that there was no difference between the records. Consequent upon this, 51 per cent immediately expressed acceptance, 16 per cent contradicted this view while 21 per cent abstained from expressing any opinion. It should be remembered that only 4 per cent of these were the only ones to use their intelligence in judging. All the others had been deceived by the prestige suggestion.

7. Auto-Suggestion. Thought has the power of suggestion. If you are always engrossed in thinking that you are not intelligent and can never score a good division in the examination, then how can you hope to study properly? Much stress has been laid by Indian thinkers upon the importance of autosuggestion in the development of character. The character that an individual develops depends upon his thanking and the thoughts that he entertains. The famous psychologist Emile Cone cured some patients of mental diseases on the basis of auto-suggestion. By studying the biographies and auto-biographies of great men one can see that they always placed the highest ideals before themselves to pursue and even in the time of extreme adversity they reassured themselves that in the end they would be victorious and successful. In this way, auto-suggestion has important influence upon the mental and physical condition, conduct and even success of the individual. The doctor always advises the patient to have faith in his cure because the fact of this belief helps to influence the health of the patient and it supplements to some extent the medicine that is being administered to him.

8. Mass Suggestion. Why is it that the behaviour of the individual undergoes considerable change when he is in a group situation? The reason why the most balanced and sane individuals who are the very essence of propriety in their private life become almost insane and exhibit animosity and pugnacity in a crowd is that they fail prey to mass suggestion. In one of his studies H. T. Moore has pointed out that students are more susceptible to mass suggestion than prestige suggestion. It is for this reason that one only too often comes across striking students who pay no heed to the utterings of the Vice-Chancellor of the University let alone the poor professor, and victims of mass suggestion that they are, they precipitate the most awful gaffe and do things that cannot be expected of them. By his experiments, C. H. Marple has proved that there is a ratio of 4 : 2 between mass suggestion and prestige suggestion.

9. Ideo-motor Suggestion. As is evident by the name given to it, in ideomotor suggestion there is no discrimination between thoughts and action, *i.e.*, action takes place almost immediately the thought arises. Hence, in this there is no time to think or to discuss. Generally, in suggestions of this kind the mind almost unconsciously accepts and adopts suggestions given to it. The famous psychologist, Alfred Binet conducted important experiments in connection with ideo-motor suggestion.

The degree to which suggestions are inherent in social life is evident from the description of the various kinds of suggestions. In trade, industry, politics, therapy, education and every other field, people acquainted with psychological facts make use of suggestion to have their ideas and, notions accepted by other people and to have the latter behave according to their wishes. Whether we like it or not we are influenced by the suggestions of others at one time or another. And, even otherwise, suggestions can be employed not only to influence others but also for self-development.

Conditions of Suggestibility

Of course, suggestion almost always elicits some response from the individual at whom it is directed, but under some special circumstances its effect and influence is enhanced. Psychologists have made detailed studies of these circumstances or conditions and have attempted to derive general principles in this connection. The conditions that influence the power of suggestion can be divided into two classes — internal and external. Under some specific conditions the suggestibility of an individual is increased and he becomes more susceptible and receptive to thoughts and activities of other people. For example, when the individual is in a fatigued state mental activity is at a low ebb and his suggestibility consequently increases.

Internal Conditions — The internal conditions of suggestibility comprehend all those that help to reduce the reasoning power of man so that he loses his immunity to the suggestions of others. The internal conditions may be said to be personal causes. These causes are the following:

(*i*) *Age.* Age influences suggestibility. According to some psychologists, the suggestibility of the child starts increasing from the fifth or sixth year and continues to increase till he attains the age of eight or nine years after which it decreases. Contradicting this opinion, Ellock has tried to show that the child does not possess the degree of suggestibility that he is supposed to have by the elders. Whatever the truth in this connection, there can be no denying the fact that the suggestibility of an individual decreases with an increase in his maturity and mental level, and that the immature people are characterised by a greater suggestibility than the mature ones. But, here it is necessary to top in mind the fact that while there may be a difference in the suggestibility of children belonging to different societies, differences are also found in the suggestibility of children belonging to the same society.

(*ii*) *Temperament*. The suggestibility of the individual is also influenced by his temperament. For example, in the opinion of some experts the extroverted individuals possess greater suggestibility than the introverted. In this way, the extroverted temperament is an internal factor of suggestibility.

(*iii*) *Sex differences*. On the basis of some experimental studies some psychologists have attributed greater suggestibility to fair sex. But, on the other hand, it has been seen in some experiments that the difference in suggestibility is seen to exist between individuals of the same sex. Hence, sex difference is not considered to be an important factor in suggestibility. In Charles Bird's opinion, the difference in suggestibility among the two sexes is due to the system of education and the social structure. In the old education system and the social structure, the large difference between individuals of the two sexes was particularly conducive to a major difference in their orientation and consequently in their respective suggestibility. Under the existing educational system and the social order the gulf between the two sexes is being constantly reduced and consequently one does not find much difference in suggestibility on the basis of sex difference.

(*iv*) *Intelligence*. Some scientists have attempted to establish a correlation between suggestibility and intelligence. In other words, according to them, suggestibility will be as much low as the intelligence is high, and as much high as the intelligence is low. But in opposition to this view, it is held by Estrabooks and some other psychologists that there is very little correlation between intelligence and suggestibility. In their studies Ewlling and Hargreaves found zero correlation between intellect and suggestibility.

(*v*) *Ignorance*. Ignorance is favourable to suggestibility. People readily accept the notions and ideas of other individuals concerning subjects of which they are ignorant. On the other hand, the individual who is conversant with the particular subject is, more or less, immune to these suggestions and he is not misled even if he is affected by the suggestions.

(*vi*) *Other internal conditions*. In addition to forementioned internal conditions that affect the suggestibility of the individual there are some other important conditions also of an eternal nature. For example, it is a matter of common knowledge that a person is prone to acquiesce to almost any suggestion when he is in an intoxicated condition. Suggestibility also increases because of lack of self-confidence, and the individual tends to accept everything suggested without discrimination. In addition to this, those physical conditions, such as hunger, thirst, exhaustion, etc., that tend to reduce physical energy and to retard mental activity also augment the suggestibility of the individual. Besides the religious beliefs and notions of individuals also tend to become factors in suggestibility. For example, in India, suggestions concerning the evil of other groups circulate very easily among people possessing a communal bias.

External Conditions. In addition to the forementioned internal factors of suggestibility, there are many external condition that also help to increase suggestibility. The main ones are the following:

(*i*) *Group situation*. In a crowd or a group the mental or intellectual powers of the individual are comparatively weaker and emotions are facilely aroused. Hence, suggestibility increases in a group situation. In a crowd, particularly, any idea circulates with contagious rapidity and in a matter of moments all sorts of individuals are seen doing the same thing.

(*ii*) *Influence of public opinion*. Suggestibility is also influenced by public opinion. In other words, the ideas that have the sanction of public opinion are more suggestible than any other and people accept them easily. It is for this reason that people profess their suggestions to be public opinion.

(*iii*) *Influence of majority opinion*. An idea is accepted generally even when it is not the accepted public opinion but it is accepted by majority of the people in society. The reason behind this acceptance is that people feel that what is accepted by so many individuals must be right, since so many people cannot be wrong. There is no doubt that some individuals pursue their own views even in contradiction of public opinion let alone the opinion of the majority but as a general rule most people prefer to imitate public opinion in matters of ideas and activity.

(*iv*) *Prestige of the suggestor*. The prestige and respect paid to the suggestor also influences suggestibility. The greater the degree of this prestige the greater will be the appeal of the suggestion made to the individual. The thoughts of great leaders, famous film actors and actresses have the power of suggesting to the common people to follow and copy the film personalities. In political matters, the ideas and notions of the leaders are adopted by the people as their own view. In the same fashion, people uncritically accept the suggestions of scientists and thinkers who are specialists in their own respective fields.

(*v*) *Confident tone*. Another factor that tends to increase the suggestibility of an idea is the confident tone of the person propounding it. If the individual propounding the idea is confident of it, and this confidence is apparent in his voice, then the idea carries more weight and hence it is more suggestible: This is the reason at the root of the influence wielded by specialists, leaders and saints etc. The truth of the matter is that even a false statement stated confidently is more influencing and powerful than a truthful statement stated weakly and without confidence.

(*vi*) *Repetition*. Constant repetition of the same phenomenon also increases the suggestibility of individuals for it because it then starts to attract the attention of the people. In this connection, it has been established on the basis of many experiments that repetition should also be marked with some small degree of variation in the suggestion since otherwise people come to look at it as a mere commonplace and cease to attend to it.

The forementioned internal and external conditions that chance suggestibility find comprehensive application in propaganda moves in the political field and in advertising in the industrial and commercial spheres. Actually, propaganda and advertising are based on the fundamental psychological principles of suggestion because the best propaganda and the best advertisement is that in which anything is suggested, and not bluntly stated, in a manner that convinces the listener and compels him to accept it.

IMITATION

When a child attempts to walk impressively like his father swinging a stick, he is imitating. Mead has characterized imitation as the conscious emulation of the behaviour and conduct of others. He writes "Imitation is self-conscious assumption of another's acts or roles."[3]

From the psychological viewpoint, the process of imitation is seen to possess the following characteristics:

1. The individual imitating does not indulge in thought or trial and error before he imitates but immediately becomes involved in the activity of imitation.
2. The person imitating does not show any previous acquaintance with the activity imitated.
3. In the process of imitation the person imitating performs exactly the same activity as the one being performed before him.

Kinds of Imitation

In Ginsberg's opinion imitation is of the following three types:

1. Biological Imitation. An animal of a particular species commences to act in the manner in which he sees others of the same species acting. In the woods, when one jackal starts crying, the others follow suit. This is biological imitation and it is unconscious. This is what Kirk Patrick calls reflex imitation.

2. Ideo-motor Imitation. The children in the family behave in the manner in which they see their elders behaving, eating, talking and performing other activities. This is ideo-motor imitation. It is motivated by emotions or thoughts. As is evident by the name given to this type of imitation, there is no distinction between idea and activity or in other words, there is no gap of time between thought and action since activity occurs immediately after the idea arises. In this way it is a kind of unconscious imitation. One often comes across individuals who can be seen copying the actions of players in the field in games such as cricket, hockey, etc. Even in audience witnessing dramatic and theatrical performances one sees people who try to imitate the actors on. the stage.

3. Rational or Purposeful Imitation. A person who is being imitated into some new function learns much by imitating the individual who is guiding him in his orientation. This is purposeful imitation and it employs reason.

William McDougall, besides accepting the above-mentioned ideo-motor type, mentioned four other types of imitation in his classification of this phenomenon.

1. Sympathetic Imitations. It is a fact of common knowledge and experience that people are seen emulating the efforts of others because of the sympathy that they bear for them. For example, one can see individuals crying, laughing or mimicking when they observe other individuals doing it. But imitation of this kind is limited only to simple physical or psychological activities.

---

3. Mead, G. H., Quoted by K. Young, *A Handbook of Social Psychology*, p. 110.

2. Deliberate Imitation. As is evident from the nomenclature employed, this type of imitation signifies willful and deliberate imitation. In this, the individual exercises himself in his efforts at imitation. The individual indulges in initial preparation for this imitation, which is based on his interests and objectives. Evidently, this type of imitation is not to be found in children.

3. Intermediary Imitation. This type of imitation falls somewhere in between the two forementioned types of imitation, and hence it partially possesses the characteristics of both these types. In this way, it is partially initiated by thought and is partially the result of effort inherent in it. Imitation of this kind is characteristic of infants. It is not based on any predetermined aim or object and does not contain any elements of preceding considerations. For example, children can often be seen unconsciously or at least effortlessly imitating some scene or situation that has affected their imagination powerfully. In this, there is no thought involved.

4. Meaningless Imitation by Infants. This particular category of imitation includes the imitation of children, which does not have any meaning because of its very nature. In fact, this is the purest and natural form of imitation. But this hardly means that the child does not benefit by it since it is one of the important sources whereby the child learns many social behaviour patterns. This is what Kirk Patrik calls spontaneous imitation in which are included all those imitative actions which the individual indulges in, according to his nature. For example, children love to whistle in imitation of the locomotive. In this way, then, this classification includes only those imitations which concur with the nature of the individual.

Besides reflex, deliberate and spontaneous imitations mentioned above, Kirk Patrick accepts the following two:

1. Dramatic Imitation. This imitation is of a dramatic nature. It is a natural tendency in children to imitate all that they see around themselves. One of the commonest things that children do is to don their father's head-wear and to walk around, equipped, with his walking stick. The little girl acts just like her mother and behaves in the same manner towards the dolls as her mother behaves towards her. The imitative impulses of the children lead them further afield and they are found imitating practically everyone and everything that they come across. They will imitate the policeman, the railway guard and even the newspaper-boy, the way he calls. This dramatic influence has much importance in the field of education. The successful teacher who knows that the children love to imitate goes through the actions of whatever he wants to impress upon them and they imitate him, and thus he is successful in his effort.

2. Idealistic Imitation. In this case, the individual places ideal before himself and imitates it. Besides deliberate imitation already mentioned, Drever has made the following distinction in imitation:

1. Unconscious Imitation. This classification is inclusive of all those imitative activities that the individual performs unconsciously and it is through the medium of this unconscious imitation that the individual adopts many patterns of social behaviour.

2. Perceptual Imitation. If the conduct that is being imitated is present in front of the individual imitating it, then the imitation is said to be of a perceptual nature.

3. Ideational Imitation. But if the behaviour pattern that is being imitated is not objective present in front of the person imitating it, but is rather present in his mind in the form of an idea or image then this activity of imitating is called ideational.

Social Importance of Imitation

Of all the living beings, it is the human child who possesses the greatly capacity for imitation. Language plays a major part in this imitation and language and pronunciation is acquired by the child only through imitation. The activity of imitation possesses much importance for social life, In fact, it would be no misnomer to say that a major part of the social conduct of the human being is adopted through imitation. It is only by indulging in imitation that he can make adequate use of the experience of his predecessors and others around him. It is imitation which provides him behavioural patterns whereby he conducts himself in the presence of others. It is only through the medium of imitation that customs, traditions and mores act in society and are maintained intact in their passage from one-generation to the next. In society many forms of behaviour such as manners, conversational modes, etc., are carried on by fashion. The reason behind this, too, is the presence of imitative activity in individuals of every society. It is an accepted norm for the ordinary individuals in society to follow the views of great parsons and leaders. Here, too, this happens because of imitation. Even educator makes use of the tendency of imitation. Education of social behaviour is based primarily on imitation. It is often remarked that one is known by the company he keeps. It is sometimes seen that the students try to imitate and adopt the behaviour, thoughts, ideals and mannerisms of their teachers and because of this good teacher succeeds in moulding the conduct of the students on desired lines. It also usually happens that people estimate the behaviour of the children according to the knowledge that they have of their predecessors. It is commonly believed, and in most cases also taken for granted, that the off-spring of cultured parents will be of cultured nature while the children of quarreling parents will be obstinate and quarrelsome. At the root of all these notions is the phenomenon of imitation. By making adequate use of the tendency to imitate that the human child possesses in abundance, an able teacher may succeed in moulding the behaviour of his students on cultured lines. It is because of the tendency to imitate that children are so much susceptible to the influences of their parents and friends whose behaviour they imitate indiscriminately. It is only because this importance of imitation has been understood that now great emphasis is laid, in every sphere of education, on the concrete presentation of the ideals before the individual that are to be inculcated into him. And particularly in the various spheres of cultural life such as dancing, music, art, etc., demonstration and imitation are of great importance.

Realizing the importance of imitation in social life, some sociologists have been led to conclude that it is the sole basis of social education. In the opinion of these sociologists, the conduct and behaviour that the individual learns is through the medium of imitation. Tarde has gone so far as to say that society is imitation. But, as can be seen from a detailed analysis of Tarde's principle, in fact imitation cannot be postulated to be the sole cause of all social behaviour although it undoubtedly has much importance in social education.

SUGGESTION-IMITATION THEORY

According to this theory, imitation is the major element in social organisation and behaviour, the origin of tribal communities, the customs of the existing societies, dogmas, mores, fashion, political and religious behaviour, art, literature, modes of life, etc. Bagehot was the first to advance the suggestion-imitation theory in 1873. He used the term imitation in a very comprehensive sense and comprehensive suggestion in it. It is for this reason that his theory came to be called the suggestion-imitation theory.

Distinction between Imitation and Suggestion

In Bagehot's view, the essential difference between imitation and suggestion has been overlooked. The distinction is in respect of the following points:

1. Imitation is a physical activity while suggestion is a mental one.
2. In imitation copying is willingly done while the influence of suggestion is unconscious.
3. The field of imitation is limited to physiological activities, while the field of suggestion is more comprehensive.
4. Intelligence has no function in imitation while in suggestion the intellect leaves its imperceptible mark.
5. Suggestion is inherent in imitation, but there is no imitation in suggestion.
6. Suggestion precedes imitation.

Tarde's Theory

Like Bagehot, Tarde has also stressed the importance of imitation. He included all sorts of mental activities in the process of imitation such as suggestion, sympathy, etc., and went so far as to pronounce society as imitation. Social progress is the outcome of the internal mental actions of the members of the group. Mental activity of covert type is manifested in three ways — repetition, opposition and adaptation. Each of these three has three forms of repetition. In its physical form it is manifested as the waves of sound (word) and light, in its biological form as heredity and in the form of imitation in his social aspect. According to Tarde, the progress of society rests upon research and the power of research is based on the relationship of new ideas. The acceptance of research is based on imitation. Imitation leads to repetition and repetition leads to social homogeneity. The advent of an invention is based on the following two social causes:

(a) *Logical.* When any new idea concurs with the prevailing social ideas it is immediately accepted.

(b) *Extra logical.* It is of the following three kinds:

(*i*) Even if the new idea is not logical it is accepted because it is attractive.

(*ii*) A new idea is accepted because of the social prestige of its proponent.

(*iii*) Imitation proceeds from the centre to the periphery. Europeans took an interest in French dress after they had become interested in French literature.

It is contended by Tarde that ideas and thoughts are imitated first, and this imitation is followed by imitation of institutions. Tarde's theory has been criticised on the following grounds:

1. It cannot be asserted that everything in society is because of imitation, however important may be the role of imitation in social life.

2. It is absolutely unscientific to employ imitation in such a comprehensive manner; it has only led to the meaning losing its precision.

3. In addition to imitation other factors that influence social behaviour are instincts, social traditions, suggestion, sympathy, etc.

SYMPATHY

When one individual shares the pain of others and also their joys then it is said that he is sympathetic towards others. It is common experience that when we meet a person who is smiling we also smile. In a serious atmosphere we are serious and we are compelled to feel jolly and happy in a colourful and gay atmosphere. In this way, the role of sympathy can always be seen in day- to-day experience and behaviour.

No definite assertion can be made about the nature of sympathy, particularly whether it is innate or acquired, and whether it is a process acquired through imitation or through some other media. What can be said without much hesitation is that sympathy is not mere imitation. In addition to imitation, it also contains a definite motive and inspiration. Lovers naturally share in the feelings and experiences of each other, but when they become husband and wife they have to share in each other's feelings even deliberately knowing that their failure to do so may shatter their matrimonial peace and calm and reduce is longevity. Sympathy strengthens their mutual love and provides psychological peace and comfort.

According to McDougall, sympathy is not an emotion but an instinct. In his treatise on *Social Psychology*, McDougall has written that one may observe the existence of sympathy, arising out of emotion and feeling, in children at an age when they cannot be said to be in a position to understand the importance of expressions that they reciprocate. An early stimulus to sympathy in the child is the crying and yelling of other children. When they have grown up somewhat, the observation of a smiling face as the expression of merriment, brings forth a smile. At an even later stage, the feelings that are communicated from one child to another in this obvious fashion are fear, curiosity and anger. Mirth is infamous for its contagion-like spreading, although it is not an expression truly born of an instinct but which rather presents the most recognised example of sympathy-originated expression of an emotional state. This immediate and unrestricted reaction to the emotional expression of other people is one of the great attractions of childhood and infancy. In this way, it is McDougall's considered opinion that children possess a natural tendency towards sympathy for others.

According to some psychologists, sympathy is an acquired activity. According to W. E. Biatz, the emotion in the person showing sympathy, which aroused as a definite reaction towards a common element uniformly present in the existing situation, is a part of his personal or individual system of emotional habits arising out of his past experience. In this way, when a child cries upon perceiving another child crying, then it means that he is only giving expression to the reaction that he has felt when confronted by a similar situation himself.

If one contemplates upon one's own experience and the behaviour of children that one comes across, then one is forced to the conclusion that both the above opinions are one-sided. All the various examples of sympathy cannot be explained by defining it as instinctive behaviour or as a conditioned reflex. Sympathy can be motivated by instinct but it can also be a reaction to the situation. In fact, all the sympathetic behaviour that man acquires in society cannot be explained by calling it instinctive or conditioned response to the situation. It is only too apparent that the child learns to sympathize or to express sympathy by imitating the behaviour of his parents and those older than himself. Briefly, then, there is much in sympathy that is acquired and much that is innate. The extent to which sympathy is acquired or innate may be learnt through observation.

Need for Imagination in Sympathy

A sympathetic individual must be imaginative. The individual who cannot place himself in the predicament of another through imagination and thereby feel his emotion, and experience cannot generate feelings of sympathy for others within himself. For sympathy, and in order to be sympathetic, it is necessary to be emotional. One may participate in the pain and suffering of another only if one has suffered similar if not identical privation or if one may experience pain of another through imagining it. Sympathetic behavior is no doubt natural but one must also learn to sympathies with others. Sympathy is innate but it is constantly developed by experience. The scope of the child's sympathy also widens. It is only because of this that every one sympathies with the friend but no one fraternises with the foe.

QUESTIONS FOR EXERCISE

1. What is suggestion? Discuss its importance in social life.
2. Enumerate and explain the various types of imitation and suggestion.
3. Discuss the role of suggestion in social life.
4. What do you mean by imitation? State the role of imitation in social life.
5. Write a short note on sympathy.

CHAPTER 4

Social Control: Meaning and Agencies

MEANING OF SOCIAL CONTROL

Social control is the control of society over the individual. Some of man's tendencies are beneficial to society while others are detrimental to its interest. There can be no question of controlling the beneficial tendencies. Thus, social control is exercised by society over the undesirable or harmful tendencies of man. But, is social control merely negative? Is controlling some tendencies its sole function? No, social control creates those conditions in which man can be socialised and be prevented from performing anti-social activities. Some control comprehends all those processes, methods, mores, patterns, etc., which render assistance in this work. In this way, the term social control is fairly comprehensive. This is not governmental control. Governmental control is based upon force and is enforced upon the individual externally. Social control is self-control. It keeps on changing in accordance with the changes in society.

DEFINITION OF SOCIAL CONTROL

The various definitions of social control, as provided by the sociologists, are not identical. Some main definitions are the following:

1. *Brearly*. "Social control is a collective term for those processes and agencies, planned and unplanned, by which individuals are taught, persuaded or compelled to conform to the usages and life values of the group to which they belong." It is clear from this definition that social control includes those laws by which an individual behaves in concurrence with the mores of the group.

2. *Gillin and Gillin*. "Social control is that system of measures, suggestion, persuasion, restraint and coercion by whatever means, including physical force, by which a society brings into conformity to the approved pattern of behaviour of a sub-group or by which a group moulds into conformity its members."

3. *MacIver and Page*, "By social order is meant the way in which the entire social order coheres and maintains itself, how it operates, as a changing equilibrium."

4. *Gurvitch and Moore*. "Social control can be defined as the sum total or rather the whole of cultural patterns, social symbols, collective spiritual meanings,

values, ideals, as well as acts or processes, directly connected with them, whereby, inclusive of society, every particular group and every participating individual member overcome tensions and conflicts within themselves through temporary equilibria and take steps for new creative efforts."

This definition of social control is adequately comprehensive. It has taken into account both the negative and creative aspects of social control and has indicated the means and processes of social control.

TYPES OF SOCIAL CONTROL

1. Karl Mannheim's View. Different sociologists hold differing views upon the types of social control. Karl Mannheim has accepted the following two types of social control:

(a) *Direct social control.* This is the control exercised upon the individual by the reactions of the people living in proximity. Such control is found existing in the family, neighbourhood, playgroup and other primary groups. An individual is deeply influenced by the opinion and views of his parents, colleagues, neighbours and those who work with him. His behaviour is determined or controlled by their criticism, derogation, praise, suggestion or persuasion, etc. This is direct control.

(b) *Indirect social control.* This is the control exercised upon the individual by factors which are separated from him. Control of the individual by secondary groups is of this type. Its prominent means are traditions, institutions, customs, rationalised behaviour, changes in situations and social mechanism, etc. The means of social control are invisible and subtle. In the existing complex society, the influence of the opinion, law, custom, etc., is conveyed in this way. It is not that there are no individuals behind this control but these individuals are not seen by the persons affected.

2. Kimball Young's View. Kimball Young has divided social control into two classes from the viewpoint of methodology. In this way, social control has been divided into the following two types:

(a) *Positive.* Reward has an immense value upon the activities of an Individual. A large part of the population of society desires to be rewarded by the society. And, consequently, they constantly endeavour to conform to the traditions, mores, values and ideals accepted by the society. For this, they are rewarded in the form of social recognition, fame, respect, etc.

(b) *Negative.* Under this are comprehended those types of social controls in which a person is prevented from doing something by threat of punishment. Society, while it encourages the people to indulge in certain types of activity of promising reward, also discourages and prevents people from many activities by fear of punishment, which can be moderate, severe, physical, or verbal or in any other form. Examples of verbal punishment are defamation, criticism, ridicule, etc. An example of physical punishment is extradition from caste. Fear of these punishments helps to prevent people from violating the socially accepted customs, traditions, values and ideals, etc.

3. Other Views. In addition to the above mentioned forms of social control two other forms, formal and informal, have also been recognised. The formal type are those which are specifically designed for control, and include government, law, police, army, jail, penal code, etc. Informal social control includes those methods which develop by themselves according to the needs of society and are, mores, traditions, customs, social ideals, etc. Hayes has accepted two forms of social control: 1. Control by sanction. In this, social control is effected by rewarding the obedient and punishing the miscreant. 2. Control by socialization and education.

AGENCIES OF SOCIAL CONTROL

It would have become evident from the foregoing description of the various types of social control, that there are many direct and indirect, formal and informal means of social control. Among the important means of social control, Ross has enumerated family, educational system, belief and religion, social suggestion, social ideal, ritual and festival, art, leadership, law and administration besides physical force. Giddings has accepted the importance of belief, social direction or guidance, religion, social ideals, social festivals, art, leadership, intellectual factors, education and propaganda, law and administration and force, as means of social control.

1. Customs. In controlling the behaviour of an individual in society, customs play an important role. They regulate the life of an individual in a way so that he experiences the minimum of pressure. Generally, the people themselves want to live according to the custom, as such a course firstly saves them from the objections and ridicule of the society and secondly they do not have to resort to original thinking on every aspect. By means of customs they are provided with a clear guidance for every activity. To take an example, among the Hindus there are various definite customs relating to their day-to-day activity, education, behavioural concepts, procedures, marriage, etc. In the Varnashram system, these customs have been organised and systematised even further. Hence, a Hindu does not have to think about these things and his life progresses comfortably and in orderly fashion according to the customs instituted after the experience of ages. It has correctly been said by Ginsberg that the role played by customs in life is comparable to the role of instincts in living beings. Instincts guide the living beings in his struggle for existence. Customs enlighten man in his social life. From his very childhood, man forms the habit of obeying them and he follows them without raising any hue and cry. He comes into possession of these customs when they come down to him in the form of his social heritage or inheritance, and it is these very customs which he bequeaths to his successors. Ordinarily, an individual does not dare oppose the customs. Sometimes harmful customs continue to prevail for long periods "because most people do not consider them, while those who do consider them harmful lack the courage to oppose them. It is an exceptional individual who transforms customs, withstanding criticism and sometimes even endangering his life, but as time passes the people become reconciled to the novel idea and in this way the customs undergo a change.

But they do not suffer a loss in their effort of controlling behaviour due to this possibility of their being changed.

2. Public Opinion. Public opinion is of no mean importance as a means of controlling the behaviour of an individual. History bears evidence to numerous incidents of great men having to make great sacrifices because of public opinion. It was on the word of a washerman of his kingdom that the great king Ram Chandra turned his wife Sita out of his palace and sent her into exile. In ancient times, many kings resorted to disguise in order to guage, and judge public opinion concerning them. In the present democratic age, public opinion is supremely powerful. It controls the government. Even the most powerful government has to resign if it opposes it. This public opinion is formed by propaganda, newspaper, cinema, radio, etc. Before embarking upon improvement of society the wise reformers first create public opinion favourable to them. An individual is more concerned with the reaction of people than even with the wrath of God. It is the fear of disgrace in society which causes most people to keep a check upon their behaviour. It is ordinarily very difficult to contradict public opinion. Some enterprising people do succeed in converting the opinion of the public towards themselves but without doing so they cannot remain in conflict with it for long. Public opinion controls the conduct, behaviour, way of living and methods, etc., of the individual to a fairly large extent.

3. Family. Family has great importance as an instrument of social control. The first place where an individual is socialized is the family. It is in the family that he learns the various methods of living, behaviour, conversation, etc. In the family he learns obedience and respect for the opinion of others. The control of parents upon the child is the control of society upon the individual. The family is a basic or fundamental form of society. It has some laws which every member has to obey. As a general rule obedience of these rules is enforced lovingly and effort is made to make the individual understand them but sometimes recourse is had to punishment. In the family, a child is taught to behave in a way which conforms to the standard of goodness of the people. A divergence from such behaviour is checked by advising the child of the bad opinion of him which may be formed by other people. In this way, the individual learns to respect public opinion and to be controlled by it. The family ingrains into the child the propriety of behaviour in all trades of life. This brings him under the control of mores and traditions. Infringement of the rules of family brings punishment in its wake and in this way he learns to accept the pressure of law. The family initiates him into the good and the bad. in this way the communal ideals, values and thoughts exercise their influence and control upon him. In the family the child finds the patterns for behaviour by imitating the behaviour of the other members of the family. In this way the family educates the individual to accept and obey social control, accustoms him to it and introduces him to the customs. Due to the family the various forms of social control become a part of the individual's life and he does not experience any difficulty in adjusting to or living under social control in future.

This control of the family over the individual is not restricted within the family but is exercised even outside its precincts. Consideration for the family honour steers an individual clear of many undesirable activities. He has at all times, and in all circumstances, to keep in mind the honour and respect of the family. In this way, the family has control over an individual not merely in his childhood but from his infancy to his senility. In this way, the family is one of the most important agencies or instruments of social control.

4. Education. According to Ruskin, "Education consists in making people polite what they ought to be." The ideals and patterns of politeness differ from society to society. An individual is trained in these through education. Here the word 'education' does not contain merely literacy but is employed in its most comprehensive sense. It is only in this meaning of the word that the sociologist studies or contemplates it. Education teaches man the use of the various capacities, abilities, intelligence, etc., bestowed upon him by Nature. Education gives him ability to succeed in his struggle for existence. Education is an art of adaptation. For man, adaptation is more social than natural. Hence, education adapts man to society. In this way, education is an important means of social control.

Education is in the family, school, playground, club, office, in fact everywhere. At every place the individual is taught something and socialized. In the family, in school, on playground, the child learns the use of polite behaviour, learns to respect the opinion and advice of others and learns to comply with the traditions and mores. Theoretical education, *viz.*, reading and writing, serves to form the intellectual base for all this and with practical education he learns to put this into practice. The organisation or system of society is disrupted and thrown into confusion when the educational systems contradict or when the activity of education does not function correctly, and social control fails to function. Hence, education is a necessary condition for the proper exercise of social control. In the absence of an appropriate and organised education social control remained merely an arbitrary pressure which cannot continue for long. Without proper education the harmony of the individual and society is not merely difficult but well nigh impossible. Education makes social control normal. It makes social control self-control and the individual does not experience its burden. It is another thing that an educated person cannot easily be persuaded to acquiesce to a wrong or incorrect form of social control.

5. Law. Law is a prominent means of social control. The state enacts laws to control the behaviour of the individuals in the society. Disobedience of these laws and their infringement is punished by the government. In this way the control of law is the control of administrative power which is vested in the government officials. Laws are enforced with the help of the court, the police and sometimes the armed forces.

According to Ross, "Law is the most specialized and highly furnished engine of social control employed by society." Ross has enumerated two functions of law: (1) to crush completely some of the homicidal activities of the individual, and (2) to persuade the individual to both pay attention to the rights of the others and to act cooperatively. In this way law does not merely protect society or ensure its existence but also contribute to its welfare. The modern state is a welfare state. Hence, in modern states, law enters into all the aspects of life. Law, on the one hand, limits the field of activity of the criminal while on the other it prevents other people from criminal activity by threatening punishment. While it protects the obedient from the disobedient of law, it also prevents every one from becoming an obstacle in the path of another. In this way law controls the conduct of the people of the state and grants everyone the opportunity to progress.

6. Communal Codes. Communal codes include all those laws of the community by means of which the community exercises its control over the individual. Customs, folkways, mores, morals and rituals, etc., are enumerated under it.

(*i*) *Customs.* Shakespeare has called custom 'a tyrant', Montaigne 'a violent schoolmistress', and Bacon the principal magistrate of man's life'. All these utterings serve to indicate the control potential of custom. Disobedience of custom brings social disgrace. Custom has great utility from the social standpoint. It is a kind of social necessity.

(*ii*) *Folkways.* Folkways are laws of behaviour in society *e.g.*, people greet each other in England by shaking hands and in India by putting the palms together vertically upward. Folkways develop in the society, unaided by the law of trial and error. Activity which violates them is not punishable but other people in the society look upon such behaviour as degenerate and ridicule it. The fear of social ridicule acts as a large measure of control on the conduct of an individual.

(*iii*) *Mores.* Mores are those folkways which are considered essential for the welfare of group. Society exhibits greater sternness in its efforts to win compliance of these folkways. The person who violates mores is turned out of the particular class of society to which he belongs, people do not converse with him and even show a disinclination to marry into his family. An example of a more is the prohibition of cow-slaughter in Hindu society.

(*iv*) *Morals.* Morals are laws concerning concepts of goodness and badness. In civilised societies non-violence, truth, justice, equality, etc., are considered moral and conduct violating them is condemned. Behind morals is the force of conscience. It is based on the social consciousness of good and bad. These conceptions of good and bad change according to their context. But in every country the current ethical concepts govern the social behaviour of the individuals.

(*v*) *Rituals.* Rituals are those forms of socially accepted behaviour which are important in times of festivals and religious celebration. These rituals are to be followed, as a matter of duty. Among the Hindus, there are many rituals to be performed at festivals such as Holi, Diwali, etc.

7. Religion. The control of religion is very strong in the social sphere. Every religion has determined some laws in the behaviour, the obedience of which is considered compulsory. At the base of these religious laws is the fear of divine displeasure and sufferings of hell, coupled with a love and respect for some invisible power. The individual feels the pressure of this belief even more than the pressure exerted by the state and the society. In this way religion is a powerful weapon of social control.

8. Recreational Group. In the recreational group a person undergoes specialization and learns the methods of behaviour towards other people. Hayes has written that "By supervised play children team by experience that the civilized life is far superior for all concerned than savagery." Games are based upon laws without following which the game cannot be played. In this way games instil in man the habit of remaining in control and obeying law. Game makes a person pliable and teaches him to obey the orders of the leader and cooperate with other people. As a result the sense of group responsibility is awakened in the participants.

9. Art. also controls the behaviour of men. Poetry, folksongs, drawings, sculpture, music, etc., have their effect on man's emotions and sentiments. Art is a pleasant social control. Its influence is universal. Folksongs are important in every society. Music makes human tendencies refined. Community feeling is enhanced by communal singing and dancing.

10. Social Ideals. The activities of individuals are affected by the social ideals. Social ideals are subject to change, and are relevant in their own context. But in every country most of the people endeavour to mould their lives according to these social ideals. In modern times, the conduct and behaviour of people of democratic countries has been influenced by democratic ideals of liberty, equality and fraternity while the conduct of the communist population has been swayed by communist ideals.

11. Leadership. The leaders have also shown the way for the masses to follow. The path followed by great men is the path to be followed by others. In this way leaders in the religious, social, political and other fields have had great influence upon the lives of people. Mahatma Gandhi and Karl Marx converted the lives of millions of people. And even otherwise, it is the leaders in every society who enforce the social control.

12. Fashion. In the present day, fashion has become an important means of social control. In civilized societies the determinant in the field of thought and conduct, dress, belief, opinions, recreations, jewellery, adornment of the house, way of talking, literature, music, art, in brief, all fields of life, is mainly fashion. With the increase in the means of transport and communication, the influence of fashion spreads over a greater range. Fashion is constantly changing but the people are ever desirous of chaging with it.

QUESTIONS FOR EXERCISE

1. Clarify the meaning of social control. Describe various means of social control.
2. What do you understand by social control? How do religion and law control the behaviour of an individual ?
3. What is meant by social control? Discuss the importance of customs and opinion in controlling the behaviour of an individual.

4. What is social control? Describe a few of the forms of social control.
5. What is social control? How is it exercised in a society ?
6. What are the agencies of social control in modern society?
7. Define 'social control'. Describe the agencies of social control in urban areas.
8. Assess the importance of mores and folkways in social life.
9. Discuss the importance of norms in the social life of the people.
10. Explain two of the following and discus the role they pay in social control:
    (*i*) Custom
    (*ii*) Law
    (*iii*) Religion
    (*iv*) Fashion.
11. Distinguish between religion and law as means of social control.
12. Define social control and discuss major agencies of social control with examples.

CHAPTER 5

Social Control in Social Groups

WHAT IS A SOCIAL GROUP?

Sociologists have presented several definitions of a social group, in which emphasis has been laid upon different characteristics of group life. Some of the important definitions of a social group are the following:

1. *Williams, R.M.* "A social group is a given aggregate of people playing interrelated roles and recognised by themselves or others as a unit of interaction."[1]

2. *Ogbum and Nimkoff.* "Whenever two or more individuals come together and influence one another, they may be said to constitute a social group."[2]

3. *MacIver and Page.* "... by group we mean any collection of social beings, who enter into distinctive social relationships with one another."[3]

4. *Gillin and Gillin.* "A social group thus grows out of and requires a situation which permits meaningful inter-stimulation and meaningful response between the individuals involved, common focusing of attention on common stimulation or interest and the development of certain common drives, motivations or emotions."[4]

5. *Edward Sapir.* "Any group is constituted by the fact that there is some interest which holds its members together."[5]

6. *Eldredge and Merrill.* "A social group may be defined as two or more persons who are in communication over an appreciable period or time and who act in accordance with a common function or purpose."[6]

7. *E. S. Bogardus.* "A social group may be thought of as a number of persons two or more, who have some common objects of attention, who are stimulating to each other, who have a common loyalty and participate in similar activities."[7]

---

1. Williams, R. M., *American Society: A Sociological Interpretation*, Alfred A. Knopf Inc., New York (1951), p. 446.
2. Ogburn and Nimkoff, *A handbook of Sociology*, p. 172,
3. Maclver, R. M. and Page, C. H., *Society: An Introductory Analysis*, Macmillan and Co., London, (1953), p. 213.
4. Gillin and Gillin, *Cultrural Sociology*, p. 196.
5. Edward Sapir, *Group, Encyclopaedia of Social Sciences*, Vol. 7, p. 179.
6. Eldredge and Merrill, *Culture and Society*, p. 19.
7. Bogardus, E. S., *Society*, p. 5.

Most of the above mentioned definitions have emphasised someone or the other trait of group life. A workable definition can be adopted by saying that social group is that aggregate of persons which is like a unit and whose members have some common aims, interests, stimulations and emotions together with mutual social relations and social interactions.

CLASSIFICATION OF GROUPS

Different sociologists have classified groups in different ways. The chief bases of these classifications of groups are functions, scope and stability. George Simmel, Von Weise and Becker have taken number as the basis. Tonnies has taken social interaction as the basis. Lovie and Malinowski have preferred age, sex and other signs and Monier has classified on the basis of blood relationship, place and action. Similarly, the groups have been classified on the basis of size, duration and choice.

Bogardus has classified groups into the following types:
(i) Informal, Formal and Bureaucratic, (ii) Voluntary and Involuntary, (iii) Genetic and Congregate, (iv) Primary and Secondary, (v) Disjunctive or Overlapping, (vi) Social, Pseudo-social, Anti-Social, Pro-social and Socialized.

Some other important classifications of groups are as following:

1. Cooley's Classification (i) Primary Groups — in which there are face to face, strong and co-operative relations between the persons such as a family.
(ii) Secondary Groups — where strong, personal and warm relations are not found as in political parties.

2. Sumner's Classification. (i) In-groups — In these groups the members have common object and common interest and a sense of well-being. The member of the in-group treat others as outsiders. These groups can be formed on the basis of relation, country, political interests and economic interest, etc.
(ii) Out-group — Groups other than in-groups are out-groups.

3. Miller's Classification. (i) Vertical, (ii) Horizontal.

4. Gidding's Classification. (i) Public, (ii) Private.

5. Elwood's Classification. (i) Sanctioned, (ii) Unsanctioned.

6. Gillin and Gillin's Classification. (i) Based on blood-relationship, (ii) Based on physical traits, (iii) Based on situation proximity, (iv) Based on cultural interests.

7. Ward's Classification. (i) Voluntary, (ii) Involuntary.

In fact, to classify groups is a difficult task. In this connection, Cuber has rightly written, "Sociologists have devoted a great deal of effort to the difficult problem of classifying groups into types.

At first, though this would seem easy to do but perhaps after further reflection, it will be found to present numerous difficulties. These difficulties are so great, in fact, that at present we have no overall systematic classification of groups, which is entirely acceptable to all sociologic scholars." The most important classification of groups is into primary and secondary. Primary groups are such in which there are face to face, strong and cooperative relations among the members. Secondary groups have impersonal and formal relations. The former are in-groups, the latter out-groups.

CHIEF CHARACTERISTICS OF GROUP-LIFE

Just as to classify the groups is a difficult task, similarly to point out the characteristics of group-life is also a difficult problem. Even then some characteristics of group-life can be described. They are as follows:

1. **The Members of a Group are Related to Each Other**. Simply a gathering of persons cannot be called a group. The members of the group should be interrelated. In fact, it is this social relation that is called a group. A number of human beings in reciprocal communication, constitute a group. Most of the sociologists have admitted the social relations to be the fundamentals of group-life.

2. **Group Involves Sense of Unity.** A sense of unity is essential for every group. By virtue of such a sense members of a group treat each other as their own and a feeling of sympathy between them develops.

3. **Members of a Group have a Sense of We-feeling.** By a sense of wellbeing, the members of group help each other in performing their duties; and they defend collectively against the harmful powers. They treat others as outsiders and try to make their group prosperous and self-sufficient.

4. **The Interests, Ideals and Values of the Group Members are Common.** A group includes those persons who are related to each other in such a way that they should be treated as one. For it the interests, ideals and values of the persons of a group should tend to be common, because this similarity promotes unity.

5. **There is Similarity of Behaviour in a Group.** As the interests, ideals and values of the persons of a group are common, similarly the behaviour of the persons also tends to be similar. A social group is not merely a group of persons, but it is a continuation of their behaviour.

6. **Control of Group over the Actions of the Members.** The main reason behind the similarity of behaviour in group-life is that actions of the members are controlled by the group. In each group there are some customs, norms and procedures which are acceptable to everyone and the members of the group have to obey them. Whenever these are neglected, the group gives punishment. Even if the group fails to punish a person disobeying these, he shall be severely criticised by the public. In this way, everyone has to obey the social norms. In fact, without some norms, the existence of group-life is practically impossible.

7. **The Members of a Group are Affected by its Characteristics.** Each group possesses some special characteristics which separate it from the similar and dissimilar groups. These characteristics affect the members constituting the group. The effect may be of a different nature for different persons, but still all the members are influenced by the group.

The above mentioned characteristics can be observed in a family group. In a family group, the members are related to each other by intimate relations such as that of husband-wife, father-son, brother-sister, etc., and all work together extending mutual help for the common good of the family and in the interest of the family. All members treat each other as their own and though their interests may be different, still their ideals and interests tend to be similar. A family works as a separate unit by virtue of this similarity of ideals and interests. All the members are controlled by the family and if they don't obey the family norms, they are rebuked.

These characteristics of group life can be observed in other groups too, though their quantity may be different.

PRIMARY GROUPS

By primary groups we mean those which are characterised by intimate face-to-face relations, close association and co–operation. These groups are primary in the sense that they play a fundamental role in forming the social nature and ideals of the individuals. Participation in primary group leads to a fusion of individualities in a common whole. This wholeness involves the sympathy and mutual identification for which 'we' is the proper expression. The best example of primary groups are family, a group of children, playmates and neighbourhood of village, etc. These groups influence the life of human beings more vitally than other groups. For example, in play group men give first creative expression to their social impulses as playmates and comrades. In these respects the primary group is fundamental in man's life. Cooley has rightly said, "By primary groups I mean those characterised by intimate face-to-face association and co-operation. They are primary in several senses but chiefly in that they are fundamental in forming the social nature and ideals of the individuals. The result to intimate association ... is a certain fusion of individualities in a common whole, so that one's very self for many purposes at least is the common life and purposes of the group. Perhaps the simplest way of describing the wholeness is by saying that it is a 'we', it involves the sort of sympathy and mutual identification for which we is the natural expression."[8]

Characteristics of Primary Groups

For better understanding of primary group, it is necessary to understand its characteristics. Some of these characteristics are internal while some of them are external. The external characteristics are as follows:

1. Physical Closeness among Members. It is characteristic of a primary group that the members constituting it should be physically close to each other. It will be very difficult to exchange thoughts or to help each other if they are not physically close. The members of the primary groups are very closely related. Therefore, physical closeness is essential for them.

2. Small Size. The size of the primary group should be so small that the desired intimate relation may be developed. Intimacy diminishes when the number of persons is increased in a class, family, team or other group. On the other hand, the smaller the size of the family the greater the intimacy there is. If the audience is in excess, everybody cannot see the speaker and also cannot listen to him clearly.

3. Stability. To promote closeness in primary group, it should be stable to some extent. New friends increase and old ones decrease if a person tends to change places too often.

8. Cooely, C. H., *Social Organisation*, p. 23.

4. Continuity in the Relations. Therefore, continuity in relations is necessary for the members of the primary group. By meeting frequently, and by exchanging thoughts, the intimacy increases. When this chain is broken, the relations do not remain so fast.

Internal characteristics of primary group are those which relate to the inner relations of the members. It is due to the external characterisitics that gradually these internal characteristics also develop. Main internal characteristics are as follows:

1. Common Aims among the Members. Memebrs of a primary group have common aims and objects. In primary groups like family, etc., every member's pleasure and pain is shared by the whole family group, and all the members work for some common aims.

2. Relations are Ends in Themselves. The relations of the members of a primary group are not based on personal interests. These relations are ends in themselves. These provide mental pleasure and contentment to both the parties. Family relations are of this nature.

3. The Relations of the Members are Spontaneous. As the relations of the members of the primary groups are ends in themselves, so they are also spontaneous. There is nothing like compulsion or pressure between them. Every member of the group feels intimacy for the other in a natural way.

4. Member have Personal Relations. Members of primary groups have personal relations and this is why the gap of one member's absence is not filled completely by the other. After the death of wife, a person may marry again, but the memory of the first wife does not end with it. One may abandon an old relationship and establish a new one but it is impossible to substitute one individual for another in a particular relationship."[9]

5. Relations of the Members are Inclusive. The relations of the members of a primary group are inclusive, their whole personality takes active part in these relations.

6. Maximum Control of the Members. Because of the intimacy, spontaneity, physical closeness, stability and the small size of the group, all the members of a primary group know each other very well, and it is difficult to conceal the affairs of any member from the other. Therefore, there is maximum control of the group on the affairs of the members of the group. The group does not permit anybody to follow a wrong path and stops him against the actions contradictory to group traditions and ideals. According to MacIver, "It is the group through which as playmates and comrades we first give creative expression to our social impulses, it is the breeding ground of our mores, the nurse of our loyalties, it is the first and generally remains the chief focus of our social satisfactions. In these respects the fact group is primary in our lives."

---

9. "A new personal relationship can be established, an old one can be abandoned, but no substitution can be made of one individual for another in the same relationship."

—Davis, K., *Human Society*, The Macmillan and Co., New York (1954), p. 293.

Importance of a Primary Group

The reason behind the foundation of social structure of primary groups is their social advantages. The members of the primary group get advantages which they cannot achieve in their individual capacity. From the point of view of an individual, the main points regarding the importance of a primary groups are as follows:

1. Development of Personality. Freud, Adler and other psychologists have maintained that the personality of a child is developed in a family and playmates group and it does not change appreciably afterwards, it only develops. Thus, the development of personality depends, in most cases, upon the primary groups.

2. Increase in Efficiency. With the development of personality in primary groups, the efficiency is also increased. Persons of a group get help, inspiration and co-operation from the others. In a family, a person works so efficiently for his children that he can never work with such an efficiency for himself.

3. Satisfaction of Psychological Needs. Primary groups satisfy many psychological needs of the individuals. They provide a sense of contentment and security to the persons and satisfy their desires of loving and be loved. By virtue of primary group, a person gets the benefits of companionship, sympathy, exchange of thoughts and satisfies most of his psychological needs.

Primary groups are equally important from the point of view of the society. They realise socialization of the individuals. They maintain the control of society over the persons. Social structure is consolidated by them and the working of the society remains smooth. They teach the persons to work in the society according to their roles. The whole society is dissolved by their dissolution. The primary groups are the foundation of whole society. It is from them that the individual acquires basic attitudes towards people, social institutions, and the world around him. The attitudes of kindness, tolerance, love and generosity are derived from primary groups through imitation and absorption of group attitude. Two important characterises of the relations of the members of primary groups are mutual concern and affection. Love for the other person is developed without any consideration of self-advantage. Members freely give mutual help in time to troubles. They gossip about each other and show concern for the absent members. Betrayal is considered unforgivable, and guarded by intense and bitter jealousies. To quote P.H. Landis, "From primary groups the individual acquires basic attitudes towards the world around him, people and social institutions. From these groups attitudes of tolerance, kindness, love and generosity are derived, probably more in imitation and absorption of group attitude than by direct teaching, although direct teaching often takes place. Mutual concern and affection are characteristic. Love and consideration for other person is placed above competition and self-advantage. Mutual help in time of trouble is freely given. Group members gossip about each other, showing an interest in and concern for the absent members. If jealousies or hatred should develop, they are intense and bitter, for betrayal is unforgivable."

SECONDARY GROUPS

The secondary groups are opposite to the primary groups. Physical closeness, intimacy and individuality are not desired in them. They are constituted for some proposes and aims after achieving which, they are not more required. Relations in them are indirect, short and temporary. They are the representatives of a cold world. In fact, the warmth of the relations in primary groups cannot be found in the indirect relations in secondary groups. The spontaneity which is obvious in primaiy groups is not found in the secondary groups. The relations in the secondary groups are formal. This type of 'cold behaviour' can be seen among members of an office. The persons do not have any interest in the pleasure and pain, and problems of others. Relations among them are rather competitive than helpful, casual and impersonal. They provide an experience lacking in intimacy. To quote P. H. Landis, "Secondary groups represent that 'cold world' into which parents in rural community have always thought of their young people going when they leave home. Secondary groups are those that are relatively casual and impersonal in their relationship. Because secondary groups make only specialised demands on the person, they receive only a segment of his time and attention. Relationships in them are usually competitive rather than mutually helpful."

Characteristics of a Secondary Group

The characteristics of a secondary group throw light on its nature. The chief characteristics are as follows:

1. Position of a Member Depends Upon his Role. In the secondary group, the position of every member depends upon his role. The persons are not treated on the basis of their births.

2. Individuality in Persons. Individuality develops in the persons in the secondary groups because their relations are based on self-interest. After satisfying interest, they are no longer interested in the group.

3. Self-dependence among Members. Therefore, the members of a secondary group are self-dependent. They have to safeguard their interests themselves. Because of the big size of the group, the relations are indirect.

CONTRAST OF PRIMARY AND SECONDARY GROUP

The chief points of distinction between a primary and a secondary group are as follows:

1. The size of a primary group is small while that of a secondary group is big.

2. The relations in primary groups are close and direct while in the secondary groups these are indirect and formal.

3. In primary groups the purposes and aims are the same for all members and the persons take others' interest as their own. In secondary groups, the aims and purposes are not the same. Every one, therefore, tries to fulfil his self-interest.

4. In the primary groups, the relations are inclusive and this is why the absence of one person cannot be fulfilled by another. Inclusiveness of relations is not found

in the secondary groups and therefore a person can very easily take the place of any other person.

5. Primary groups are the foundation stones of the society. Secondary groups are not so important.

6. Primary groups are generally found in old and rural societies while the secondary groups are generally found in the urban areas.

7. Primary groups do not include other groups in them. Secondary groups may include several groups because of their big size.

8. The position of a person is fixed according to his birth order and age in the primary groups while it is fixed according to roles in the secondary groups.

9. Primary group is concerned with the total personality of a person and it develops his personality. Secondary group is concerned with a particular aspect of personality and it develops only that aspect.

10. Qualities like love, sympathy, mutual help, etc., flourish in the primary groups while secondary groups promote self-interest and individuality.

11. There is a fixed routine in the primary group which is controlled by the aged persons and the rules which have to be obeyed by all the members compulsorily. There is less control on the affairs of the persons in the secondary group and these are controlled by police, jail, court, etc.

SOCIAL CONTROL IN PRIMARY GROUPS

Social control is a pattern that aims at maintaining social organization. This control is both formal and informal. The formal control consists of the laws of society and the state which are enforced through the police and law courts, etc. The informal control takes the form of customs, etiquette, manners, etc.

Informal Control

In primary groups the social controls take an informal form. The means of informal control are folk-ways, mores and group ideals. They exercise their influence through the medium of public opinion and gossip. For example, in primitive societies and rural societies such as India the conduct of the individual is guided by the dogmas, traditions, customs and ideals of society. In the villages of India many of the conflicts are resolved peacefully through negotiation and promotion of common understanding. These ingenuous villagers are controlled by the village committees known as panchayats and groups of elders within their own clan. Every individual fears of the social ostracism that will invariably result if he takes it on himself to violate the wishes of his guides. People fear to violate the laws of society or of their own clan for they fear the loss of their reputation and good name. At certain places and under some circumstances, this fear is an even more powerful antidote than even the fear of legal or judicial punishment. The violation of the laws of the state can lead to a punitive fine or at most to prison sentence that will end some time or the other but when a man is defamed in society, he dare not show his face for the rest of his life.

Influence of Public Opinion

According to Ogburn and Nimkoff, "The group in itself is frequently able to exert more effective control over the conduct of its members than can an outside individual charged with special authority." Further elucidating this influence of public opinion upon members of society, Ogburn and Nimkoff have adduced the example of a child reformatory. The inmates of this reformatory were very naughty. The director threatened them with physical punishment but could not meet with any success. When he was replaced by another director, the new person thought of reforming them by controlling them through public opinion. Previously, the children used to create pandemonium while eating and they would throw all edibles at each other. The new director divided the children into different groups. Members of each group would sit within their own group at separate tables. A new law was introduced to the effect that group behaving best at the dining table would get a double ration of all the best things besides a flag in prize. Now, if any child tried to be naughty the other members at his table would prevent him from doing so or would criticize him because each of the groups wanted to win the prize by exemplary behaviour. In this way, some sort of organization and control was established among the children. Thus, the control of the group was achieved which the former director could not. This one example is sufficient illustration of the fact that in primary groups, the informal forms of social control can often prove even more effective and efficacious than those of formal groups. The pressure of the group itself maintains order within the members. Public opinion as a mode of social control is all the more effective when the group with which it is concerned is of members of a common age and having common interests.

The Family Example

The family is the best example of the primary group. In the family the conduct is guided and controlled in the case of each and every member since every senior member performs the function of guide to his and her youngers. The parents govern the conduct of the children while elder brothers and sisters guide their younger brothers, and much the same function is performed by husband and wife for each other. This government and organization in the behaviour of the family members does not find its parallel in any secondary group or any of its institutions, whatever the moral or internal influence of the group upon its members. Mutual love, affection and sympathy usually and naturally compel the members to conduct themselves towards each other decorously. The scolding administered by the parents or other senior members of the family and even oblique glances convey much meaning and work wonders where guidance is concerned. At times even this is not necessary since the desired effect is achieved through coaxing and persuasion.

In this manner, the methods of social control in the primary group are informal, moral and internal.

SOCIAL CONTROL IN A SECONDARY GROUP

Formal Control

Contrary to the primary group, the methods of social control in the secondary form of groups are formal. The basis of this difference is the fundamental distinction between the primary and secondary group. As opposed to the primary group, the number of members in the secondary group is very large and they manifest a large diversity in thoughts, behavioural patterns and moral or ethical ideals. The relations between them tend to be impersonal. They are not very easily influenced by the opinions of each other. An example of this would be the urban society. In the urban magnitude of population. It is possible for any person to commit some crime and lose his identity in mass of humanity to the utter despair of his pursuers. In the town, the cultural difference that is to be found even between neighbours is enough to dispel any feeling of love and attachment. They have not the time to bother with each other. In the fast routine of life relationships assume a mechanical air so that men grow impervious to all the attacks to public opinion, and this insensibility increases to such an extent that they even appear to be oblivious of their neighbour. As a consequence of all these reasons, the informal method of social control proves ineffective while it becomes necessary to resort to the formal methods of social control such as the police forex, law courts, jails, etc.

Legal or Constitutional Control

Social control in secondary social groups necessitates the use of law or constitution. All associations formulate rules and regulations that serve to control and regulate the behaviour of their members, and they incur punishment if they disregard the rules of their association. Some common examples of such rules would be the rules framed and exercised by labour unions and college unions. School is a secondary group. It lays down certain principles that regulate conduct within the school and class, the infringement of which results in fines and punishments and even rustications in case of serious infringement. In this way, it is evident that in secondary groups, the constitution is resorted to in order to affect social control. It is mad, affective through the channel of force rather than that of common morality. It is external rather than internal, indirect rather than direct.

QUESTIONS FOR EXERCISE

1. What is the role of primary groups in social control? How is social control exercised by family ?
2. Distinguish between primary and secondary group.
3. What is a social group? What are its characteristics.
4. Define secondary group and describe its characteristics.

CHAPTER 6

Social Control in Family Group

In common parlance people sometimes interpret the word family to mean wife but the child is an indispensable part of the family. Again, from the sociological point of view, a temporary alliance between a man and a woman for sexual gratification cannot be said to constitute a family. In order to constitute a family the sex relationship should necessarily be permanent and definite enough to allow for the procreation of children and for an appropriate arrangement for their upbringing. In this way, the family as a part of society is a system of relationship. The family does not mean a place or location but rather web of mutual relationships between the family members in the same way in which the meaning of society lies not in its being a group of human beings but in constituting a web of relations between them.

ESSENTIAL CHARACTERISTICS OF FAMILY

Some idea of the essential characteristics of the family must have been conveyed by a perusal of the definition of family. The essential characteristics of the family are the following:

1. Permanent Relation between Husband-wife. The family is constituted of the husband and wife and their children. Thus, a permanent relation of some kind between, man and woman is the main characteristic of the family. Marital relations in different countries may be more or less permanent, but the relations between man and woman have some degree of permanency in all cultures. Without this, neither can the children be brought up nor can there be any family. Even in societies where polygamy and polyandry are customary the husband-wife relationship does possess some degree of permanency.

2. Permanent Sexual Relationship. The family rests on permanent marital relations because one main object of it is the establishment of permanent sexual relationship. Without marriage there can be no family even though there may be sexual relations. When the marital relations break up, as in the case of divorce, the family disintegrates. Proper upbringing of children can be expected only when there are permanent conjugal relations.

3. Attachment of Blood Relations. Another necessary characteristic of the family is the existence of blood relationship among the members. These blood relationships may be real or imaginary. The members of the family are generally the descendants of the same ancestors. The relation between adopted children and their parents is accepted as legal but blood relationship means no more than that among the members of a family there should exist an attachment of the degree of blood relationships. It is generally believed to be necessary that there should exist no blood relationship between husband and wife.

4. Financial Provision for the Subsistence of the Members. In a family there is financial provision for the upkeep of its members, senile-folk, children, women-folk, etc. The earning members of the family arrange for the subsistence of the other members. In this way the members of the family are bound in the ties of duties and rights. In different cultures the burden of earning may fall on different members. At some places the women go out to work while the men do the domestic chores but the principle that there should be provision in the family for the sustenance of its members is accepted almost everywhere.

5. Common Habitation. If the members of a family reside at different places, it would be difficult to call them a family in spite of their being blood and other relationships. It is a different matter for a member to leave temporarily or for the entire family to change its habitual but generally all the members of a family live in one residence be it one room or an entire palace, rented or the ancestral home of the family. In the nomadic people also the members of one family stay together at one place.

6. Nomenclature. Among the essential characteristics of the family is a distinct nomenclature which serves to identify the family.

In this way the family is a group of individuals in which men and women have the permanent sex relationships of husband and wife, which is distinguished by a name, in which there is adequate financial provision for the sustenance of its members, in which there is the attachment of blood relations among the members and who live in a common habitat.

SOCIAL IMPORTANCE OF THE FAMILY

Family is the first institution in the history of man. In the ancient age men lived in small families, which lacked any kind of organisation or permanence. But they served to fulfil simple biological and psychological needs. Generally, the family consisted of husband and wife and their offspring. The powerful men possessed many wives and thus they lived in big families with their wives and children. When men became oriented in agriculture, many families formed a group and stayed permanently at some place for farming. When these people started partaking of each other's pain and happiness as neighbourly gestures, social relations multiplied and in this way many families formed a community and the next step was the creation of nation.

Family is a fundamental unit of human society. Its foundations rest upon man's biological and psychological needs. In the modern age, many functions of the family have shifted to other institutions but, nevertheless, there are many biological and psychological needs which man cannot satiate without a family. Havelock Ellis has shown in his penetrative essays, that the value of the mother's milk for the child cannot be obtained in any other manner. Psychologists have proved that the absence of family affection has a serious impact upon the child's development. Sexual passions can be satisfied even outside the family but it can never be the source of emotional fulfilment. That 'man is a social animal' implies that man cannot live without a family. Thus, family is a fundamental unit of society.

The family has a nuclear situation in human society. In primitive societies the entire organisation is based on family units while the division of labour in society is also based on the family. In the complex structure which is society today, the family has lost some of its importance, but even today, the activities of most members are for the family or contiguous to it. It is seen that people work and labour more for the comfort of their wives, children and other members of family than even for personal comforts. Thus, even now the family is the nucleus of a major part of man's activities.

Proper social organisation depends upon proper organisation of families. If the families disintegrate in some society, then the society will never be safe. One major cause of social disorganisation is family disorganisation. Families develop the characters of the members of society. Freud and other psychologists have proved that a child exhibits the same character and mental tendencies in adult age which he acquires in the family. In the opinion of Adler, a man's role in the family determines his role in society.

In this way, a person is socialised in the family. Family is an enduring association of parents and children. Its primary functions are the satisfaction of the members and socialisation of the child. It is a social agency for the education and protection of the race. It is in the family that the child acquires such important qualities as sincerity, sympathy, self-submission and consciousness of responsibility, etc. It is the character developed in the family which helps the child in becoming an important and responsible member of society. In every family, the child gets an opportunity for free expression of thought and development of his entire personality. Psychologists have incontestably proved that proper development of the child is impossible without a good environment in the family. The tendencies and habits which he acquires in the family, he finds impossible to shed later on. According to Freud, the viewpoint of a child towards the elders in the family determines his attitude and viewpoint towards the elders in society. The child's first school is his home and family. Th child's education should be in the hands of the parents in family. The parents should participate in all the child's activities. A child learns much by imitating his superiors. Mahatma Gandhi and such thinkers paid personal attention to the development of their children. It is the family which imparts practical education to the child concerning the customs in society, conduct, other important elements of culture, conservation of health, love, sympathy, co–operation, etc. In the words of Burgess and Locke, "The family is a fundamental agency in the cultural conditioning of the child, the family tradition provides the child with his earliest behaviour patterns and standards of conduct."[1]

It is evident from the above account that family is the primary and fundamental unit. Confucious remarked quite correctly that if you want to improve society, improve family. Society will improve automatically when the families improve.

The family moulds the character and personality of an individual. It is through the family that society imparts its culture to the individual. Thus, in the form of a socialising agency the family is very important. In the essay, *The Family Conveyance of Tradition*, Paul Schreker rightly maintained that a particular function of the family is to sanction children. Like marriage, the institution of family is constituted of different elements of culture. It is due to this reason that it has religious, judicial, political, artistic and linguistic aspects. Whenever a new thought impresses itself on an age, the family takes a new form from it in order that the upbringing and mental tendencies may be harmonious to that thought. Politics and law were dominant in Rome, so the family organisation was such as to ensure the upbringing of children in harmony with the culture. Today, the economic order is predominating. So the family has changed its form, it makes the mental tendencies concur with the new culture. In this way, the family makes the individual harmonious with the culture of society. In the family, the child acquires knowledge about the current customs, mores, traditions, etc.

SOCIAL CONTROL IN THE FAMILY

A social life is a web of relationships. In order to maintain these relations properly a system of rights and duties is organised which avoids conflict between the members of society and allows them to develop as complements to each other. In order to avoid any breach of this harmony between the individuals in society, the society applies numerous kinds of control on the individual. They are taught to obey the elders, have sympathy for the young and for others. Control over sex relationships is necessary for maintaining the social order otherwise disintegration will spread over the complex social life. Relationships between men and women will lose their solidarity. Illegitimate children will be born with no one to lode after them. Although the anthropologists Mead and Malinowski have discovered societies where control over sex relations is inordinately lax without disturbing the social order but such an order is completely contradictory to the thinking of today's cultured persons. It is the family which does this work of controlling sex passions for society. In all cultures the families exercise some degree of control over the unmarried members till they attain the matrimonial state. In the same way, the family acts as a preventive to the individual in keeping him from bad habits and crimes like drinking, thefts, etc. Not many parents would like their children to embark on careers of crime. Even the worst person tries to prevent his children from adopting similar habits and consequently any objectionable behaviour on the part of children is punished and laudable effort suitably rewarded. They thus drop bad habits and leant good things. In this way the making of a good citizen in society depends upon the parents.

1. Burgess and Locke, *The Family* (1950), p. 212.

In every society some values and ideals are regarded as high, and signs of culture. Whichever person exhibits, these, in greater quantity, is respected in society. For example, Indian society treats religious and spiritual qualities as supreme, and a person, who is possessed of them, is appropriately respected everywhere. Besides, in India, premarital and extra-marital sexual relations are controlled as a necessary measure. The responsibility of creating these values in the individual which are treated highly in society lies with the family. It is true that the character of every person is different from any other by nature but the family environment also has a big hand in forming them. Many of the famous religious preachers of the world over were deeply influenced by some religious person of their family. In the making of great men the mothers have always had a major part to play. The differences in the ideals of people related to different cultures are born in their families.

In every society the culture, conduct and values are very strongly related to the languages spoken. Literature is the mirror of culture in society and literature is based on language which plays, by no means, a mean part in man's socialization. The credit for the complex order of human society must go to man's linguistic superiority over other animals and the language one picks up in the family. Human children brought up by animals in the forest are seen completely ignorant in matters of language. They communicate their wishes by signs in animal language, walk on all fours, eat raw meat and exhibit the least signs of humanity. A child brought up by an animal family grows like an animal as a child brought up in human family grows into a human being. To go even further, a child developing in a cultured family is cultured while one brought up in baser circumstances is coarse. The child is first taught language in the family. This is his mother tongue through the medium of which he exchanges thoughts. If an Indian child is brought up in some English family, English will become his mother tongue. Thus, the major element in the child's socialization in the form of language comes to him in his mother's lap.

Besides the above mentioned elements, an individual receives a number of other things from his family. Mot unusually, even the person's occupation in society is decided by his family. Even in the modern age many people carry on the paternal business and occupation for which they are trained in the family from the start. It is no uncommon occurrence that a jeweller's child shows interest in the same business from his infancy and becomes expert very soon.

Thus, in brief, the family educates the individual in culture, conduct, behaviour, customs, tradition, religion, laws of thinking, ideals, values, occupations, obedience of duties and proper use of authority, etc. It would be no exaggeration to say that the family is the most important institution in man's moral development.

RELIGION AND FAMILY

In ancient India, a life of domesticity was regarded as the basis for the fulfilment of duty. The name 'Patni' in Hindu implies that woman who accompanies the man in the performance of his religious duties. According to the Hindu scriptures no man can complete religious activities without a wife. Even today it is in the family that the individual is educated regarding religious customs and functions. The important work of imparting elementary religious education to the members of society was everywhere the responsibility of the family. But now the relation of religion to the family has weakened and has been much reduced, since now-a-days the interest in religion is declining, and in addition to this, religion is looked upon as a private affair in which the family need not interfere.

FAMILY FROM THE ECONOMIC VIEWPOINT

Family is the centre of economic activities. It is the family which utilizes the production of society. Sometimes the entire family jointly pursues an occupation. Agriculture, especially, is an occupation which is pursued jointly by the entire family. In it the men do the work of plantation, irrigation and sowing, the women that of cutting the crop while the children take over light work such as grazing the herds of animals. Inheritance also stems from the family. The family protects property, makes arrangements for an adequate income and endeavours to fulfil the needs of the members. It is the family which provides the support for the old, disabled, unemployed and helpless.

FAMILY FROM THE POLITICAL VIEWPOINT

In the ancient Roman family, the head had all the authority of an absolute ruler vested in him. In the Roman law it was prescribed that the father could put his sons into jail, sell them and execute them. In this way, in ancient times the right of administration was the possession of the *Pater Familia.* Now-a-days the family no longer possesses such unbridled authority to punish the individual. Only the state has the authority to sentence a person to imprisonment or death. Nevertheless the family does much to assist the state in running the government machinery. It exercises control over the conduct of the individuals and prevents them from indulging in anti-social activity. The government consequently finds it easier to maintain order. The family inculcates in the child the habit of discipline from the very beginning. The family presents to the child an environment which enables him to become a successful citizen of the future. In the absence of training of this kind the child grows up to become obstinate and criminal.

In this way, although the importance of the family from the viewpoints of religion, economy and the government has wanted, it still is an important social institution. In all these spheres it assists other agencies.

ORIGIN OF THE FAMILY

Family, as an institution, is to be found even in the most primitive of human societies in the world. Since the earliest time in human history, the family, too, has been constantly prevailing. Thus, the family is perpetual. There can be no question of its having originated.[2] Yet there is much controversy and difference of opinion with regard to the question of the origin of the family. Some of the important theories in this connection are as follows:

---

2. Maclver, R.M. and Page, C.H., *Society: An Introductory Analysis,* Macmillan, London (1952) p. 345.

1. Theory of Sex Communism. According to some sociologists in ancient times, any man or woman could establish sexual relations with any other man or woman. There was no restriction on sexual relationships. Such a stage is called the stage of sex communism. In order to prove this theory, the support of such customs of primitive tribes is invoked, which make it appear that in ancient times control over sexual relationships amounted to nothing. Many customs of this kind have been noticed by anthropologists studying ancient societies. Customs such as freedom concerning sex on occasions of festivity, presenting wives and daughters to a guest for sexual gratifications as sign of hospitability, and exchange of woman, etc., have been found practised in many primitive tribes. In many primitive tribes the father of the offspring is not ascertained. But in spite of extreme diversity of restricting customs concerning the establishment of sex relationship, incest has been forbidden in almost all tribes. Hence, the theory of sex communism does not appear to be tenable.

2. Patriarchal Theory. In ancient times it was Aristotle and Plato who supported the patriarchal theory while among its modern proponents Sir Henry Maine is notable. According to this theory, the family in its most ancient form was patriarchal in which the father was the most powerful and the unquestionable authority. In Rome, he was empowered even to the extent of sentencing his sons to death. He was called the patriarch.

This theory is defective in as much that it, too, cannot be applied to some human societies because in many societies the mother instead of the father, was the supreme authoritarian.

3. Matriarchal Theory. Hence, on the other hand, some people propounded the matriarchal theory of the origin of the family. Briffault has supported this theory in his book *The Mothers*. Briffault has written that in ancient societies people were not aware that the offspring has any relation with paternity. And in societies which practise promiscuity there is no knowledge of the father of any child. But mother is known definitely anywhere. Consequently, it seems more reasonable to believe that the ancient family was matriarchal. The patriarchal family originated in these matriarchal families. The importance of the father, increased with the progress of civilization and the development of agriculture.

The matriarchal theory is as much one-sided as the patriarchal theory because in different human societies one can see families of both kinds. MacIver has written that in the tribal society existing today, it is the patriarchal family which is to be seen. Hence, Briffault's theory of the origination of the patriarchal from the matriarchal family does not find universal application.

4. Theory of Monogamy. Westermarck has propounded the theory of monogamy in his book *History of Human Marriage*. Among its supporters are Darwin, Zuckerman and Malinowski. According to Darwin, the family originated in the male's feeling of ownership and jealousy. In ancient society the powerful male wanted to possess individual ownership of the female and he succeeded in his design by virtue of his physical prowess. Later on, this right of the male was normally accepted in society. Zuckerman and Malinowski with Westerpiarck, agree to and support the fact that this same custom is found in semi-human societies and also among the apes who are believed to be man's ancestors.

According to MacIver, the monogamic theory does not offer a complete explanation of the origin of the family. It cannot be accepted that the family originated in this manner everywhere.

5. Evolutionary Theory. The American sociologist Morgan has put forward the evolutionary theory of the family. According to him the family has passed through the following five stages:

(*i*) *Consanguine family*. In this stage of the family, marriage between blood relations was not forbidden.

(*ii*) *Punaluant family*. Evolving further the next stage saw the imposition of restriction on incestuous marriage and the family group arrived at the stage of the marriage of brothers in a family with the sisters of another family. Even in this stage sex relationships among different persons were not definite.

(*iii*) *Syndasmian family*. In this stage one man married one woman but the sex relationships of the women married into the family were not clearly defined and certain.

(*iv*) *Patriarchal family*. In this stage man's ascendancy and dominance in the family had fully blossomed. He could marry many women and have sexual relationships with them.

(*v*) *Monogamous family*. This is the present stage of the family. In this, one man can marry one woman at one time.

Evolution in the institution of family can be believed but what cannot be believed is the same sequence of stages in evolution of the family in all societies, Thus, Morgan's theory does not appear to be correct in its practical application. Besides, there is no reason for believing the monogamous family to be the ultimate stage of the family. Actually, historical facts do not bear out Morgan's theory. Morgan's theory is hypothetical.

6. Multiple Factor Theory. According to many contemporary sociologists, the sequence of the evolution of family has been different in different societies. In the words of Ralph Lindon, "Societies have not followed a single consistent line of evolution but a multitude of diverging lines." In this way the modern sociologists accept the multiple factor theory of the origin of the family. MacIver and Page have written, "Rather a complex of human desires and conscious needs finding different expressions in different environments, everywhere gave birth to some kind of family system."[3] In this way, many factors conspired in the origin of the family.

According to MacIver, the various factors in the origin of the family may be classified under the following heads:

(*i*) *Sex*. This is a fundamental or innate tendency in man. The family originated in the need for permanent means of its satisfaction and gratification.

3. *Ibid.*

(*ii*) *Reproduction.* The family originated in the strong desire for reproduction and the need for a permanent co-operation between man and woman for the nourishment of the offspring.

(*iii*) *Economic Organisation.* From the economic viewpoint, women and children depend upon the male. Consequently, a permanent institution of family was required.

Actually, it is difficult to make definite assertions with regard to the truth of and the factors in the origin of an institution as complex and as human as the family. This subject must be considered from a more comprehensive and more sympathetic viewpoint.

TYPES OF FAMILY

On the basis of different viewpoints, in sociology, many forms of the family have been described. Many distinctions in family have been based upon nature of residence, name of ancestry, power, dominance of mother or father, etc.

1. Distinctions of Family According to the Nature of Residence. The following distinctions of family are made according to the nature of residence:

(*i*) *Matrilocal residence.* In this kind of family the husband goes to live in the home of her wife.

(*ii*) *Patrilocal residence.* In this kind of family the wife goes and lives in the home of her husband. Now-a-days most families conform to this type.

(*iii*) *Changing residence.* At some places it is customary for the husband and wife to alternate continuously between each other's residence. For example, one year the husband lives with the wife and the next year the wife lives with the husband.

2. Distinctions of Family on the Basis of Ancestry. These forms of the family are also classified on the basis of traditional ancestiy. The main forms are:

(*i*) *Matrilineal Families.* In these the mother is the basis of ancestry. A man is believed to be the prime ancestor of the family. Ancestral tradition and inheritance are affected through the mother. The rights of each member of the family depend on his relation to the mother, hence they are also known as the mother right families.

(*ii*) *Patrilineal families.* In these families the ancestor of the family is the man and traditional ancestry continues through the father. Now-a-days this type of family is the most common.

3. Distinctions of Family on the Basis of Authority:

(*i*) *Matriarchal Families.* In these the mother wields the authority. But the actual administrative power is in masculine hands even in societies where the womenfolk rule. Hence, in the opinion of some sociologists the word matriarchal is misleading and should be replaced by the word maternal. Matriarchal families are to be found in the Nayar and Tiya castes of Kerala and Khasi and Garo tribes of Assam in India.

(*ii*) *Patriarchal Families.* In these the entire authority is in the hands of the father. In ancient Rome and Greece, the patriarch used to be the absolute ruler.

4. Distinctions of Family on the Basis of Marriage. On the basis of marriage also some distinctions of family have been made. The major forms among them are:
(*i*) *Polygamous or Polygynous Family*. In this one man marries many women and lives in a family with his wives and children.
(*ii*) *Polvgandrous Family.* In this one woman marries many men and lives in a family with all of them or with each of them alternatively.
(*iii*) *Monogamous Family*. In this one man marries only one woman and establishes a family.
5. Other Distinctions of Family. The following distinctions of family are based on the dominance of the mother or the father in the family:
(*i*) *Matronymic.* In these the name of the family or ancestry is the name of mother such as Gautami, Saumitra, etc.
(*ii*) *Patronymic*. In these the family is named after the father.

Some other distinctions of family are the following:
A. *Immediate Family*. This consists only of the mother, father and their children.
B. *Conjugal Family*. In the conjugal family the husband and wife live together and sexual relations exist between them.
C. *Extended Family*. In this type of family, besides the wife and husband other relatives also live.
D. *Consanguine Family*. In Consanguine family live only those who are related in blood such as brother and sister, father and son, etc. In the Nayar families of Malabar, the husband does not conduct his wife to his house after marriage and the daughter, though married, stays in her mother's house.

Classification of the Functions of the Family

Functions of the family show its importance in a culture. Different sociologists have classified the functions of family differently. Ogbum and Nimkoff have divided family functions into six categories: (i) Affectional function, (ii) Economic function, (iii) Recreational function, (iv) Protective function, (v) Religious function, (vi) Educational function.

Groves classified family functions in the following manner:
(*i*) Protection and care of the young, (ii) Regulation and control of sex impulses, (iii) Conservation and transmission of the social heritage, (iv) Provision of opportunity for the most intimate contacts.
Reed has attributed the following functions to the family: (i) Race perpetuation, (ii) Socialization, (iii) Regulation and satisfaction of sex needs, (iv) Economic functions.

MAJOR FUNCTIONS OF THE FAMILY

From the foregoing classification of family functions it is evident that the main functions of the family are of two types:
1. Basic and universal, and 2. Traditional.

Basic and Universal Functions of the Family

The following are the basic and universal functions of the family:

1. **Biological Functions,** the most fundamental biological functions are as follows:

(a) *Reproduction.* According to the Hindu scriptures procreation is the main function of the family. Commentators on the Hindu scriptures have written that the religious activities of man cannot be consummated unless he has a son and he cannot repay his ancestral debts. He has to suffer in hell if he has no son. In almost all societies of the world barren women are the objects of scorn and derision. In the words of Ogburn and Nimkoff, "The sex and parental functions are distinctive of the family."[4] And in some societies marriageability is attributed only to a woman who gives evidence of her fertility by conceiving a child before marriage. Hindu scriptures permit a second marriage if there is no issue from the first wife. The woman was permitted to conceive a child from another man through 'niyoga' if the husband is impotent or otherwise incapable of procreation. In most human societies of the world the child is believed to be the nucleus of the family. Procreation perpetuates the family. It increases the population of the country. Some Hindu thinkers have considered reproduction to be the sole aim of marriage. In the rituals of Hindu marriage the groom says to his bride that I accept you in order to obtain good progeny. To quote Sutherland and Woodward, "The basic biological function which the family has been performing, is a function absolutely essential to the survival of any human or animal society."[5]

(b) *Provision of food, housing and clothing.* Food, housing and clothing are indispensable to the existence of human life. A major biological function of the family is the provision of these amenities for its members. The earning members of the family provide food and clothing for all the rest. Every family has a house to live in and the food for the family members is generally cooked at home. In the words of Dennis Chapman, "Each new family establishes an independent home as soon as possible after marriage, the new home reflecting the interest and the culture of both husband and wife."[6]

2. **Psychological Function**. The second fundamental and universal function of the family is psychological. Ogburn has included affectional functions in the necessary or vital functions of the family. According to Groves, it is the function of the family to provide opportunities for the establishment of intimate relations. Burgess and Locke have written, "Mutual affection is becoming the essential basis of marriage and the family."[7] The individual receives affection, sympathy, love and psychological security in the family. The relations between man and woman in the family are not exclusively physical. Profound conjugal affection for each other is generated in husband and wife by working together in the family and by sharing each other's joys and sorrows. In the absence of family love an all round

4. Ogburn and Nimkoff, *A Handbook of Sociology*, p. 459.

5. Sutherland, R. L. and J. L. Woodward, *Introductory Sociology* (1948), p. 610,

6. Dennis Chapman, *The Home and Social Status* (1955), p. 93.

7. Burgess and Locke, *The* Family from Institution to Companionship.

development of the individual is not possible. The family plays an important part in the development of the child's personality. Ralph Linton has written that merely the satisfaction of bodily needs is not sufficient for the proper development of the infant. Children are in greater need of individual attention, love and satisfaction of response.

3. Satisfaction of Sexual Need. The fundamental function of the family, according to Reed, is to regulate and gratify sexual needs. Manu accepts sexual satisfaction besides reproduction as the aim of family. Vatsyayan also looks upon sexual satisfaction as the primary objective of the family. In the modern age, the fulfilment of sexual needs is one of the primary function of the family. When sexual needs remain unsatisfied in the family, it starts disintegrating. To quote Havelock Ellis, "With failure of sexual harmony, the marriage structure rests on shifting sand."[8]

4. Protection and Care of the Young. According to Groves the protection and care of the children is a necessary function of the family. The human child is the most helpless and weak being. A family is needed in order to maintain its existence and to ensure its coordinated and balanced development. Its balanced development is achieved with difficulty without the care of the parents and other family members.[9]

TRADITIONAL FUNCTIONS OF THE FAMILY

The following are the traditional functions of the family:

1. Economic Functions. The family performs many economic functions some of which are the following:

(a) *Division of labour.* In the family, the work is divided among the members of family according to their status and role. The male members generally do the work which means outdoor movement. The women generally take care of the domestic chores while the children undertake only such work as can assist in their development. While this division of labour prevents putting excessive burden on the shoulders of one individual, it ensures the systematic performance of the family activities. All people undertake responsibility and work co-operatively.

(b) *Arrangement of income.* Money is needed for such of the family requirements as food, cloth, habitation, etc. The family is the centre of economic activities, consumption etc. The family makes arrangements for an income in an effort to fulfil the need of the family members.

(c) *Organization and care of property.* Most families possess some property in the form of a house, farm, jewellery, money, etc. The family looks after this property and in case such a contingency arises it also equitably distributes it among the members. The family is the judge of what property an individual shall receive, and who shall look after the property and how, these and other important questions.

2. Social Functions. The social functions of the family are important since the family is the fundamental and primary unit of society. Among many social functions the following deserve mention:

---

8. Ellis, H., *Little Essays on Love and Marriage.*

9. "Home is the place where when you have to go there they have to take you in." Robert Frost, *The Death of the Hired Man,* Complete poems of Robert Frost, Henry Holt and Co. Inc., New York (1940), pp. 43-55.

(a) *To establish status*. An important function of the family is the determination of an individual's status in the society. The modes of earning wealth of an individual are also generally determined by the family.

(b) *Socialization*. The family imparts learning to the individual on all those subjects whereby he can become an ideal member of society. It carries out the socialization of the individual and teaches the etiquettes of eating, conversing, coexisting, etc.

(c) *Social control*. Another function of the family is to exercise social control over the individual. The prevalent moral norms are enforced upon the individuals and their conduct and thoughts are controlled so that the order in society may remain intact. In the family, the anti-social tendencies of the individual are watched.

(d) *The accumulation and transmission of social heritage*. The family keeps the social heritage intact and hands it over to the generations to come. As a result, the social traditions, customs and ideals, etc., are transmitted continuously from one generation to the next.

(e) *Assistance in the choice of a life partner*. The family renders assistance to the individual in his choice of a life partner. Although, in the modern age, people have started preferring personal choice of a life partner, yet in India even now in most cases the choice of the bride or the groom is still the province of the other family members.

3. Religious Functions. In the Hindu scriptures family life has been considered the basis of the fulfilment of religious duties. The scriptures prescribe the wife as essential in the fulfilment of duty. The literal meaning of Hindi equivalent of the word wife (patni) means the woman who accompanies the man in the performance of the religious rituals, which were considered incomplete in the absence of the wife. Besides this, the performance of religious activities also demanded the presence of a son. Thus, in the ancient Hindu system the main function of the family was the fulfilment of duty. Living in the family the members fulfilled their religious duties. Now, the religious activities of the family have been materially reduced.

4. Cultural Functions. The family keeps the culture of society alive. It moulds its members according to the social culture. The children are educated in the various aspects of culture from their infancy. The family creates such an environment for them that they learn to live and to behave in accordance with their culture. The senile members of the family impart education in matters of conduct, thinking, religion and ethics, etc., to the children.

5. Recreational Functions. The family provides entertainment for its members. The love between husband and wife, the halting utterances of the children, the scoldings and preachings of the elders and other such occurrences serve to create an atmosphere in which everyone can find an object which can interest him or her.

AGENCIES PERFORMING THE FUNCTIONS OF THE FAMILY

In the modern age the functions of the family are changing because other agencies are taking over its functions. The main agencies of this nature are: (i) Maternity hospitals, (ii) Women hospitals, (iii) Baby clinics, (iv) Creches, children parks and the kindergarten, (v) Baby sitters, (vi) Hotels and restaurants, (vii) Public aid to the family, (viii) Club, cinema and other means of recreation.

1. Maternity Hospitals. Previously, children were born at home and midwife was called in at the time of delivery. Now in the prosperous families this is done in the maternity hospitals. During pregnancy the women constantly consult doctors and are confined to the hospital some days in advance of the delivery. They remain for some time in the hospital after the child has been delivered. This system is very beneficial. In this the mother and the child are constantly in the care of expert physicians and can get any and every kind of medicine whenever required. Even if there is difficulty in the delivery, operations can be performed without delay. There can be neither the facility of medicine nor the arrangement for operation in the family house. This creates much travail and the lack of these facilities can even be a danger to the lives of the mother and child in certain cases. One cause of the increase in the use of maternity hospitals for child delivery is the disintegration of the joint family. In the modern societies the newly wedded people live separately from their families. At the time of delivery there is no old and experienced woman near them who can give them proper advice and can take the matter into her own hands. Secondly, the houses in the towns are so small that it becomes difficult to accommodate relatives. Under these conditions the easiest course to follow is to confine the pregnant woman to a maternity hospital or a delivery home to avoid all kinds of worries and dangers.

2. Women Hospitals. In the modern age of specialization there are specialists for every kind of disease. Now-a-days one can secure specialists in the peculiarly feminine diseases in all big towns and cities. Thus, it is they who treat the women for their diseases. Previously, this work was done in the family being performed most incompetently and dangerously.

3. Baby Clinics. Now-a-days, in addition to the treatment of women, there are doctors who specialise in the treatment of children. Previously, the more common infantile diseases were treated at home but now this is done in the baby clinics. In this way much of the responsibility for the care and treatment of the diseased is on the doctors' shoulders. This, however, does not mean that this function has been completely taken away from the family.

4. Creches and Children Parks. Creches and children parks are being developed in modern progressive countries. Employed women who work in factories leave their bottle feeding children at the creches where educated women look after them, feed them at the proper time, and keep them occupied with toys, etc. Institutions of this kind have developed very much in modern countries, particularly in the U.S.S.R.

Similarly, in the Western countries, Montessori schools, nurseries and children parks have been developed for children between three and six years of age. In these, every care is taken of the children. The number of nurseries and creches in India is very small.

5. Baby Sitters. In the Western countries much of the chores of caring for and upbringing children has been taken up by baby sitters, in addition to the creches and nurseries. These baby sitters are generally females. Their duty is to keep the children busy and for this they receive payment by the hour. In America when a woman has to go out of the house on an important mission on which it is inconvenient to take children, she leaves them with the baby sitters.

6. Public Aid. Previously, one of the fundamental functions of the family was caring for and assisting the old, the invalids and the unemployed. Now-a-days in many European countries the government undertakes to assist the old, helpless, unemployed people and orphaned children. There is a similar system in Canada and America also. Women work in factories and get paid leave along with free medical facilities. Everywhere the government assists the old people and the orphans through the media of pension and insurance. In many countries an extra allowance is paid by the government when the number of children increases. There is a special arrangement for this kind of assistance in Russia, Sweden, Germany and Italy.

In this way, many institutions render assistance to the family in the performance of its duties. Hotels and restaurants provide food and rest while the picture houses and clubs provide the recreation. In this way these institutions share much of the family's work. But these can never replace the family, they can only supplement its efforts.

CHANGES IN MODERN FAMILY

In the modern period, the institution of family is undergoing rapid change and modification. The main changes, in this connection, are as follows:

1. Reduction in the Economic Functions of Family. In the modern age, many of the economic functions, which were previously being performed by the family, are now being performed by factories, government aid and other associations.

2. Reduction in other Activities of Family. Many of the other functions of the family have now been taken over by other agencies. The work of looking after and bringing up children is now being performed in creches, children parks, kindergarten schools and by baby sitters. Hospitals undertake the work of delivering children and of treatment. Restaurants provide food to thousands of families.

3. Increase in Family Recreation. With the inventions of radio and television, and the advent of indoor games modern families have been transformed into centres of recreations.

4. Changes in the Relationship of Man and Woman. Now that the women have gained equal rights with men, their mutual relationships has undergone much change. Mowrer has correctly written, "The husband is no longer the head of the household in many families, in spite of the fact that he still provides the family name as well as the Christian name which his wife uses upon more formal occasions. Within the family circle however, he is no longer the autocrat whose word is law. In fact he is lucky if his children look upon him other than as a meddlesome outsider or as an alley to be catered to when support is needed in breaking down his wife's opposition to some programme of the children.

The wife on the other hand finds herself equal to her husband in the family circle, if not superior. She rules the destiny of the family group with a sympathetic, but nonetheless determined hand. She is no longer the drudge and slave of the other days. So far as the children are concerned, her commands are even more to be taken into account than those of father."[10]

5. Laxity in Marital and Sex Relationships. The rigidity traditionally associated with marital and sexual relationships no longer characterises the modern family. To quote Sutherland and Woodward, "The family has been greatly affected by the changes in sex mores."[11]

6. Increase in the Importance of Children. In the modern family the importance of children has increased. They are now only rarely physically punished but are instead taught lovingly. The modern families tend to become child-centred families.[12]

7. Decrease in the Importance of Blood Relationships. In the modern family there has been a continuous decrease in the importance of blood relationships. The family is now constituted of a husband, a wife and their children.

8. Disorganisation of Joint Family. The modern family is no longer joint. The joint family is rapidly being disorganized.

9. Smaller Family. Due to the prolific use of contraceptives and the tendency to regard children as an obstacle in the progress and enjoyment of life, the birth rate is continuously falling and the modern families are becoming smaller.[13]

10. Family Disorganisation. The process of disorganisation is quite apparent in the modern family. The number of divorces is on the increase. The control which the family exercises over the individual is being lessened.

11. Instability. The modern family is no longer a permanent association. It is precarious and can be rendered void at any time. Marriage has been reduced to a mere social contract which is not difficult to break in the event of even the slightest friction. In comparison with the ancient and medieval families the modern family is weak and unstable.

NEW PROBLEMS CONFRONTING THE FAMILY

In this way the modern family is beset with many new problems the major among which now follow:

1. Problem of Adjustments of the Husband-wife Relationship. In the modern family the most difficult problem is that of the mutual adjustment of husband and

10. Mowrer, Earnest, R., *The Family* (1932), pp. 274-275.

11. Sutherland and Woodward, *Introductory Sociology*, p. 603.

12. "They In fact tend to dominate the scene, their wishes determining the policy of the family. Thus the trend seems to be towards the filiocentric family to which the child plays the dominant role."

—Earnest, R. Mowrer, *The Family*, University of Chicago Press (1932), p. 274.

13. "The two child family is now the prevailing social standard or ideal."

—J.K. Folsom, *The Family and the Democratic Society*, p, 188.

wife. The educated and enlightened woman of today wants to be the equal of her husband in every sphere of life. But the husbands have not yet adjusted themselves to this situation. Hence, a conflict between the two is inevitable. Laxity of sexual relations and the instability of marital relations also tend to create conflict between the husband and the wife and to spoil their relationship.

2. Problem of Sexual Adjustment. The modern family is also faced with the problem of sexual adjustment, it being the outcome of changes in sex values. D. H. Lawrence, among the Western authors, has presented a graphic and revealing sketch of this problem in his novels. Psychoanalytic literature has also adversely affected the ancient ideal of fidelity in sex relationship. Some scholars have gone so far as to declare variety in sex relationships not only desirable but also necessary. This tends to encourage pre-marital and extramarital sex relationships. All the factors have the effect of creating sexual disharmony between husband and wife and as a result numerous families are disorganised.

3. Marriage Based on Romantic Love. The third major problem that confronts the family is that of marriage being based on romantic love. After marriages of this nature when the dreams of the husband and wife do not materialise in the family they are seriously frustrated. They start blaming each other and either live out their life in a state of perpetual strife or break the ties of marriage. In their book Social Disorganisation, Elliott and Merrill have described divorces as the inevitable consequence of romantic marriages.

4. Problem of Broken Marriage. A major problem faced by the modern family is an increase in the number of broken marriages. Marriage has been reduced to a mere social contract. Materialism, individualism and rationalism are the causes of paucity of such feelings at benevolence, love, etc. Greater stress is laid on sexual pleasure. The women are far less dependent upon men. The laws of divorce are also not very stringent. All these causes have the cumulative effect of increasing the number of divorces.

5. Problems of Working Women. Now-a-days there are more women who are employed outside the precincts of the home. They consequently do not get sufficient time to look after their children. Returning exhausted from their work they do not have the energy left to attend to their husbands or their children. This hinders the development of children and increases conflict and misunderstanding between husband and wife.

6. Laxity in Family Control. A major problem has been created for the modern family by the decrease in the control exercised by the family over its members. This has undermined the administration of the family. Boy, girl, husband, wife, brother, sister each wants to pursue his own course and does not relish any interference, be it advice or be it rebuke.

7. Family Conflict and Strife. Changes in the values of life and a reduction of the family control in the modern family have led to increased conflict between husband and wife as well as between parents and children. This conflict is usually not apparent but it does disturb the peace of the family, destroy the faith in one another and remove the sense of psychological security.

8. Lower Birth Rate. The birth rate is felling constantly due to late marriage, frequent use of contraceptives, and a tendency to consider children a burden. This tends to accentuate the instability of the family since the absence of children reduces the sense of responsibility in the husband and wife, besides preventing intimate family relations.

DISORGANISATION OF MODERN FAMILY

The modern family is gradually becoming increasingly disorganised. According to Elliott and Merrill, "In the broadest sense family disorganisation may be thought to include and sort of non-harmonious functioning within any of several types of family."[14] Family disorganisation is the disruption of the harmony among family members. Some signs of this phenomenon can be seen in the following changes in the family:

1. Lack of Family Unity. Men, women, boys and girls each have their own ideals, their own plans, individual programmes and individual thoughts, in which they welcome no interference whatsoever. In this way, even while living together, eating and moving together, no one is concerned with another. The house becomes almost a hotel where the family members gather only to take food and rest. Where both the husband and wife are employed a similar distance is seen to exist between them.

2. Decrease in Family Control. In modern times, the control of the family over its members is continually decreasing. No one wants to be lectured by anyone else. The younger generation finds a bitterness in the wisdom of its predecessors. They do not want to be controlled by them in any sphere. They want to be separated from the family immediately after they start earning or after they are married. In this way, the disorganisation of the family is obvious.

3. Strife. The strife within the family is presently on the increase because of the absence of family control as well as the absence of a sense of unity among the members. Joint families are rapidly becoming disorganised. Violence, litigation, etc., are common enough occurrences. Faith in one another is decreasing. There are many separate families within one house. The disorganisation of the family is only too evident from this.

4. Laxity in Marital Bonds. The tie of marriage is the basis of family. Weakening of marital ties results in a weakening of family ties. Now-a-days marriage is no longer a religious ritual but merely a social contract which can easily be cancelled or annulled on grounds of boredom or some kind of misunderstanding. Consequently there is a constant increase in the number of divorce. A major cause of the weakening of marriage ties is the failure of men to adapt to a new circumstance created by the education of women. Previously, women were completely dependent upon their husbands. Now, being educated they also earn

14. Elliott and Merrill, *Social Disorganisation*, p. 352.

as much as their husbands or at least possess the capacity to do so. They have come to recognise their rights. They want to be equal of the men in every aspect of life. They now demand the same fidelity which their men demand of them. When the men do not want to have women on a equal footing with themselves, the result is a struggle due to which the family tends to become disorganised.

5. Conflict between Parents and Children. Now-a-days an important element indicative of family disorganisation is the conflict between parents and children. The control of the old people over young men and women is constantly decreasing. They do not want to be ordered by their parents in their behaviour, marriage, society, etc. Consequently, the misunderstanding between the two parties increases and the family becomes further disorganised.

6. Lack of Security. As a result of conflict between husband and wife and parents and children, psychological security is being continually diminished due to which mutual trust is decreasing and the family organisation is being shattered.

It is obvious from the above mentioned causes, that the family is being rapidly disorganised in the modern age. The families are becoming smaller. The number of divorces is increasing. Mutual intimacy and faith are being reduced and their place has been taken by selfishness and frivolity.

CAUSES OF THE INSTABILITY OF MODERN FAMILY

The modern family is instable. An increase in the number of desertions, separations and divorces, etc., are a proof of this.

The main cause of this instability are the following:

1. Less Social Protection in Family Crises. Previously conflicts between husband and wife were overcome by the constraining influence of the elders, kinsmen, social mores and traditions and the family was saved from disintegration, but with the existing loss of respect for these modes of social control the husband and wife are deprived of any guidance of mediator and in a fit of temper or even vengeance they destroy the delicately and lovingly nurtured sapling which is the family no matter how much remorse they may experience when they have cooled down. Previously, being financially dependent upon the husband the wife silently bore much injustice and did not dare think in terms of a separation. Now, the women who are capable of earning their livelihood marry only for love and when that is not forthcoming there is almost nothing to deter them from dissolving their marriage. At some places extreme laxity of divorce laws has led to very great instability and impermanence of the family.

2. Replacement of Domination by Co-operation. The basis of husband-wife relationship in the modern family is no longer domination but co-operation. Previously, everywhere, be it in the East or in the West, the wife was dominated by the husband and hence the family stability survived despite the husband's dictatorship. But with the removal of this dominance, in the modern time, the stability of the family can be maintained only by benevolence, sympathy and co-operation. Normally, it is not easy to create these qualities. Hence, the instability of the modern family.

MODERN CIVILIZATION AND FAMILY DISORGANISATION

Many factors of modern civilization have a major hand in the disorganization of the modern family. The main causes are the following:

1. Industrialism. In the modern industrial system women and children work in factories along with the men. This reduces the unity of the family and increases disoragnisation.

2. Ideal of Romantic Love. Modern marriages are based on the ideals of romantic love. When the dreams of the two partners do not materialise in the family, hatred increases and is gradually transformed into conflict.

3. Hedonism. Modern culture is hedonistic. People pay more attention to their rights than to their duties. This breeds selfishness and the occasions for conflict.

4. Individualism. Modern civilization is individualistic. Few want to consider the interests of the family. Everyone is engaged in the consideration of solely his own interests. No one is prepared to sacrifice his smallest for the benefit of others. As a result of this conflict in the family increases.

5. Lack of Control in Sexual Relationships. Another consequence of modern civilization is a change in the values concerning sex. This tends to diminish control in sex relationships, to reduce fidelity in marital relation and also to increase chances for family disorganisation's.

Future of Modern Family

This has led some people to doubt whether the family will escape the present crisis in the highly industrialised and mechanised societies of the West. Sorokin writes, "Accordingly, contractual family, in the progress of its development has unexpectedly reached the point where it has lost most of its functions and prerogatives, even those it retains are often atrophied and poorly performed. It has shrunk in size. It has become increasingly unstable and fragile. Less and less does it furnish even pleasure and comfort, the primary objects of the sensate contractual family. When any institution finds itself in such a situation it is in the process of decay. This is precisely the position of the contractual sensate family to-day."[15] Will the family survive to continue in the form of a primary association? What will be the future of the family? Actually, there can never be any doubts concerning the continued existence of the family since it is based upon the fundamental needs of human beings. It would be no exaggeration to say that the family will assuredly exist in whatever varied or transformed form, as long as the human society exists. The desire for procreation is a natural desire in men. Outside the family there can neither be any legal offspring nor any proper arrangement for its upbringing. Some or the other kind of marriage system and a family are needed to afford a remnant means for the gratification of the sexual impulses of men and women. The family satisfies not merely the physiological needs of the male and female but also their psychological needs, the desire to love and to be loved, the sense of psychological security, etc. The family exercises the control of society upon the

15. Sorokin, P., *The Crisis of Our Age*, p. 192.

individual. The family creates an environment in which the child can be brought up to develop his personality fully and to become an ideal citizen. Many studies have revealed that among people aged more than thirty, the death rate among the unmarried men and women is twice that of the married women and men. Among people who die as a result of tuberculosis, accidents, suicides, alcoholic indulgence and sexual diseases, the proportion of unmarried is greater than that of the married. Mutual affection of family members guards against many of the mental and physical difficulties of a complicated society. This is clearly indicative of the benefits which accrue to man from the institution of family. Actually, the family is a primary and fundamental unit of society. It is the foundation of all social life. It socializes the individual and assists him in the choice and selection of a life partner. It determines inheritance and procures property. It is difficult to describe all the direct and indirect benefits of the family. It is an inseparable part of human nature. It is the foundation of the social structure. Hence, one will agree with Burgess and Locke when they say, "It seems safe to predict that the family will survive, both because of its long history of adaptability to changing conditions and because of the importance of its functions of affection giving and receiving in personal satisfaction and in personality development."[16]

QUESTIONS FOR EXERCISE

1. Critically discuss the main theories of the origin of family.
2. Write a short note on The Family.
3. Discuss the different forms of family and state your views on their comparative virtues.
4. Is family an institution or association? Give reasons for your answer. Discuss briefly the importance of family.
5. Define family and bring out its importance in society.
6. 'Home is the primary school of civil virtues.' Justify the remark giving illustration.
7. What is the value of the institution of family to human society? Can society dispense with this institution?
8. Discuss the ethical importance of the institution of family. Can family be abolished?
9. Critically discuss the role of family as a social institution. What is the future of the institution?
10. Discuss the role of modern family in controlling and directing human behaviour.
11. What is the role of family in the socialization of an individual ?
12. Explain how family is the primary and fundamental unit of society.
13. Discuss the main functions of the family as social institution.

16. Burgess and Locke, *The Family* (1950), p. 715.

14. What are the functions of family? Describe its advantages and disadvantages.
15. Describe the educational and economic functions of the family. What in your opinion, are the circumstances that tend to weaken the family?
16. Does the function of family change? If so, will family wither away?

Chapter 7

Social Control in Political Institutions

According to Aristotle, the state is a union of families and villages having for its ends a perfect and self-sufficing life. This definition by Aristotle applied only to city-states. Some of the more popular definitions of the state are as follows:

1. *Burgess.* The state is a particular portion of mankind viewed as an organised unit."

2. *Bluntschli.* "The state is the politically organised people of a definite territory."

3. *Laski.* "The state is a territorial society divided into government and subject, claiming within its allotted physical area a supremacy over all other institutions."

4. *Garner.* "The state as a concept of political science and public law is a community of persons more or less numerous, permanently occupying a definite portion or territory, independently or nearly so, of external control and possessing an organised government to which the great body of inhabitants render habitual obedience."

Modern states are not limited to merely villages. Modern thinkers point to four characteristics of state: (1) Public, (2) Defined geographical areas, (3) Administration of government, (4) Sovereigenty. In brief, state can be defined as an organised people living in a definite territoiy which has its own sovereign government.

TOTALITARIAN THEORY OF STATE

The description of the rights of a state is the most important part in the discussion of state. This question arises in connection with the limit to which state can control an individual. As usual, a number of thinkers have offered their opinions. According to the totalitarians the state has complete authority over individuals. Its authority supersedes all others such as that of family, religion, community, etc. Before he is a father, son, businessman or scientist, Hindu or Muslim, an individual is a member of the state and all other duties are negligible before his duties to the state. The state rights render secondary the rights of family, caste, community, etc. The state is supreme. It demands complete self-submission of the individual. It says, "Forget that you are peasants, workers, businessmen, scientists, wives or mothers and remember only that you are a citizen. Forget all others' claims upon you, for none of them compares with mine." Dictators tried to establish similar states in Fascist Italy and Nazi Germany. The tyranny in Italy and Germany and the degradation of Mussolini and Hitler are evidence of the fact that monopolistic authority of state over the individual is incorrect. The above mentioned quotation is not an appropriate description of the powers and functions of the state. To say that the sovereign has the complete disposal of the life, rights and duties of the individual is completely immoral. To assign such absolute authority to the state is to deal a serious blow to the moral freedom of the individual. Especially, an effort to control the thoughts and feelings of a person will put an end to his individuality. Ultimately, all social institutions are merely the means to an integral development of mankind and the state is no exception.

Limits of State Rights

Actually, even the legal viewpoint sets some limits upon statutory rights. The factors which limit the rights of state are as follows:

(1) Fundamental Rights. The citizens of every state are accorded certain fundamental rights. These fundamental rights are immune to any state control.

(2) Rights of Social Organisations. There are many social organisations within a state which have their own rights and which are essential to social life. Normally, the state does not violate the rights of these social organisations.

(3) Rights due to Social Traditions, Customs and Conventions. Normally the state does not interfere with the social customs, traditions, conventions and the rights ensuing from them.

(4) Constitution of the State. The constitution of the state, too, limits the rights of the state. The rights of the citizens in democracy, dictatorship and various other constitutions are different from each other.

(5) International Conditions. In asserting its authority, the state has to pay due attention to other states and international bodies. Any overlooking of this aspect can even endanger its existence. Thus, when a state uses its rights it keeps in view not only its own citizens and their social institutions but other states as well.

In brief, the fundamental rights of citizens, social customs, traditions and conventions, rights of social organisations and nature of the state and international institutions limit the rights of the state, otherwise the state is sovereign in its limited area. Thus, even from the legal or practical viewpoint the rights of the state are not unlimited.

Functions of the State are Limited

From the totalitarian point of view it seems that the state can perform every act, but such an idea is false. Actually, from the viewpoint of means, too, the state is incapable of working for ail the necessities of individuals. Thus, the state cannot even be recognised the sole means, let alone an end. MacIver and Page have rightly pointed out that while some functions are within the province of the state only, other functions are such for which the state is comparatively more suitable, still others are those which would fare better if left alone by the state and there are finally those functions which the state is incapable of implementing. Having understood these four distinct kinds of functions, it will become obvious that the state cannot be treated as the sovereign over the individual.

1. Characteristic Functions of the State. There is a general difference of opinion in respect of this class of functions but generally only the state can organise justice, peace, education and order, determine the scales of measurements and arrange for currency, etc. No other institution can perform these functions.

2. Functions to which the State is Well Adapted. There are many functions which the state can carry out more efficiently than other institutions. Such functions include protection of forests, looking after the foodstuffs, protecting animals, arranging for education, constructing recreation grounds and installing public conveniences, etc. In the state, natural resources may be exploited by other organisations too, but in order to maintain a standard of efficiency an authority is required which only the state is capable of supplying. Similarly, the state can conduct plans of social welfare and security better than other institutions who will have to make larger pecuniary sacrifice and would yet not achieve the same standard as would the state at less monetary expense to itself.

3. Functions to which the state is ill-adapted. There are many cultural, religious and class addicted activities for the welfare of which the state is ill-adapted too. These functions can be done better by other organisations.

4. Functions which the State cannot Perform. There are many functions which cannot endure state control at all. For example, the state cannot control public opinion, formulate laws for the conduct of individuals or change and transform social customs, traditions and conventions. Public opinion is formed due to many social and other causes, people's conduct depends upon their individual characters while social customs, traditions and conventions are perpetually involved in a process of autonomous altercations.

The foregoing description of the functions of a state has made it obvious that the state cannot perform all functions. The state cannot be treated as the sovereign authority. An individual is the member of a family and society before he is the citizen of a state. And before he is a member of society he is human being, a self-conscious being. In this way, the duties and responsibilities which he acquires by virtue of being a human being, and a member of society and family, are outside the province of the state which cannot interfere with them on this account. Actually, when compared to the rights of the individual the state has rights for their development, though it will have full authority to dissuade an individual from hindering the development of another fellow-being.

FUNCTIONS OF A MODERN STATE

The functions of a modern state may be divided into two classes — compulsory and voluntary.

Compulsory Functions of the State

The functions of a state are as comprehensive as its rights. Among them some functions are compulsory. Functions in this category are the following:

1. Defence Against Foreign Attack. The most urgent function of a state is the defence of the country against foreign attack. It has to make adequate preparations in the form of weapons and land, sea and air forces. It has to take special notice of things which can create the danger of attack from other countries.

2. Internal Peace and Security. The policy of a state at home is quite as important as is its foreign policy. It is prime duty of the state to maintain internal peace and security. An increase in communal riots, thefts, cases of dacoity and rebellion can endanger the existence of the state itself. The state maintains peace and order through police and army.

3. Protection of the Rights of Citizens. In every state the citizens possess certain rights like rights to life, property, freedom of thought, etc. It is incumbent upon the state to protect these rights, for which it has to formulate essential laws, arrange for proper administration and organise justice.

4. Justice. In this way justice is the compulsory function of the state. This provides for obedience of laws in the state, maintains order aud protects the rights of everyone.

Voluntary Functions of State

1. Provision of Education. In the modern age, all states consider it their duty to make adequate arrangements for the education of their citizens. A state of uneducated citizens can never progress. Thus, state makes arrangements for primary schools and colleges and universities so that higher eduction in sciences, agriculture and the humanities may become possible. Arrangements are made for opening research centres, libraries, zoos, store house and art classes, etc. Efforts are made to provide free primary education. Capable students are awarded scholarships by the state. But the state should avoid unnecessary interference in the affairs of the educational institutions.

2. Maintenance of Health. Along with education, modern states try to provide for the protection of health. Provision is made for sanitation, hospitals, free medicine, vaccination and essential energizing foods for the poor. Medical colleges are opened to end the dearth of capable doctors. Government research centres and training schools for nurses are opened.

3. Protection of the Old, Poor and Invalid. Modern states have also begun making arrangement for the old, unemployed and invalid citizens. They are given financial aid. The old people are given pension. The facility of insurance insures the security of everyone. Orphanages and homes for destitutes are created.

4. Arrangement of Public Welfare Services. The state organises the railways, postal and telegraphic facilities, wireless, etc. It is the duty of the state to make arrangements for means of transportation such as buses, railways, aeroplanes and ships, etc.

5. Social and Economic Improvement. Another of the state's duties is affecting social and economic improvement. The state lays down laws against harmful customs and makes necessary arrangements for their enforcement.

6. Encouragement of Trade and Industry. It is also the duty of the state to encourage trade and industry and to develop it as well. Almost everywhere in the world, it is the state which controls economic system and the mint. It is the state which standardizes the scales of measurement and weighing. The country cannot benefit by international trade if it does not make proper laws for import and export. The state should establish factories of the key industries in order to implement and initiate other industries in the country. The state should also encourage cottage industries.

7. Organisation of Labour. The state should direct its efforts to the improvement of conditions of labourers and lay down rules to obviate the probability of their exploitation. It is the responsibility of the state to make efforts towards labour welfare.

8. Proper use of Natural Resources of the Country. A country can become powerful by land, forests, rivers, minerals and agricultural products. Maximum benefit should be extracted from them. On this subject, the state should direct the necessary precautionary measures, research and search for new mineral products and lay down laws for the utilisation of forests, mines, land, etc.

9. Arrangement of Recreation. In order to maintain novelty and excitement in the life of the public the state should provide means for recreation. For this film industry, dramatic societies, etc., may be encouraged.

Actually, the function of a modern state is not merely administration but an integral welfare and development of its subjects. Thus, its functions have been aggrandized. The turbulence of local situations does make an appreciable though slight alteration in them, while different political schools of thought have recognized different functions of the state. Thus, nothing final can be said upon this subject. The only theory which can be universally acceptable is that the state should function in a manner calculated to add to public welfare but the scholars differ in their opinions about that in which lies this public welfare. It is here that guidance of the sociologist is needed. He has to determine the supreme and ultimate objective of the individuals. The state shall collect the means to the attainment of this ideal. For example, while the supreme ideal of an individual Is self-realization or an integral development, it is for the state to utilize the means to his physical, mental and spiritual development.

STATE AND COMMUNITY

Many people come to treat the state as a community. But the state is only a political association in the community. State is a means which organises particular human society, both in its internal and external relations, into a corporate body. Accordingly, the state is actually the means for the welfare of a community. It may be described as a part of community. It is organised for the fulfilment of certain objectives.

When compared to community a state is more limited. It is, of course, true that it does control a major part of social functions and relations but still many aspects of human life are excluded from it. A communal life is more comprehensive than the life of a citizen. In a community, the individual is a member of many other associations, besides the state. The laws of the state exert their influence upon a very small part of the person's life. As social beings, men are more than merely citizens. They enter into many relationships, and carry on many social activities as social beings and not as members of state. As a self-conscious being the individual thinks independently of others and attempts self-development. Moral life is wider than the political and social life. An individual acts more as a social being than as a citizen and more as a self-conscious being than as a social being. And this moral nature of his is the most comprehensive of all.

Actually, despite some differences which it professes from other associations, the state is an association. The state is here referred to as an association in the sense that its establishment is motivated by particular objectives. It has some special functions to perform. It can neither perform all functions nor does it exercise sovereign authority over the individual. Besides the state, there are other associations in society which cannot be replaced by state and in the implementation of whose functions the state is neither appropriate nor capable. In some countries like Italy and Germany the state was made the sovereign but the experiment did not prove a success. Though the state can effectively supervise the external aspects of life, it can never be a substitute for those cultural organisations which express beliefs, opinions, interests and ideals of the different groups in society. Actually the state is a political association whose objective is to maintain peace and order in the community and to raise the standard of living while creating circumstances conducive to the free integral development of every citizen. There are a number of activities like religious, moral, economic, social and psychological which the state cannot perform. Even the sovereign state of Germany could not take into its hands the functions of the church.

In this way, state is not an end in itself. It is a means to which rights are assigned for governing over society and individual for their own benefit. When the state ceases to be of any use to the individual its need will also end. At this stage, according to Engels, the state will dissolve of itself. Many thinkers including Marx, Engels, Gandhi, Kropotkin, Tolstoy, Sri Aurobindo, etc., have recognised the uselessness of state in an ideal order. The theories of the origin of society also support this view that it is a means, not an end. The end is the integral development of the individual and society. The state is accorded its rights by the society and individual. It governs because that is what it is meant for. It is created for the proper utilization of natural resources, maintaining peace and order, defence of the country from external aggression, protection of health, arrangement for means of transport and communication and other activities of a similar nature. It does not annihilate other associations but organises and encourages them. Even in totalitarian states like the U.S.S.R. the state has not interfered in the activities of the family. In Germany the state never triumphed over the Church. Actually, a good state is one which makes its objective the benefit of community and works for its attainment. It is useless in the event it fails to achieve the communal benefit and is changed by revolutionaries. It is an agency of the community with very broad and important though limited functions. From the moral viewpoint the state is a means to the integral development of society and the individual.

QUESTIONS FOR EXERCISE

1. What is the need of social control? How is social control exercised by the state?
2. What is the state? Describe the role of state in connection with morality.
3. Describe clearly the elements of the state. How does the state differ from society and Government?
4. Explain the nature and scope of the laws of a state. Must the individual obey all of them?
5. Define state and describe the functions of the state in the modern society.
6. What is the prospect of nation-state in the world community of the future?
7. Give reasons for conceiving the state as an agency of the community.

CHAPTER 8

Social Control in Economic Institutions

Economic associations and institutions are shaped by the economic structure prevalent in the country. This economic set-up may be capitalistic, socialistic or communistic. A discussion of the institutional complexes in these systems will be useful for the understanding of the role of economic associations and institutions in society.

CAPITALISM

Economic Institutions in Capitalism

In the words of Ogbum and Nimkoff, "The activities of man in relation to food and property constitute economic institutions."[1] The major economic institutions of capitalism are private property, large scale production, money and credit, business organisation, profit, wages, competition, price mechanism, etc.

1. Private Property. The institution of private property constitutes the basis of economic structure in capitalist societies. Private property is the *terra firma* of capitalism. In capitalism, every person reserves the right to maintain private property and increase it to any extent. The right to private property is considered a sacred right in which no one can interfere. Accordingly, many businessmen in the capitalist states own property worth millions. Originally, no one could come into possession of such vast sums of money due to agriculture dominated business. Industrial revolution popularised gigantic machines by means of which a person, with a small number of assistants, could carry on agriculture on a big farm. But the basis of capitalistic private property is modern industry which, due to machines, gives more importance to capital than to labour and the capitalists start making unlimited profits and exploiting the labourers.

2. Large scale Production. In this way, it is large scale production which has made possible the recent development in the institution of private property. Factories accommodating thousands of labourers are the result of the utilization of big machines and use of electric or steam power. International trade was encouraged by the development of the means of transport and communication. This again

1. Ogburn and Nimkoff, *A Handbook of Sociology*, p. 375.

made it possible to send goods to any part of the world. Countries came closer to each other and fulfilled the needs of each other. The advent of new inventions everyday led to an increase in the quantity of production and factories producing new commodities were set up. Thus, large scale production is an important institution of capitalism.

3. Money and Credit. With the success of large scale production in the development of capitalism, the institution of credit has become important. People got money on loan from the banks on their credit. Business and industry developed. Thus, despite a lack of capital, the people in the capitalist order increased private property on the basis of credit.

4. Business Organisation. Another important institution of capitalism is big business organisations and corporations. In these, the capital of numerous shareholders is pooled and industrial or business concerns set up. This reduces the risk of shareholders and personal calamity concerning any one of them does not affect the company. Big business and industrial organisations may reduce competition and increase profit.

5. Profit Institution. In capitalism the investors have enjoyed an increase in their profits due to large scale productions and business organisations. Economic activities like production, exchange and consumption have increased in large proportions. The capitalist invests money, the labourers cany on the production. Salesmen and traders bring the commodities into the market and only then do they reach the consumer. In the process, salesmen and traders make huge profits. In this order; with the increase in the importance of capital, capitalists exploit labourers as they pocket the major share of the profit. Actually, as Marx has proved, capitalism cannot even exist in the absence of the institution of profit.

6. The wage Institution. In this way, using the law of supply and demand, the capitalists started haggling the labour of the labourer. Their objective was to pay minimum wages to the labourer and to take maximum work out of him. Wherever the labourers organised, they forced the capitalist to pay adequate wages but more usually the capitalist took advantage of the helpless state of the labourer and abstracted his share in the form of surplus profit.

7. Competition. Thus, competition is the inevitable result of a capitalist economy. There is extreme competition and rivalry between millowner and millowner, salesman and salesman, in order to increase the price of commodities, thousands of tons of foodgrain are dumped into the sea. Demand is artificially increased. Advertisements are in the whole lot of things. In this cut-throat competition, the interests of nation and humanity are discarded in the face of personal and vested interests.

8. Price Mechanism. Thus, in capitalism the price of a commodity is determined not by its cost of production or utility but by the law of demand and supply. People concentrate their production upon commodities which are in greater demand and short supply in order to make large profits. But an increase in production again increases the supply.

Social Consequences of Capitalism

A detailed review of the social consequences of capitalism will help in its sociological analysis. Some consequences of capitalism are good, while other bad and harmful. The good consequences are as follows:

1. High Standard of Living. Capitalism increased the production of novel things. Necessities were easily available. This raised the standard of living as evinced by the average standard of living in U.S.A.

2. Economic Progress. Capitalism led to economic progress. Due to economic freedom people exerted themselves utmost for earning wealth. A tendency towards more efforts replaced fatalism, unemployment decreased and the consequence of a constant increase in business and industry was the economic progress of the country.

3. Exchange of Culture and Civilization. Capitalism was instrumental in increasing large scale production and businesss which, in its turn, increased international trade and the means of transport and communication. People inculcated in different cultures and civilizations came into contact with each other with the result that culture and civilization were exchanged.

4. Increase in the Sense of Co-operation. Capitalism caused an increase in specialisation in business and industry. This involved the need of increased co-operation because it became impossible for one to progress without another. Co-operation helped to decrease the sense of differences based on race, creed, nationality and caste.

5. Economic Freedom. In the view of the supporters of capitalism its most momentous social result is economic freedom. In this order even an ordinary person can become a millionaire by dint of personal effort, and progress in life as far as he may wish.

Disadvantages of Capitalism

But, nevertheless, capitalism has proved a curse to humanity instead of a blessing. Its bad consequences far outweigh the good ones of which the major ones follow:

1. Class Struggle. Class struggle is the worst social consequence of capitalism. Capitalism created a big gulf between person and person on the basis of economic situation or financial status. In order to achieve the economic interests of capitalists and middle class people, the labourers were exploited to the extreme. If the capitalists do not resort to exploitation then how can they augment their wealth by leaps and bounds? This way the capitalists and labourers are involved in an unceasing struggle and conflict. Lockouts, strikes and other such means disturb the run of social life. Obviously, capitalism increases the immorality in the lives of groups and the individuals.

2. Intense Economic inequality. In a capitalist order, an intense economic inequality between the different classes of society is apparent. As a consequence, a wide difference in their living and opportunities for progress is obvious. In capitalism, the rich become richer and the poor poorer. In this way, the gulf of economic inequality is widening. And this inequality in society is a great obstacle to the moral development of the individual.

3. Unemployment. A capitalist tries to make a maximum use of mechanical appliances in the industry thus reducing the demand of labour. The advent of one machine sometimes spells the unemployment of as many as fifty to a hundred people. An unemployed person cannot realise his own development, nor can he pursue his moral ideals.

4. Social Disorganisation. The capitalist order established big factories in which many labourers work at minimum wages. These people live in dirty slums. Poverty instigates crime and prostitution. An increase in poverty helps to make the life of people degenerate. Social life cannot remain organised in the face of terrible poverty, extreme class differences, unemployment and extreme economic inequality. Its structure may seem imposing and glorious from outside but its foundations are continually being weakened. Freedom in capitalism gives rise to exploitation. Proper order and synthesis are mere fancies in the absence of economic equaity. Actually, capitalism is bad both for the exploited as well as the exploiters. It brings the moral degeneration of both.

Impact of Capitalism on Modern Culture

The capitalist order has had major impact on modern culture, as it did on modern society. These influences have been good and constructive in some instances and bad and destructive in others. The good impacts of the capitalist system on modern culture are as follows:

1. Spread of Education. Due to capitalism, books and other media of education have spread on a wide scale, and the spread of education among the common people has become considerably easier. With the development of the means of transport and communications people come into possession of news from foreign strands and education has become a possibility in the most secluded spots.

2. Increase of Scientific Research. Capitalism greatly assisted scientific research. In capitalist countries all types of scientific research has been encouraged. The big industries have their own laboratories. Capitalists have invariably been a source of encouragement to research in business and industry. This has increased the richness of culture.

3. Advantages of Industrialism. Actually, the advantages of industrialism are, more or less, the advantages of capitalism because the capitalists have concentrated their attention on gigantic machines and large scale production. Architecture has come in for some surprising development. The techniques of constructing buildings, canals, factories, bridges, dams, etc., have progressed very rapidly. Capitalism has had a big hand in the development of modern civilization.

4. Progress in Literature, Music and Art. Literature, music and art progress only when the country is rich. Many of the institutions of literature, music and art flourish merely on the patronage of the capitalists. The progress of science and large scale production of radio, television, newspapers, magazines and books have put the enjoyment of literature, music and art within easy reach of the millions.

But a careful observation will reveal that the above mentioned favourable influences in the development of culture are the result, not of the capitalist system but rather of wealth, industrial revolution and scientific progress. If these things are available, all these results may be seen in every communist nation contradicting capitalist systems. Even if the communist nations are not ahead of capitalist countries in scientific research, spread of education and advantages of industrialism, they are, in no way, trailing behind their contemporaries. Of course, the capitalist system may admit more freedom in literature, music and art. But even in this direction much efforts have been directed by and in the socialist countries and they can, in no way, be said to be lagging behind. On the other hand, capitalism has had some bad influence upon modern culture. The more prominent ones are:

1. Greed for Wealth. Capitalism is based on greed for wealth. It has elevated wealth to the pedestal of deity. Wealth is its God, its ideal and its sovereign. Wealth has become the objective of human life. This greed for wealth has been made universal by capitalism and it is steadily and unremittingly on the increase. A person earning a thousand wants to earn a million and one who is earning a million wants to earn ten millions. Wealth is no longer a means, having become an end in itself, and the idea of morality or immorality does not enter into the means of earning it. This greed for wealth is generating extreme moral degeneration.

2. Wealth the Sole Criterion. In a capitalist order, everything has come to be measured by wealth. All values of human life such as art, literature, music and love, sympathy, benevolence, pity, affection, etc., are evaluated in terms of silver coins. Every person wants to get his maximum market value. The sol; criterion is wealth, not labour or value. Such a condition is frankly immoral.

3. Materialism and Atheism. In this way, a capitalist order manifests materialism at its extreme. Big multimillionaires have attachment for their wealth even if they have to strangle humanity to this end. While people are starving to death due to famine, the millionaires do not hesitate in throwing tons of foodgrains into the sea in order to raise the price of foodgrains. Religion and spirituality are mere remnants and have become hypocricy and ostentation. This worship of wealth is an indication of the moral degeneration of man.

4. Artificiality. Capitalism has transformed modern culture into something extremely artificial. Modern tourist does not enjoy Nature on his tour but feels proud in collecting photographs of it. A person who is considered cultured today is an expert at false courtesy, hello, shaking hands, *au revoir*, etc., but one cannot find much geniality, love and sympathy. One may see artificiality, advertisement, false prestige and hollow culture even in art and literature to say nothing of the more commonly perceptible modes of life like living, food, clothes, etc. The drawing rooms of the so-called cultured people are decorated with a view to exhibiting their wealth, not for comfort. Boys and girls coloured in the modern trends are absorbed in fashion. Life for the modern man is artificial. Obviously, the hope of an integral development of man has turned into despair.

5. Emphasis on Sex. Capitalist culture places extreme emphasis on sex, as it does on wealth. Matrimonial bonds have degenerated into a mere agreement for the satiation of the sex urge of man and woman. Family disorganisation is on the increase. Pre-marital and extra-marital sexual relations, infidelity, illegal children, abortions and divorces are increasing in number. Literature based on sexual passions, pictures meant to arouse sexual desires and similar artistic pieces are the order of the day — an outcome of capitalism. How can ideals and spiritual values flourish in such circumstances?

6. Frivolity. Though individual freedom is stressed in capitalism but being based on wealth, freedom has been transformed into frivolity. Everywhere, in literature, art, society, family, education, conduct, thought, people are breaking through all bonds. This is degenerating the individual and as a consequence, the society too, is being similarly affected. Real freedom is not in lack of control, but in self-control, in moral life.

Actually, one needs a complete text to enumerate the evil influences of capitalism on modern society. Erich Fromm in his *The Sane Society* and Elton Mayo in *The Social Problems of an Industrial Civilisation* have pictured human life in a capitalist society and both throw sufficient light upon this subject. Among the eminent people who have written upon this subject are Aldous Huxley, Spengler, Toynbee and Sri Aurobindo. Obviously, the capitalist order is not suited to the moral development to man. It is injurious both to society and the individual.

INSTITUTIONS OF SOCIALISM

Socialism is the economic organisation in society in which the society has the right over all physical means which are controlled by representatives of the society who are responsible to society, and all the members of society have a right to obtain the profits of results of such a production conducted on a specialist basis. As stated in the 11th impression of the *Encyclopaedia Brittannica*, socialism is "that policy or theory which aims at securing by the action of central democratic authority a better distribution and, in the subordination thereto, a better production of wealth than now prevails." Some of the more popular definitions of socialism are as follows:

1. *G.D.H. Cole*. "Socialism denotes a classless society in which economic activities are directly conducted under public auspices on a basis of public ownership of the means of production and democratic control of the uses to which capital and labour are to be applied."

2. *Hughart*. "Socialism is a political movement of working class which aims to abolish exploitation by means of collect the ownership and democratic management of the basic instruments of production and distribution."

3. *Sellers.* "Socialism is a democratic government whose purpose is to secure an economic organisation of society which will give the maximum possible, at any time of justice and liberty.

The following are the main institutions of socialism:

1. State Ownership. In socialism, the state owns the entire wealth of the country comprising land, industry, means of transport and communication, banks, etc. It is the state which arranges social amenities like education, sanitation, health, recreation, etc.

2. Equality of Opportunity. Socialism provides everyone with equal opportunities for progressing. No distinctions based on sex, caste, race or class are made among them.

3. Maximum Distribution of National Income. The national income is distributed among the maximum number in socialist societies. This does not allow extreme inequality in the incomes of people.

PRINCIPLES OF COMMUNISM

The major principles of communism are:

(1) Economic Interpretation of History. Communism is based on the economic interpretation of history. According to it, the society undergoes fundamental changes along with the transformation in the means of production and distribution.

(2) Class Struggle. According to Marx the society has always been comprised of two classes, the exploiters and the exploited, a conflict between which is indispensable to progress. The objective of communism is to destroy the capitalist order of the bourgeoise and to establish a communist state of the proletariat.

(3) Theory of Surpuls Value. The difference between the cost of production of a commodity and its selling price is the surplus value. According to Marx, it is the labouicr who has the right over this surplus value because it is his labour which is the cause of this increase. The capitalists generally appropriate this share belonging to the labourer. Thus, their property is augmented by exploiting the labourer and it is this exploitation which communism wants to end.

(4) Dictatorship. Communism does not put faith in the democratic method. It wants to establish, by revolution, the dictatorship of the proletariat.

(5) Stateless Society. Communism treats the state as a transient institution. It will cease to exist when the class does so, too. Engels has written, "In proportion as anarchy in social production vanishes, the political authority of the state also dies away."

(6) Inevitability of Labour. In a communist order, every person must, of necessity, labour. From each according to his ability, to each according to his needs is the communist principle.

The following table classifies the main distinctions between socialism and communism:

Socialism	*Communism*
1. Equal ownership of all people over the means of production and distribution.	1. Equal consumption of all objects besides this equal ownership.
2. No opposition to private income and private property.	2. Opposition to private income and private property.
3. Reward of labour according to the needs of the individuals.	3. Reward according to utility of labour and effort.
4. Slow evolutionary change in the society.	4. The establishment of dictatorship of the proletariat by revolution and force.
5. Faith in democracy.	5. Against democracy.

DISTINCTION BETWEEN CAPITALISM AND COMMUNISM

Capitalism and communism differ with regard to ownership institutions like right of property, distribution of property, communications, education, health, transport, insurance, credit and the organisation of the price mechanism, etc. Due to these differences, these complexes have acquired different characteristics in these two orders.

1. Right to Property. In capitalism, property is private and an individual's right over it is recognised. In communism, private property cannot increase beyond a fixed limit and the state owns all the property in the country. State controls not merely productive objects and agents of production but even the objects of consumption. Land, factories, mines, means of transport, etc., are all controlled by and belong to the state, all are nationalised. The entire property of a communist country is treated as public property.

2. Distribution of Property. Under communism, every individual has to work to the best of his ability and he is given wealth according to his needs, from the public wealth. The system does not admit of the exploitation of the workers. He is paid his wages according to his labour and his needs. He does not have to resort to any quarrelling for it. In communism, public properly is equitably distributed and effort is directed to use it for national welfare. On the other hand, the distribution of property under capitalism is extremely inequitable. There certainly is a difference between the income of people even in communist society but not so wide as to make one a beggar and another a multimillionaire, whereas in capitalism the difference between the income and financial status of individuals and classes is extremely wide. There is no limit to which an individual can increase his private property. The state does not intervene in any way because the control of the government is in the hands of rich or their representatives. In this way, while the individual has complete freedom of all kinds and descriptions to improve in this system there is also, at the same time, grave exploitation of the poor helpless workers. The rich keep on getting richer and the poor keep on getting poorer. The attention of the capitalist producer is directed towards his own personal interest and not towards the national interest and for this he does not even hesitate in injuring the interest of the nation.

3. Social Stratification. Due to these reasons, the standards of living and the amenities of life which classes possess are of a widely differing nature in capitalism, and this tends to increase the class struggle and harm the interests of the nation. In communism, the difference between the ruler and the ruled is, no doubt, perceptible but not among economic classes of millionaires, beggars who sleep on the roads and slum dwelling workers. It is not a fact that a person has no economic freedom under communist system. In this system too, a person can increase his personal property to some extent but he cannot exploit anybody. On the other hand, in capitalism, there is no restriction on the means to wealth.

4. Competition. In this way, the efforts towards money making, in the economic field under the capitalists lead to cut-throat competition. Every person wants to earn the maximum sum of money. Business organisations are created to this end. In communist system, along with business organisation and monopoly, one is not confronted with unemployment, poverty and hunger. Every person must be employed and he must labour. Besides work, he gets wealth enough for his needs. In communism there is competition in working and the people who produce the most win recognition and awards from the state. In communism, competition in labour is encouraged in place of economic competition.

5. Insurance and Credit. Insurance and credit institutions are controlled by individuals under capitalism whose objective is the personal benefit of the people who run these institutions. Communism also has these institutions, but the state has authority over them and they aim at public benefit. The public gets the opportunity to make the maximum use of them.

6. Control of Price Mechanism. In capitalism, the basis of the price mechanism is the law of supply and demand. It is not controlled in any way with the result that capitalists, by virtue of monopoly and business organisations fix any price of commodities which suit them. In this way, the public in general is exploited while the wealthy keep on getting wealthier. The communist state controls the prices and retains them within some limit. This tends to elevate the standard of living and eliminates any possibilities of exploitation.

7. Other Institutions. Actually, one can broadly state that in communism the government is in control of most of the institutions while in capitalism, such institutions are individually controlled. Thus, under capitalism, such institutions as transport, advertisement, education, health, etc., are controlled by individuals or business concerns. On the other hand, under communism, these are nationalised and controlled by the government in the public interest.

From the preceding description of capitalism and communism, it is evident that communism creates better conditions for the development of the individual But the sovereignty of state authority sometimes deals a serious blow upon the freedom of the individual and intervenes in his moral development. Thus, the best alternative is socialism. It has neither the violence nor the dictatorship of communism. Only in this can the circumstances conducive to the integral development of man be created.

QUESTIONS FOR EXERCISE

1. Discuss the influence of capitalism on present day culture.
2. Compare and contrast socialism and communism. Write a short note on socialism.
3. What are the main features of communism?
4. Define socialism. Is socialism incompatible with individualism?
5. Estimate the value and drawbacks of communism as a social theory.

Chapter 9

Social Control in Religious Institutions

Religion is instinctive to man. Man is the only religious being. As reason distinguishes him from animals, he can similarly be distinguished through religion. Man is finite-infinite being. From the time when man opened his eyes on this planet, he has been desirous of knowing and being acquainted with the conscious power latent in nature. As and when he was compelled to face natural hardships and dangers, storms, floods, lightning, epidemics, deluge, famines, scarcity, dangerous animals, etc., man has looked up to some invisible power for assistance, motivation, strength and help. Thus, this religious tendency awoke in man when he was gripped sometimes by fear and at other times by curiosity. And, man tried to realise this intangible power for reasons such as to obtain salvation from the sorrows and transience, death, birth and old age. Similarly, man, when he got fed up of the worldly sensual love, conceived God as the object of love in the supreme aesthetic idealistic forms. There is no relation which the man did not attach to God. People tried to attain God in the form of father, friend, husband, master, lover, beloved, verily in every form. In this way man, time and again, attempted to quench his urges in that Power the search of which is religion.

VALUE OF RELIGION IN HUMAN LIFE

Here, religion is definitely an advance upon man's rational culture, science and ethics, art and literature and even philosophy, "for religion is that instinct, idea, activity, discipline in man which aims directly at the Divine, while all the rest seem to aim at it only indirectly and reach it with difficulty after much wandering and stumbling in the pursuit of the outward and imperfect appearances of things."[1] Religion has always been a dominant tendency in the human history not only in the East but also in the West.

Spirituality is the Essence of Religion

Thus, spirituality is the essence and criterion of religion. The success of religion as a method of social development depends on the spiritual element in it. Religions are serviceable only so far as they are spiritual. When spirituality is missing, religion is

1. Sri Aurobindo, *The Human Cycle*, p. 192.

a mere activity of man, powerful yet never a principle of guidance in his life. And spirituality is the very opposite of limitation, fixation, systematization. It is fulfilled by freedom which means the power to expand and grow towards perfection by the law of one's nature. True religion, as Sri Aurobindo has rightly pointed out, is the following of the spiritual impulse in its fulness, and spirituality is "the attempt to know and live in the highest self, the divine, the all-embracing unity and to raise life in all its parts to the divinest possible value."[2] A religion founded on spirituality will give freedom and perfection to Philosophy, Science, Art, Social and Political activities and illumine them for a many-sided finding of their greatest, highest and deepest potentialities.

SOCIAL FUNCTIONS OF RELIGION

Religion has been a powerful agency in society and has performed many important social functions of which the main are the following:

1. Religion and Service. Religion manifested itself in man's social tendency. Human beings learned to love each other in the relationship of children of the same father. Finding God present in everybody the devotees sacrificed their life for the Divine Power who is inherent in the society. With regard to many saints, it is said that they licked clean the wounds of lepers while serving God manifested in the form of the lepers. In the Gita the worshipper of God has been ordered to engage in the service of all living beings. Love and service are accorded considerable importance in the Christian religion. Christ served the poor, culminated in his crucification. Islamic religion has encouraged the tendency of brotherhood. Buddhist religion has preached non-violence, compassion and sympathy. Similarly, even in ancient tribal religions, the people recognizing the same totem as object of worship were well organized. Religion has always generated a sense of belongingness in society.

2. Religion and Education. Religion has served humanity through the spreading of education. In almost all places in the world, the spread of education has had an important place in all religious campaigns and the activities of religious institutions. Priests in Christian churches and their contemporaries in Islamic mosques, Hindu temples and Buddhist monasteries, have long been engaged in the spreading of education. Religion also caused much encouragement to higher education. While Nalanda and Taxila were the centres of Buddhist religion they were at the same time the seats of knowledge and consummate mastery. Men of different communities made serious efforts to diffuse education among the members of their community.

3. Religion and Benevolence. There has been a tradition of medical service in society in the name of religion. The fundamental reason for such a move is that the religious person treats the service of the helpless and ill as a part of his worship to God. In order to stock up virtue and due to a feeling for service it is a tradition among rich people to open hospitals, distribute medicines and necessary clothes, etc. An important aspect of the daily life of saints is service.

2. Sri Aurobindo, *The Renaissance in India,* p. 75.

4. Religion and Alms-giving. To religion is conjoined alms-giving. Christianity, Buddhism, Islam, Hindu and all other religions have accepted the importance of alms-giving. In Hindu religion, a person who consumes without giving alms is thieving. Given in Islam, it is a religious instruction to give a part of one's income as alms. The purpose of alms was the economic assistance to the poor members of society. It prevented in quality in society and maintained the balance. Even today one comes across people indulging in such activities as distributing clothes. Some people go to the extent of giving everything in the name of religion.

5. Religion and Non-violence. All religions have emphasized sacrifice and forbearance. Christ said that if a person begs you for your cloak, give him your coat as well and if slapped on one cheek, present the other. This religious tolerance is in evidence from Christ to Martin Luther, Buddha to Ashoka, and from ancient Indian saints to Gandhi.

6. Religion and Non-violence. All the founders of religion the world over Christ, Buddha, Mohammed and Hindu seers and saints have preached love and non-violence. Jains and Buddhists treated non-violence as the supreme duty. Mohammed himself suffered many kinds of cruelty. Even when Christ was mounting the cross, he begged God to forgive those who were responsible for this gross misdeed. Although Gandhi had been shot, he politely addressed the assailant and bowed.

Religion also augments the sense of world brotherhood. As far as a religious person is concerned, everyone has been made by God and all worship Him in different forms and names. In this way religion generates a sense of the 'world as a family'. Christ, Gandhi, Buddha and Mohammed, not to mention other religious sages, have all preached world brotherhood. Religion teaches the lesson of sacrifice and service, removing selfishness and material tendencies.

IMMORAL ACTIVITIES UNDER A RELIGIOUS PRETEXT

But all these good activities in the name of religion in society do not imply that immoral acts have not been done under a religious pretext. The society has also been harmed as it has been assisted by religion and consequently some people want to eradicate the name of religion from society. One may consider the following points on this subject:

1. Dogmatism. Religion had been the basis of dogmatism. Fearing God and the next world religious people do not have the courage to break ancient traditions and customs. In this way religion has become the negation of child marriage, and the sati custom, etc. Religion has handicapped social progress.

2. Exploitation. In this way, in human history women have been mercilessly exploited in the name of religion. The religious priests have stripped her of all rights and made her the slave of man. The principle of Karma prevented the poor and injured from revelant things against exploitation.

3. Laziness and Fatalism. Religion encouraged fatalism and people became addicted to laziness. Even today, thousands of men in different religions live a parasitic life, a burden to society on religious pretensions. In India thousands of people garbed as sages live a lazy life, becoming a burden upon society.

4. Violence and War. Bloody wars have been fought for centuries both in the East and West on the same pretext. The pages of human history are cluttered with accounts of the bloodsheds of the crusades and the jihads. In Europe alone, in medieval times, some four hundred men and women were burnt alive in the name of religion. In India, such religious fenatics as Aurangzeb wielded cruelty to other religious people, again in the name of religion.

5. Despise and Hatred. In this way, religion was responsible for currents of hatred and despising which pulsate in society. If God had lent his ears to these religious people in their pleasure for the destruction of others, man would not have soiled the face of this planet today. In Hindu-Muslim communal riots in India, naked women were taken out in procession and beaten with whips, the breasts of women severed, unweaned children thrown into the fire, and people turned out of their countries and compelled to beg and roam. Viewing these inhuman activities in the name of religion, one doubts whether religion makes man a saint or devil.

Religion and Religionism

But even after a perusal of these defects religion cannot be deported from society. Religion cannot be irrevocably condemned for their sake because similar deeds have been done in the name of politics, science, race, country and state. Whenever any ideals and thoughts are transformed into institutions in society their life energy becomes petrified as it gets entangled in external limitations and the essence of religions was destroyed as it had become involved, not inextricably, in scriptures, churches, methods of worship, priests and other fry of the congregation. Separating the latter from true religion, Sri Aurobindo has christened it religionism. All defects attributed to religion are the defects of religionism. Religionism is as false and harmful as racism, casteism, groupism and narrow nationalism.

RELIGION AND MORALITY

Actually, both religion and morality formulate laws of conduct in society like abstention from theft, being veracious, acting honestly, etc. These laws are obeyed by internal urges or pressure. In religion this internal pressure is the fear of God and in morality it is the pressure of conscience, Some thinkers have thought it fit to do away with distinctions between religion and morality on account of this similarity. In the words of Matthew Arnold, "Religion is morality touched with emotion." F.H. Bradley and J. S. Pringle Pattison have also assented to an intimate relation between morality and religion. F. H. Bradley writes, "It is a moral duty not to be immoral and that is the duty to be religious."[3]

Contrast of Religion and Morality

But Bradley and other savants seem to overlook the dissimilarity between religion and morality. To be religious is not a duty. Religion is instinctive. The forms of

3. Bradley, F.H., *Appearance and Reality*, p. 388.

religion change but it is spontaneous and dominated by emotion. One major point of difference is that morality does not require any external sanction. Its sanction is internal. The violation of its law is treated as wrong whereas the violation of the laws of religion is a sin. Some supernatural force is accredited with the formulation of these religious laws to them are attached the notions of heaven and hell. It is believed that the individual, guilty of violating them suffers numerous cruelties. This religious force is suprasocial but its fear supersedes even the fear of a social or political force. Religious laws exercise indirect control over social relations because of their foundation in the fear of a suprasocial power. On the other hand, moral laws are based on inner conscience. Moral laws change with the necessities of society but religious laws are treated as permanent even if they may prove to be harmful in some situation. Moral laws are based on rational judgement while religion is predominantly emotional and non-rational.

Priority of Religion or Morals

Scholars are not agreed as to which of the two, religion or morals, can claim priority. One group believes that religion precedes morality. According to August Comte, religion conceives morality. Rene Descartes, John Locke and Paley believe that morality is born in religion. God's mandate or censor judge the good or bad of things. Supernatural laws are the moral standards. God creates morality according to his desire although he himself is not compelled by any moral law. We acquaint overselves with his order through seers and divine texts. On the other hand, some scholars have believed morality to precede religion. According to Kant, morality precedes religion. According to Tonnies and Emile Durkheim religion was conceived in order to grant sanctification to social and moral notions. A third opinion besides these two is one which treats religion and morality as distinct. Herbert Spencer assures that the original religious remnants revealed no element of morality. At that stage man used to perform cruel sacrifices for destructive evil spirits. According to MacIver, the distinctions between morals and religion have resulted from the changing social evolution and this view does seem more appropriate in regard to the question of the priority of morals and religion. Actually, the two were so interminate in primitive society that neither can be said to be prior to the other.

Conflict between Religion and Morals

Religion is dogmatic and morality progressive. Religion is based on divine sanction and morality on internal sanction. Thus, religion and morality often conflict. Many traditions are granted licence by religion even though morality considers them wrong. Many traditions, though morally acceptable, are objected to by religion. Consequently, some thinkers have come to regard this conflict of religion and ethics as inevitable.

As far as facts go this view is quite correct but it is vitiated by logical fallacy. It is a fallacy common to all opinions treating the conflict between morals and religion as inevitable. Religion and morality both possess one aspect each of dogmatism and one each of a progressive nature. The dogmatic aspect has always been a hindrance to the progressive aspect whether it is religious or moral being of no consequence. And this dogmatic aspect is popular with the public in general. Accordingly, at one time slavery was treated as perfectly moral. Have not many young men and women been strangled in the name of morality of the family? Hedonism is a moral theory but does it make individual or social welfare possible? In its dogmatic aspect morality is no less an obstacle to progress than is religion. The progressive and pure forms of religion and morality are not conflicting. For example, no conflict is apparent in the religion and morality of Gita. Morality conflicts with religionism, not religion. Sri Aurobindo writes, "True religion is spiritual religion, that which seeks to live in spirit, in what is beyond the intellect, beyond the aesthetic and ethical and practical being of man, and to inform and govern these members of our being by the higher light and law of the spirit. Religionism, on the contrary, entrenches itself in some narrow pietistic exaltation of the lower members or lays exclusive stress on intellectual dogmas, forms and ceremonies, on some fixed and rigid moral code, on some religio-political or religo-social system."[4] The pure and comprehensive form of religion does not conflict with morality.

QUESTIONS FOR EXERCISE

1. Discuss the significance of the role of religion in society.
2. How far does religion help man in progressive realization of social value?
3. Discuss the place of religion in social life. Can religion be dispensed with?
4. What is religion? Explain its role in present day society.
5. What is religion? Enumerate a few defective forms of religion.
6. What is religion? What are its main defects? Discuss in detail.
7. Discuss the importance of religion with reference to social control.
8. What constitutes the essence of religion? Describe the defects of religion.
9. How does Religion influence the behaviour of men?
10. Discuss the significance of religion and morality as social sanction.

---

4. Sri Aurobindo, *The Human Cycle*, Ist Edn. 1949, Sri Aurobindo Ashram, Pondicherry, p. 197.

Chapter 10

Social Control Through Propaganda

In the world of today, propaganda is an important element in the political, economic and social spheres. The word 'propaganda', derives from the Latin 'propagare' which means to produce or to spread or to plant the branches in order to grow a new plant. In this way, propagare implies production or spreading which is artificial, not natural. Evidently, in its literal meaning the word propaganda means the artificial propagation or spreading of something. According to Kimball Young, "For our purposes we shall define propaganda as the, more or less, deliberately planned and systematic use of symbol, chiefly through suggestion and related psychological techniques, with a view first to altering and controlling opinions, ideas and values, and ultimately to changing overt action along predetermined line."[1]

To quote Doob, propaganda is "...a systematic attempt by interested individuals to control the attitudes of groups of individuals through the use of suggestion and consequently to control their action."[2] In this way stated briefly, propaganda is a psychological process in which suggestion is systematically employed to influence or to control the ideas, ideals and tendencies of the people indirectly.

KINDS OF PROPAGANDA

The main kinds of propaganda are as follows:

1. Direct and Indirect Propaganda. From the foregoing definitions it should not be supposed that propaganda is affected only indirectly. In actual fact, propaganda can be both direct and indirect. In direct propaganda the people upon whom it is being used are cognizant of the individual who is doing it and the purpose why he is doing it. For example, the present Indian government is directly propagating the schemes of life insurance, family planning, small savings, etc., besides its many major projects. The people are frilly aware of the fact that this propaganda is governmental and in it, the government points out the benefits accruing to the public from these schemes and asks the people to adopt them. On the other hand, some propaganda can also be indirect, just as the propaganda against India by

1. Young. K., *Handbook of Social Psychology* (1951), p. 506.

2. Doob, L.W., *Propaganda, Its Psychology and Technique.*

Pakistan is guided by their intention of taking possession of Kashmir. In direct propaganda, people are not aware of the objective or purpose of it. For example, it is the practice adopted by many people who resort to propaganda never to reveal their intention which motivates the propaganda. They change the views and ideals of the people in a subtle manner and succeed in forcing it to act in the manner they desire. In war time many leaders try to arouse the national sentiment and the patriotic fervour in their fellow country-men, the intention behind such action being to persuade more and more men to enlist in the army.

2. Other kinds of Propaganda. Psychologists have classified propaganda further such as primary and secondary propaganda. Primary propaganda consists in the instigation and excitation of attitudes and prejudices that already exist. To take a common example, the state of tension between the Hindus and Muslims continues from the past into the present. Taking advantage of this the Azad Kashmir government always excites and tries to force the Muslim population of Kashmir to mutiny and revolt. This is an example of primary propaganda. In secondary propaganda no tendency or mental set is present previously. In it, new tendencies and thoughts are instilled into the people. Some psychologists have also affected distinction between conscious and unconscious propaganda. Conscious propaganda, apparently enough, is done purposely and is preplanned. Unconscious propaganda happens accidently and is not affected knowingly.

PSYCHOLOGICAL BASES OF THE APPEAL OF PROPAGANDA

The foregoing description of propaganda throws light upon its various psychological bases and the appeal which it has for the public. Roughly stated, in the background of propaganda are suggestions, motivations, tendencies, beliefs, emotions and feelings. Propaganda is aimed at influencing these factors in the people, these are employed and these are transformed and controlled. If the psychological bases of propaganda are to be properly understood, the relation between these elements and propaganda must be delineated easily.

Propaganda and Suggestion

As has been pointed out earlier, the main basis of propaganda is suggestion. Through the medium of suggestion, all kinds of desirable changes can be made in the thoughts and ideals of people. The suggestibility or the power of reacting to a suggestion is not alike in all individuals but even then every individual is influenced by suggestion to some extent. In suggestion, some factors are of particular importance. As a general rule, the suggestions of political leaders, actors and religious saints are respected and imitated. People quote them in their own works. This power of suggestion is due to their prestige. Hence, this is called prestige suggestion. It is proverbially said that the path that the wise and the great tread is the one which ought to be taken. Similarly, the people are also want to imitate the majority. This is named Suggestion of Majority. People tend to adopt those activities that are considered good and are indulged in by the majority of individuals. This imitative tendency of human beings is because of their socialization. The individual who remains unaffected by and indifferent to public opinion and majority is a rare being indeed. In this way, all kinds of practices are propagated in public through the media of the opinions of respected individuals and the suggestions of the majority. For example, much of the propaganda indulged in by Indian National Congress is prefaced by the names of Pt. Nehru and Gandhi.

Propaganda and Motives or Needs

Every activity of the human being is dependent upon his motives and his needs. Without this the human individual cannot be instigated to indulge in any activity at all. That which is not needed, and that which holds no inspiration or motivation cannot be the object of propaganda. Only that can be the object of propagation which is either needed by the public or the need for which it is created. For this reason people who are successful in propaganda appeal to the motives of the people. Although the motives and the needs differ from individual to individual, yet in their general form these motives and needs of most individuals concur. To take an example, the desire to be respected in society and to be considered good is an almost universal desire. Almost every individual wants to obtain power. Every individual desires the security of his family and of his own self. And every individual wants to improve and raise his standard of living. Generally speaking, every one has love for his country and his religion, if any. Everyone stands in perpetual need of food, clothing, occupation, name and comfort. In propaganda, these needs and motives are aroused and this awakening is exploited by those conducting the propaganda.

Propaganda, Belief and Attitudes

One aim of propaganda is the control and transformation of the beliefs and attitudes of the people. As has been said before, primary propaganda makes use of the existing attitudes while in propaganda of secondary nature, the attitudes are transformed or created anew. In the same way, in propaganda, old beliefs are replaced by new ones, or at least, an effort is made in this direction. For example, every political party tries to convince the public that it is the true and the only representative of the people and it is the only one which can bring about the true welfare of the people. Everyone speaks of himself as the true representative of the people and wants to create distrust concerning his rivals in the minds of the electors. But in changing beliefs, it is essential to be aware of attitudes because otherwise propaganda cannot be effected forcefully. If the public is not at all tendencious in a particular direction, it is of no avail to start propagating in it without any preparation. Before this, the mind of the public should be prepared for it and a tendency towards it created.

Propaganda in Relation to Feelings and Emotions

The things that most easily influence the individual are those that arouse feelings and emotions. It is for this reason that while indulging in propaganda, the people who succeed are those who make progress in creating a favourable attitude towards themselves in the people. According to the need of the moment, they endeavour to excite fear, anger, hope, despair and hatred, etc., in their audience. For example, the communal groups excite the emotions of fear, anger and hatred in their own people with regard to other communities. In attempting to oust the British from the rule of India, different people aroused various emotions in the Indian people and instigated them against the Britishers and propagated the idea of independence of the country among the people. Gandhi aroused the sentiment of love of the country. The revolutionaries performed the task of spreading hatred and anger towards the British. All kinds of slogans were shouted. The objective of slogans is the excitement of the feelings and emotions of the public. 'Inqalab Zindabad' is a slogan that aroused the feeling in men when it was heard or uttered. People express their anger by abusing the government in their slogans. The successful leaders control the feelings of the public and turn them into the desired channels through their inflamatory speeches. In development plans, the government tries to win active participation of the people in such movements as prohibitions, family planning, life insurance, co–operation, etc., by the display of various kinds of posters and pictures. This, too, is one form of propaganda.

METHODS AND TECHNIQUES OF PROPAGANDA

In New York, U.S.A., there is an Institute of Propaganda Analysis. This institute has classified the various methods of propaganda. According to it, the different methods are the following:

1. Name Calling. In propagating for somebody, whether in his favour or against him, some names are employed when referring to him. This name calling in itself is fairly good propaganda, favourable and unfavourable. It is not uncommon, and may serve as a good illustration, for individuals of one particular political party to refer to another party by speaking of them, or calling them, traitors. Some people employ propaganda against another party after giving them communal names.

2. Transfer. In transfer various unrelated feds, ideas or objects ate conjoined. For example, many preachers adduce many unrelated facts in favour of their own specific contention.

3. Glittering Generalities. There are some words which attract everyone and are acceptable to all. Some words of this kind are world brotherhood, equality, liberty and fraternity, etc. Propaganda concerning many things is based upon these glittering common conceptions. In the field of international politics, both Russia and America indulge in the propagation of their own views while ostensibly they speak of world peace. The communist party use the; slogan of equality and fraternity to further and popularise its own principles. The slogan of world peace and progress of humanity won recognition and consequent employment even by a dictator of the mettle of Hitler.

4. Testimonials. In trying to propagate their own products, thoughts or views, people often solicit and make use of the testimonials of great leaders and renowned individuals. In India, most political parties resort to the age old cliche that they are adopting the principles of M. K. Gandhi and are putting them into practice while all others are treading the wrong path. In the election days the Congress turned to presenting the testimonials issued by J.L. Nehru and M.K. Gandhi.

5. Plain Folk Appeal. In propaganda regular appeal is made to the plain folk concept of the public because the people have a propensity for adopting the folkways. Keeping this idea well focused in their minds, politicians all over the world adopt signs which bear a close relation to common life. For example, the election symbols of the various parties in India are: a pair of bulls for the Congress, a lamp for the Jan Sangh, a cottage for the P.S.P., and the well known hammer and sickle of the Communists. All these implements and objects are very near to folk life.

6. Band Wagon. The influence of the band wagon is also utilised for the purpose of propaganda. People have a tendency to accept the majority opinion, because majority opinion has the power of suggestion. Hence, every preacher tries to convince the public that it is his opinion that is accepted by the majority. This method is seen in extensive use at the election time. Even though they have received very few votes, the different political parties keep on announcing that they have received many votes and are leading by a wide margin.

7. Card Stacking. In this propaganda method, as is evident from its name, facts are twisted and moulded in order to make them appear favourable to one's own view while facts favouring the rival party are by hook or crook proved to be false. In this way, this is one-sided propaganda Evidently, this method of propaganda is immoral and misleading. Yet it finds extensive use both in the national as well as the international field. In the national sphere, the government newspapers print news favouring the government policies while the newspapers published by the other political parties print news which are prejudicial to the government's policies, but in both cases the actual news gets transformed because of its modifications to suit the needs of the two rivals. The common place fact is brought into prominence while the important fact is made to appear as if of secondary importance. And, the opposition has a peculiar tendency of blaming one particular department for almost everything that happens to go wrong. Much the same sort of thing happens in the international field also. The Chinese newspapers are persisting in their propaganda against India and are continuing to say that it were the Indians who attacked their soldiers, and the aggression was performed by the Indians who invaded their territory. Similarly, the Pakistan newspapers are also persistently stating that India is making military preparations that threaten the sovereignty and independence of Pakistan.

ESSENTIAL ELEMENTS IN EFFECTIVE PROPAGANDA

Social psychology can do much towards rendering propaganda measures effective. Social psychologists conducted many experiments to discover the means whereby propaganda could be rendered more effective. In all these experiments it was seen consistently that the effect of propaganda is dependent upon the strength of its psychological basis. Kimball Young has defined the following four factors as the psychological basis of propaganda:[3]

1. The object of propaganda as related to the audience.
2. Every element on the basis of which propaganda is made more effective and concise.
3. Specific suggestions related to the propaganda and other psychological methods.
4. The effect of propaganda on ideas, viewpoints, values and actions.

The foregoing description of effective propaganda can be condensed into the following seven laws of successful propaganda enunciated by Kretch and Crutchfield, based on different experiments conducted by them:[4]

1. Suggestions pertaining to the satiation of some need or motive are easily and promptly accepted. Hence, the orator should base his propaganda on the needs and motives of the people.
2. Suggestions offered in indistinct and indeterminate circumstances are accepted more easily than when the suggestions forthcoming pertain to a distinct circumstance. For this reason, the successful orator creates confusing circumstances and then offers suggestions for their solution.
3. The suggestions that concur with the prevailing beliefs and notions in whatever human group the propaganda is being conducted are the easily acceptable ones.
4. Indirect propaganda is more effective than direct propaganda. People should not come to know of the subject which is being thus propagated among them.
5. The propaganda should have the sanction of society. The suggestions that are given should be in keeping with the general needs of the common people. People should be matte to feel that the orator is giving expression to their and not to his own thoughts.
6. In order to arouse effective excitations it is necessary that the language, choice of words, pronunciation and the mode of speech should be such that it may impress the audience at which the propaganda is directed.
7. Propaganda can be countered by contradictory propaganda. The best countering thought or idea can be that which includes the proposal for the most prolonged appeasement of most of the social and economic needs of the people.

DIRECT AND INDIRECT MEDIA OF PROPAGANDA

Of the various media of propaganda, the platform is the most direct. Besides this the press, radio, cinema and literature, etc., are the indirect media of propaganda. Among the direct media of propaganda can be included processions, meetings, slogan shouting etc. In these methods the orator of the person involved in the propaganda personally appears before the public and informs them of whatever he wants to get off his chest. In this, his physical appearance also influences the audience. In the case of the indirect media the orator himself is not present before

3. Young, K., *Handbook of Psychology* (1951), pp. 507-508.

4. Kretch and Crutchfield, *Theory and Problems of Social Psychology*, P.P., 357-360.

the audience. His ideas and thoughts become known to the public through the medium of literary magazines. His voice is heard over the radio and can be seen speaking upon the cinema screen. As a general rule, the direct media of propaganda are more successful than the indirect media. But, on the other hand, indirect media have the added benefit that their propaganda can comprehend a greater number of people which is not the case with the means of direct propaganda. To take an example, the lecture given over the radio can reach a few million people, whereas the speech delivered from the platform can be heard at most by a few thousand people. In actual fact, the type of means of propaganda depends upon the type and the object of the propaganda. In case where the actual personality of the speaker is very effective, direct propaganda can be far more beneficial than the indirect means of propaganda. As it generally happens, the presence of a leader and speaker of high calibre is enough to attract a few thousand people to present themselves at his speech. They are influenced not only by what he speaks but also by his action and personality.

There can be any number of the media of propaganda but only the main ones shall be mentioned here. These media are the following:

(1) Platform (2) Press (3) Radio (4) Television (5) Cinema (6) Religion (7) Education (8) Literature (9) Meetings, Processions and Slogans (10) Use of Force.

1. Platform. The platform is the oldest, and even today, the most important medium of propaganda. In the field of politics, all political parties make use of platform for proposes of propaganda of the party's policies. The contestants contest the elections to gain the votes of the electors by speaking from the platform. Not only in India is the platform an important medium of propaganda, but also in such progressive countries as the United States of America, the platform is the main medium of political propaganda. The late President of U.S.A., J.F. Kennedy, made extensive use of this medium in his election campaign. Often, the great leaders are also very good orators. Their speeches have the influence of magic upon the public listening to them. The medium of platform is possessed of some advantages which are not available in the other forms of propaganda. Its greatest advantage arises from the fact, which has been mentioned earlier, that the speaker is personally present in front of the audience. In this he has the opportunity of entrancing and attracting the public by his personal qualities and his personality. The platform exerts much influence from the point of view of communal guidance. Through this medium the speakers often succeed in arousing the desired emotion in the audience and coaxing it to perform the deed that they want it to perform. This particular characteristic is not available in any other medium of propaganda. One main cause of this phenomenon is that the people collect in crowds to listen to a speech. Hence, mob psychology prevails in the audience. People are more influenced by emotions and their prudence and logical mind do not function. For this reason it is not at all difficult to come across incidents where the orator has aroused the public and instigated it so much that the crowd has indulged in worst things from arson to murder. It is not possible to achieve this frenzy of emotion by any other means such as radio, cinema, etc., because the recipient of inflammatory speech is an individual and not the member of a crowd, and hence there is no occasion for blind emulation.

2. Press. The invention of the press led to almost a revolution in the sphere of propaganda. Propaganda affected through the medium of the press comprehends millions of people distributed over great distances. In every country millions of individuals read newspaper habitually. Thus, the propaganda material published in them is transmitted easily to the public. The ideas expressed in the newspapers are more balanced and logical and it is for this reason that the press is considered the best means of propaganda in the educated society. It is now the regular practice of the leading political parties to have some special newspapers and magazines of their own. These newspapers and magazines regularly propagate the views and ideals of the party. Then, there are some government newspapers also which explain and express the political opinions and views of the government and put them before the people.

3. Radio. The most important medium that science has gifted to the field of propaganda is that of the wireless or radio as it is more commonly known. It is an established psychological fact that auditory perception is more effective than visual stimulation. The speech that is heard is more effective and influencing than the speech that is read. This is so because the recipient then hears the voice of the propagandist and in this way is to some extent influenced by his personal contact. It is the accepted thing for the prosperous families today to listen to the radio. There are public radios in the villages and many individuals collect to listen to them. In the towns, there are radios on the betel shops, restaurants and the public places and it is only rarely that the blaring of these instruments does not fall on human ears. In this way, while the press may carry its propaganda only to the educated, the field open to radio includes the uneducated. Its only limitation is in the case of the deaf. Another characteristic of the radio as a medium of propaganda is that its broadcasts are more balanced and acceptable because it is under the control of the government. Propaganda heard over the radio is believed to be more valid than that heard from the platform or read in the newspaper. Another characteristic of the radio is that one may immediately know what is going on in a particular place even though one is a thousand miles away from the spot and one feels that he is seeing the incident occur with one's own eyes. The eyewitness account of the Independence Day celebrations in Delhi is broadcast over the radio. Hearing this account when the listeners hear the Prime Minister speak, they feel as if they are physically witnessing the occasion.

4. Television. Among the various media of propaganda gifted to this sphere by science the second is the television. The radio succeeds only in carrying the voice of the propagandist to the people but in the case of television he or she can be seen on the television screen alive and kicking. It need not be pointed out that the propaganda projected over the television will be more comprehensive and more effective than in the case of radio. Recently, in America it happened that while viewing a fight over the television one person became so excited that he died of heart failure. In this way, television sometimes becomes a direct medium of propaganda. Being behind the Western nations in matters of technology beside others, television has as yet not been fully developed in India. But in Western countries the television has become an important medium of propaganda.

5. Cinema. Generally speaking, the cinema is a means of recreation but it can also be used for purposes of propaganda. The government uses the cinema to propagate its policies and the plans for the nation's progress and various other programmes. The government has only recently made a film to propagate India's view on the Kashmir issue. Similarly, the government had made many films for propaganda in the public concerning Family Planning, Life Insurance, Co-operation, Small Savings, Prize Bonds etc. In times of war and national crises the government makes use of the medium of the cinema to propagate knowledge of the actual situation among the people. The medium of the cinema has the advantages of both auditory and visual perception and hence propaganda through it is more accurate and more effective. Compared to the television, the screen of the cinema is bigger and the persons and places seen on the screen appear to be real. Hence, the cinema may arouse and stimulate the feelings, emotions and motives of the people more effectively. In this way the propaganda projected through cinema is more effective in its psychological import. Propaganda through the medium of the cinema has another advantage. The same film for the propagation of the same subject may be simultaneously displayed at hundreds of different places and thus many thousands of people can be influenced at the same time. The main characteristic of the cinema is that by means of it the actual incident can be displayed in all its details without any question of its validity. The films that are made of war and of disturbances are so alive that the members of the audience feel that they are themselves present at the scene and witnessing it in its original form. Hence, they accept it without any reservation and the propaganda through it is completely accepted.

6. Literature. Even though it is considered a defect in literature to possess the tendency for propaganda yet Literature has always been one of the important media of propaganda. Communist Manifesto propagates the communist viewpoint, Gandhi and Vinoba have written many books aiming at propagating the concept of sarvodaya. Books such as these are directly aimed at propaganda. Besides them, propagation of thoughts and ideals also takes place through the medium of the various forms of literature, novel, drama, story, poetry, essay etc. Almost all the forms of literature have been utilised for the propagation of the communist viewpoint and thought in all countries. Besides political thought, concepts concerning the philosophy of life are also propagated among the masses through the medium of literature. To take a well known example, a great amount of literature has ten created to support the material viewpoint, and it hardly needs to be pointed out that material and empirical concepts and ideals are hereby propagated. When a country is faced with a crisis the authors and poets of the country propagate the feelings of patriotism and self-sacrifice among the people.

Propaganda through the medium of literature has an advantage in as much as it profoundly influences the feelings and experiences of the individual who reads it. No other medium of propaganda can affect this internal and hidden aspect of the human emotions with the same degree of profundity and neither is the influence of any other quite as long lasting as that of literature. Thus, literature has proved to be particularly effective in the case of an indirect nature. The reader unconsciously accepts the notions and ideals expressed by the various characters in the books that he reads. In this way, propaganda through the medium of literature, the personality and the individual skill of the author or the propagandist is of great importance. The greater the degree of indirectness in propaganda through literature the greater will be its effectiveness.

7. Religion. Religion and education have ten used as the media for propaganda since the olden times. Religion has a very deep influence upon the general public. The ideals or thoughts which possess the sanction of the religious texts or of saints or of great religious men find easy acceptance among the common people. Actually, religious sanction is further backed by divine sanction, or to put it differently, it is believed that God himself is amenable to these ideals and thoughts. Further, to this is conjoined the popular conceptions of heaven and hell. It is generally believed that an individual attains heaven if he obeys the orders of God whereas he lands in hell and suffers all kinds of privations and troubles if he behaves in contradiction to the wishes of God. Hence, the things that have religious sanction are easily propagated and circulated. Realizing this importance of religion many people try to show agreement between their views and the views expressed in the religious texts. One of the main causes of the wide acceptance of the views of M. K. Gandhi was his religious influence,. Had he not ten a great soul, a Mahatma, his thoughts could not have found such great popularity in a religious minded country as India.

8. Education. Education is the chief medium for the propagation of thoughts, ideals and values. From the very ancient times the leaders in every nation have favoured the idea of imparting national education of the public in order to circulate nationalistic thought among them. Even if some foreigners want to propagate their own thought in any country, they turn to education for this. The Christian missionaries made comprehensive use of the medium of education in the propagation of their own religion. Now-a-days, many governments resort to education to propagate views favouring them among the coining generations. In Germany, Hitler made every effort to change the views of the boys and girls to concur with his own through the medium of education. In communist countries the government everywhere has control over the education and propagates its own ideals among the future generation. The children are taught to think in a particular way. A major characteristic of education as a means of propaganda is that through it only proper and logical facts can be propagated. And because education develops the personality of the individuals and increases the degree of prudence in him it may propagate only those thoughts and notions that are propounded with the help of profound and subtle arguments.

9. Meetings, Processions and Slogans. Meetings, processions and slogans have their own importance for propaganda concerning the political, economic unions of various kinds of employees hold meetings to give currency to their views and to circulate them among the public. They take out processions and shout slogans. The special importance of these media of propaganda is that they arouse and stimulate violently the passions and emotions of the people. People participating in meetings and processions behave just like the people in a crowd. They lose much of their prudence and gain in suggestibility. And thus they are easily amenable to being led in favour of or against any particular subject. Slogans are words in which the fundamental idea of the propaganda is conveniently condensed. These words are so composed as to facilitate their easy memorisation and repetition. These words are such that they easily attract the attention of the audience and effect them emotionally. Slogans are shouted in a state of emotional instability and at the top of the speaker's voice. If slogan shouting is done collectively, the emotional disturbance spreads rapidly from the epicentre to the people. In the days when the independence movement was at its height, the slogan 'Britishers! Quit India' was seen deeply affecting the public. Similarly, slogans concerning the swarajya and swadeshi were fairly sufficient to propagate the viewpoints in the public.

10. Use of Force. Of course, indirect propaganda is more effective than direct propaganda, and hence it does not call for the use of force but even then the use of force has always remained one of the important weapons of propaganda. According to Hadamovsky, force and propaganda have never been completely antagonistic towards each other. The use of force can be a part of propaganda. From the very ancient times, rulers and governments resorted to the use of force in order to propagate their own respective views among the public. And in the field of religion, force has been the main weapon of propaganda. The Muslim religious preachers raised the flag of their religion in many countries on the strength of the sword. The Christians also fought wars in the name of religion, and where they did not fight they suppressed the people by other means and propagated their own religion. For example, the Christian missionaries in India loaned money to the Hindus of backward tribes on the condition that they get their religious stock of hair cut. Failing to do this, the Hindus had to return the principal along with the interest. If they accepted the conversion to Christianity, even their loan was wiped out. Dictators such as Hitler, Mussolini and Stalin made extensive use of force in propagating their own ideas and ideals. But all these examples do not prove that the use of force is an appropriate medium of propaganda, nor do they adduce any justification for it. Its greatest defect lies in the fact that in this method something is externally forced upon the people. The people continue to pay respect to it as long as the force is maintained but the moment the force is removed the people want to give it up. Besides this, the use of force for the purpose of propagation leads to the fostering of revolutionary and mutinous force within society and a time may come when this force may explode with such violence that it may succeed in destroying the propagandist as well as his propaganda. In history, the people who resorted to the use of force in their campaigns of propaganda are remembered with loathing and disgust. Hence, now the use of force is no longer recognized as an important and appropriate medium of propaganda.

PROPAGANDA PROPHYLAXIS

The counteracting of misleading and deceptive propaganda is an important and serious problem. Consequently, modern governments have started paying attention to it. Many psychologists have experimented upon this problem. The experiments of Biddle and Collier are important. In a general way, the following suggestions can be made for counteracting misleading propaganda and advertisement:

1. Informing the Public of the Misleading Propaganda. In order that misleading propagation should be cheked, it is necessary that some social and governmental institutions should constantly carry out research in this direction and should inform the public of its findings. The Institute of Propaganda Analysis, New York performs this function. The public can be warned to beware of misleading propaganda through the medium of newspapers, magazines, radio, posters, books and pamphlets.

2. Contradicting Propaganda. An important method of counteracting misleading propaganda is contradictory propaganda. For example, if the people can be made to understand thoroughly that there can be no panacea of all ills or that the energy and power lost over many years cannot be recovered in a few hours, the public can be prevented from being deceived by propaganda of this nature. Healthy tendencies and beliefs can be created in different spheres in the public by contradictory behaviour of propganda.

3. Legal Prohibition. The government should take strong legal steps to prevent false propagation and threaten the unscrupulous individuals who indulge in such activities. Propaganda of this kind should be declared to be illegal and people who are found indulging in such practices should be punished sternly by the government.

4. Education. Generally, it is the uneducated individual who is likely to be influenced by misleading propaganda. The educated people are not so easily misled. Hence, the most important means to counteracting misleading and deceptive propaganda is education. Through scientific education the people in the public should be taught to judge everything on the basis of logic and intellect so that they may not be deceived.

5. Economic Welfare. Under some economic conditions people are easily misled. For example, it is usually seen that it is the poor who is easily deceived because he is always on the look out for some thing which costs less and provides greater utility. Hence, the skilled individual succeeds in making false promises and giving them something spurious in place of the genuine goods. Hence, some economic improvement is also necessary in order to counteract false propaganda.

6. Social Emancipation. There are many social situations that create such superstitions and prejudices that it becomes easy to practice deception even in the field of propaganda. In order to counteract this, some degree of social emancipation is also necessary.

To conclude, it may be said that if misleading and deceptive propaganda is to be counteracted, it is necessary to attack the problem from all angles. The public should be educated. The misleading propaganda should be exposed. The government should sternly punish the miscreants. Propaganda contradicting it should be disseminated, and all circumstances, whether social or economic, should be eliminated from the society.

QUESTIONS FOR EXERCISE

1. Define propaganda. State and illustrate its techniques.
2. Write short note on propaganda.
3. Explain the mechanism of propaganda. How would you use propaganda to bring about changes in beliefs and attitudes which are conducive to a healthy and secular democracy in India.
4. Distinguish between propaganda and education. What is the role of propaganda in a democracy?
5. Examine the role of propaganda in the formation of public opinion.
6. Discuss the importance of propaganda in modern societies.
7. Propaganda is a good word turned bad. Comment.
8. Write a short note on Techniques of Propaganda.
9. Describe the various means of propaganda. Which of them do you consider most effective and why?

CHAPTER 11

Social Control Through Public Opinion

The very title, public opinion, suggests that it is the opinion of the public. The public is not a group or a crowd. Public denotes the people of a country. It further refers to the people of the nation or the community. In this way, this conception is more complex and comprehensive than the concept of a group. The members of the public are found to possess 'we-feeling'. According to Kimball Young public is "...a non-contiguous and transitory mass of individuals with a common or general interest."[1] The public lacks the feature of organization mid is generally distributed over a large area, but it is not necessary for it to be organised. Besides this general form of public, there is a public related to particular problems such as economic public, political public, etc. These are short period groups. One single individual can be the member of any number of such groups simultaneously. Such a group or public dissolves when the problem for which it was assembled is solved.

Characteristics of Public

The following characteristics of the public will serve to clarify its nature:

1. Public is a Non-contiguous Mass of Individuals. As has been stated earlier, it is not necessary for the individuals to collect at a definite place and to assume an organised form in order to comprise public. In the words of Kimball Young, "The public is not held together by face to face or shoulder to shoulder contacts, a number of people scattered in space react to a common stimulus, which is provided by indirect and mechanical means of communication."[2]

2. Public is a Transitory Mass. The public as a group is not permanent. Yet this should not create the impression, eminently mistaken, that it is as transitory as a crowd. In fact, the permanence of the common interest is responsible for its coming into existence. Public loses its identity the moment the subject of interest loses its existence.

3. Public is Related to a Particular Problem. In this manner then, public is concerned with some particular problem that is of common interest, be it social, political, economic or of any other sphere.

1. Young, K., *Handbook of Social Psychology*, p. 429.
2. *Ibid.*

4. Public Group Ends when the Problem no Longer Remains. It is the concern over a common problem that constitutes the binding force between the members of the public. Once the necessity for this problem vanishes, the public also loses its existence.

5. An Individual can be Member of many Public Groups Simultaneously. If an individual has wide interests, he can be the member of various such public groups as are concerned with political, economic, social or other problems without prejudicing his membership of any one of them.

6. Interstimulation among Members of Public is not Essential. The exchange of ideas among the members of the public takes place through the medium of mechanical means. Hence, no Interstimulation is necessitated.

7. Members of the Public have We-feeling. The public has the force of manpower and it is also respected. Hence, the members possessing the we-feeling is only a natural consequence.

8. It is Difficult to Oppose the Opinion of the Public. It is this force or power of the public that makes it difficult to oppose the public opinion. Ginsberg, in his book, *The Psychology of Society* has written, "The public is in modern societies enormously large and complex and its prestige is correspondingly greater than that of a mere crowd. Very few individuals can resist an opinion which is widely accepted and diffused and which comes with the authority of a vast public."[3]

PUBLIC AND CROWD

The nature of public can be understood even better if it is studied in contrast to crowd to which it evidently bears some resemblance but from which it differs considerably. Roughly speaking, the points of distinction between public and crowd are the following:

(1) The very constitution of a crowd necessitates the presence of its members in one particular area whereas no such physical assembly is essential when the members form a public and not a crowd.

(2) In this way, the absence of physical contiguity renders possible the formation of the public even when the means of communication between members are completely mechanical. On the other hand, the contact and the communication between the members of a crowd is face to face and as near as possible.

(3) Physical contiguity also results in heightened suggestibility among the members of a crowd. Its absence has the result of a much lower level of suggestibility among the members of the public because they lack this physical proximity.

(4) In this way, crowd gives the impression of being collected and compact while the public is obviously scattered.

(5) Excessive suggestibility leads to excitement in the crowd with the result that a condition of pandemonium exists. The members of the public have a better claim to decorous behaviour because no such excitation and hubbub exists among them as they are widely scattered.

3. Ginsberg, M., *The Psychology of Society* (1951), p. 138.

(6) In a crowd the media of mutual exchange are direct and present on the spot. Its unity arises from its being limited to a particular spatial context while the unity of the public increases through such mafia as the newspapers, radio, press and propaganda. Even its existence is known only through this media.
(7) A public is relatively constant or permanent whereas a crowd is more fickle.
(8) In a crowd, relations are established through direct stimulation and excitation whereas in a public the basis of these relation is more indirect stimulation.
(9) In a crowd, the behaviour of members is excited and irrational. The conduct of the members of a public, on the other hand, shows no sign of any such execution or irrationality, other than that which can normally be attributed to human beings. The lack of such excitement is another reason for its greater reasonableness.
(10) Whatever its size, the crowd can almost never exceed the extension of a public.
(11) An individual member of a crowd can be a member of only one crowd at any given period of time but there is no such restriction on the member of a public since his physical presence within the public is not required.
(12) The members of a crowd are imbued with a sense excitement and an experience of power but the sense of respect or honour is not as pronounced as among the members of a public.
(13) In addition to the sense of respect, the members of a public also evince a mental unity. The members of a crowd exhibited physical contiguity rather than mental unity or identity.
(14) The members of the crowd express an emotional excitement. The behaviour of the members of a public shows a greater degree of rationality and balance.
(15) The effect of a crowd is as temporary as its existence. Comparatively, the influence wielded by a public is permanent. The crowd disperses and collects with equal facility because its very existence is the result of some accidental occurrence. On the other hand, the public takes greater time both in its formation and disintegration. It disintegrates whereas the crowd disperses. Its formation is based on common interests and not on chance occurrences.
(16) The various kinds of crowd have a definite and specific and clear physical form but the public has no such definite physical form for its members are scattered over a large area.
(17) The members of a public evince a mental identity. The members of a crowd are characterised by a physical unity in addition to mental identity.

The foregoing account should not convey the impression that there is no similarity between crowd and public. As Ginsberg has written, 'Though therefore the mentality of the public is at any rate in normal times, more rational, and less explosive, it does have many elements in common with that of crowd in the narrower sense of the term."[4] For example, during any revolution or crisis, any individual witnessing congregation would be hard put to it to distinguish between crowd and public and say definitely which is such. Both are psychological groups.

4. *Ibid.*

And both groups take their existence from the identity of interests and objectives of their members, aiming at the achievement of some common objectives.

PUBLIC OPINION

Having considered the concept of public at adequate length, it is now necessary to turn to a definition of the term opinion. In this connection, Kimball Young, in his work, *Handbook of Social Psychology*, has written that, "An opinion is a belief somewhat stronger or more intense than a mere notion or impression but less strong than positive knowledge based on complete or adequate knowledge. Opinions are really beliefs about a controversial topic or with respect to the valuative interpretation or moral meaning of certain facts."[5] This particular explanation of the term opinion might lead to a confusion between opinion and belief. Opinion is conjoined to some particular belief but belief and opinion are two different words and it is necessary to distinguish between them. For example, many of the opinions are only formed after considerable discussion on some polemical subject while some beliefs are adopted before any discussion of the subject is held. Secondly, opinion has not the strength and invincibility of belief. Contrarily, belief is stronger than opinion and is hence also relatively more permanent. Yet, it can be said with perfect composure and fidelity that opinion is a particular kind of belief which is formed and which relates to some controversial subject or the explanation of some facts.

After analysing the meaning of public and opinion, we may take into consideration the definition of public opinion. "Public opinion consists of the opinions held by a public at a certain time,"[6] writes Young in his book, *Handbook of Social Psychology*. In Cooley's opinion, "Public opinion should be regarded as an organic process and not, merely as a state of agreement about some question of the day."[7] According to Akolkar, "Public opinion simply refers to that mass of ideas which people have or express on a given issue."[8]

From the foregoing definitions of public opinion, it is evident that in public opinion are assimilated the opinions of individuals concerning various specific problems in addition to their judgements, ideas and notions. Here it is not necessary that every individual should possess identical views and ideas. In fact, public opinion represents the opinion of the majority and the views of the powerful groups. There are always some individuals who are opposed to the public opinion but this does not have the effect of changing the public opinion. It is further not necessary that public opinion should be the opinion of a great many individuals. Actually, as Lowell has indicated, public opinion shows not the preponderance of numerical superiority but the preponderance of influence. Public opinion concerning some subject shows that viewpoint which is most powerful. In Mcdougall's opinion, "public opinion is the moral conception of

5. Young, K., Handbook of Social Psychology' (1951), p. 431.

6. *Ibid.*, p. 431.

7. Cooley, C.H., *Social Psychology* (1959), p, 244.

8. Akolkar, V.V., *Social Psychology* (1959), p. 244.

the people."[9] But, as is evident in practice, public opinion is concerned not only with moral and ethical considerations but is also addressed to political and even administrative problems.

Ginsberg has prescribed that the presence of the following characteristics as essential to an opinion if it is to possess the authority to which public opinion is entitled:[10]

(1) Public opinion can be only that opinion which is acceptable to all. In order to be generally accepted, it is not sufficient for it to be the opinion of the majority but it should accord with the interests of the group as well.

(2) Public opinion is not the belief of one individual but it is rather the assimilated and combined opinion of all the members of the group.

(3) Public opinion is formed by common acceptance by the group.

(4) For the public opinion it is necessary that there should be social and cultural unity among the members of the group.

(5) In order that public opinion may be formed, the members of the group should possess the facility of exchanging ideas and views.

(6) It is indispensable that all members of the group should have the freedom of exchanging views of each other.

(7) Only that view is called public opinion, which has the firm belief of the public opinion at its back.

PROCESS OF FORMATION OF PUBLIC OPINION

The process which results in the formation of public opinion is a very complex one as public opinion is not formed in an instant but is a continuous process. The opinion of the leaders has an important hand in forming public opinion. The process is set in motion when some people draw the attention of other members of the group to some particular problem and stress its importance. These later individuals then slowly devote their attention to this problem and put forward their respective opinions concerning it. The conclusion that derives from the comparative analysis of opinions so expressed is public opinion. The administration of government also has its influence in this but it is not inevitable that government officials must have a hand in the public opinion. It is the opinion of some psychologists that the formation of public opinion is the result of the alteration between individuals in the group. On the other hand, it is contended by some others that the basis or root of public opinion is the unbiased or unprejudiced discussion and argument of the people. It is contended by some other individuals that the elements at the root of the formation of public opinion are of an effective or emotional rather than of an intellectual nature. And these elements are basal on mob psychology. Some people have also tried to explain public opinion on the basis of the group mind. In fact, the formation of public opinion is based on the instincts of man. It is not formed through intellectual consideration or on the

9. Win. Mcdougall, *The Group Mind*, pp. 898-199.

10. Ginsberg, M., *The Psychology of Society* (1951), p. 141.

basis of moral standards. It is further influenced by unconscious desires and complicated and tangled thoughts. It is only because of this that some intelligent leaders turn the public opinion with complete facility. In addition to instincts and motivations another element that contributes to the formation of public opinion is imitation. When some individuals see other people holding some particular view on some specific problem they also do the same because they argue to themselves that the opinion must have some element of truth as these people are holding that opinion. In this way, any opinion can become public opinion if it is the opinion of the majority. As has been mentioned earlier, some leaders direct public opinion in the process of its formation but in this directive effort, the greater influence is wielded by the individual who is a specialist on the subject rather than the propagandist. In addition to these elements, the sense of self-respect is also an important constituent of public opinion. Allport has laid great emphasis upon this element. The feelings of self-respect collectively influence the individual and help in the establishment of public opinion. Besides this, common problems and public beliefs are also important constituents of public opinion. The common beliefs or faith towards the public problems is converted into public opinion.

FACTORS IN THE FORMATION OF PUBLIC OPINION

Factors playing an important part in the formation of public opinion can be divided into two classes — individual and social.

(A) *Individual factors*. As a general rule it is the social circumstances that influence social processes more than other factors but in the case of pubic opinion and its formation some individual or personal factors are also of importance, in particular the opinion of influential individuals. These great men become the ideals of the men and women.

(B) *Social factors*. The following are the main social factors influencing the formation of public opinion:

1. Cross Pressures. In society the beliefs and assumptions of the individuals are influenced by cross pressures from different institutions and different directions. Public opinion is formed of these beliefs and assumptions. It is apparent that the process of formation of public opinion is rendered more complex by these cross pressures and it is diffiiclt to say as to which institution has a greater hand in some or the other particular pressure.

2. Economic and Professional Institutions. Economic and professional institutions are also of some moment in the formation of public opinion. It is because of differences in them that there appear differences between the opinions of the various economic groups and classes. Economic interests have an important hand in the formation of public opinion. It is seen that different classes or groups collectively possess different opinions concerning the same problem because of the different economic and professional interests that are current in their particular groups.

3. Caste and Religion. Among the factors that influence public opinion formation are caste and religion. Religion is a social matter and not a private affair as most people are prone to consider it. Even though most states today are secular, religion does influence social life and in particular rural social life. For example, in India public opinion is considerably influenced by religious considerations in connection with most social and political problems. The influence of religion is further strengthened by caste and together they put considerable influence upon public opinion. Hence, caste, too, is an important factor in the formation of public opinion. Although the caste system is being continuously modified, casteism is increasing in India and is being encouraged because of the vested interests. Both in the political as well as in the social spheres one can see difference in the public opinion, the difference being caused by the various caste interests in the consideration of the problems. It need hardly be pointed out that such conditions are most undesirable for a healthy democracy.

4. Effect of Particular Social Phenomena. The formation of public opinion is further amenable to the influence of some specific social phenomena in addition to the forementioned factors of a social nature. In this connection, Kimbal Young has mentioned following seven kinds of phenomena — (1) Specific economic phenomena. (2) Other specific incidents. (3) Incidents influencing the international situation. (4) Change of the individual's direction of action by specific incidents. (5) Social phenomena related to the intellectual viewpoint. (6) Delusive phenomena related to rationalisation. (7) Phenomena influence upon the formation of public opinion.

5. Education. Education plays an important part in the formation of public opinion. Education helps both the formation as well as the modification of public opinion. As a general rule, the urban population is generally more educated than the rural population in a country. Hence, one finds difference in the public opinion of rural area and that of the urban area. Generally speaking, rural public opinion is dogmatic and stigmatized whereas public opinion in the urban area is progressive.

PUBLIC OPINION FORMATION IN DEMOCRACY

The process of the formation of public opinion passes through the following stages in democracy:

(1) Definition of the problem or subject,

(2) Introductory examining of thoughts or ideas,

(3) Practical solution or the presentation of plans,

(4) Formation of public opinion.

In this way, the first step towards the formation of public opinion in democracy is that some individuals or a groups of individuals draw attention to a particular problem and define it. For example, it was the activity of some social reformers who attracted the attention of the public in India towards problems related to the dowry system, the sati system, widow remarriage, etc. The problem is examined and studied at the same time that it is defined, in addition to which notions are advanced for its solution. Individuals who are specialists in that field present their views to the public. The educated people try to clarify the problem by argumentation and discussion, this clarification of the problem being facilitated by the co-operation of the radio, press, newspaper, pamphlets, etc., because different individuals shed light on the problem from their individual viewpoints and thus help to light up all its various aspects. In this way, after the problem has been clarified, plans and solutions are put forward for its solution. Simultaneously with the presentation of these plans people put forward their views concerning these suggestions. In this way, after argumentation and discussion when one solution is unanimously or at least generally accepted it slowly becomes the public opinion. In fact, the formation of public opinion is not one of the steps in this process but is rather the result or culmination of the first three steps.

It is time now to take an example of the formation of public opinion in a democracy. In India, people favouring the idea of widow remarriage threw light upon the deplorable state of widows in the society. Everyone was that unanimous on the point that their condition should be improved. In this way, the plight of the widows became clear to all the people although they were not all agreed as to the solution of the problem of widow remarriage. Different solutions and plans were suggested. And slowly, widow remarriage was also legally recognized. Hence, public opinion also turned in its favour even though somewhat hesitantly and slowly. Now-a-days, public opinion may be generally said to be in favour of widow remarriage although even today there are great many individuals who look down upon it and oppose it.

METHODS OF MEASURING PUBLIC OPINION

The main methods by means of which public opinion can be assessed are the following:

1. Historical Qualitative Methods. In this particular method efforts are made to assess the qualitative aspect of public opinion. Besides, it also procures the knowledge of the history of public opinion or the history of the changes that occurred in public opinion. In this method, the changes that take place in the views and beliefs of people within a definite time period are examined. In this process the help of such methods as life history, subject study, visualisation etc. is solicited. In this the research worker keeps track of his own experiences and obtains assistance from the data published by newspapers, radio, etc. In addition to public opinion the feelings, motives, inspirations, imaginings, stimuli, etc. also have a hand. In the historical method it is necessary to attend to all these also. Many important facts concerning the public opinion are revealed by the historical method. For example, the historical method shows just how the public opinion concerning anything becomes custom, dogma or law consecutively.

2. Gallup Poll Method. The most famous method of assessing public opinion is the gallup poll method. Now-a-days this method is employed to find out the public opinion concerning different problems. For example, the Daily Mirror, a newspaper in England, used this method more than once to find out the public opinion concerning capital punishment that prevailed in England. In this method public opinion is examined and assessed with the help of the questionnaire and projection method.

3. Polling Method. In democratic countries the polling method is used to find out the opinions of the public in order to form a government. In the Indian adaptation of this method the public expresses its opinion by marking the name of the party which has the individual's approval on the ballot paper. The polling method is also utilised to find out public opinion concerning other problems and for this the following three methods are used in a particularly prolific manner—1. by distribution of ballot papers among the people through newspapers, 2. by sending ballot papers by post to selected citizens, 3. through interview. Sometimes these methods are used to know the results of the general elections that are to be held subsequently.

4. Interview Method. In the interview method, as is evident from its name, the research worker personally meets the individuals and interviews them and finds out public opinion by asking questions of them. Its one great advantage lies in the feet that the information thus gleaned is accurate and hence fairly valid. But its greatest disadvantage lies in the fact that its implementation on a large scale requires enormous amounts of both time and money. If it is to be successful, the interview should be unprejudiced or unbiased because otherwise it cannot yield correct information.

5. Questionnaire Method. In the questionnaire method some questions are selected that deal with all the important aspects of the problem and are put to the subjects being examined. The questions should be short and precise and should be answered with equal brevity. This particular method has the advantage that many things about which the individual is reticent in the presence of the interviewer can be put in the questionnaire.

6. Mass Observation Method. As is evident from the name, observation of an entire group are made and efforts are also made to make generalizations. In this method the danger of prejudice is always present and hence this particular method does not possess much in the way of scientificity.

7. Letters to Public Officials. It is not unusual for people to send letters to the editors of newspapers or to senior public officials containing their views on various problems, and evidently letters of this nature can be indicative of the public opinion."[11]

8. Quasi Experimental Method. In is not possible to make any experiment upon public opinion because it is generally open to far too many influences only a very few of which are controllable. And an experiment under these indefinite conditions would be more or less useless. For this reason the quasi experimental method is used to assess public opinion. In this method the people are given some controlled stimuli and their views are obtained. Peterson and Thurstone used this

11. Wyant, R. and Herzog, H., Voting Via the Senate Mail Bag, *Public Opinion Quarterly*, v (1941).

method to find out the opinion of the public concerning [12] the social attitudes of children and attitudes towards the cinema. Using this method Meier and Annis discovered that in the people the more active values are the effective[13] ones rather than the rational values.

AGENCIES OF PUBLIC OPINION FORMATION

The agencies that are essential to the formation of public opinion have particular importance for a democratic society since here before any change can be introduced in any particular direction it is necessary to create public opinion in its favour as a preliminary step to the modification. The major agencies to the formation of public opinion are the following:

1. Newspapers. The most popular agency of the formation of public opinion is the newspaper. Through the medium of the newspaper the government and the leaders transmit their views to the general public. In order that the opportunity supplied by the papers should be fully utilized, it is necessary for the published news to be valid and true. The different newspapers consider the same problem from different points of view. The collective result of this is that all the various views are put before the public and all the different aspects of the problems are examined. The newspapers can both guide public opinion as well as mislead it. Hence, impartial newspapers ought to be encouraged and the newspapers represent different vested interests should be kept under close check.

2. Radio. The second important means for the formation of public opinion is the radio. It is a psychological fact that what is heard is more effective than that what is read. Hence, the radio is more effective than the newspaper. Many scientific studies of propaganda through the radio have been made in connection with psychological effect upon the public. In their book *The Psychology of Radio* Cantril and Allport have mentioned the following important facts concerning the radio:[14]

(a) Greater amount of the broadcasting should be done by female announcers because their voices are more pleasant and liked by the public.

(b) The speeches of the practised speaker are liked over the radio.

(c) It is necessary to stress the importance of clear pronunciation.

(d) The general description of any subject should be also accompanied by a specific analysis.

(e) Repetition should be indulged into some extent because it is effective.

(f) The sentences should be shortened or lengthened to suit the subject matter; generally the shorter sentences are better but they can also be made longer if the subject is an interesting one.

(g) The speed of talking should not be too fast. It is proper to speak between 115 and 160 words in a minute.

---

12. Peterson, R.C., and Thurstone, L.L., *Motion Pictures and Social Attitudes of Children* (1933).

13. Annis, A.D. and Meier, M.C., *The Indiction of Opinion Through Suggestion by Means of Planned Contest* (1934).

14. Cantril and Allport, *The Psychology of Radio* (1935).

(h) On an average, a programme should be not longer than 15 minutes although it may be so if it is a dramatic programme,

It seems frivolous to point out that if the above principles are adhered to, the entire power of the radio in the field of the creation of public opinion may be utilized to its fullest extent. Radio influences not only the ideas, opinions, beliefs and tendencies of the audience but also the existing social values.

3. Television. In the present age, along with the radio, the television has also become an important tool for the formation of public opinion. It has the advantage of visual stimulation over and above the radio's auditory stimulation. Apparently, it will be more effective.

4. Cinema. The cinema also has an important role in public opinion formation. Through the medium of the cinema the ideas, values, etc., are modified in practically every field of human efforts, such as the social, political, religious, etc. As for changing the patterns of fashions the cinema has proved the most powerful tool. The main cause behind the effectiveness of the cinema is that the shadows cast on the screen appear almost indubitably real and hence it has great effective influence. It is true that It lacks the coverage that is possible in the case of newspaper or radio but as far as the question of motivations is concerned the cinema is far more effective than any other means.

The forementioned agencies of the formation of public opinion allow both of proper as well as improper use depending upon the intention of the individual who employs them. In a democracy they should be employed for the good of the public. A democracy is a government of the people intended for the good of the people. Hence, if any change is to be effected in it, it is necessary first of all to convert public opinion because in a democracy the most important determinant of the propriety or otherwise of governmental actions is the public. Before any change in the public can be affected it is necessary that public opinion should be assessed and it is only after considerable propaganda concerning the problem has been affected and the problem has been clarified to the public that any effort to convert the public opinion to any new direction can be made.

QUESTIONS FOR EXERCISE

1. Define public opinion and discuss the factors which affect public opinion.
2. What is public opinion? Discuss the major agencies which bring about change in public opinion.
3. What is public opinion? How is it (a) formed, and (b) measured?
4. What is the nature of public opinion? How is it formed? How is it controlled?
5. Write a short note on public opinion.
6. Write a note on the nature and importance of public opinion. What methods do psychologists adopt to measure it?

7. Explain the nature of public opinion. How is public opinion on a controversial issue formed and crystallized?
8. Define public opinion. How is social control exercised by it?
9. What is public opinion? How is it formed?
10. What is public opinion? Discuss the relative merits of poll and open-end questions in public opinion research. What is public opinion?
11. What do you understand by public opinion? Discuss the methods utilised for assessing public opinion.

CHAPTER 12

The Social Codes

The social laws have their unique place and importance in human society. In the herds or groups of animals we do not find any existence of social laws, customs, traditions and folkways. Animals exhibit no organization or system which may entitle their groups to be called societies in the accepted sense of human society. Social laws are products or outgrowths of the process of cultural orientation. Man learns by virtue of the fact that he lives in a society and comes into various types of contacts with its members. Thus, he acquires knowledge of social laws and some of these become part and parcel of his existence. Some of the laws are believed in and observed by man because their non-observance results in unpleasant and painful consequences. Besides, he may or may not believe in them or admit their validity but he cannot by any means escape being affected by them. Their impact on him is in no way determined by his acceptance or non-acceptance of these laws. Social laws bring cohesion in society and provide social organizational structure. By analyzing and understanding social laws we can understand the nature of society.

A systematic collection of social laws is called a Social Code. The social laws which are included in a particular social code are determined by their thematic unity of similarity.

The important social codes can be classified as following:

(1) Religious Code
(2) Moral Code
(3) Customary Code
(4) Code of Fashions.

Besides the above-mentioned codes, there are some other means and methods of social control. These will be dwelt upon shortly.

Though the external form of social codes undergoes little or no change and is more or less permanent, yet the rules under a social code keep on altering or modifying in keeping with the time and other circumstance. Accordingly, social codes are not rigid iron laws, rather it is a dynamic and flexible concept.

IMPORTANCE OF SOCIAL CODES

The various social codes are of grave import and they play a very crucial role in maintaining the equilibrium in a society. They mediate between social change and social stability. Thus, it is because of these codes that in spite of drastic changes in our social and moral concepts, the social behaviour of man is kept under check and remains within the socially accepted norms. We shall soon discuss the role and importance of social codes as means of social control. This will make explicit the extent and form of social control exercised by Religion, Traditions, Customs and Fashions.

CLASSIFICATION OF SOCIAL LAWS

The social laws in any society are too numerous and too diverse to be enlisted in entirety. Thus, it is difficult even to classify them adequately. There are different ways of classifying the social codes. Sometimes social acceptability is taken as the basis; sometimes social importance is made the basis and sometimes changeability or communicability is used as basis of classification. Broadly, the social laws are codified on the bases of Mores, Folkways, Laws, Customs, Fashions, Conventions and Etiquette. These laws have an obligatory character which constrains the members of a society to follow these. Of course the social laws are not uniform or universal in character. They are subject to amendments and modifications to suit the interests of a particular society under particular circumstances. Not everyone follows them in the same manner. Depending upon social and individual reactions the social laws undergo change or modification. Though the social laws are flexible and quite changeable, this does not mean that they are dispensable or that we can have an organized society in which everybody acts as per his conscience or impulse. As a matter of fact the very idea of society is inconceivable without the presence of social laws. Now we shall describe the process whereby social control is maintained and exercised through social codes. This will make clear the various means of social control.

1. Mores and Folkways

Mores and folkways are the two chief means of exercising social control. In order to understand the full meaning of mores and folkways, we need examination of various definitions of these terms. Some important definitions are given below:

MacIver and Page: "Thus, it is reasoned that when the folkways have added to them conceptions of group welfare, standards of right and wrong, they are converted into mores."[1]

Dawson and Gettys: "Mores are folkways which have added to them through some reflection the judgment that group welfare is particularly dependent upon them."[2]

Like folkways, mores also develop automatically. Sometimes the folkways get converted into mores. The only difference between folkways and mores is

1. MacIver and Page, *Society*, p. 20.

2. Dawson and Gettys, *An Introduction to Sociology*, Ronald Press Co., New York (1984), p. 50.

that of obligation or sanction. As compared with folkways, mores have greater obligation or sanction, that is, it is more hazardous for an individual to violate or deviate from the mores than folkways. Following are the chief characteristics of mores:

(1) Mores cany a sense of moral obligation. Lack of the observance of mores carries social disapproval and there is provision of some kind of punishment.

(2) Mores are socially accepted and it is obligatory to observe them.

(3) Folkways tend to become mores.

Generally there are three types of mores:

(*i*) *Mores pertaining to conduct*, e.g., respecting of elders, speaking truth, etc.

(*ii*) *Taboos*, e.g., non-violence to animals for Jains, prohibition on use of beef by Hindus, etc.

(*iii*) *Laws*. These are backed by fear of punishment by the state in case of non-observance or violation of these.

Some important definitions of folkways are given below:

E.S. Bogardus: The folkways of a group include the mores and all other ways of behaving that are considered interesting but not essential to the welfare of the group."[3]

A.W. Green: "Those ways of acting that are common to a society or a group and that are handed down from one generation to the next are known as folkways."[4]

Thus, folkways are the social laws of traditional acts and behaviour of men. Folkways have following important features:

(1) Folkways act as guide to social behaviour.

(2) Folkways exercise restraint and control on social conduct.

(3) Folkways keep modifying to melt the changes of time and place. Old folkways give way to new. But this happens gradually. On the whole folkways have conservative influence in a society.

Distinction between Mores and Folkways

As a matter of fact, there is little difference between folkways and mores. As compared to mores, folkways are less rigid. The amount and gravity of social disapproval and infliction of moral or social penalty is less in case of the violation of folkways than in the case of the violation of mores. The common man equates mores with morals, that is, for him whatever is customary or traditional is moral and vice-versa. Such is not the case with folkways. The non-observance of mores is considered hurtful to social welfare and society, therefore, tries to inflict economic, moral or social punishment on the violators of mores. The non-observance of folkways entails mild social disapproval but no tangible punishment.

3. Bogardus, E.S., *Sociology*, p. 6.

4. Green, A.W., *Sociology: An Analysis of Life in Modern Society*.

2. Customs

Like mores and folkways, customs also play an important role in the exercise of social control. In every society there are definite rules, procedures and ways regarding eating of foods, housing, relationship between elders and youngsters, the manner of social speech and conduct. For example, in some societies everyone eats in strict privacy while in others communal eating is encouraged. In some societies, privacy of bed and bath is considered absolutely necessary, while in some societies communal bathing is practised. These socially approved and accepted ways of behaviour are customs. According to MacIver and Page, "The socially accredited ways of acting are the customs of society."[5] Because of these customs, man does not have to think afresh about these ways of acting. As a matter of fact they are followed almost blindly. For example, during fairs and festivals by the riverside in India, people take bath in full public view without the least feeling of shame or reserve, whereas womenfolk do not even show their faces to some of their relations at home. These customs keep passing from one generation to the other. These are considered most natural ways of acting and people generally do not like to disrespect or violate them. According to E.S. Bogardus, "Customs and traditions are group accepted techniques of control that have become well established, that are taken for granted and that are passed along from generation to generation."[6] The difference between folkways, mores and customs is one of degree and not that of kind. For example, marriage is an institution which includes many mores, customs and folkways.

3. Law

Law is the chief means of social control. The state frames laws to regulate and control the behaviour of citizens. The non-observance and violation of these laws is met with punishment from government machinery. Thus, the control by law is the control by means of governmental power and force which reside in the various governmental agencies and its agents. The laws are enforced by police force and if needed the might of the army is also used to enforce them and punish the violaters of law.

According to Ross, "Law is the most specialised and highly furnished engine of social control employed by society" Ross has described the two functions of law: (1) to suppress violent acts, and (2) to compel individuals to respect the rights of others and to cooperate with others in actions which promote common welfare. Thus law not only protects the rights of people but also helps in ushering in welfare state. Thus, law is having its jurisdictions extended to every part of the social life in modern times. Besides limiting the scope of crimes, the law deters people from committing crime for the fear of governmental relation. The law protects the life and security of the law abiding citizens, but, furthermore, prevents others from interfering with the interests and rights of the citizens. Thus, law keeps the actions

5. Maclver and Page, *Society*, p. 18.

6. Bogardus, E.S. *Society*, p. 415.

of its citizens within the prescribed and socially acceptable limits and provides everyone opportunities to make progress.

The Difference between Law and Custom

According to MacIver and Page, "Law is the body of rules which are recognized, interpreted and applied to particular situations by the court of the state."[7] But while defining law, MacIver and Page observe, "Law means the code upheld by the state, which because of its inclusive applicability, is thus a guardian of society itself."[8] Now we see that according to these writers while customs develop and grow through a fairly long period of time, the law comes into existence and force the moment a state upholds a particular customs or set of customs and adopts them through various governmental agencies. Ultimately, the law courts act as its guardians and see to it that it is properly observed and followed in actual behaviour of the members of a society. Whereas customs remain in force through social acceptance, the law has the backing of governmental power. In this respect, law differs from the rules of any other organization. The rules of other organizations that do not have the sanction of state are powerless, unless, of course, adopted by the state. If you violate law, you will be punished and made to respect it, whereas if you violate any rule of an organization, you may at most be expelled from its membership and having come out of it your obligation to follow its rules is finished. But even if you have been jailed for theft, you are liable to re-sent to jail if you repeat the act of theft. Moreover, the violation of laws of state carry the extreme penalty of death, but no organization can inflict such a penalty. While custom is a social law, the law is custom of a state. Customs are unwritten and therefore indefinite, whereas laws are written and precise. According to MacIver and Page law has the dual function of maintaining security and preventing internecine feuds of the members of a society.

PLAY GROUPS

In a play group the child experiences social interaction and interplay and is thus socialized. He also learns the manners and etiquette from others. According to Hayes, "By supervised play children learn by experience that civilized life is far superior for all concerned than savagery." Games are played according to rules; and it is not possible to play a game without following the rules governing it. Thus the rules of game inculcate in the players respect for rules and sense of fair play. He learns to live under discipline. By playing games one learns to follow the leader and obey his command. Playing games also develops a sense of collective responsibility among children.

ART AND SOCIAL CONTROL

In a society, the art determines and controls the feelings and emotions of the individuals. The artists creating poetry, music, dance forms, painting and sculpture

7. MacIver and Page, *Society*, London (1957), p. 175.

8. *Ibid.*

influence the emotions of the other people. In an organized group the emotions play a crucial role. It is only due to the feeling of unity and emotional attachment that any society becomes a cohesive structure. Emotional unity alone provides the bond of unity in a society. Accordingly control of emotions is an effective means of social control. Whenever there is danger to the integrity of a nation or society through internal or external threat, an appeal to emotions is made to increase and heighten the feeling of unity. In ancient India and also in other countries in old times as well as now the soldiers going to the battlefield were encouraged and their feeling of patriotism aroused by chorus singing of patriotic songs. In the tribal and primitive societies, collective dancing plays an important role in maintaining and sustaining the tribal unity. The dances arouse emotions and relax tensions. This in turn leads to welding up of mutual feeling of love and fellow feeling. Dance and song affect the emotions of participants but even the spectators are influenced by emotional vibrations released by these art forms. Accordingly art has the same role in social control as the role of play. Both help remove mutual suspicions and relax tensions. They promote the feeling of unity, brotherhood and fellowship. In primitive societies, dance and music are very widely and universally employed to procure desirable results. The communal singing and dancing accompany celebration of fair and festivals, preparation of battle and the sowing and harvesting of crops. Thus, art has a universal role and its appeal is very wide and deep. Art is pressed in service of religion, politics and social affairs. In India singing of national anthem at the end of every picture in the cinema hall has the same function.

Art exploits the aesthetic feeling of people in order to serve social ends. By the use of painting, sculpture and architecture national heroes are immortalized. Their constant presence in society serves as a reminder of the paramount value of social and national interests. The nefarious persons are caricatured by artists and in dance, play and drama the evil wages of their evil acts highlighted. In Indian temples the gods and heroes are glorified and satanic characters degraded. Thus art influences the ideals and general thinking of people. The good is represented beautiful and the evil is represented ugly in art. This helps to wean people from evil-doing. In every form of art — dance, drama, music, painting, etc. — the evil tendencies of man like thieving, debauchery, falsehood, murder, rape and loot are shown to prosper only for a shortwhile and ultimately duly punished. Such acts are shown to be ugly, villanous and degrading. On the contrary, the good actions like love, sympathy, charity and sacrifice are glorified and shown as beautiful.

Art glorifies our national symbols. For example, the colour combination of a national flag is made as aesthetic as possible. Our national tricolour with its Ashoka lions is perfect and beautiful aesthetically. The flags of different countries portray different feelings. The hammer and sickle combination in Russian flag highlights the contribution of labour. In India there are hundreds of statues and buildings celebrating national heroes and martyrs. These constantly infuse spirit of patriotism in the onlookers. A visit to Jalianwala Bagh is most certain to stir emotions of intense patriotism. The presence of these signs and symbols serves as a source of national unity and integration. Thus, art helps objectification of dear, sacred and worthwhile memories of a nation. Art also beautifies and glorifies national festivals, ideals, traditions and institutions.

Art establishes the dignity of labour, too. The giant statues of man and woman with hammer and sickle bring to everyone's mind the value of labour. Similarly, the paintings of workers building a dam, working on roads and engaged in various crafts celebrate the dignity and worth of labour. The workers are true sons of the soil. They have a great role to play in national reconstruction. They have to throw the yoke of economic, cultural and sexual slavery. Many a dance, opera and drama celebrate this theme and thus help in raising the prestige of labour.

Thus, we find that by means of art, society exercises a control on the ideals, traditions and mores of a society. By art man is persuaded to pursue the high ideals and make any sacrifice needed to fulfil them.

BELIEFS AND SOCIAL CONTROL

Beliefs, suggestions and ideals have tremendous importance in social control. Ross has discussed in great details the importance of beliefs in social control, Gillin and Ross have classified beliefs in five categories. These are as follows.

1. Belief in the Eternal and Natural Character of Social Laws. The implications of this belief are that social laws have their sanction in the Nature and that like laws of Nature social laws are also eternal and immutable. Negatively the belief implies that any violation of social laws entails punishment by Nature. That is, violation of social laws calls forth the wrath and anger of Nature.

2. Belief in the Law of Karma. Hindus believe in the Karmaic law according to which the force of cause and effect is always equal. That is, as one sows so one reaps. The good deeds lead to reward and the bad deeds lead to punishment. This belief is closely attached to belief in metapsychosis or rebirth or transmigration. According to the law of re-birth each soul is re-born after physical death to reap the good and bad results of actions done in the previous life. Even animals are believed to be covered by this law. An animal earning exceptional merits may be re-born as a man and a Brahmin doing excellent work may be elevated to kingship or godhood. Bad deeds lead to demotion as good deeds lead to promotion. Thus, the belief in Karma helps to regulate social behaviour. Men desist from bad deeds on pain of being demoted and punished in future lives.

3. Belief in Austerity. According to this belief, a man who has been excommunicated from his society due to wrong deeds may re-enter the social fold by undergoing the punishment and acting virtuously and piously.

4. Belief in the Other World. Almost all societies believe in the other world or heaven and hell. Puranas are full of description of hell and heaven. These descriptions prevent men from committing bad and evil deeds, and inspire them to follow the path of virtue and piety.

5. Belief in the Departed Soul. According to this belief souls are immortal and after the death of the body do not become wholly detached but maintain some kind of relation with people living on the earth. The souls who are very intimate with us keep a sympathetic watch on our activities on this earth. Mother, husband, wife, keep a watch on the activities of their daughter, wife, husband, respectively. This belief provides us with great energy and confidence in our life on this earth, shows us the correct path and prevents us from slipping into wrong pathways.

The above account makes it quite clear how important a part these beliefs play in controlling our social activity. These are effective and efficacious and require no monetary investment. As regards self-control, these prove even more effective investments of control than laws of the state. Law is not concerned with motives and intents nor can it have an ascendance over our hearts. But beliefs are inalienable parts of our conscience. Due to beliefs in heaven, natural justice, law of Karma and rebirth and watchful care of departed souls on our activities we are guided on right path and kept away from the wrong path. Moreover, due to these beliefs man becomes anxious while doing wrong and feels joy and peace while doing good actions. 'God Surveys All' is a belief which can control our behaviour more effectively than any state government agency, legal code or relative or neighbour. These beliefs exercise most effective control on our unsocial tendencies. These beliefs also become inspiring sources of our activities. These beliefs are responsible for social control in primitive as well as civilized societies. Their efficacy and strength is directly proportionate to the intensity of our beliefs in them. With decline in our faith or raising of doubts the efficacy of these beliefs vanishes.

SOCIAL CONTROL BY SUGGESTION

Suggestions are indirect means of social control. Man is unable to grasp his unconscious motives underlying his activities. Many a time the real motives are directly opposite of his known and conscious motives. Social control is thus exercised through this medium of unconscious motivation. If we can influence unconscious motivation by appropriate suggestions, we can easily exercise the desired social control on human behaviour. As we know in the world of advertisement business thrives on this simple psychological fact. A very fine example of social suggestion and its control on behaviour is found in the well- known fact that people coming from foreign lands take to the ways of the people of their adopted countries. This is particularly the case as regards children. A useful method of social control by suggestion is to honour and reward people displaying desirable behaviour. This will in turn motivate people to follow the example of persons who have been haloed or glorified by society. The national heroes whose conduct is considered most useful for the society are honoured by raising memorials in their honour and people gather on these memorials from time to time and the good deeds of these heroes are recalled. This serves to stimulate people to emulate the example of these honoured persons. Thus, people are influenced by the examples of saints, heroes, social reformers and martyrs. This influence is deep and affects our unconscious so that we try to behave in the same way as these heroes did though we may not be quite conscious of this fact.

Another method of using social suggestion is to emphasize and stress the dormant powers in the individuals and thus infuse in them a spirit of self-confidence and capability for great deeds and big achievements. By steeling one's will one can succeed in doing the impossible. Systematic encouragement helps release of deep reserves of energy and man becomes capable of great accomplishments. This fact is widely exploited by leaders, generals, social and religious reformers. Social suggestion also works through written expressions of the ideals and great deeds performed by honoured persons. Propaganda is also a type of social suggestion. In modern times, the radio, the television and the press are used by interested persons to propagate their ideas or goods. By systematic use of propaganda, Germany and Italy organized themselves into powerful nations having world conquest as their mission. People believed they were destined to conquer and rule the world and they worked relentlessly towards this end. They even committed inhuman and most reprehensible acts believing them necessary for the accomplishment of their mission. By propaganda people are drugged into a state of utter submission and are made to follow unquestioningly the command of the leader.

The most effective technique of social suggestion is education. In educational process a very wide use of social suggestion is made. For example, sermonizing, drilling for discipline and cultivation of democratic procedures are cases of social suggestion. Like education, the custom and the tradition also make use of social suggestion. The customs and traditions help production of uniform behaviour in a society.

SOCIAL CONTROL BY SOCIAL IDEALS

Likewise social beliefs and suggestions, social ideals also have important role to play in social control. What an important role has been played by the ideals of Freedom, Equality and Fraternity in ushering in democracy and sustaining the democratic societies! How marvellously did Hitler weld German society into a powerful war machine by exploiting the ideal of 'Conquering Race'! The ideals of equality and proletarian power are the backbones of communist revolutions. Kantian ideal of non-exploitation and respect for personal integrity of every individual is a great source of strength to all fighting against tyranny and exploitation. The ideal of world brotherhood has helped breaking of quite a few parochial barriers. Similarly, the ideal of Justice has prevented many a injustice. Of course, the strength and efficacy of ideals depends upon the strength of feeling for ideals amongst people.

Thus, beliefs, suggestions and ideals are powerful techniques of social control and have an important role to play in every organised and civilized society.

THE ROLE OF PUNISHMENT AND REWARD IN SOCIAL CONTROL

In every society we find a system of punishment and reward which determines and controls the various activities of the individuals. Of course, the system of reward and punishment differs from one society to the other. The kind of social control, that is, the kinds of activities permitted and prohibited depends upon this system. For example, in some primitive societies a woman getting divorce maximum number of times receives a place of honour. This is seen as a proof of her tremendous capacity for sex and child bearing. This, of course, encourages the tendency to seek divorce. In Nagas, a youth is not considered fit for marriage by any maiden unless he has beheaded someone, while such a youth will be least suited for marriage among Hindus. Due to this difference in the system of reward and punishment, head-hunting is common among Nagas while it is not found among Hindus.

There are various types of rewards sanctioned, in different societies. A man may be rewarded by conferring of a title, presentation of cash, woman or certificate of merit. Deprivation from these goods is punishment. Man by nature wants to do deeds which will bring him honour, social acceptance or cash reward and refrains from activities which invite punishment. Thus, by a definite system of punishment and reward a society exercises powerful control on the conduct of its members. For example, in some societies only those girls are considered fit for marriage who have been pregnant before marriage. This ensures that marriage shall not be childless. Obviously, in these societies premarital sexual relations are no stigma and virginity is not prized. In some societies a woman is allowed to have more than one husband while in others a husband may have many wives. In Hindu society loss of virginity before marriage is a stigma and forfeits the chances of marriage. Sometimes back, even now caste system held a great sway over Hindu society and inter-caste marriages were condemned and invited the punishment of excommunication. Now, of course, there is some change in the public opinion and in some advanced urban arms inter-caste marriage is tolerated. Love, charity and sacrifice are prized virtues in many societies and, therefore, people tty to earn these virtues. Incurring debts, indulging in debauchery, violence, etc., are considered vices and people try to avoid these. Man by nature tries to avoid social ridicule and is prepared to make sacrifices to earn social prestige and honour. People are rewarded for increasing productivity in Soviet Union, therefore workers strain their every nerve to achieve maximum production. This earns them laurels. As regards reward, wealth plays a very great part. Man is capable of doing virtually anything for the sake of monetary gain.

Man is social being. Therefore it is but natural that his conduct should be affected by the fear of punishment and desire for reward. We all wish to earn social prestige, laurels and status and equally wish to avoid social disapproval and stigma. All our conduct is guided and governed by these factors. If any act will bring us social ostracisation or loss of face, we shall not do it unless too strongly impelled. A Brahmin boy enamoured of a Harijan girl is unlikely to marry her for the fear of social stigma, unless, of course, he is too passionately in love with her or is likely to earn governmental favour. Thus, we conclude that reward and punishment play very vital role in social control.

LAUGHTER AND SOCIAL CONTROL

In social relations of man, laughter makes a special contribution. It is through laughter that diversity, intimacy and alacrity of social relations is maintained and sustained. Laughter is a safety-valve through which excess of tension is released. Man feels light and refreshed after a bout of laughter. By means of good humour we can bring home to others unpleasant facts which if seriously told would provoke others. Thus, comics and hilarious narratives make the task of social control easy. In political and social satires the corruption and evil deeds of politicians are brought home to audience without directly offending the persons concerned. Thus satire amuses as well as teaches. By the medium of cinema people are kept amused. Cinema also provides educative information. The education material presented visually on TV or screen is grasped without effort.

Every strata of society is kept under check and control through laughter. In the rural areas the traditions and mores of the rural society are critically reviewed in folk songs, collective dance and drama. By this means rural societies kept amused and suitable reforms in the traditions and mores initiated. Moreover the people who participate in the light variety programmes find their tensions relieved. People belonging to different cultural groups and religions can be made to mix up best through light and humorous programmes and in a jovial spirit and atmosphere.

Thus, in every sphere of social life some provision for laughter and joke is made. The social atmosphere itself provides the source of laughter and amusement. Laughter and amusement cements the bonds of friendship in people and helps to remove tension and smoothen the rough edges. Psychologically speaking, laugher is a natural tendency in man and some scholars consider laughter to be the basic human-instinct which distinguishes man from other animals.

Ridicule is a form of laughter and the fear of ridicule keeps the unsocial tendencies of people in check. For example, a person going to a marriage party may feel tempted to pick up handful of fruits or dry fruits and put them in pocket but the fear of discovery and consequent ridicule prevents him from doing so. Nobody wants to expose himself to a situation in which people may laugh at him. An artist, a sculptor and a craftsman try their best to produce artistically worthy goods because inartistic products will expose them to public ridicule. The kind and amount of laughter relevant in a particular social situation is determined by the nature of situation.

There are various theories regarding the origin of laughter. According to some it is intended to release extra energy of man while others believe that through laughter we try to regain the lost energy. Laughter is a natural tendency in man and it fulfils both purposes. Mankind, in its long experience has discovered laughter to be useful for both individual and society.

QUESTIONS FOR EXERCISE

1. What are social codes? What is their importance in social life?
2. Describe the means of social control. Which of these means is most effective and why?
3. Write short note on Social Norms.
4. Bring out the role of law as agency of social control.
5. Explain the difference between Mores and Folkways.

297

Bibliography

Allen, F. R. et. al, *Technology and Social Change*, New York, Applet Century, 1957.

Eqbert De Vries, *Man in Rapid Social Change*, Garsten City, New York, Doubleday, 1961.

Evevelt, E. Hagen, *On the Theory of Social Change: How Economic Growth Begins*, Home Word, Dorsey, 1962.

Kenneth E. Boulding, *A Primer on Social Dynamics*, New York, Free Press, 1970.

National Bureau of Economic Research, *Demographic and Economic Change in Developed Countries*, Princeton, Princeton University Press, 1960.

Ogburn, W. F., *Social Change*, New York, The Viking Press, 1950.

Pitrim Sorokin, *Social and Cultural Dynamics*, Boston, Porter Sargent, 1957.

R. M. MacIver and C. H. Page, *Society*, New York, Rinehart, 1949.

Robert A. Nisbet, (Ed.) *Social Change*, Oxford, Oxford University Press, 1972.

—, *Social Change and History*, New York, Oxford University Press, 1969.

—, *Evolution and Culture*, Ann Arbor, University of Michigan Press, 1960,

Theodozius Dobzbansky, *Mankind Evolving*, New Haven, Yale University Press, 1962.

Wilbert E. Moore, *Social Change*, New Delhi, Prentice Hall, 1978.

—, *The Impact of Industry*, Englewood Cliffs, Prentice Hall, 1965.

—, *Man, Time and Society*, New York, Wiley, 1963,,

—, *Technology and Social Change*, Chicago, Quadrangle Books, 1972.

Zimmerman, Carle C., *Pattern of Social Change*, Washington D. C., Public Affairs Press, 1956.